Fourth Edition

Diagnostic Teaching of Reading

Techniques for Instruction and Assessment

Barbara J. Walker

Oklahoma State University

Merrill,
an imprint of Prentice Hall

Upper Saddle River, New Jersey   Columbus, Ohio

To Lorrin, Sharon and Chris

Preface

As our national diversity grows, teachers must increasingly celebrate our likenesses, empathetically discuss our differences, resolve that we know of no *one best* way to teach all children to read. The Great Debate has continued, but the conclusions have been the same. No one approach is better in all literacy situations and with all learners that it should be considered the one best method. However, we have increasingly expanded our concepts of the instructional process. At the core of this knowledge has been the continued assertion that effective instruction is executed by effective teachers. This text provides a tool for teachers to understand the various instructional frameworks underlying diagnostic teaching techniques.

Text Purpose

Embodied within this text is the strong belief that as a nation of readers, our strengths lie in our individual differences. These individual differences need to be nurtured within our instructional programs, building upon the unique strengths that each student possesses. Furthermore, sensitive teachers use these strengths to expand students' conceptual knowledge, creating intelligent citizens.

Teachers are often keen observers and reflective thinkers. This text promotes the idea that teachers can make sophisticated diagnostic judgments and can identify appropriate instructional techniques through a process of diagnostic teaching. Using this knowledge to make informed instructional decisions leads to a renewal of teachers' decision-making power.

Diagnostic Teaching of Reading is designed to supplement course work in the diagnosis and remediation of reading difficulties. It can ultimately be used in a reading practicum or as a guide in reading clinic experiences. Furthermore, school psychologists, learning specialists, and Title I teachers will find it a useful reference. The instructional techniques are written in a step-by-step fashion so that classroom teachers and practicum students can readily follow the prescribed procedures. The goal is to increase communication between the practitioner and diagnostic specialists as well as the practicum student and the college professor.

Text Development

The text grew out of a need encountered in translating theory and test results into practice that would effectively help the problem reader. When I began writing diagnostic evaluations, I used the traditional battery of tests, and from these tests, I made an educated guess about how a particular problem reader would respond to instruction. I sent my report (based on both normative test data and criterion-referenced tests) to the parents, who in turn took the report to the school. *But nothing changed.* I was not really communicating because I had not told how to *teach* the problem reader. They did not know how to translate the test data into effective instruction.

Then I began using teaching lessons during the diagnostic evaluations and writing down how to implement specific teaching techniques. And so Chapter 11 was born.

One astute graduate student asked, "How do you know what will work?" What I had learned to do as a clinician was intuitively to measure the sparkles in the reader's eyes. When I analyzed why specific techniques had worked with certain students, the decision-making cycle of diagnostic teaching became less intuitive and more understandable based on theoretical rationales. This text is the outcome of writing down this analytical process.

Changes for This Edition

This new edition reflects my growing commitment to diagnostic teaching as assessment.

1. New to this revision is Chapter 9, Selecting Instructional Materials, which outlines the various materials available to the diagnostic teacher. The abundance of reading material increases the complexity of the decision-making process, but it also enhances the success of selecting appropriate and interesting stories for problem readers.

2. In the appendixes, I have listed my favorite predictable books according to levels; computer programs that have been successful with problem readers; and series books that I have used to develop fluency with older problem readers.

3. New techniques in this edition focus on decoding and identifying words within a balanced framework. The techniques represent a

variety of instructional frameworks and theoretical perspectives. These techniques include *Word Analogy Strategy, Making Words, Word Walls, Word Probe Strategy, Retrospective Miscue Analysis, Framed Rhyming Innovations, Summary Experience Approach, Paired Reading,* and *Collaborative Reading.*

4. In the assessment chapters, I have highlighted how diagnostic teaching assessments are conducted with beginning readers because they cannot read the text before instruction occurs.

5. In the diagnostic lesson framework, I have added *familiar text time* as an essential element in the framework to provide opportunities for readers to use their developing strategies in authentic textual situations.

6. A companion Website is available as a resource for both instructors and students. It can be accessed at www.prenhall.com/walker.

Text Organization

The efficacy or validity of any text is its inclusion of content. The following is a brief description of each chapter's focus.

Chapter 1 presents the decision-making process of diagnostic teaching. It outlines some common initial diagnostic decisions and lays the groundwork for the rest of the text. Chapter 2 describes the various influences on diagnostic decisions. Factors impacting a student's reading performance are the reader, the text, the task, the technique, and the context. Chapter 3 presents strategies for effective diagnostic teaching, while Chapter 4 develops a framework for a diagnostic teaching session.

Chapter 5 explains how to gather diagnostic data, while Chapter 6 shows how to formulate hypotheses using the collected data. Chapter 7 provides the procedures for using teaching (rather than testing) as a method of reading evaluation. Chapter 8 discusses how to use portfolios for gathering and assessing diagnostic information.

Chapter 9 describes the various kinds of instructional materials available for a diagnostic teacher to use. Chapter 10 classifies the diagnostic teaching techniques on the basis of several methods: the instructional framework implemented, the type of text used, the response mode used, the strategy taught, the targeted skill taught, the source of information targeted, the structure of instruction selected, and the cognitive process emphasized.

Finally, Chapter 11 presents a simple description and the procedures for 70 techniques. Following each description is an explanation of when that approach is most effective in teaching reading. It describes the view of reading underlying the technique and provides a checklist for the diagnostic teacher to use in assessing its effectiveness with a particular student.

Acknowledgments

This text represents a point of view developed over years of clinical experience. During that time, several people have been an inspiration to me. First, I want to thank Darrell D. Ray, Oklahoma State University, who has been my mentor and advisor. As the cornerstone of this text is his strong belief that children who experience reading difficulty need instruction that uses their strengths, which is continually adjusted to meet their changing needs. I thank him for initiating my quest to understand individual differences in learning to read. Also, I want to thank my knowledgeable friends who read parts of the text and offered suggestions, criticisms, and support for my efforts. I am especially grateful for the ideas and comments of Claudia Dybdahl, University of Alaska, regarding qualitative assessment, and William Powell, University of Florida, regarding quantitative assessment and classifying techniques. Their professional critique of my initial ideas set the course for the view of assessment in the text.

Special thanks are extended to my reviewers: Carole Bond, Memphis State University; Mary Anne Hall, Georgia State University; Michael W. Kibby, University of Buffalo; and Bonnie Konopak, Louisiana State University. I have also appreciated the astute judgment of the staff at Merrill, especially Jeff Johnston for his encouragement and perspective as I have grown as an author; Brad Potthoff, editor for this edition; and production editors Mary Irvin and Holly Henjum for their untiring efforts to keep the project moving at all times. I am especially thankful for the editorial work of Cheryl Wilms.

I owe a great deal to each of the eager students who willingly let me test my ideas about instruction. I am especially indebted to my own two children, Chris and Sharon, who let me teach them in different ways. They were especially patient in sharing their mother with the reading profession. Last, I would like to thank my husband, Lorrin, and my good friend, Marleen Moulden. They have listened to my ideas about instruction, offered counsel, and shared my belief in children throughout the writing and revision of this text.

Adjusting instruction to meet the changing needs of students in our classrooms and clinics is a challenging and rewarding task. This text is designed to facilitate that decision-making process.

Barbara J. Walker

Discover Companion Websites: A Virtual Learning Environment

Technology is a constantly growing and changing aspect of our field that is creating a need for content and resources. To address this emerging need, we have developed an online learning environment for students and professors alike—Companion Websites—to support our textbooks.

In creating a Companion Website, our goal is to build on and enhance what the textbook already offers. For this reason, the content for each user-friendly website is organized by topic and provides the professor and student with a variety of meaningful resources. Common features of a Companion Website include:

For the Professor

Every Companion Website integrates **Syllabus Manager**™, an online syllabus creation and management utility.

- **Syllabus Manager**™ provides you, the instructor, with an easy, step-by-step process to create and revise syllabi, with direct links into Companion Website and other online content without having to learn HTML.

- Students may log on to your syllabus during any study session. All they need to know is the web address for the Companion Website, and the password you've assigned to your syllabus.

- After you have created a syllabus using **Syllabus Manager,** students may enter the syllabus for their course section from any point in the Companion Website.

- Class dates are highlighted in white and assignment due dates appear in blue. Clicking on a date, the student is shown the list activities for the assignment. The activities for each assignment are linked directly to actual content, saving time for students.

- Adding assignments consists of clicking on the desired due date, then filling in the details of the assignment—name of the assignment, instructions, and whether or not it is a one-time or repeating assignment.

- In addition, links to other activities can be created easily. If the activity is online, a URL can be entered in the space provided, and it will be linked automatically in the final syllabus.

- Your completed syllabus is hosted on our servers, allowing convenient updates from any computer on the Internet. Changes you make to your syllabus are immediately available to your students at their next login.

For the Student

- **Topic Overviews**—outline key concepts in topic areas

- **Electronic Blue Book**—send homework or essays directly to your instructor's email with this paperless form

- **Message Board**—serves as a virtual bulletin board to post—or respond to—questions or comments to a national audience

- **Web Destinations**—Links to www sites that relate to each topic area

- **Professional Organizations**—links to organizations that relate to topic areas

- **Additional Resources**—access to topic specific content that enhances material found in the text

To take advantage of these resources, please visit the *Diagnostic Teaching of Reading: Techniques for Instruction and Assessment* Companion Website at www. prenhall.com/walker.

Contents

1

What Is Diagnostic Teaching?

Diagnostic teaching uses instruction to understand how students read and respond to what they read. During instruction, the teacher assesses how problem readers approach the reading event. Using this information, she establishes the instructional conditions necessary for problem readers to learn. Diagnostic teaching, then, is the process of using assessment and instruction at the same time to establish the instructional conditions that enhance learning. Instruction that fits the needs of problem readers enriches their engagement in literacy activities and enhances the likelihood they will be able to construct meaning.

The report *Preventing Reading Difficulties* states, "The critical importance of the teacher in the prevention of reading difficulties must be recognized. . . . It is imperative that teachers at all grade levels understand . . . the role of instruction in optimizing literacy development" (Snow, Burns, & Griffin, 1998, p. 9). With knowledge about reading and reading instruction, teachers can adapt instruction to meet the needs of problem readers. Instruction that is tailored to their needs heightens students' engagement and enhances their ability to construct meaning when reading.

The diagnostic teacher identifies specific instructional alternatives for problem readers to enhance their literacy. As a reader begins to experience success, he attributes his reading improvement to using strategic processes. This attribution, in turn, increases his engagement during subsequent literacy events. The diagnostic teacher's task is to monitor this improvement and identify the instructional modifications that produced it. Therefore, she formulates her diagnostic hypotheses by observing the instructional conditions that improve reading. This process is outlined in Figure 1–1.

The decision-making cycle of diagnostic teaching begins in the midst of a *reading event,* where the teacher can observe the reader's strategies for constructing meaning. From these observations, she develops various types of assessment activities. She uses the information from the assessment activities and her observations within the reading event to *formulate diagnostic*

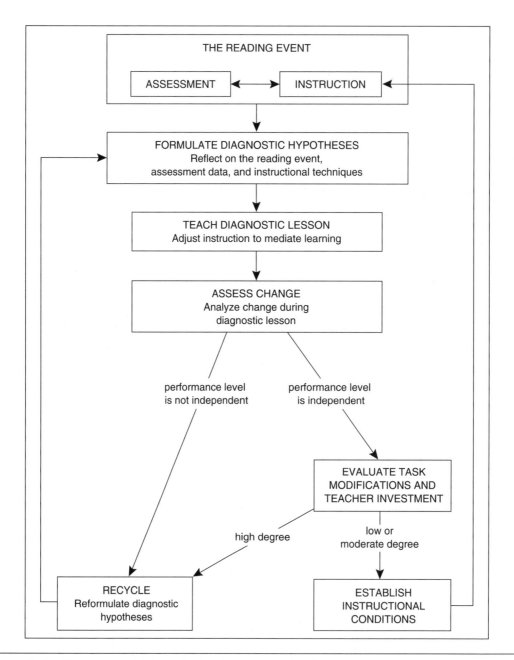

Figure 1–1   The Decision-Making Cycle of Diagnostic Teaching

hypotheses and select instructional techniques that will advance the student's reading. As she *teaches the diagnostic lesson,* the teacher adjusts her original plan to ensure learning. After the lesson, she *assesses the changes* the reader made, as well as *evaluates* the effectiveness of the adjustments she made. Using this information, she either *establishes the conditions* for learning (how she will teach) or *recycles* (reformulates or makes new hypotheses). In this decision-making cycle, the diagnostic teacher shifts between assessment and instruction to create evaluations that emerge from, and immediately influence, instruction within the reading event.

> Diagnostic teaching is the process of using assessment and instruction at the same time to identify the instructional modifications that enable problem readers to become independent learners.

The diagnostic teacher is an active problem solver. She is much more than a test giver. She is first and foremost a teacher. As she teaches, she explores how a particular student reads and responds. She knows that his reading is affected not only by what he knows but also by the strategies he uses. Thinking about what the student already knows and does when he learns, the diagnostic teacher selects techniques that will facilitate learning in the most efficient way. Rather than looking for causes of reading disabilities, the diagnostic teacher focuses on what students can do, then coordinates their strengths with suitable reading experiences.

Active Reading

The diagnostic teacher makes instructional decisions based on her understanding of how reading occurs. In this book, reading is viewed as a process that involves using both (a) information from the letters and words in the text and (b) information that the reader already knows to construct meaning within a social context. The reader is an active learner who interprets and responds to what he reads using what the text says (text-based information) and what he knows (reader-based information). The student strategically combines these information sources when reading; he also relies on both text and personal knowledge when communicating his own ideas about text within a social context. Effective readers use the following processes.

1. Effective readers coordinate the reading process, combining both the text and personal knowledge. While reading, such readers construct

a tentative model of meaning based on inferences about the author's intended meaning. They shift between using what they know (reader-based inferencing) and what the text says (text-based inferencing) to construct their model of meaning (Pearson, Roehler, Doyle, & Duffy, 1992).

2. Effective readers elaborate what and how they read (McNeil, 1992). They think about how the text they are reading relates to what they know and elaborate the strategies they are using to construct their understanding. Thus, they make connections that help them remember and interpret what they read. These new connections become part of what readers know. Likewise, readers expand their strategy options as they read and embed new strategies within their repertoire of strategies.

3. Effective readers monitor their understanding to see if it makes sense (Paris, Lipson, & Wixson, 1994). If it does not make sense, effective readers check their purposes for reading to see if they are on the right track, check their own knowledge and compare it to what they are reading, and vary their strategies to remove difficulties as they try to construct meaning.

4. Effective readers use their knowledge and perceptions of the social context to select both their strategies and the information they use. In essence, the situation in which literacy occurs—such as a classroom group, friends talking on their way to school, a one-to-one tutoring session—influences what students select as important to discuss, what they elaborate, what strategies they use, and how they engage the text in order to construct meaning. When their engagement seems inappropriate, they think about the literacy situation as well as past situations and ask themselves, "What response would be appropriate for this situation?"

Reading is an active process in which readers shift between sources of information (what they know and what the text says), elaborate meaning and strategies, check their interpretation (revising when appropriate), and use the social context to focus their response.

The following scenario illustrates the process of active reading when a reader encounters an unknown word. A text has a picture of a baseball diamond with a figure running toward second base at the top of a page and the following sentence at the bottom of the page: "The girl hit the home run." From the picture of the baseball diamond, Bobbie guesses that the story is about a boy. However, when he reads the sentence, the graphic cue *g* instead of *b* helps him figure out that the story is about a girl rather than a boy. Bobbie's initial hypothesis, that the story is about a boy, is based on his previous experiences with similar situations and stories.

The reader selects cues from the text and measures them against his own background knowledge and important textual information already established *(combines sources of information)*. If the response is confirmed, or fits, reading continues. For example, when Bobbie could not confirm the expected response in the baseball story because the word *girl* does not look like *boy,* he asked himself, "What word is like *boy* that begins with a *g*?" In other words, he wanted to know what word semantically and graphically fits *(monitors reading)*.

Our experiences and the language used to describe them build our schema, or our personal world view. Although in their own experience, children may know that both boys and girls play baseball, they may view baseball as more associated with males because of the professional games they see on TV and the many baseball books available about male stars. Because of this knowledge *(use of situational context),* Bobbie in the baseball story example expected the main character to be a boy. He then revised the expected response of *boy* according to grapho-phonic information, and he read the sentence in the text as "The girl hit the home run." Reading this story caused the reader to refine the schema that "stories about baseball usually have boys for heroes" to be more specific, namely that "stories about baseball usually have boys for heroes, but sometimes they have girls *(elaborate)*." With this experience, along with other similar experiences, Bobbie began to elaborate strategies for reading and at the grading period was able to name some things good readers do when they read *(elaborate strategies)*. See Figure 1–2, for example.

The model just described can provide a framework for analyzing the behaviors of problem readers. As Bobbie did in the example, readers consider many factors within any given reading event to make sense of what they are reading. Thus, all readers "draw on their prior experiences, their interactions with other readers and writers, their knowledge of word meaning

Name some things good readers do when they read.

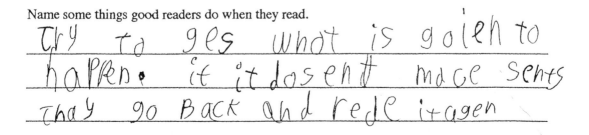

Figure 1–2   Second Grade Explanation of What Good Readers Do

and of other text, their word identification strategies, and their understanding of textual features" (*Standards for English Language Arts,* 1996). This active process is at the heart of instructional decisions made by the diagnostic teacher. The report *Preventing Reading Difficulties* points out that "Effective reading instruction is built on a foundation that recognizes that reading outcomes are determined by complex and multifaceted factors" (Snow, Burns, & Griffin, 1998, p. 313). Therefore, the diagnostic teacher examines the strategies and knowledge of problem readers in relation to active readers. Thus, a reading problem, rather than being a static deficit within the reader, is a set of strengths and weaknesses affected by interactions among many factors and instruction.

Problem Readers

Although readers use their strengths to solve problems in interpreting text, sometimes these strengths can result in compensatory behaviors that actually inhibit rather than enhance the reader's construction of meaning. While effective readers combine sources of information, problem readers vary in their use of strategies. The point of view of this text is that problem readers often experience a deficit in either a strategy or a skill that causes them to shift away from one information source. They compensate by using their strength and thus eliminate a need to use their deficient knowledge source (Taylor et al., 1995).

This overreliance on their strength often results in inefficient reading. For example, readers who easily learn to decode words and recall text-based information often develop the idea that reading is simply repeating a string of words from the text. They become bound by the text and *do not combine both the text and their experiences.* This behavior is often coupled with the likelihood that the student will be placed in a text that is difficult for him and asked to read fewer authentic texts (Allington, 1995). Effective readers elaborate both the content and their strategies, but when reading overly challenging texts, problem readers cannot readily elaborate either the content or their strategy deployment. For example, if Bobbie could not read the words *baseball* or *hit,* the sentence would have been difficult to read and Bobbie would have allocated most of his resources to constructing meaning. In this case, Bobbie's *elaboration would be restricted,* and he would not expand his content knowledge (sometimes *girls* can be baseball heroes) and his strategy use ("When the word that I said doesn't look like the text, I can think of another word that fits").

After an extended period of failing to combine sources of information or elaboration strategies, problem readers become accustomed to understanding only bits and pieces of what they are reading. They *refrain from monitoring* and passively read words without constructing meaning (Walker, 1990b). For instance, if Bobbie had an extended period of time reading difficult text, he might have continued to read the story miscalling *boy* for *girl,* thus misconstruing a major character in the story. Habitual passive reading fails to build an expectation that reading is a strategic process in which readers combine their resources to make sense of text. While effective readers readily monitor their understanding, problem readers passively read text without checking understanding, thus compounding their reading difficulty.

If readers continually fail to construct appropriate meaning when reading, they alter how they perceive themselves within the literacy context (Ruddell & Unrau, 1997). They attribute their continued failure to an ability (a fixed characteristic) that they do not possess rather than to lack of a strategic process that they can acquire. This attitude reinforces the belief that if they try to read, they will fail; and if they fail again, they are admitting their lack of ability. Knowing they have facilities in other academic situations, for instance, in mathematics, these problem readers reduce their effort, cease to try, and thus disengage from literacy activities. By disengaging, they can attribute failure to "not having tried" rather than to their lack of ability. Effective readers can choose among different strategies as they read, while problem readers come to *view literacy situations as self-defeating* and decrease their engagement.

> Rather than actively constructing meaning, problem readers perpetually read with one or more of the following characteristics. They (a) overrely on a single information source (usually a strength), (b) read difficult text with little or no elaboration of content and strategies, (c) read without monitoring meaning, resulting in passive reading, or (d) define reading as a failure situation, and decrease their engagement.

Instructional Process

The goal of diagnostic teaching is to establish appropriate learning opportunities for problem readers. If the students use effective strategies and make adjustments for themselves, a simple framework of readiness, active reading, and reacting is sufficient. Problem readers, however, have difficulty making adjustments and employing effective strategies. Inefficient readers often need to be shown exactly how to use effective reading strategies. They need instruction that is modified during the lesson framework. The diagnostic teacher, as a result, continually assesses what and how problem readers are learning and makes instructional adjustments to ensure successful reading. The process of adjusting instruction to ensure learning is called *mediating learning.*

> The diagnostic teacher mediates learning, which means she adjusts instruction to ensure successful interpretation of text.

The diagnostic teacher specifically selects activities that will directly mediate learning for each problem reader. She establishes what the student already knows and adjusts instruction to overlap his present knowledge with new information. Furthermore, she evaluates how the student learned what he knows to establish strategy strengths. A problem reader often relies heavily on his strengths; therefore, the diagnostic teacher selects a technique that allows him to demonstrate these strengths. During instruction, the diagnostic teacher discusses these strengths with the student and shows him how to use these strengths in various literacy situations. As the student experiences success with the new reading task, the diagnostic teacher selects techniques that have a more integrated instructional approach. This approach allows the diagnostic teacher to use the learner's strengths (what he already knows and does) to show him how to use his weaker information source when reading.

Diagnostic teaching techniques were developed from different views of reading and learning. Four views are described briefly here:

- **Text-Based View.** Simply stated, this view of reading focuses on text-based processing as the major instructional concern of teachers. Learning to read is viewed as a series of associations or subskills that are reinforced until they become automatic. Letters are linked to form words, words are linked to form sentences, and sentences are linked to form ideas; that is, the parts of reading are put together to form the whole in text-based processing. Processing text shapes the learner's response.

- **Reader-Based View.** This view of reading focuses on reader-based processing as the major instructional concern of teachers. The reader is viewed as an active thinker who predicts what the author is saying. Then he samples textual information to check his predictions. Readers may actually verify their ideas about what the author is saying with a minimal amount of textual cues. Thus, reading is viewed as negotiating meaning between an author and a reader. In reader-based processing, the reader's ideas create his response.

- **Interactive View.** The interactive view of reading focuses on the active-constructive nature of reading as the major instructional concern of teachers. The reader is viewed as using both reader-based processing and text-based processing to form a model of meaning. Although he is active, his predictions are formed on the basis of what the text says and what he already knows about this information; that is, reading is viewed as constructing meaning using various information sources. Thus, reading is an interactive process where the reader strategically shifts between the text and what he already knows to construct his response.

- **Socio-Interactive View.** This view focuses on situating understanding as a major instructional concern of teachers. As a reader discusses his response, he shifts between constructing ideas about what he personally understands and considering the ideas others have. Thus, during the discussion, he reconstructs his understanding as a result of rethinking his ideas and those of his peers. Thus, reading is viewed as a socio-interactive process in which the reader responds to text using his personal knowledge and feelings, framing and reframing his response according to the social situation.

The diagnostic teaching techniques associated with differing points of view can be matched to learner strengths and needs. The diagnostic teacher chooses techniques for guided reading based on strengths and allows the student to read authentic literature to construct meaning. On the other hand, she is cognizant of techniques that would develop the strategies and skills the learner needs to learn. In this process, the diagnostic teacher strives for balance in her instruction. She understands the various views of reading and "makes thoughtful choices each day about the best way to help each child become a better reader and writer" (Speigel, 1998, p. 116). The diagnostic teacher readily balances her instruction among the various views of reading, always mindful of learners' needs. The diagnostic teacher considers both text-based approaches and reader-based approaches to plan and modify her instruction. She balances supported, teacher-directed instruction with learner-centered, inquiry approaches. Likewise, she balances techniques that promote active discussion in a group of peers with settings in which the student responds on his own. The diagnostic teacher uses her understanding of students, instruction, and assessment to select instructional techniques that allow students to use their strengths. Then she uses these strengths to show students how to solve their reading problems.

Assessment Process

In diagnostic teaching, assessment is continuous. As the student learns, diagnostic information is immediately incorporated into the lesson. The teacher thus deals with the problem as she teaches, not after she has gathered the facts. For example, a teacher discovered at midpoint in her instruction that a student could not sequence the events of the story. Rather than continue trying to teach using the planned instructional format of pre-dict, read to find out, and summarize, she introduced a story map (see "Story Map" in Chapter 11), a visual arrangement of the sequence of events. Using the story map, the student and teacher reviewed information from the beginning of the story and placed it on the map. In the course of instruction, the lesson format was changed to summarize what was on the map, make a prediction, and read to find out what happened next. The final step became to add to the story map, tell how the new information fits into the story, and how it fits with the previous prediction. The lesson format changed because the teacher assessed the difficulty during the lesson and *changed the instructional conditions,* or format. This modification increased student learning.

Diagnostic teaching means that assessment occurs during the lesson. Thus, the assessment information derived is both practical and valid because it is gained through authentic literacy activities. Furthermore, the assessment is efficient because learning does not stop in order to test. The assessment process becomes an integral part of the learning.

> Diagnostic teaching means that assessment is continuous as the student is learning. The diagnostic teacher adjusts instruction as she teaches, not after she has gathered the facts.

To lead students to more efficient reading, the diagnostic teacher looks for recurring patterns among the variables of the reading event (see Chapter 2 for further discussion) and uses this information in her teaching. She changes her instruction in order to mediate learning, thus showing students how to use what they already know to solve more challenging reading tasks. This process leads readers to improved reading.

As materials and activities are adjusted to the needs of the problem reader, the diagnostic teacher maintains a close match between the text and the student's reading, making sure that the text is not overly challenging. Although this precision permeates all instruction, the degree to which the diagnostic teacher uses continuous assessment is not practical for the classroom teacher. The classroom teacher cannot continuously assess and modify her instruction in 25 different directions at once. The classroom teacher, however, collects authentic assessments through the use of portfolios. In a portfolio, both the teacher and student collect literacy samples over time and discuss how literacy is developing (see Chapter 8). However, in the midst of instruction, the diagnostic teacher assesses how the problem reader is learning and adjusts her instruction. Assessment becomes an integral part of diagnostic teaching.

Diagnostic Teaching Process

Diagnostic teaching is a dynamic process in which decisions about what the reader needs change as the student learns. Initial diagnostic information can be gathered through screening or from classroom instruction. This initial information is then expanded through informal assessment (see Chapter 5). The informal assessment allows the diagnostic teacher to identify the major problem and establish an instructional range that is challenging for the student. From this information, the diagnostic teacher makes tentative decisions about instruction.

As she teaches, the diagnostic teacher also analyzes the effects of the variables of the reading event (see Chapter 2) to help her formulate her hypotheses. She gathers and analyzes further data about the strategies the student uses to construct meaning with text (see Chapter 6). After the lesson, she reflects on the information she has gathered, the reading event where instruction occurred, and her role (see Chapter 3) during instruction to formulate and refine her diagnostic hypotheses. Reflecting on this information, the diagnostic teacher selects materials (see Chapter 9) and techniques (see Chapter 10) to adjust instruction in order to mediate learning for the problem reader.

The diagnostic teacher then instructs a lesson. The lesson can be conducted in an individual setting or within an instructional group. In any setting, the teacher assesses the specific reader's growth during instruction. To establish the amount of the reader's change, the teacher assesses the reader's growth that resulted from the instructional adjustment (see Chapter 7 for the format to assess growth). If no change took place in the reader's performance, the diagnostic teacher cycles back through the process and instructs another lesson based on the new diagnostic information gathered during instruction. If the reader's behavior did change, then the diagnostic teacher establishes instructional conditions for this reader, which includes much more than whether the student's learning increased. Because the diagnostic teacher collects data as she teaches, she also analyzes how she modified her initial plan in order to mediate learning. After the lesson, she assesses the amount and type of support *(teacher investment)* a student needed to make a change in his reading behavior. As she teaches, the teacher alters her instruction systematically, providing support for student learning. The amount of teacher investment indicates whether the selected techniques are working and when they are not (namely, when a high degree of teacher investment is required). If a high degree of teacher investment is required, the diagnostic teacher also recycles through the process, selecting new instructional approaches. Likewise, the diagnostic teacher can orchestrate reading tasks in a variety of ways, such as introducing graphic aids (story maps) or asking students to read aloud. These changes are made to foster strategic reading. Again, the teacher records the adjustments *(task modifications)* that she devises during the diagnostic lesson. If a high degree of task modification is needed, the diagnostic teacher may choose to recycle and select a new instructional technique. In some cases, the task modification may be precisely what is needed to increase student learning, and the teacher then establishes these modifications as part of the instructional conditions for the student.

The decision-making cycle of the diagnostic teacher illustrated in Figure 1–1 is a continuous process where instruction informs the assessment and subsequent instructional choices.

Summary

The process of diagnostic teaching uses instruction to understand how the problem reader approaches the reading event. The goal of diagnostic teaching is to identify instructional alternatives that create enhanced reading performance for the problem reader. Instruction mediates learning; instruction is adjusted to ensure that readers construct meaning with text. The teacher focuses on how the learner constructs meaning by gathering data as she teaches. Furthermore, she views reading as an active process in which the reader uses what he knows to interpret what the text says within the social interactions of the literacy event. Therefore, the diagnostic teacher uses the student's strengths (knowledge and strategies) to lead the student to integrate new information as well as new strategies into his reading repertoire. She then assesses the reader's change as a result of her instruction. She bases her decisions regarding the next steps in a student's instruction on this assessment as well as on her reflections about the student's learning as a result of the instructional adjustments. These decisions become increasingly more refined as the diagnostic teacher considers the reading event, evaluates the strategies of the problem reader, and matches those with appropriate techniques.

2

The Reading Event

Diagnostic teaching establishes those instructional conditions that will advance students' literacy. The diagnostic teacher bases his decision making on the patterns of interactions during the reading event (see Figure 2–1). Those patterns that recur are considered the most representative of the student's reading processes. From these patterns, the diagnostic teacher predicts what instructional setting will positively affect a student's reading; the goal of assessment, therefore, is to identify instructional conditions that advance a student's literacy.

During instruction, the diagnostic teacher analyzes five variables of the reading event—reader, text, task, technique, and context—and evaluates their effect on the reader's performance. The variables do not act in isolation but affect one another during the course of instruction. The diagnostic teacher evaluates how changing any one of them affects a reader's response.

Through repeated instructional opportunities, the teacher evaluates the interactions of these five variables. During the lesson he evaluates the diagnostic *task* (*what* he asks the *reader* to do) and the *technique* (*how* he asks her to complete the task). He evaluates the *text* (*what is read*) and how it affects reading performance. The diagnostic teacher evaluates the *reader's* knowledge, strategies, and engagement during the reading event. Equally important, he evaluates the social *context* or where instruction occurs. As shown in Figure 2–2, these five variables influence reading performance during any given reading event and continuously interact as instruction occurs. This chapter elaborates each variable.

Task

Students are often mystified when trying to figure out the *purpose of the task* they are to complete during an instructional lesson. To demystify reading tasks, the diagnostic teacher needs to create authentic, functional tasks in his classroom. Authentic activities have been found to provide opportunities for students to discuss ideas both before and after reading. The tasks are

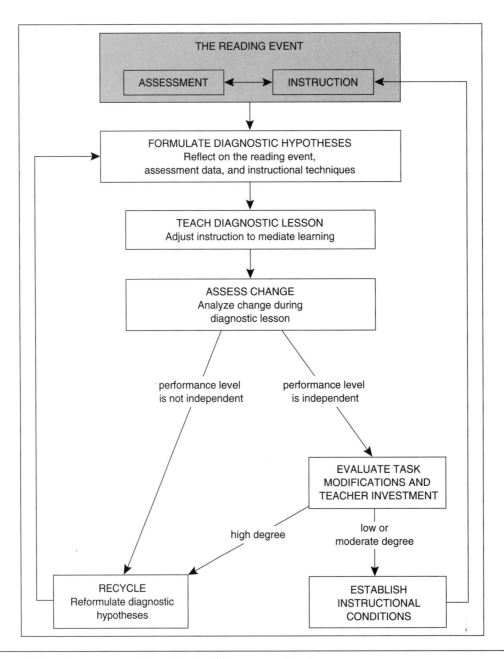

Figure 2–1   *The Decision-Making Cycle of Diagnostic Teaching*

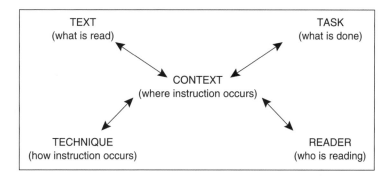

Figure 2–2 *The Reading Event*

generally more cognitively challenging and engaging (Hiebert, 1994). Teachers need to choose activities that will show children the variety of functions that reading can serve: reading for pleasure, reading for information, or reading to remember. Tasks are understood in terms of the context in which they are embedded. If learners complete authentic tasks that are familiar and functional, they will generate responses easily and view literacy as a challenging cognitive task (Turner, 1997). However, if the task is contrived to teach an isolated part of reading, then students must define the task as well as its function. In fact, many teachers evaluate precisely this factor: the rapidity with which students can figure out the task. Thus, contrived tasks make instruction less effective for the problem reader.

Therefore, the kind of task students are asked to do affects their reading performance. For instance, the diagnostic teacher uses either *silent or oral reading* during the diagnostic lesson. Sometimes oral reading is performed for students to prove a prediction that they made before a silent reading of a text; thus, students are reading material aloud that they previously read silently. Therefore, they use already-obtained meaning to facilitate their oral reading. At other times, however, the oral reading occurs on an initial reading of the passage, which places an additional demand on the processing of information (Allington, 1984b). In this instance, readers must attend not only to meaning but also to oral production of the text. Whether the text is read orally or silently is a task condition.

As the diagnostic teacher varies the task demands, the students produce widely varied responses. After reading a paragraph and being asked literal questions, students often ask for a second chance, once they know what the teacher wants for an answer. Students who are repeatedly asked one *type of question* pay more attention to that type of information (Hiebert, 1994). In other words, the type of question typically asked narrows a reader's purpose for reading and therefore limits comprehension. In one study, when students were given formal, text-based questions and assignments, they tended to report more story elements and interpret the text objectively. But when these same students were given questions and task assignments that were more personal, they included fewer story elements and interpreted the stories in light of their prior experiences (Newell, Suszynski, & Weingart, 1989).

Reading comprehension can be assessed using two formats. The teacher can use direct questions: "How did Johnny solve his problem?" Or he can ask students to retell the story: "Tell me this story in your own words." However, the kind of information required and the organization of the response make these tasks quite different. Direct questioning asks for information from the text that relates specifically to the stem of the question. An oral retelling, however, asks students to organize a response according to what they think is important. These two types of task have different *production demands*. Answers to direct questions frequently require a short, circumscribed response; while a retelling usually involves an elaborated response.

Likewise, the type of response can require different *types of reasoning*. Sometimes the diagnostic teacher uses a series of direct, literal questions: "Who were the characters? What did they do? What was the outcome?" Answering these questions is different from answering questions about the overall theme: "What was the author trying to tell you in this story? Do you think the author has a reason for including this character?" The two types of questions require different kinds of reasoning (Fitzgerald, 1989). The first group of questions requires the students to recall factual information stated in the text. The second group requires that readers use inferential thinking about the author's intended meaning. The readers have to use several parts of the text to construct a rationale for their answers. Still other questions ask students to respond personally to information in the text: "Have you had experiences similar to Jack's? Did you feel the same way?"

Besides the reasoning requirements, the order in which the teacher asks the questions can also change the task. Questions can probe a logical sequence of story development, or they can require nothing more than a random recall of unrelated facts. These two tasks are quite different. Questions that probe a logical sequence of story events cause students to think about story development and, therefore, increase their comprehension of the story (Pearson, Roehler, Dole, & Duffy, 1992). Unrelated literal questions, however, are harder to answer because they offer no relationship among the responses. Furthermore, asking students to relate story comprehension to their own experiences can prompt them to associate what was read to what they already know and thereby increase their comprehension of the text.

The questions that the diagnostic teacher asks change the task, making it harder or easier for the student to understand stories. Likewise, the task changes if the readers have the *text available* for answers. The difference in the responses when the text is available and when it is not becomes a task condition. If the teacher prompts the student to clarify a response or asks the student to search the text, he influences comprehension and changes the original task demands. This change often increases comprehension. When the teacher does not probe incomplete student responses, a valuable learning occasion may be lost. When possible, the diagnostic teacher probes the students' responses and records the task modifications that increase reader performance.

In summary, the task can vary during reading instruction. As tasks change, the way the reader perceives the purpose of the task and approaches the text may change. Likewise, the task can be oral or silent reading of sentences, paragraphs, or stories. After students read the story, the task can vary from answering direct questions to elaborate, unaided recall of textual information. Questioning can also vary from literal teacher-generated questions to nonliteral student-generated questions. Furthermore, responses can require different kinds of reasoning; they can vary from factual recall to personal application. Sometimes responses require students to locate the answer in the text, while at other times they do not use it to answer questions.

Consequently, different task conditions result in various instructional procedures, which can be modified by the diagnostic teacher. Altering any of the task conditions changes the nature of the information obtained during a diagnostic lesson. It is the diagnostic teacher's responsibility to analyze the major task features of the diagnostic lesson and vary them (when necessary) to enhance the students' ability to construct meaning with text. The following list provides task considerations that establish what the student is asked to do and can be used to focus the teacher's reflective thinking about the reading event.

What the teacher asks students to do affects the kind of information he obtains about them. Many beginning teachers evaluate only oral reading and believe that students have no reading problem. If the teacher had asked questions after silent reading, he would have found that the students did not comprehend what they read silently. They did not know how to think about what they were reading. The diagnostic teacher thinks about what he asks students to do when they read. Then he formulates tentative decisions about the students' reading processes.

- Purpose for the task
- Oral or silent reading
- Question type
    Literal, nonliteral, main idea, vocabulary
- Production requirements
    One-word response, retelling, finding answer in text
- Reasoning requirements of task
    Factual recall, inference, application
- Availability of text

Text

Traditionally, variation in a student's reading is attributed to the difficulty of the text. However, the influence the text has on reading performance is much more complex. The diagnostic teacher, therefore, systematically evaluates what the student is reading. He thinks about the possible textual characteristics that affect reading performance. He thinks about the content, length, and complexity of the passage, as well as its coherence, words, and structure. The *length of the passage* (sentences, paragraphs, stories), for example, can affect both miscues and understanding. Many short passages are extremely dense, requiring an extraordinary amount of comprehension in a short span. Longer passages, on the other hand, often contain *examples,* diagrams, and explanations that aid comprehension. For some students, however, reading a long passage orally often reduces comprehension because of the attention demanded by oral production over a long period of time. Other students' strategies improve as they read longer passages. The diagnostic teacher thinks about how passage length, *density of information,* and use of examples affect reading performance.

Reading performance also changes with different *text formats* (narrative or expository). Each text format requires different kinds of reading strategies. Narrative text is organized using characters who have problems that are solved. The story line is developed through characters' actions, consequences of their actions, and events that occur in solving the problem. Expository texts are organized around main ideas and the supporting details that explain the main idea. Because each text format is organized differently, readers do not have the same experiences with them, which increases the variability of their performance (Pearson & Camperell, 1994).

The way the text is *structurally organized,* moreover, influences what is remembered. Authors who logically organize the text using the expected formats for narrative or expository text facilitate reader performance. If a text follows a logical organization, then it is easier to comprehend and remember (Hare, Rabinowitz, & Schieble, 1989). Thus, the style the author uses will affect reader performance. High-quality literature provides students with authentic reading experiences that motivate them to read (Rasinski & Padak, 1996). When expository text is written in a more *engaging style* (more like a novel), it is also more easily remembered. Thus, *coherent organization* and engaging style affect reading performance.

The *type of content* likewise affects reading performance. Students differ in what they already know about the topic they are reading. The more students use what they already know about a particular content, the more they will remember when they read the text (Paris, Wasik, & Turner, 1991). The diagnostic teacher analyzes the content of the text and how much *prior knowledge students need* to know before they read the text. For example, the sentence "She wore a parka" requires more prior knowledge on the part of the reader than "She wore a parka to protect her from the cold wind."

The diagnostic teacher evaluates the effect that text content and required prior knowledge have on reader performance.

Grammatical complexity also affects constructing meaning with text. Some texts are constructed of simple sentences that require the reader to infer causality. For example, the pair of sentences "The chair fell. The dog ran." requires that the reader infer that the dog ran because the chair fell. Other texts are constructed with more complex sentences that reveal causality and thus facilitate comprehension. The wording "The dog ran because the chair fell" describes the relationship between the dog running and the chair falling. Sometimes the simple sentences do not tell a readily comprehensible story. If the sentences are combined to form a well-structured story and connections between ideas are explicitly made, text is easier to understand.

The *predictability of the sentences* also affects reading performance. If the text contains repeated language patterns, the child can predict a word by using the pattern of the language (Fountas & Pinnell, 1996). For example, the language pattern in the following paragraph allows readers to use a minimal amount of visual cues to guess the words: "There was an old fisherman who swallowed a shark. He swallowed the shark to catch the piranha. He swallowed the piranha to catch the crayfish. He swallowed the crayfish to catch the gnat. He swallowed the gnat as he yawned on the shore."

In addition to predictable patterns, other types of *word choices* affect comprehension of text. Some texts have words that are easy to read but do not convey the exact meaning. For example, "This boy had that" uses easy words, but it does not describe the exact meaning of the story. In another text, the words may be harder to read but more precise in conveying the intended meaning of the text: "The tall boy had the ice cream cone." This sentence uses harder words, but the meaning is clearer because the words are more precise.

During initial reading instruction, word choices are highly related to reading performance. For children who have profited from instruction in phonics, a text that is decodable is easier to read ("The pig went to dig a hole") than a text that consists primarily of sight words ("The children have gone to the house") (Barr, Blachowicz, & Wogman-Sadow, 1995). As children apply the rules of the phonetic system to a text that has a high percentage of sight words, the error pattern will reveal a set of problems different from what might appear if the text contained decodable words that followed the rules they had been taught (see Chapter 6).

The diagnostic teacher thinks about the words in the text. He evaluates whether the words can be easily decoded using phonic rules. If the students were taught to read using a sight word approach (see "Sight Word Approach" in Chapter 11), the diagnostic teacher evaluates whether the words in the text are the words that students have been taught in the program. If so, students can use this knowledge to read the unfamiliar text. They figure out a word by thinking, "What word do I already know that starts with a *b*?" If the words are unknown, the diagnostic teacher checks to see if the new words have similar letter patterns to the words that the students already know. If the new words have the same pattern as the known words, students can figure out a word by thinking, "What word do I already know that looks like this word?" However, if many words are unfamiliar or words do not have patterns similar to known words, students will stumble over words, substituting words that make sense but do not look like the words in the story. Therefore, the diagnostic teacher evaluates the words in the text to assess their influence on student performance.

The text can help or hinder reading performance. The kind of text that is read will affect the information the teacher gathers about students' reading. For example, an informal reading inventory placed a student at the sixth-grade reading level; however, this same student had difficulty when she read the 10-page story in the sixth-grade reader. Three text characteristics had changed. The content had changed from information about sunflowers to a story about a boy who was cleaning his room. The text length had changed from short paragraphs to a long story. The text format had changed from expository to narrative.

A reflective teacher looks closely at the kind of text he has asked students to read. He asks himself, "Which features of the text will affect students' reading?" Then he asks, "Have these same features affected the reading before?" In other words, "Is it a consistent problem?"

In conclusion, a variety of textual characteristics affect student reading performance. Passage length, as well as the density of information and the elaboration of information by the use of examples, pictures, diagrams, and headings, influences student performance. Equally important are the passage format (expository or narrative) and the organizational structure of the text. Furthermore, an engaging style (whether the text is expository or narrative) facilitates comprehension of the text. Authors can require an extensive background knowledge or coherently organize the text to clarify and elaborate word meanings. Likewise, the grammatical complexity and the authors' word choices affect how the student constructs meaning. In other words, the diagnostic teacher examines the text to evaluate these features, which affect student reading performance:

- Passage length
- Density of information
    Elaboration, or use of examples
- Passage format
    Expository or narrative
- Organizational structure or coherence
    Headings, diagrams, etc.
- Engaging style

- Type of content
- Background knowledge required of reader
- Grammatical complexity
    Predictable sentence patterns
- Word choices
    Decodability, distinctive meanings

Reader

Bringing to the task and the text their own knowledge and strategies, learners construct meaning in distinctively different ways; therefore, the diagnostic teacher observes students' interactions and engagement within the reading event to assess learner differences. Readers differ not only on *what* they already know (knowledge-based dimensions) but also on *how* they integrate new information into what they already know (strategy-based dimensions). Likewise, readers differ in their engagement during reading events.

Initially, the diagnostic teacher evaluates *knowledge-based dimensions.* He establishes *reading levels* for instruction by matching the readability of the text with the level of reading performance for the students. Concurrently, he finds out what the readers already know about the task of reading and the content that he is to teach. As the instruction begins, the diagnostic teacher looks for patterns within the reading event to analyze *skill knowledge.* Word identification skills (e.g., sight word knowledge, phonic knowledge, and context use), vocabulary knowledge, and fluency are evaluated in relation to how the student constructs meaning. Comprehension skills (e.g., identifying the main idea or problem, key details or events, and the theme or the resolution) are also evaluated during instruction.

Equally important to skill knowledge is the student's general knowledge as indicated by *language facility.* Some students have a rich variety of experiences and are able to talk about these experiences. This ability indicates that students are organizing and classifying their worlds of experiences. When they read, they are able to use their prior experience and the words they know to express them. Other students have limited experiences or limited word knowledge, which results in difficulty when reading. Therefore, students' knowledge of the world and the words they use to describe their experiences influence comprehension and word identification (Daneman, 1991).

These knowledge-based dimensions are accentuated by differences in readers' strategy deployment *(strategy-based dimensions).* Students differ in their strategy deployment (Paris, Lipson, & Wixson, 1994). Some students select meaning cues, while others select graphic cues. Some students rely heavily on their background knowledge, while others use only the text to form hypotheses while they are reading. Some students revise and monitor their model of meaning readily, while others need explicit information in the text before they revise their models.

Students' use of strategies can be evaluated by their patterns of verbal responses and miscues (words miscalled) as they read and answer questions. Looking for consistent patterns, the diagnostic teacher notices students' selection strategies (the way they find cues and use sources of information), monitoring strategies (the way they check their understanding), and elaboration strategies (the way they relate new information to what they already know). Initially, the diagnostic teacher notices the student's *selection strategies,* or how the reader selects from a range of information sources to enhance comprehension and correct miscues. To repair mistakes, students can use the overall meaning ("Oops, that doesn't make sense") or the way the word fits into the sentence ("That doesn't sound like a sentence"). Sometimes students use what the word looks like or sounds like ("Oops, I didn't say what those letters say") to restore comprehension. Efficient readers select appropriate cues and flexibly use sources of information; however, inefficient readers often use only a single source of information when selecting cues.

Readers also differ in their *monitoring strategies,* or when and how they check their understanding. Students' strategies for monitoring word identification and comprehension are evaluated through oral reading and story discussions. Young and less skilled readers monitor their reading less frequently (Paris, Lipson, & Wixson, 1994). They tend to read a string of words without checking to see if the words they are reading make sense. When their understanding breaks down, students differ in their persistence to regain meaning. Many poor readers tend to give up when repeatedly encountering problems, while good readers persist in employing a variety of strategies to solve problems.

Finally, readers differ in the way they elaborate responses *(elaboration strategies)*. During a discussion, some students answer literal-level questions with exact, text-based responses, while others answer questions by relying heavily on the overall theme of the story and inferring facts about the story rather than recalling specific information. Retellings can also indicate students' ability to organize and elaborate verbal responses. In an oral retelling, the brevity or elaboration of the story theme is noted to determine the student's preference for either generalizing or using specific facts.

Through instructional interactions, the teacher notes the students' involvement in literacy activities *(engagement dimension)*. The students' engagement is based on the reasons and expectations that they have for participating in a reading event. They formulate these reasons from past experiences and their personal coping strategies.

The value the students place on reading differs based on their experiences and model for literacy within their environment. When students see parents, grandparents, and friends reading in their daily life, then they too begin to value literacy as these role models do. Thus, if students value reading and see its usefulness, then they are more likely to engage in literacy activities. One part of valuing literacy is the interest value placed on not only literacy activities, but also on the tasks and topics that are read. When reading an interesting story, students are often more engaged than when reading incoherent expository text (Schallert & Reed, 1997).

Engagement can also stem from a reader's ability beliefs or their belief in their competence as a reader. These beliefs are usually pervasive and difficult to change. If a student views herself as unable to read, it is difficult to change her perception of herself as a reader. These beliefs affect the perception of task success and the student's engagement. If students believe they can succeed in a reading task, then, they are more likely to choose to read. The reader's perception of her success at a task influences the amount of effort she will expend and her persistence in reading (Wigfield, 1997). Because prior experiences with reading vary as well as reading success, students differ in their beliefs about their success or self-efficacy when they read. This belief, in turn, affects their engagement.

The diagnostic teacher also notices how the students respond to their own successes and failures or their attributions of success or failure during instruction. Some readers persist when confronted with a difficult task, while others give up easily and are more likely to attribute failure to lack of ability (Wigfield, 1997). When these readers are successful, they attribute success to luck or an easy task. These attributions affect their subsequent engagement.

Similar to this response of attribution, some students view reading as a strategic process and are reinforced simply by revising their thinking and thinking new thoughts. Other students, however, view reading as getting the words right, and when they falter, they lower their perception of themselves as readers and in turn decrease their engagement. They do not understand how to apply strategies when reading becomes difficult; therefore they do not expect a successful outcome of their engagement.

Further, students differ in their evaluation of how they are doing. Some students easily evaluate their performance, and if the evaluation is positively related to their effort, they increase engagement (Schunk & Zimmerman, 1997). Other readers have a rather hazy notion of what constitutes proficient reading. They therefore often have a confused idea of their performance and disengage in literacy activities.

The teacher also notes the students' need for "sense making." Some students like to work practice examples and actually love workbook exercises, despite the fact that these exercises may have little substantial purpose. Such students believe the teacher is right and are externally motivated to please the teacher. Other students, however, continually search for meaning (Oldfather, 1992). These students are intrinsically motivated to read and experience learning as deeply personal. Their engagement is sustained by the ideas and emotions that emerge from constructing meaning.

Students have different preferences for the social interactions within the classroom. Some students like to read and respond independently. They prefer to work alone or simply with a partner. However, other students like social settings in which they share their learning with group members. They are constantly learning from their peers as they discuss ideas. In fact, most of these learners increase their engagement when they work as part of a group. The group offers support for ideas and a chance to share and modify thinking. According to Almasi (1996), students who talk with their friends about what they read are more active, engaged readers. Thus, social interaction and the expectation that individuals will listen to their perspectives creates increased student engagement.

How readers approach the reading event affects the kind of information a teacher has about them. A teacher makes many diagnostic decisions about differences among the learners in his classroom based on what his students know, how they learn, and their engagement. Although this assessment is appropriate, a teacher should also evaluate how the other variables of the reading event affect the reading patterns that the readers use. He asks, "Is what I am observing a pattern that I always see in these readers, or has something in the reading event affected their performance?" Therefore, to assess readers, he looks for consistent responses over different reading events.

In conclusion, readers differ not only on what they already know as evaluated by level of performance, skill knowledge, and content knowledge, but also on the strategies they possess. These strategy-based differences include patterns of cue and strategy selection, monitoring and shifting of these strategies, as well as elaboration strategies. Students also differ in their engagement. The value students place on literacy activities varies, as do their perceptions of their abilities when completing literacy activities. They differ in their perception of the strategies available to them to recover meaning as well as their ease of self-evaluation and subsequent attributions of success or failure. The students' need for sense making and their interactions within a social group also vary. Each of the attributes affects their engagement in literacy activities. The diagnostic teacher evaluates the following dimensions of reading performance:

- Knowledge-based dimensions
- Reading level
- Skill knowledge
- Language facility (General knowledge)
    Word and world knowledge
- Strategy-based dimensions
    Source of information selected
        Text or prior knowledge
    Monitoring—active or passive
    Elaboration
        One word or embellished
        Literal or nonliteral

■ Engagement dimension
    Engagement dimension
    Value of literacy tasks
    Ability beliefs
    Attributions of success or failure
    Perception of available strategies
    Sense making
    Social interaction

Technique

A key to effective instructional decision making is an analysis of the intervention, or the techniques, that the diagnostic teacher employs. During the lesson, the diagnostic teacher thinks about how the readers will best profit from instruction. Subsequently, he analyzes how various techniques approach instruction so that he can match readers' strategies with the most efficient instructional techniques. Several considerations inform the analysis of instructional techniques.

Techniques can differ in their function within the *instructional framework*. Some techniques develop prerequisite knowledge in order to understand the content of the story. Techniques that introduce vocabulary and develop background knowledge are used prior to reading, while other techniques focus on developing active reading during the reading of the text. Techniques such as the directed-reading-thinking activity, reciprocal questioning procedure, and reciprocal teaching (see Chapters 10 and 11) are used during the reading of the story to promote active comprehension. Furthermore, after a story is read, techniques can extend the comprehension of the story (see "Story Map" in Chapter 11) or reinforce word identification and fluency (see "Repeated Readings" in Chapter 11).

Different techniques were designed to be used with different *types of text*. Some techniques fit narrative text and would not be appropriate for expository text. For example, it would be difficult to story map an expository passage about volcanoes. However, making a vocabulary map or a K-W-L sheet (see Chapter 11) is ideal for expository text.

Techniques also differ in the *mode of response* that readers are asked to use. Some techniques ask students to discuss what they learn when reading. By sharing their thoughts through a discussion, students select what is important to reconstruct the story. They actually construct an answer rather than merely recall events. Other techniques ask students to write about what they have read, which facilitates meaning construction. Again, students must decide what is important, as well as how they will communicate what they learned. Readers vary in their ability and preference for response modes. Some students like to discuss what they have learned and share ideas and thoughts. Other students, however, prefer to write what they are thinking so that they can revise their understanding before communicating what they think. The diagnostic teacher selects a response mode that will mediate learning for a particular student.

The diagnostic teacher also decides whether a technique is to work on a *strategy or a skill*. Some techniques incorporate strategy instruction as they teach skills, while other techniques focus only on the skills. Question-answer relationships (see "Question-Answer Relationships" in Chapter 11) is a technique developed to teach the skill of answering comprehension questions. Students learn to analyze questions according to the source of information needed to answer the question. Not only are they taught the skill of answering comprehension questions that are literal or inferential, but they are given strategies for how to use the skill. On the other hand, a typical synthetic phonics lesson (see "Synthetic Phonics Approach" in Chapter 11) may focus only on skills. The lesson teaches the skill of blending sounds together to form words. However, students are not taught how that skill is used as a flexible strategy when miscues occur as they read.

As discussed in Chapter 1, techniques also differ according to what *source of information* is emphasized during instruction. Some techniques ask students to use their prior knowledge, or reader-based inferencing. In using these techniques, the diagnostic teacher helps students focus on what they know to figure out what the text may say. In other words, they use a reader-based approach. Message writing (see "Message Writing" in Chapter 10) is an approach that begins by using what students know and then helps them construct rules for word analysis. In this approach, the students use what they want to say (reader-based inferencing) to figure out unknown words as they write. Other techniques, however, ask the student to use the information in the text. In using these techniques, the diagnostic teacher helps the student focus mainly on the text to figure out the meaning. For example, in the synthetic phonics approach (see Chapter 11), the student is asked to decode words letter by letter, focusing on the text to figure out the words. After the word is decoded, the student is asked to think about what it might mean. In these approaches, the students are continually asked to refer to the text when problems in print processing occur.

Techniques also differ in the *nature of the structure* that is provided by the diagnostic teacher during implementation. Some techniques require that the teacher present the information in a rather nondirective format and simply provide thoughtful questions and support for reading. These techniques rely on students to construct their own rules. When using these techniques, the diagnostic teacher immerses students in contextual reading and then facilitates their inquiry. It is assumed that students will be able to discover the meaning of the text on their own. The language experience approach (see "Language Experience Approach" in Chapter 11), where students read stories that they have dictated to the teacher, is based on an implicit, nondirective approach to learning. This technique allows students to learn to read by encountering in print the language structures they use.

Other techniques require that the teacher direct learning by modeling how the strategy or skill is to be used in the reading process. Furthermore, students are directed in how to incorporate this strategy or skill into their reading. Reciprocal teaching (see "Reciprocal Teaching" in Chapter 11) is a technique that uses explicit instruction. Students are shown how to summarize, ask good questions, clarify difficult parts, and predict what will be discussed. First, the teacher models the strategy; then the students lead the discussion with the teacher offering encouragement and talking about when it is best to use the strategies.

Not only do techniques differ in their function as exemplified by their instructional frameworks, they also differ in the cognitive demands placed on learners by the *instructional sequence*. Some techniques present reading tasks as a whole and simultaneous and show students how the parts are organized within the whole. These techniques are called *simultaneous*. The predictable language approach (see Chapter 11) is an example of a technique that introduces the story as a whole. Children read along with the teacher to discover the predictable pattern. After the story has been read as a whole several times, students are asked to identify individual words.

Other techniques present the parts of the reading task in a sequential, step-by-step progression that leads to the formation of the whole. These techniques are called *successive*. They emphasize verbalizing the separate parts, logically structuring these parts into a whole, and explicitly stating rules for organizing the parts into a whole. Synthetic phonics is an example of a technique that is sequential in nature. The synthetic phonics approach begins by teaching the sounds of letters. These sounds are then blended to form words, and finally rules for the different sound combinations are given.

How the teacher directs the reading event affects the information he gathers. Techniques vary in the demands placed on learners. For example, a teacher explicitly tells a student to look at the sounds of letters and blend the sounds together to form words; however, the student prefers to create her own rules, and thinking about sounds is her weakness. The ineffective teacher continues to teach the letter sounds, providing a high degree of feedback about her miscues and finally concluding that she is passive and a nonreader.

However, the effective diagnostic teacher probes further. He changes the technique to include predictable stories that have phonetically consistent words. When the student self-corrects, the teacher asks, "How did you figure that out?" The student then tells how she has used her knowledge of phonics: "I thought about other words that looked like this word and then I substituted the sounds. You see hopping looks like popping. Words that look alike at the end usually sound alike." The diagnostic teacher changed the technique from explicit instruction in letter sounds to implicit instruction in a text that required the student to create her own rules for phonics. The reflective teacher thinks about how he is directing instruction. He asks himself, "In what other ways can this task be presented so that this student can learn more efficiently?"

Although evaluating techniques seems to present an either-or situation, in reality, the techniques can be placed upon a continuum of instructional features. For example, a technique is neither a totally explicit nor a totally implicit one; rather, each technique falls along a continuum with a tendency to approach instruction from a more or less explicit to a more or less implicit structure. The relative effectiveness of its approach depends on the learner's task knowledge and task independence, as well as the teacher's execution.

In conclusion, the diagnostic teacher can use different teaching techniques to vary the manner in which instruction is offered. The techniques can be more appropriately used either before, during, or after instruction. Some techniques are more appropriate for narrative text, while others are better for expository material. Likewise, some techniques require oral discussion while others require a written response. Techniques are designed to teach skills or strategies or both. Techniques vary in the source of information stressed during implementation (reader-based or text-based). Techniques also vary in the amount of teacher direction necessary for their implementation. Some techniques present information as a whole (simultaneously) and then show the parts, while other techniques present information in separate parts (sequentially) and then show how the parts fit into the whole. The diagnostic teacher evaluates the instructional features of each technique, as well as the students' responses to the techniques. He then selects the most efficient techniques to mediate learning for his students. Instructional features include the following:

- Instructional framework
    Before, during, or after reading
- Type of text
    Narrative or expository
- Mode of response
    Discussion or writing
- Strategy instruction
    Predict, monitor, elaborate
- Skill instruction
    Word identification, fluency, vocabulary, comprehension, or study skills
- Source of information
    Reader-based or text-based
- Instructional structure
    Implicit or explicit
- Instructional sequence
    Simultaneous or successive (sequential)

Context

The social context plays an important role in influencing the learning that occurs during an instructional event. How teachers and students exchange information about what they are reading affects construction of meaning. In one study, for example, students' story retellings were more complete when conveyed to a peer who had not read the story than when they were told to a teacher who had read the story (Harste, Burke, & Woodward, 1994). In other words, the students and the teacher read more than the story in the book. In essence, they also read the context, such as the authority structure of the classroom (whose understanding will count?), the teacher (what are the expectations), the social dynamics (what are the question-answer patterns) and the sociocultural setting (Ruddell & Unrau, 1997). Thus, how teachers and students exchange information about what they are reading affects construction of meaning. Likewise, whether it is assessment or informal discussion, affects their responses. A fifth-grader explained it simply: "It is like school has a big circle around it. Once I walk into this circle, I don't talk. Outside this circle, I talk a lot. I talk with my friends about the ideas I have. But in school, I don't talk about the ideas that I have" (S. R. Walker, personal communication, February 17, 1982).

This example illustrates the status of schooling. Schooling has become a culture of its own where students are taught formal rules within well-structured problems. Unfortunately, problem solving, particularly when reading, is a complex, dynamic activity that depends heavily on the context in which it is situated. Vygotsky (1978) stressed that social interaction provides individuals with an opportunity to interact with more knowledgeable peers, thus increasing their level of understanding. Students "gradually internalize some of the interpretative behaviors that are associated with higher levels of thinking" (Almasi, 1996, p. 15). Their thinking is expanded by rethinking what others view as the meaning of a text. Thus, knowledge is reconstructed within each experience as the learner reflects on how a particular context affects his interpretation. As students read and resolve ambiguities in a variety of literacy contexts, they refine and generalize their knowledge and strategies. As a result, knowledge and strategies are constantly evolving with each new situation.

Often, however, instruction does not focus on an exchange of ideas about content and the strategies used to derive meaning from texts. Much of the time teachers ask questions to assess learning rather than discuss ideas. Continual random assessment after students read a story can inhibit an exchange of relevant information. By focusing on irrelevant facts without connecting them to the reader's knowledge, the teacher inhibits reading comprehension and reinforces a context of interrogation rather than discussion. This recitation format does not allow students to participate in engaging discussions where they can construct meaning (Almasi, 1994).

Rather than using a recitation format, the diagnostic teacher moves his interactions to a discussion where students naturally engage in constructing meaning. When a teacher *shares meaning construction,* he changes the situational context in order to engage everyone in constructing meaning rather than merely to answer questions. Meaning is negotiated during the discussion with all students sharing and reconstructing their ideas. The diagnostic teacher listens closely to the discussion focusing comments on the students' ideas (Peterson & Eeds, 1990) and encouraging reflection by saying, "Let's think more about that idea." Thus, meaning is co-constructed among group members, and shared understanding is created by students' framing and re-considering themes and concepts.

The diagnostic teacher thinks about the *composition of the instructional group* and how he responds to students during the lesson. The context can vary by who is a member of the instructional group and the students' perception of their membership in that group. Sometimes the diagnostic teacher uses whole-group instruction; however, sometimes he uses small groups or partner reading, which can be heterogeneous (grouped by different traits) or homogeneous (grouped by similar traits). At times, he might even decide to have an individual conference or lesson with a student.

As well as the group composition, the diagnostic teacher decides at what *points he needs to provide assistance* to support dialogue and active thinking. If he provides assistance before the lesson, students might read the story with ease; however, they might profit more from talking about reading strategies as they read the story. If he intervenes at the appropriate instructional points during the reading event, he is able to support students' construction of meaning by listening closely to students' ideas, thus, building more appropriate student-teacher interactions. In this situation, the diagnostic teacher evaluates his responsiveness to students' comments, examining their intended meaning and tailoring the discussion to meet the developing understanding of the students (Roskos & Walker, 1998). These analyses can foster an engaging and dynamic relationship between the diagnostic teacher and his students.

Thus, in discussions and assessment, the diagnostic teacher analyzes his own dialogue, focusing on how he *elicits student responses*. He thinks about how he formed his questions and how the formulation influenced the response. He evaluates whether his questions and comments truly assist the students' thinking. The diagnostic teacher probes and rephrases his instructions. For example, he can suggest students work together to look for the page in the text where the topic is discussed, and then he can ask students to read the page orally. He can rephrase the text, eliciting from the students what similar experience they might have had, and encourage the students to tie together their experiences with the text. This process can prompt the students to elaborate information from the text with background knowledge. If students cannot construct meaning, the teacher thinks about how he can assist them. He asks himself, "Do I need to focus on what the word means or do I need to reread the text with expression?" These on-the-spot analyses create a context where meaning can be co-constructed.

Teachers also can change when and how they *prompt* students. When the teacher gives the student the word or tells her to sound it out, the student loses an opportunity to construct a meaning base for reading. The student will continue to focus on the words in the text without thinking about their meaning (Rasinski & Deford, 1988). Other times teachers interrupt at the point of error and prompt with a word-level prompt. However, with some students, teachers wait until the end of the sentence and then say, "Try that again; that didn't make sense" (Cunningham & Allington, 1999). Allowing students to read to the end of the sentence rather than interrupting at the point of error facilitates more active reading strategies and communicates to readers that they can think through problems when they read (Cunningham & Allington, 1999). Thus, the diagnostic teacher is aware of the silent time between responses *(wait time)* and the scaffolds, or prompts, he uses to promote meaning construction within the social context.

When teachers interrupt students when students make errors, they are focusing on accuracy rather than meaning and are interacting in a recitation format; they are thus encouraging students to develop a helpless approach to problems. Many times this focus is based on teachers' expectations for students. *Teachers' expectations* about students' abilities frame the context of the reading interaction. If teachers expect students to fail and to expend little effort, then teachers' language, wait time, and prompting will convey this expectation to the readers. Consequently, the readers respond according to the teachers' expectations (Ruddell & Unrau, 1997). They slowly change their perceptions of the literacy context and begin to judge themselves as unable to read, which contributes to their associating reading events with failure.

Often school reinforces negative expectations by focusing on weaknesses. When teachers focus on skill weaknesses and repeatedly evaluate these skills using criterion-referenced tests, they reinforce the reader's association of reading with failure. Likewise, when teachers use norm-referenced evaluations, they reward students who learn easily and quickly rather than assist problem readers who may require adjustments in their learning. Although the problem readers try hard, they do not meet the standard created by other rapid learners in the classroom. Over time, problem readers change their perceptions of the context and view literacy events as experiences to avoid because their efforts do not result in positive evaluations by their teachers.

A key to reversing students' association of reading with failure is an instructional context where students *focus on strengths* and discuss with their peers what they know and can do. Likewise, conversations about *strategy use* (Walker, 1996) refocuses the classroom climate on how each student constructed meaning rather than on how to get right answers to narrowly defined questions. Discussing how students interpret text increases the likelihood that they will define the context of literacy as a place to refine and elaborate their knowledge and strategies.

Along with focusing on strengths and conversations about strategies, the diagnostic teacher changes the context by using *collaborative assessments* rather than evaluating students against their peers using norm-referenced assessments. The students and teacher construct assessments when they evaluate how the students did on a particular task. The students construct self-assessments when they evaluate how they did on a particular task. For instance, one teacher had his students evaluate how they retold a story. They used a short "yes or no" format of story elements to evaluate their story summaries (see Chapter 8). This assessment focused on how the task was completed rather than on a comparison among students. Then the students and their teacher talked about how the students could improve their performance on retelling. Two of the students were going to pay more attention to main characters while three were going to focus on key events rather than naming all the events. All the students were going to reread the last of the stories to figure out the resolution. In other words, the assessment had shifted from only the teacher making judgments to the students and teacher discussing performance and setting goals for improvement. This approach changed the context from simply looking at the number of points each student received to a collaborative process where individual goals were based on students' strategies and performance. Portfolios (see Chapter 8 for further elaboration), where students need to think about how to show their expertise and reflect on selected pieces that show what and how they are learning, also change the contextual interactions. When portfolios are used, the classroom climate changes from looking at how we are alike on a specific task to looking at how we all did the task well but differently. In portfolios, individual differences are highlighted by changing the context to one of accepting uniqueness rather than evaluating sameness.

The context of the reading event is a powerful influence on readers' performances. The situational context affects the information the teacher gathers about students' reading. For example, an informal assessment that used only factual questions after silent reading placed a student at the third-grade level; however, this same student was able to answer inferential questions at the eighth-grade level. When she discussed the same story with her peers, she recalled 80 percent of the facts as she needed them to support her interpretation. In this case, the context had changed from silent reading and answering factual questions in a relatively sterile context to reading and discussing the story in an interactive instructional group.

The diagnostic teacher thinks about how he negotiates meaning within a sociointeractive context that requires collaboration among group members. As the teacher becomes a sympathetic partner in understanding text rather than an assessor of students' deficits, he increases students' reading power through an instructional context that focuses on meaning. As an active listener responding creatively and consistently within the reading event, he carefully analyzes his own behavior and its effect on students' reading performance.

In conclusion, the context (or where instruction takes place) influences diagnostic decision making. A format that promotes shared meaning construction is encouraged. The context, therefore, can vary by who is a member of the instructional group and the student's perception of her membership in that group. The form and timing of teacher assistance are influential factors in creating a collaborative context for learning. Teacher expectations and classroom focus also influence the context. The diagnostic teacher evaluates all these factors in the following list in order to make diagnostic decisions:

- Format of discussion
  Shared meaning construction
  Group composition
  Point of assistance during the lesson
  Responsiveness
- Type of assistance
  Elicitation of responses
  Prompts
  Wait time
- Nature of teacher expectations and classroom focus
  Focus on strengths
  Focus on strategy use and effort
  Use of collaborative assessments

Summary

In summary, five interrelated variables establish the parameters of the diagnostic teaching that occurs in an interactive learning situation rather than a static, product-oriented situation. By evaluating these five variables, the diagnostic teacher identifies the instructional conditions. Reading instruction and assessment are redirected to the interrelationship of the variables rather than just student deficits.

3

Roles of Diagnostic Teachers

Effective diagnostic teaching involves making instructional decisions before, during, and after the reading event. At the core of decision making is the effective teacher who reflects on her instruction. As she teaches, the diagnostic teacher thinks about her role within the context of the reading event. This chapter delineates five roles of effective diagnostic teachers: reflecting, planning, mediating, enabling, and responding. These roles are supported by eight instructional guidelines that help focus diagnostic teaching and encourage students to realize their individual potential as learners. As the effective teacher assumes these roles, she views readers from different perspectives. As she reflects on her decision making, therefore, she considers each of these roles and its influence on her instruction. Figure 3–1 suggests the interrelationships between the roles and guidelines discussed in this chapter.

The first role of the effective diagnostic teacher is reflecting. Central to effective diagnostic teaching is the teacher who reflects on teaching before, during, and after the reading event. She checks the instructional decisions she makes with her personal assumptions about reading and cross-checks her plans with students' learning. As she is teaching, she analyzes how she modifies instruction and the language she uses to mediate learning. Teaching as reflecting means that every interaction is analyzed so that appropriate instructional adjustments can be made.

The second role of the diagnostic teacher is planning. As the diagnostic teacher plans her lesson, she thinks about the *whole act of reading* and selects experiences for students to share their ideas. As she plans her lessons, she selects activities that will not only stimulate learning, but *ensure success*. To do so, she uses familiar and interesting stories. At the end of the lesson, the diagnostic teacher encourages students to evaluate their experiences focusing their attention on their developing strengths. Teaching as planning means that the diagnostic teacher focuses on the whole act of reading, ensuring success for each student.

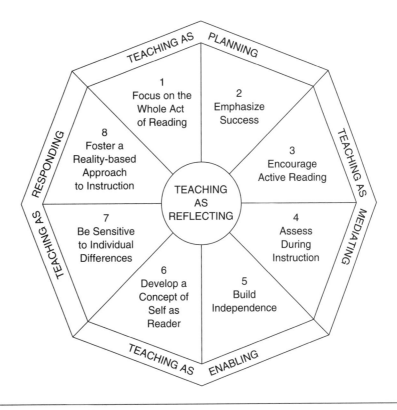

Figure 3–1   Roles of Diagnostic Teachers

The third role of diagnostic teaching is mediating. The effective diagnostic teacher *encourages active reading* on the part of learners by asking questions that not only lead students through the story but also relate the events and key ideas to what students already know. As she teaches, the diagnostic teacher actively aids students in sense making, phasing in to support reading and phasing out to promote self-directed learning (Singer, 1989). During the lesson, the diagnostic teacher *assesses while she instructs* so she can modify her instruction to meet students' changing instructional needs. Teaching as mediating means that the diagnostic teacher uses students' present strategies to lead them to more active reading strategies.

The fourth role of effective diagnostic teaching is enabling. She helps her students develop a *concept of themselves as readers*. Immersing her students in relevant and successful reading experiences, she attributes their success to the effective strategies they use. As she plans lessons, she thinks about how to *build students' independence*. She plans lessons where she models her own internal thinking, asks students to share in thinking through the problem, and actively listens and encourages students to tell her how they construct meaning. Teaching as enabling means that the diagnostic teacher provides students with the resources to understand themselves as readers, thinkers, and problem solvers.

In the fifth role, the diagnostic teacher views teaching as responding to individual human needs. An effective diagnostic teacher *accepts the individual differences* among her students. She knows that the experiences of her students vary widely and plans her instruction to account for the differences in what her students already know. She thinks about the different ways her students solve problems and plans lessons that use their problem-solving strengths. In accepting their individual differences, the effective teacher *fosters a reality-oriented environment* by accepting individuality but expecting all students to read. She uses humor and laughter to develop a relaxed atmosphere where students learn to cope with their mistakes and produce well-thought-out ideas. She also reacts personally to literacy, sharing her personal change as a result of being literate. In other words, she shares how literacy has changed her life. Teaching as a human response means that the diagnostic teacher treats individuality and making mistakes as human conditions.

These roles and the instructional guidelines they represent work together to create an instructional environment where all students learn. This model fosters instructional interactions that focus on the whole reading event, giving students control of their own learning and creating a coherent learning experience for them.

Reflecting

The reflective diagnostic teacher considers and selects among instructional alternatives and, at the same time, anticipates the consequences of differing decisions before, during, and after a reading event. This reflection helps teachers know why they teach as they do and facilitates their explanations to others (Roskos & Walker, 1994). The diagnostic teacher shifts between immersion in the reading event and distancing herself from it in order to critically analyze the experience. This distancing helps the diagnostic teacher reconsider reasons for her instruction and refocus on the theoretical framework that underpins these decisions (Walker, 1990a). Thus, in reflecting, the diagnostic teacher continually evaluates her guiding theory of reading (see Chapter 1) and expands her awareness of individual differences among students.

Before the lesson, the diagnostic teacher plans her instruction based on her guiding theory of reading. She thinks about students' strengths and needs in relation to students' knowledge, strategies, and engagement. She reflects upon the instructional sequence as she plans each lesson. Diagnostic lessons are much more than a set of activities selected because they are fun. Diagnostic teaching involves the systematic orchestration of reading instruction. At this stage in the teacher's thinking *(reflections before teaching)*, the students' attributes are matched with an instructional framework (see Chapter 4), and her plans are cross-checked with her guiding theory.

As the lesson is taught, the diagnostic teacher observes how the student is responding to the lesson *(reflections during instruction).* Using these observations, the diagnostic teacher changes original plans to modify instruction and thus to mediate student learning. Every day teachers make decisions that are often intuitive and unconscious. These changes enable problem readers to employ independent strategies. For example, after a fourth-grade teacher finished working with a student she reflected in this way:

> *"During the lesson, I discarded the story map, modeled self-talk, self-questioning, and especially prediction. I used the story map as a summary. . . . The student elaborated and answered with background knowledge the comprehension questions, today" (Jordan, 1989).*

In this example, the teacher makes adjustments during the lesson to improve the student's reading. The teacher is constantly sensitive to how the student-teacher interactions affect the goals of the lesson.

After the lesson, the diagnostic teacher evaluates what specific part of the lesson produced the desired reading behavior, and she considers how the on-the-spot adjustments fit into the overall diagnostic lesson. She considers the amount of energy expended in order to encourage student understanding. Likewise, she reflects on the scaffolding, or prompts, she used to improve reading performance. Then she makes adjustments in subsequent lesson plans as she reflects on what occurred and how the interactions were consistent with her plans as well as her beliefs about reading.

The reflective teacher analyzes her own preferences for learning and how these preferences affect her teaching. She focuses on how she learns and how she teaches, not only on what she is teaching. She watches herself to cross-check strategies for teaching with personal beliefs about reading. The teachers' beliefs about reading affect how they teach, (Ruddell & Unrau, 1994). Reflective teachers review their assumptions about literacy.

Finally, the diagnostic teacher thinks about how this instructional event brought a new understanding to her theory of reading instruction. For example, one diagnostic teacher was uncertain how to measure passive reading; she had a student who was not constructing meaning but simply repeating the words in the text. After teaching, she decided to review several articles on passive behavior in reading. She later commented: "I understand that there is no testing that particularly tests this element. It is determined by observation and analysis of the reader and the reading event." After analyzing the characteristics described in the research literature, she felt she knew enough to identify one of her students as a passive reader. These reflections led the diagnostic teacher to become more confident in her own knowledge. By reflecting on the various aspects of an instructional event and thinking about how they fit together, the diagnostic teacher elaborates and changes her model of the reading process. Through reflection, she actively constructs her theory of reading and reading instruction.

Thus, the diagnostic teacher reflects on her plans (the diagnostic session), her observations during instruction, and her intuitive decisions (adjustments). She uses these reflections as she plans lessons, mediates learning, enables student independence, and responds personally during the reading event.

Planning

Prior to the reading event, the teacher thinks about how instruction will occur. She thinks about the variables of the reading event: task, text, reader, and context. Then she selects teaching techniques that focus on reading stories that ensure student success. As teachers focus on the broad aspects of reading, they talk with students about why and how the strategies of reading will improve their reading performance. Through this interaction they create activities that are both challenging and successful.

This planning creates an expectation that the reading event will produce independent readers. Effective teachers expect the students in their classrooms to read and interpret stories. Furthermore, this planning allows the effective teacher to think about the strategies needed to complete the assigned reading task; therefore, she can attribute students' success to both their strategy use and efforts. Teaching as planning means that the teacher sets up her lessons both to focus on the whole act of reading and to ensure success. These two planning guidelines are delineated in the following section.

Guideline #1: Focus on the Whole Act of Reading

As the diagnostic teacher plans her instruction, she creates a literate environment by focusing on the whole act, rather than the parts, of reading. Furthermore, she realizes that students learn what teachers teach. If teachers instruct students to recognize vowel sounds, they will learn vowel sounds. If teachers emphasize literal comprehension, students will, in fact, become excellent fact finders and comprehend the literal information of a story. However, if teachers instruct students to respond to whole stories using important textual information and their own prior knowledge, students will actually become comprehenders who flexibly shift between reader-based and text-based knowledge. As a result, focusing instruction on the whole act of reading is extremely important.

Effective teachers focus on having students *read entire stories* and relate them to relevant personal experiences. They encourage sustained silent reading of stories. However, studies have shown not all students receive the same amount of contextual reading instruction. A longitudinal study that investigated children's reading progress in first through third grade (Juel, 1988) found that poor readers read less than half as many words each year as good readers. In another study, good readers were observed to be engaged in contextual reading 57 percent of the time; poor readers, only 33 percent of the time. Poor readers, in fact, spent an extended amount of time practicing the skills of reading in short, isolated drills (Allington, 1995). The results are even more astounding in remedial programs. In these programs, students read fewer than 50 words a day (Allington & Cunningham, 1996). Even though research supports the premise that skill knowledge is best mastered during contextual reading, it appears that remedial instruction in both classrooms and clinics continues to focus on the parts rather than the whole act of reading. However, classrooms with high reading achievement are characterized by reading of selections followed by small-group discussions where students exchange ideas about the meaning of the story (Gambrell, 1996). Through the small-group discussions, students justify their interpretations by relating the text to what they already know, which focuses instruction on meaning rather than decoding.

As teachers focus on the whole act of reading, they engage students in a *discussion about both the content of the story and the strategies* they use to construct meaning. This social interaction is critical to the process of constructing knowledge. As students explain and defend their ideas to their peers, they refine and reorganize their knowledge (Spiegal, 1998). Likewise, students who hold misconceptions about the content need to be challenged by others to redefine their understanding and create new knowledge. By communicating ideas in discussion groups, students share their interpretations, focus their purposes, and think about the functions of reading and writing. The diagnostic teacher plans time for discussing stories in both small-group and large-group settings so that students can explore their own interpretation with classmates.

The diagnostic teacher plans for the *engagement of all students* in an instructional group. Research shows that remedial instruction focusing on individualization means that each child "will work, primarily alone, on a different skill sheet. . . . Each child receives but a few moments of teacher attention" (Johnston & Allington, 1991, p. 994). Realizing that learning is a social activity, the diagnostic teacher makes sure all students interact in discussion groups, sharing their ideas about stories they have read. Therefore, as she plans for student engagement, she reminds herself of the social nature of literacy development and thus encourages active engagement in literacy for all students within her classroom.

In summary, the effective diagnostic teacher encourages students to discuss ideas during the reading event. She explains the process of shifting between reader-based knowledge and the text and how the strategies of reading will influence reading efficiency when problems in text interpretation arise. The diagnostic teacher carefully orchestrates these discussions to engage all students.

GUIDELINE #1: FOCUS ON THE WHOLE ACT OF READING

- Focus on reading entire stories.
- Plan time for discussing content and strategies.
- Plan for the engagement of all students.

Guideline #2: Emphasize Success

As the diagnostic teacher focuses on the whole act of reading, she must at the same time ensure successful reading for students. Students' reading achievement is directly related to their engagement in successful literacy activities. It is not only the amount of time engaged in reading that matters, but also important is a high level of success. Thus, in order to develop a notion of efficient reading, students must first experience numerous successful reading experiences. When students have success, they tend to repeat the successful activity. Obviously, success is a powerful motivating factor.

On the other hand, if students experience numerous failures in an activity, they often give up and avoid subsequent opportunities to engage in this activity. Poor readers often read material that is difficult for them (Allington & Cunningham, 1996). They have either a low rate of recognizing words or understanding the content, which discourages them from further reading. These unsuccessful reading experiences contribute to an unsystematic evaluation of reading performance. These students have a serendipitous notion about success. Success is attributed to external factors such as "It was baby reading material," "It was my lucky day," or "The teacher gave it away when she helped me."

To encourage a healthy attitude toward success, the diagnostic teacher creates a *series of consistently successful reading events*. She keeps a close match between the students' abilities and the texts that she chooses for reading instruction. When choosing texts, the diagnostic teacher not only considers an appropriate difficulty level but also the extent of students' prior experiences. She chooses material that contains familiar concepts so that students can readily use their prior knowledge to predict, monitor, and elaborate their understanding. She, then, plans for the students to read a greater amount of material and to express ideas based on what they have read.

Not only does the diagnostic teacher plan successful reading experiences by placing the students at the appropriate reading level, but she also carefully selects *authentic texts that are familiar and interesting* to her students. Good children's literature presents characters who share similar experiences with readers, thus promoting students' ability to read for meaning. When children's literature is matched with students' experiences, the problem readers readily identify with the main character's conflict and can successfully predict solutions out of their own experiences. Therefore, the diagnostic teacher selects high-caliber children's literature and reads with students to establish a successful reading experience. The students can continue to read on their own and feel the success of reading an entire book. This success can spill over into other literacy activities by giving students confidence in writing or in taking on other reading tasks.

However, many problem readers have a hazy notion of success and do not recognize when they are successful. Therefore, besides creating successful experiences, the diagnostic teacher designs activities that concretely show students how they are progressing. The diagnostic teacher *encourages self-assessment,* which helps readers evaluate and recognize their success. Portfolios, where students choose what is included in their assessment folder, can help them evaluate their success on various activities and show them their progress over time. Periodically, the teacher uses these portfolios to show students their growth in strategic reading and knowledge acquisition. Students can also evaluate their success on individual reading activities as they complete them by using teacher-developed check-sheets related to the task. For example, a check-sheet was designed with story grammar questions (see "Story Mapping," Chapter 11). The students marked whether their retelling included main characters, setting, problem, major events, and problem resolution (Glazer, 1992). Using the check-sheet, the students and teacher assess literacy and discuss student success. Self-assessment helps problem readers develop a more systematic evaluation of reading performance and attribute their success to internal factors such as knowledge and strategies rather than to luck or easy materials.

GUIDELINE #2: EMPHASIZE SUCCESS

- Create a series of successful reading events.
- Use authentic texts that are familiar and interesting.
- Encourage self-assessment.

Mediating

The diagnostic teacher mediates learning by phasing in and out of the reading event as she adjusts her instruction to students' needs. She asks questions that help students actively interpret the text. She listens to the students and uses what they understand about the story to elicit more elaborate interpretations. She gives them time to develop predictions and formulate answers. When students are unsure of a response, she asks them what they know so far about the story. Then she asks them to explain how they came to that conclusion. From this information, the teacher develops leading questions or examples that will guide the students' interpretation. Using students' responses, the diagnostic teacher assesses their learning as she teaches. Teaching as mediating means that the teacher phases in and out of the reading event in order both to encourage active reading and to assess learning as she teaches. These two mediating guidelines are detailed in the following section.

Guideline #3: Encourage Active Reading

Reading is an active, problem-solving process that involves predicting (or guessing) what the author is going to say, based on expectations about story events. After making a guess, students select clues from the story to confirm their guesses and then check this knowledge with what they already know. The diagnostic teacher engages students in this active problem-solving process so they construct meaning as they read. This engagement fosters students' exploration of their own concepts and strategies. From a young age, children strive to make sense of their world and the diagnostic teacher builds on this natural aptitude by supporting students in *making sense of reading and writing events.* The diagnostic teacher, then, encourages students to evaluate their guesses from a "sense making" perspective. She assists students to extend ideas, revise misconceptions, develop opinions, and prove beliefs. In their search for meaning, students invent their own explanations for print, examine and justify these hypotheses, and finally refute or rework their explanations. To mediate learning, the diagnostic teacher constantly engages students in an active meaning search.

To do so, the diagnostic teacher checks her behavior with both proficient and problem readers to see whether her prompts focus on meaning. Research shows that teachers treat their less proficient readers differently from their proficient readers (Johnston & Allington, 1991). When working with proficient readers, teachers are more engaged using meaning-level prompts and letting good readers continue reading to see whether they are going to recover meaning. However, when working with less proficient readers, teachers often allow more interruptions, interrupt poor readers at the point of error, and use more word-level prompting before correcting them. These teaching behaviors often cause poor readers to miscall words or ideas and continue reading without checking these words or ideas against an overall meaning to see whether they fit. For these readers, the diagnostic teacher needs to frame her prompts from a sense-making perspective. As students miscall a word or miscomprehend an idea, she indicates her inability to make sense of their response and encourages them to rethink their explanation. This approach focuses the problem reader on making sense of text.

As the diagnostic teacher responds to the discussion, she thinks about how to orchestrate her support. The effective diagnostic teacher *phases in to support the students' sense making and phases out to allow students to think independently* (Singer, 1989). Initially, she allows three to five seconds between her probes and the student's response. Increasing the wait time from one second to three seconds positively affects the number of student responses as well as the organization of the response (Allington & Cunningham, 1996). Furthermore, the amount of time between the students' responses and the teacher's response affects the elaboration of the answer. Thinking takes time. Silence may mean that students are constructing thoughtful responses.

Not only should the diagnostic teacher increase her wait time, but she must also deal effectively with inappropriate responses. Initially, the teacher uses part of the student's response to probe reasoning. Sometimes she rephrases or repeats part of the student's response to clarify the interpretations. At other times, she asks students to justify their answers by supplying information from the text. She probes student reasoning by asking "How do you know that?" and "What makes you think that?" Finally, if the line of reasoning is justifiable, the diagnostic teacher accepts the response as a valid point of view. As the diagnostic teacher increases her wait time and deals creatively with inappropriate responses, she develops an atmosphere that promotes active interpretation of text.

The diagnostic teacher can encourage active reading by *creating instructional conversations* (Goldenberg, 1992–1993) and focusing on constructing ideas rather than giving right or wrong answers. The diagnostic teacher creates a shared activity in which the students and teacher can discuss their ideas rather than the traditional recitation format used in classrooms. As they discuss ideas, the diagnostic teacher connects the students' statements, helping students build a cohesive understanding. She interjects open-ended comments that encourage rethinking of ideas, and she invites students to expand their thinking by saying "tell me more," encouraging them to connect important ideas in the text with their own knowledge.

In summary, the diagnostic teacher encourages active reading by focusing students on making sense of text and probing student responses in order to support their active reflection. She phases in and out of the lesson to create an atmosphere that promotes thinking rather than interrogation. To increase students' understanding, she engages students in conversations about text where they elaborate their thinking.

GUIDELINE #3: ENCOURAGE ACTIVE READING

- Focus on "sense making" with text.
- Phase in and out to support active thinking.
- Create conversations about the text.

Guideline #4: Assess During Instruction

As the diagnostic teacher implements the lessons that she planned, she keeps a mental log of the students' responses. Her instruction, therefore, not only creates active readers but also provides a means for assessment. As the diagnostic teacher mediates learning, she observes how she modifies the initial reading task to create learning. In other words, she *assesses changes in the readers' performances occurring as she mediates learning.* This record of students' responses to instructional modifications is called dynamic assessment. Dynamic assessment evaluates students' performances as they are guided to use more effective reading strategies. This type of assessment focuses on the students' acquisition of strategies during instruction rather than unaided levels of competence.

During dynamic assessment, the teacher *probes responses.* For example, when a student read a story about two mountain climbers in Chile, South America, he miscalled the word *Chile* (actually he pronounced the *ch* sound and then mumbled). In the oral retelling, he referred to Chile as the location. When the diagnostic teacher probed how he knew the country was Chile, the student said, "Well, the author talked about the Andes Mountains, and I know the Andes Mountains are on the west coast of South America . . . so I decided that the country must have been Chile."

From this information, the teacher assessed that this student had a wide range of prior experiences and used them to interpret text. He was also able to mentally self-correct word recognition errors. This sign told her that he was an active rather than a passive reader. His reading problem stemmed from overrelying on his background knowledge when he encountered several words that he could not recognize. Probing the student about how he arrived at a response gave the diagnostic teacher a more accurate picture of the student's potential for learning new information.

Finally, as the diagnostic teacher assesses learning while she teaches, she evaluates whether her instruction is appropriate for her learners. She evaluates the reading event and *asks whether there is another way* to interact with the students. She asks herself:

1. Am I leading students through the task according to their present strategy use? If not, should I try another way?

2. Is this text appropriate for these students? If not, should I try another text?

3. Am I using the students' strengths as I am teaching? If not, should I try another way?

4. Is this technique appropriate for these students? If not, should I try another way?

5. Is this learning context appropriate for these students? If not, should I try another situation?

As key variables of instruction are changed, assessment is based on the resulting changes in reading performance. The diagnostic teacher evaluates students' improvement as a result of her instruction. If students do not improve, the diagnostic teacher looks for another way to modify instruction in order to enhance literacy.

GUIDELINE #4: ASSESS DURING INSTRUCTION

- Assess reading change as a result of mediated learning.
- Probe students' responses to understand their thinking.
- If reading behavior does not change, try another adjustment.

Enabling

During the reading event, the diagnostic teacher enables students to be independent learners and therefore think of themselves as readers. To enable students, the diagnostic teacher helps them develop independence by sharing how she thinks while she is reading. The students and teacher work together to figure out a story and then discuss how they reached their conclusions. As the teacher shares her thinking and works with the students, she enables them to control their own learning and talk through their own understanding of a story. To build students' independence, she finds ways to show them that they can read and think. She acknowledges the effective strategies they use when they read efficiently. At times, she allows students to read for their own purposes without teacher questions and discussion. These guidelines for enabling students are elaborated in the following section.

Guideline #5: Build Independence

The fifth guideline requires that the teacher both instruct the strategies of reading and systematically plan how students will assume responsibility for their own learning. Not only does the diagnostic teacher direct the learning process by explaining the steps and guiding the practice, she also gives students ownership of their learning by encouraging them to think about their thinking. Efficient readers monitor their understanding. As they are reading, they actively choose alternate strategies when reading does not make sense. Poor readers, on the other hand, are characterized by disorganized strategies and failing to spontaneously self-monitor. Consequently, they continue to rely on the teacher to monitor reading performance.

Passive readers, therefore, need instruction in effective monitoring behaviors so that they can move from teacher-directed to self-directed learning. The initial step is to redirect assessment from the teacher to the student, with the teacher demonstrating how to self-monitor reading. To do so, the teacher purposely makes mistakes while reading so that she can *demonstrate* how she monitors an active meaning search. Too often poor readers perceive proficient reading as error-free reading. By making mistakes, the teacher can demonstrate her own coping behaviors.

The teacher begins by saying, "Oops, that didn't make sense." Then she demonstrates alternative strategies. She shows readers that they can ignore the mistake and read on to see whether they can figure out the meaning—or that they can reread the sentence to check the overall meaning to see what might fit.

As she continues to demonstrate this active meaning search, the teacher illustrates the self-questioning process that goes through the mind of an active reader:

> *If I don't understand, I ask myself a series of questions, the first one being "What would make sense?" If I can't regain the meaning, I ask more questions. Most of the time I need to figure out either a word I don't know or what the author was trying to say. I can use two different sequences.*
>
> *First, to figure out a word, I ask myself, "Can I say it that way?" (syntactic fit) or "What word does it look like?" (graphic fit) or "What does it sound like?" (phonic fit).*
>
> *Second, to figure out meaning, I ask myself, "What does the text say? What do I already know about what the text says? How does this information fit together?"*

After modeling the self-questioning process, the teacher and students work through a couple of examples. The students follow the teacher's model and think aloud, asking themselves questions about their reading. The students actually talk about how they solve the reading task. As the students talk aloud, the teacher *supports their thinking by giving them hints and encouraging them to talk through their thinking.* As the students talk aloud, the teacher names the strategies that they are using. She comments, "Did you notice how you reread that sentence to see whether it made sense? That was very effective." One student reflected on her self talk when she wrote her portfolio reflection, as shown in Figure 3–2.

As processes are demonstrated and practiced, the teacher explains when it is most appropriate to use them. For example, for different types of text, the teacher explains why or why not to use the particular reading strategy that she is teaching. If the teacher is demonstrating how to formulate predictions based on prior knowledge, she explains that if the student does not know anything about the topic, he must read two or three paragraphs,

I like this because, I could write what I was thinking. This shows that you can get off track & stay on track. Self-talk helps me think of what I am thinking wails I read

Figure 3–2   Portfolio Reflection on Self-Talk

summarize the information, and then create a prediction based on the just-learned information. Teacher and student thus *collaborate in thinking* about various ways strategic reading changes in different situations.

The diagnostic teacher builds student independence by demonstrating the process of active reading and the corresponding troubleshooting strategies that efficient readers use. In addition, the teacher thinks out loud, showing students how she knows what she knows. In turn, students think out loud using the steps of active reading, and the teacher supports their thinking process rather than focusing on right or wrong answers. Finally, the teacher and students collaboratively discuss how they use strategic reading in various situations.

GUIDELINE #5: BUILD INDEPENDENCE

- Demonstrate thinking.
- Support thinking by encouraging self-talk.
- Collaborate in thinking about when to use strategies.

Guideline #6: Develop a Concept of Self as Reader

Children come to school with well-developed problem-solving abilities; they have learned to walk, to talk, and so on. Through their everyday living, they have learned many of the principles of communicating their ideas through language. However, because problem readers repeatedly fail when learning to read, they develop a concept of themselves as nonreaders. This self-assessment is difficult to change. As inefficient readers learn to read, often, word identification is difficult for them, and the sympathetic teacher assists these students more readily, allowing them to depend on teacher assistance. This type of interaction inhibits learners' active search for meaning and encourages a passive view of reading.

While listening to such readers, the diagnostic teacher notices that they read as if they do not expect the text to make sense. They read as if they believe getting every word right is reading (Goodman, 1996). This passive attitude is also exhibited when comprehending text. These readers seem to monitor their reading less frequently and accept whatever argument is presented in the text without applying their prior knowledge. They seldom reread text to check initial interpretations and try to maintain interpretations even in light of contradictory information (Paris, Lipson, & Wixson, 1994). These ineffective strategies can be altered by the teacher who is sensitive to her influence on the students' concept of themselves as readers. This concept can be developed using three teaching strategies: immersing students in reading, attributing success to effective strategy use, and allowing time for personal reading.

To be engaged in the actual reading of text is the first important requisite for developing a concept of self as reader. *Immersing students in relevant reading activities* will increase their concept of themselves as readers. As students read material that is relevant, repetitive, and rhythmic, they can feel themselves reading. Poor readers, however, have few opportunities to read connected text. In first-grade classrooms, Allington (1984a) found that children in high reading groups read 10 times as many words as children in low reading groups. In this study, children in low reading groups silently read a total of only 60 words during the five-day sample period. It is difficult to consider oneself a reader when one reads only 12 words a day. Therefore, increasing the amount of fluent contextual reading students engage in each day is the first step toward helping them develop a concept of self as reader. Difficult reading material causes students to focus on the word level of reading, precluding an active search for meaning. Reading text fluently at an independent level allows students to read enough words correctly so that they can engage in an active search for meaning.

Inefficient readers, however, need more than easy reading material to change their concept of themselves as readers. As the children build their self-concepts as readers, a second major task of the teacher is to talk about the strategies used to derive meaning from text and *attribute active reading to effective strategy use and effort* (Schunk & Zimmerman, 1997). Because of the repeated failures of problem readers, they do not recognize the effective strategies that they do use. When asked how they got an answer, students often respond with "I don't know." These students do not have enough experience with successful reading to recognize when and how their effective strategies work. They have developed a view that reading is simply calling words correctly and waiting for teacher assistance when reading breaks down. They attribute their reading performance to forces outside their control rather than to effective use of strategies. To change this attitude, teachers show students how their strategies influence reading performance. Then changing reading behavior becomes a mutual responsibility demanding effort from both teacher and students. The teacher acknowledges students' strategy use by charting their reading progress (see Chapter 4). In this way, the students' attention is refocused on those behaviors that they can control. When effective strategies are supported, students can attribute their comprehension not only to the product but also to the process of active reading. They begin to see themselves as active readers who can construct meaning from text.

The purpose for reading can also influence students' concepts of themselves as readers. When students read for their own purposes and enjoyment, their interactions with text are perceived as real and relevant reading; consequently, they perceive themselves as readers. Teachers need to set aside time in the classroom for children to *read for their own purposes* and then share their reading. In building the students' concept of themselves as readers, the teacher allows time for them to share the knowledge they have gained from reading in a creative way with their peers. She creates a "read and tell" time that reinforces individual variation in text interpretation. This activity allows students to have ownership of their own responses to the text and builds the concept of themselves as readers.

When students think of themselves as readers, they actively engage in text interpretation. They view themselves as in control of their reading. The sensitive teacher creates independent readers by having them read a lot of text, stressing the strategies of active reading, and having them read relevant materials for their own purposes.

GUIDELINE #6: DEVELOP A CONCEPT OF SELF AS READER

- Immerse students in reading.
- Help students attribute active reading to effective strategy use.
- Allow students to read and write for their own individual purposes.

Responding

In all her interactions, the teacher responds as a person. She responds to the different students in her classroom and challenges them according to their individual needs. She uses what they already know to present concepts in the way they learn best. Using the unique strengths of the individual learners in her classroom, she reduces stress for each learner. Furthermore, she acknowledges the realities of the educational situation. Using personal statements about her own reading process and laughing about her own mistakes increase students' awareness that reading is constructing a response rather than getting the answer right.

Guideline #7: Be Sensitive to Individual Differences

Students bring to the reading task their own sets of experiences and knowledge, which affect their reading behavior. At the same time, they bring their own strategies for dealing with the world. Some children are impulsive, some are extremely verbal, and some are quiet, while others are highly distractible. Even though each of them is different, seldom do these differences affect instruction in public schools, partly because the exploration of how learners are alike and different is limited. Understanding human similarities can increase one's sensitivity to human differences. When learning something new, people are alike because new learning creates disequilibrium, or stress. As people solve the problem or learn the information, they reduce this stress (Elkind, 1983).

People learn new information in two ways. First, they all use what they already know to formulate hypotheses about new information (Pearson,

Roehler, Dole, & Duffy, 1992). Second, they use their strengths to reduce this stress (learn the information). Therefore, in this state of disequilibrium (new learning), people use what they already know to make sense of the new information. However, people differ not only on *what* they already know (knowledge-based differences) but also on *how* they integrate new information with what they already know (strategy-based differences).

Knowledge-based differences are evident in the scope of vocabulary knowledge and the variety of experiences that students have. Some children come to school with a rich variety of experiences and well-developed oral language. Some children have had repeated experiences with books and have developed concepts about print. Other children come to school with limited experiences with reading events and require more exposure to a variety of experiences with both print and concepts.

These knowledge-based differences are accentuated by differences in problem-solving strategies. All students do not learn the same way. Some students select meaning cues, while others select graphic cues. For example, Clay (1993) found that many young readers did not integrate cueing systems. Some of these students used a visual cueing system: they matched the missed word with the initial letters of other words they knew. Other students used the phonic cueing system; they matched the missed word to the sounds they knew.

Some students rely heavily on their background knowledge to form hypotheses while they are reading. These students check what they already know without thinking about the text. Other students rely heavily on the text to form their hypotheses while reading (Taylor et al., 1995). Some students summarize stories, giving the overall gist of the text, while other students give explicitly stated information. Some students revise and monitor their model of meaning readily, while others need concrete facts before they revise their model of meaning (Paris, Wasik, & Turner, 1991). Some students organize information within broad, overlapping categories, while others organize information in discrete, hierarchical categories. Being sensitive to individual differences, the diagnostic teacher *adjusts instruction, incorporating not only what students already know but also what they can do.*

However, the diagnostic teacher thinks carefully about the individual students in her classroom. Because the reading event is more stressful for remedial readers (Gentile & McMillan, 1987), the demand for instruction using background knowledge and processing strengths is greater for them. The diagnostic teacher *reduces stress by using students' strengths.* By using appropriate instructional methods, the diagnostic teacher can reduce the stress and increase learning. For example, teachers have differentiated prompting by using language that emphasizes the preferred cueing system and then encouraging the integration of other cueing systems (Clay, 1993). For instance, the student using the visual cueing system can be prompted to use meaning-based and phonics cues by asking "What makes sense?" or "What begins with the letter . . . and makes sense in the sentence?" Teacher prompting can effectively focus instruction on using students' processing strengths and then encouraging them to incorporate more flexible strategies.

Furthermore, *individual sense making is encouraged through the use of* I *statements*. The teacher models "I think . . . ," talking about her own reading and thinking aloud about how she figured out a particular answer. Showing the *how* and modeling "I think . . ." release students from the necessity of having to do the process in the same way. "I do it this way" implies that others can do it a different way. Furthermore, this attitude eases the need to conform and acknowledges that even though a particular process or strategy for solving problems is not an effective strategy for reading, it may be effective in other situations. For the impulsive child, the teacher often remarks, "Someday your rapid-fire decision making may help you become a great artist, but when you are reading text, you need to think about what the author is trying to say."

Being sensitive to individual differences requires that the diagnostic teacher evaluate two broad categories of learner differences. First, she evaluates what the students already know, because using what they already know will increase what is learned. Secondly, she assesses the way the students learned what they already know so that new information can be presented using the students' strengths. These two categories, knowledge-based differences and strategy-based differences, help the diagnostic teacher adjust instruction for individual students. As the teacher learns to meet the needs of her students, she uses their strengths and models *I* statements (which release everyone from doing things in the same way). Thus she encourages individual variation in problem solving.

GUIDELINE #7: BE SENSITIVE TO INDIVIDUAL DIFFERENCES

- Adjust instruction to what students already know and do.
- Reduce stress by using students' strengths.
- Use I statements to acknowledge individual variation in problem solving.

Guideline #8: Foster a Reality-Based Approach to Instruction

Even though each child is different and some are harder to teach than others, the diagnostic teacher interacts with each of her students as a person. She is a participant in the learning process, sharing with them her reactions to reading events and student learning. Honest communication and sharing of the knowledge of the students' reading strategies set the stage.

The diagnostic teacher helps students develop a realistic assessment of their own reading behavior, as opposed to a tense, perfectionist view of their learning. Continually she demonstrates that *real life requires coping with mistakes.* She becomes human as she talks about her own mistakes and coping behaviors, focusing on the process rather than the products of reading. As the teacher finds humor in her mistakes and proceeds to correct them, so too will her students learn to reflect on their mistakes in a light-hearted manner, realizing that they can correct incongruencies as they read. Mistakes become a tool for learning rather than an indication of failure. Modeling self-correcting strategies in a relaxed atmosphere helps students develop a risk-taking attitude toward reading (Goodman & Marek, 1995) and increases their active reading behavior.

Likewise, effective teachers expect students to think, cope with their mistakes, and resolve problems as they read. As such teachers adjust instruction, they *maintain high expectations.* They expect students to read lots of words and to express ideas based on what they have read. A major characteristic contributing to the success of all readers is the teacher's expectation that all students will read and learn. Maintaining appropriate expectations is extremely demanding for the diagnostic teacher. It is important, however, not only to maintain high expectations but also to share with students how those expectations are to be met. Once the diagnostic teacher has made adjustments during instruction, she tells students she expects them to complete the necessary reading. She emphasizes that real life involves coping with limitations and using one's strengths to solve difficult problems.

Finally, the diagnostic teacher engages students by personally responding to literature *discussing her own personal change as a result of reading and writing experiences.* This personal response draws students into discussing their own individual reactions to literature. Consequently, both the students and the teacher talk about how their world view is changing as a result of being literate. In this way, she fosters reality-based instruction that gives the student more than a reading experience; it provides a model for how literacy stimulates people to expand their own knowledge.

In her classroom, the effective teacher creates a relaxed environment where students can take risks and correct mistakes as they try out new ideas. She expects that all students will grow and learn from their mistakes. She interacts with her students personally sharing with them her own interpretations and growth. Thus, a reality-based approach to instruction is just that: it makes reading a real, personal event.

GUIDELINE #8: FOSTER A REALITY-BASED APPROACH TO INSTRUCTION

- Teach that real life requires coping with mistakes.
- Maintain high expectations.
- Discuss personal change as a result of reading.

Summary

Effective diagnostic teaching is coordinated by the reflective teacher, who bases her decision making on individual assessment of the readers' responses during instruction. Thus, at the core of diagnostic teaching is reflective teaching. The effective diagnostic teacher plans instruction, mediates learning, enables thinking, and responds honestly so that students experience success when reading interesting stories that require personal interpretation. Consequently, diagnostic teaching requires planning a whole reading event, the emphasis of which is success. Furthermore, the diagnostic teacher's goal is to create active, engaged readers who use what they already know to interpret text.

With this goal in mind, she encourages active reading by assessing reader response while she teaches. She is sensitive to the individual differences among her students and accepts the uniqueness of each reader in her classroom. She enables students to read with confidence, creating the expectation in students that they can read. She reacts to the instructional event not only as the planner, mediator, and enabler, but also as a participant in the reading event. She acknowledges her own personal response to literature and fosters in her classroom real responses to reading and thoughtful sharing of responses.

4

The Diagnostic Teaching Session: An Overview*

The diagnostic teaching session places a premium on tailoring programs that specifically fit problem readers. It provides a structure for lesson planning that uses the processes of assessment and instruction to identify instructional alternatives and monitor their effectiveness. The session is composed of the following five elements: (1) familiar text time, (2) continuous diagnostic assessment, (3) guided contextual reading, (4) strategy and skill instruction, and (5) personalized reading and writing. Each element performs a distinct function and combines with the others to form a complete diagnostic teaching session that can be completed in an hour. However, the session may be spread out over several days or a week, depending on the amount of individual contact the teacher has with the student.

Each of the five elements has specific purposes within the session framework. *Familiar text time* provides a time for the student to flexibly use their reading strategies and skills while reading easy material. It provides a balance between easy reading and the challenging tasks that lie ahead (Roskos & Walker, 1994). *Continuous diagnostic assessment* uses the principles of dynamic assessment to monitor the effect of instruction on students' learning. It is a way for the teacher to assess growth by gathering data about students' unaided performance in the text that is used for guided contextual reading. In this way, assessment occurs during an instructional setting, a critical aspect of diagnostic teaching. *Guided contextual reading* focuses on meaningful interpretation of whole stories, while allowing students to demonstrate their strengths. It involves the planning and mediating roles of

---

*The diagnostic teaching session is based on a teaching procedure developed by Darrel D. Ray and used in the Oklahoma State University Reading Clinic. The author is grateful for the perceptive insights gleaned from her work in that clinic.

the diagnostic teacher. The diagnostic teaching session also includes the other two elements embedded in the reading event. *Strategy and skill instruction* focuses on specific areas of concerns that might be inhibiting students' active reading. By engaging in strategy instruction, the teacher promotes student independence. During *personalized reading and writing,* both the students and the teacher engage in reading and writing for their own purposes and self-fulfillment. This element extends aspects of the diagnostic teaching session by helping students develop concepts of themselves as readers and assuring success. The students define their own goals during this element. This chapter explains the instructional premises of the diagnostic teaching session as well as discussing its features, which are further elaborated in the chapters on instruction and assessment that follow.

Premises

In addition to the components of the reading event and the roles of the diagnostic teacher described in previous chapters, the diagnostic teaching session is based on several premises:

1. Effective diagnostic teaching results from monitoring the effect that instructional adjustments have on reading performance. Continuous diagnostic assessment provides baseline data about students' reading performance prior to instruction and is done prior to guided contextual reading. During this phase, the reading lesson is adjusted so that the reader can construct meaning with text. The difference between performance without aid (continuous diagnostic assessment) and performance with aid (guided contextual reading) is recorded using the data from these two elements.

2. Effective diagnostic teaching allows students to demonstrate their strengths (what they already know and do) by overlapping what is known and done with new information and new strategies. In other words, the diagnostic teacher uses the students' strengths, thus enabling problem readers to read with success.

3. Effective diagnostic teaching results in a balance of contextual reading with strategy and skill instruction. Guided contextual reading uses whole stories to teach reading as the students interpret and discuss text. Strategy and skill instruction provides minilessons in specific strategies or skills that are inhibiting a student's active reading.

4. Effective diagnostic teaching results from a balance of implicit and explicit instruction. Guided contextual reading is characterized by implicit (guided) instruction during which the teacher acts as guide and participant in the learning process. The focus is on constructing meaning with text. Strategy and skill instruction, on the other hand,

is characterized by minilessons that explicitly demonstrate needed strategies and skills.

5. Effective diagnostic teaching results from a balance of challenging and easy reading tasks. Thus, reading materials are validated by the diagnostic teacher, and texts are chosen to maximize student success on both independent and mediated reading. Guided contextual reading provides instruction in material that is moderately difficult for the student, while personalized reading and writing are characterized by easy reading material. During strategy and skill instruction, the diagnostic teacher uses a combination of moderately difficult texts and easy texts, depending on the instructional needs of the learners.

These premises underlie the elements of the diagnostic teaching sessions. Taken together, the elements provide a vehicle for monitoring the effect of instructional adjustments and the balance between instruction using strengths and instruction in areas of need, between contextual reading and strategy lessons, between implicit and explicit instruction, and between challenging and familiar reading tasks.

Familiar Text Time (FTT)

Familiar text time (FTT) is the rereading of books and poems that the student enjoys. These easy and often predictable books are authentic children's literature that can be read repeatedly because of the rhyme, rhythm, and repetition. Like singing a favorite song over and over again, this procedure engages the readers in active reading and sets a supportive tone for the entire session.

In this part of the diagnostic session, the diagnostic teacher invites the reader to choose among four or five familiar stories. Allowing the reader to choose what he will read increases engagement. By choosing, the reader establishes a reason for reading the selected text. He might think, "I like how the bird scares the spider so I will choose this one." Thus, the student is in control of this aspect of the diagnostic session.

Familiar text also increases the amount of easy reading that the student accomplishes during the diagnostic teacher session, which establishes a balance between easy and challenging tasks. During FTT students use their developing strategies and skills within the context of already known material. As they try out and refine their new strategies and skills while immersed in known information, readers concentrate on implementing the new processes. The interaction between the teacher, the student, and the text provides a safety net for making and correcting mistakes, which in turns increases the active engagement of readers. They enjoy the risk-taking activity that begins the session and continue the rest of the session with this same attitude.

Continuous Diagnostic Assessment (CDA)

Continuous diagnostic assessment (CDA) is an unaided assessment taken from the text used during guided contextual reading. It is the vehicle used to monitor reading performance. During the other elements, the diagnostic teacher adjusts instruction as the students read; therefore, this element assesses the student's reading performance. No teaching is done at this time. Continuous diagnostic assessment allows the diagnostic teacher to collect a sample of reading behavior prior to or after instruction. Then the diagnostic teacher compares performance data without guided instruction (CDA) and reading performance during guided contextual reading (GCR). These samples of reading behavior allow the diagnostic teacher to develop hypotheses about the changing reading needs of the students.

Conducting Assessment Prior to Reading for Guided Reading Approaches

The assessment before guided contextual reading provides two kinds of information. First, it provides information about the appropriateness of the text that is being used during the guided contextual reading element. If the material proves too difficult (at frustration level) or too easy (at independent level), an alternate text is selected and checked for an appropriate match (see Chapter 5 for procedures to determine performance level). Basically the teacher asks himself, "Am I using an appropriate text (moderately difficult) in GCR?" Second, this assessment provides baseline data so that the teacher can analyze the difference between unaided reading performance and the students' reading performance with instruction. He asks himself, "Is the student profiting from my instruction? Is there a difference between the reading performance in GCR and CDA?"

To monitor progress, the teacher follows the procedures found in Chapter 5, "Gathering Diagnostic Data." First, a segment from the text to be used in guided contextual reading is read without prior instruction (at sight). A passage about 50–125 words long is selected and questions written that focus on the main idea or problem, key facts or events, key vocabulary words, and inferences. The selection is read orally or silently, depending on the focus of instruction (see Chapter 5). Error or miscue rates and percentage of comprehension are calculated. These data are compared to the criteria of performance for independent level found in Table A–6 in Appendix 1. Decisions are made as to the appropriateness of the text. If the selection is at frustration reading level (more than one miscue out of every ten running words and comprehension below 50 percent), the teacher immediately moves to easier reading material in the GCR segment. For example, Chris reads a selection from a trade book with a rate of one miscue every seven words and a 50 percent comprehension rate on constructed questions. Since these results indicate frustration-level reading, the diagnostic teacher selects an easier text to use during guided contextual reading.

If the selection reflects the mediated reading level, the diagnostic teacher continues using the material and records miscues to establish a pattern of reading performance. For example, Sally reads a selection from a novel with a rate of one miscue every fifteen words and 80 percent comprehension. After three samplings in this text, the error pattern indicates that the substitution miscues most prevalent are on key vocabulary words, which limits comprehension. The diagnostic teacher develops a program of word identification based on word meanings related to both the text to be read and background knowledge. He adapts instruction during GCR by using a vocabulary map of key words to increase both word identification and word meanings of those words (see "Vocabulary Maps" in Chapter 11). After the story is read, he returns to the map and adds new understandings to reinforce word meaning with word identification.

If the selection is at an independent level, a more difficult text needs to be evaluated in the continuous diagnostic assessment phase. The diagnostic teacher then selects a more difficult text and prepares a segment for evaluation. For example, Toni, whose instructional focus is on meaning processing, can silently read a segment from a third-grade text with 100 percent comprehension. No previous instruction was provided before this segment was read. Therefore, a text at the fourth-grade level is selected. To evaluate suitability of that text, an on-level assessment is conducted and scored. Toni reads the on-level evaluation silently with 70 percent comprehension on the constructed questions. As a result, the text used in GCR with Toni is changed to the fourth-grade text, which reflects a level that is challenging to her and has a moderate success rate.

Conducting Assessment after Reading for Supportive/Shared Reading Approaches

When a student and teacher read a story together before the student reads the story on her own, the teacher uses a different approach to monitor progress. This supportive beginning allows students to read text beyond their instructional reading level; therefore, the teacher assesses performance after instruction waiting at least 20 minutes before asking the student to read part of the selection for an assessment. The student should be able to read the text at independent level. The assumption is that if the student is learning, a text that initially would have been at frustration level will convert to independent level when taught using the supportive reading techniques of predictable language, language experience, and collaborative reading.

To monitor progress, the teacher follows the procedures found in Chapter 5, "Gathering Diagnostic Data." A segment from the text already taught in guided contextual reading is read orally. A passage about 50–125 words long is selected, and questions that focus on the main theme are written. Error or miscue rates and percent of comprehension are calculated. These data are compared to the criteria of performance for independent level found in Table A–6 in Appendix 1. If the selection is read at independent level, then the procedures and the level of difficulty are probably creating the appropriate cognitive stretch for the learner. The diagnostic teacher carefully reviews the amount of support given to attain independent level. If support is moderate, he continues his approach. If a high degree of support is needed, such as rereading the text together six times rather than just once or twice, then the diagnostic teacher considers selecting easier material (see Chapter 9). However, if the diagnostic teacher is giving the student very little support, then he might consider moving to a more difficult text or changing the technique. For example, Jenny was reading together with the teacher, keeping a fairly good pace. After reading the selected text together, they briefly discussed the story and then Jenny read alone. The next day Jenny read the entire story again with no miscues. The diagnostic teacher decided rather than move to a more difficult text, he would try an "at sight" assessment (see "Using Guided Assessments" this section) in the trade book, *Frog and Toad*. Jenny read this sample passage at an instructional level. Thus, the diagnostic teacher changed his instructional approach to increase the cognitive stretch for Jenny.

In all the elements, the diagnostic teacher is assessing the response of students to instruction. As a more systematic monitor of progress, however, the students read a segment of a text without immediate instruction. Continuous diagnostic assessment is an integral part of the diagnostic teaching session because it provides the framework for dynamic assessment by providing immediate data about the students' performance in the selected text without instruction.

FOCUS OF CONTINUOUS DIAGNOSTIC ASSESSMENT

- Monitor reading behavior.
- Analyze patterns when reading.
- Analyze reading growth.

Guided Contextual Reading (GCR)

Each teaching session includes a guided contextual reading lesson (GCR), which focuses instruction on the communication of ideas gleaned from reading whole stories. Guided contextual reading encompasses 60 percent of the instructional time in the diagnostic teaching session; therefore, students are reading contextual material for the majority of the time. The reading selection is of sufficient length to allow for comprehension of story line and character development; however, it is short enough to provide a sense of closure for the reader. During GCR, the diagnostic teacher differentiates instruction according to the strengths and reading levels of the students. Texts are moderately difficult and are chosen to maximize student performance.

The diagnostic teacher thinks about the kind of instruction needed before, during, and after the student reads the selected story or chapter. He considers the support needed before the story to enable the student to construct meaning with text. The teacher asks himself, "Can I provide support before reading to help the student anticipate the meaning?" If support is needed, he reviews the charts that suggest techniques to use before reading a story (see Tables 10–1 and 10–2 in Chapter 10). Then the student's attention is focused on the key concepts of the story prior to reading. These concepts are then related to the student's own experience. Together teacher and student develop predictions related to the story theme, thus increasing the student's active reading of the story. Open-ended questions need to focus on predictions that will engage the student in active reading through the entire length of the story. Therefore, purposes or predictions that can be answered on the first page of the story hardly represent the main story theme.

During this brief discussion, the teacher anticipates problem vocabulary words and, if needed, provides instruction in either word identification or word meaning. This instruction needs to be directly related to the story to be read, predictions that have been made, and the key concepts or story theme. Time is of the essence in diagnostic teaching. Consequently, only the important words, meanings, and concepts need to be stressed.

The second step of guided contextual reading occurs while the students are reading and includes silent reading to construct meaning. The diagnostic teacher thinks about what kind of support is needed as the students read the story or chapter. If support is needed, he reviews the charts that suggest techniques to use during instruction (Tables 10–1 and 10–2 in Chapter 10). While discussing the story, the teacher needs to elicit responses from students that focus on the main theme. Rather than focusing on responses and questions that are text-based, literal, and unrelated to the story theme, the teacher can use questions and lead discussions that focus students on understanding the purposeful actions of the characters to resolve the problems in the story. In other words, a thematic focus and logical questions help students summarize the main actions and themes that occur in the story.

After the text is read, the students respond to the passage as a whole. This requires the students to analyze the story in terms of the characters' motivations, the author's purpose for writing the story, and other stories and experiences with similar themes. A key component of this phase is students relating the story to similar personal experiences and analyzing the effect these experiences have on the comprehension of the story. Experiences may include other stories, movies, songs that the students have encountered with similar plots and characters, as well as personal experiences. Students should focus on the similarities and differences among these cases, using textual and nontextual information to support statements.

These aspects form the framework for guided contextual reading, the major component of the diagnostic teaching session. Basic to the development of guided contextual reading is an instructional sequence that uses the students' strengths; therefore, specialized techniques are selected so that the reader can construct meaning. In other words, the diagnostic teacher asks, "What can I do to make these stories more understandable for my students? Do I need specific reading techniques to ensure active reading of these stories? At what point in the instructional sequence do I need to adjust my instruction?"

For example, students who have a limited ability to deal with oral language could receive vocabulary development and direct experiences with the prerequisite concepts that are necessary to read a particular selection with understanding. For these students, GCR requires an increased amount of instruction before they read the story. Maps (see "Vocabulary Maps" in Chapter 11), which require students and teacher to construct a visual diagram relating the vocabulary words to background knowledge, are used to introduce the story. In this case, the instructional adjustment occurs prior to reading the story. This approach facilitates the students' understanding of the concepts in the story and increases their ability to construct meaning.

When students experience little difficulty with understanding what the words mean, however, the instructional adjustments are different. For students who show extreme difficulty with print processing, the diagnostic teacher spends more time on word identification and less time on developing word meanings. Before a story is read, for example, a language experience story (see "Language Experience" in Chapter 11) might be written using the targeted vocabulary words. The teacher encourages rereading of this story so that the students encounter the vocabulary in text. After the selected story is read, readers theater scripts (see "Readers Theater" in Chapter 11) could be constructed from the story so that increasing oral reading fluency becomes purposeful. The diagnostic teacher incorporates specialized techniques both before and after the students read the story. The adjustments facilitate their ability to construct meaning with text. During GCR, the diagnostic teacher differentiates instruction according to learner strengths. The ultimate goal is to focus on the whole act of reading in connected text that will allow the students to integrate their prior knowledge with the text and to develop personal interpretations.

FOCUS OF GUIDED CONTEXTUAL READING

- Have the students read whole stories.
- Focus on meaning.
- Support active reading before, during, and after the lesson.
- Differentiate instruction so that the reader can construct meaning.
- Encourage personal interpretations.

Strategy and Skill Instruction (SAS)

Strategy and skill instruction (SAS) consists of a series of minilessons planned to develop and modify reading strategies. As such, the diagnostic teacher selects texts to teach a designated strategy or skill. He carefully selects varying levels of text difficulty to provide for an interplay of easy and challenging reading. Three requirements form a basis for the effective execution of strategy and skill instruction. First, prior to teaching a strategy or skill, the teacher conducts a task analysis. Task analysis of reading performance pinpoints specific strategies or skills that could increase students' reading (McCormick, 1995). Second, after the task analysis has identified those strategies and skills inhibiting proficient reading, lessons that explicitly teach those strategies are developed. Strategy instruction (See Chapter 11) is a minilesson that is constructed so that the teacher can easily explain and model how to use a particular strategy or skill. Finally, the targeted task is monitored by the students and teacher, using a graphic representation of progress that calls for self-assessment.

Task Analysis

Task analysis identifies behaviors inhibiting student reading and isolates the specific strategy or skill to be taught. Using the constructs of informal assessment, miscue analysis, and think-aloud procedures (see Chapter 5), the diagnostic teacher identifies particular reading strategies and skills that if learned would *readily* increase student performance.

An initial informal assessment of Mary, for example, identifies fluency of word identification as inhibiting her reading performance. Further analysis indicates that she can decode words in isolation. During the diagnostic lesson, however, it is evident that when miscues are made, Mary does not use what the word looks like or means in the story to correct the miscue. In other words, she does not ask herself, "What makes sense and starts with the letter(s) . . . ?" This analysis indicates that she would benefit from instruction in applying a "sense making" framework or from using the overall context to self-correct errors. Therefore, the task analysis results in recommending strategy instruction in self-correction.

Strategy Instruction

After the task analysis has identified those strategies and skills inhibiting proficient reading, lessons that teach those strategies are created. For most minilessons, the diagnostic teacher selects an easy text to introduce the targeted strategy or skill, which limits other possible problems in text interpretation. As the task is learned, the diagnostic teacher increases the difficulty level of the text so as to lead students to use the targeted strategy or skill in reading situations that are moderately difficult. The activities need to be carefully chosen so that the teacher can model active reading. For Mary, therefore, an effective diagnostic technique would be an adapted repeated reading (see Modification #2 in "Repeated Readings" in Chapter 11) that incorporates strategy instruction of the self-talk "What would make sense and starts with a . . . ?" as an intervention between the first and second readings.

Initially, students are informed of their inefficient strategies and shown the efficient counterpart (see "Strategy Instruction" in Chapter 11). After stating how the strategy or skill works, the teacher gives students a rationale for its inclusion in their program and tells them why doing these specific activities will increase strategic reading. Then students are led systematically through a series of short activities. In the first examples, the teacher demonstrates the active reading process. Then students use the teacher's example to modify their previous strategy use.

In Mary's case, after the first reading of a selection, the teacher reviews miscues and suggests that reading would be more effective if Mary would check the miscue to see whether it made sense. Then he explains how he would self-correct those miscues using a sense-making framework and checking the initial letter of a word. For example, before the second reading, the teacher explains that when reading breaks down, Mary should ask what would make sense and starts with the same letter as the word in the text. "If I had made this mistake," says the teacher, "I would have asked, 'What would Dad use that starts with a *sh?*' Then I would have corrected the sentence to read 'Dad shoveled the garden' and said, 'That's good! I can make sense of my reading by fixing up my mistakes.' Then I would continue to read. Now *you* try the next sentence with a miscue." As Mary rereads the next sentences, the diagnostic teacher scaffolds her attempts with strategy conversations. He focuses the conversations on the targeted strategies and discusses the active thinking process involved in using a particular strategy or skill. Furthermore, he encourages self-evaluation. For Mary, the teacher says, "I like the way you reread that sentence to correct your mistake. What did you think about as you changed your original response?" This approach engages Mary in describing her thinking. The teacher responds by supporting active thinking and highlighting Mary's strengths in strategy deployment. These on-the-spot conversations help Mary talk about her strategy use as well as expand her strategy options. These conversations lead into the third aspect of strategy and skill instruction, self-assessment.

Self-Assessment

The third aspect of strategy and skill instruction is helping students evaluate their increasing use of strategic reading processes. Self-assessment, therefore, directs the students' attention to the use of various strategies and to the effect their implementation has on their reading. It also helps students draw relationships among their strategy use, skill knowledge, and personal effort.

Table 4–1 *Chart for Self-Evaluation of Fluency*

How I Read Today	M	T	W	Th	F
Fluently in Phrases					
Mostly in Phrases				●	●
Sometimes Word by Word		●	●		
Mostly Word by Word	●				

Constructing a graph or self-assessment rubric of strategy use provides an avenue for the students and teacher to discuss the strategies that the students are using and how the strategies or skills will enhance active reading. For example, using the chart in Table 4–1, Mary evaluated her fluency when she completed her second reading. This evaluation encouraged her to discuss how the strategies she was acquiring were influencing her reading fluency. Thus, Mary, as other students, assumes increasing responsibility for changing her reading behaviors. Charts can be skill-oriented, as in the fluency chart in Table 4–1. Or they can be charts of strategy use such as the chart in Table 4–2. Self-assessment charts can vary in complexity; however, the focus of charting should be the evaluation of strategy and skill use and discussing how changing strategic reading enhances constructing meaning

Table 4–2 *Chart for Self-Assessment of Comprehension Strategies*

Today when I read,	Not at All	Sometimes	Most of the Time
I made predictions throughout.			
I revised my predictions as needed.			
I justified my thinking.			
I thought about the information in the text.			
I thought about what I knew.			
I used important information.			
I used the text information and what I knew together.			

Today my reading was _____ because _____

_____.

with text. Thus, the students assume the role of monitoring strategic reading; the teacher discusses their troubleshooting strategies, thus encouraging self-assessment.

Strategy and skill instruction is like many regular classroom lessons; however, it is different because it is specific to the readers' targeted concerns in reading. In diagnostic teaching, it is important to identify those strategies and skills that are limiting active reading. The diagnostic teacher asks, "What strategies and skills are limiting reading improvement? Will instruction in these strategies or skills advance active reading?" Identifying and working with these strategies and skills will improve overall reading. Therefore, the key characteristic of SAS is the identification of specific strategies and skills that problem readers need and that, when taught, will enhance constructing meaning with text.

FOCUS OF SKILL AND STRATEGY INSTRUCTION

- Conduct a task analysis of inhibiting strategies and skills.
- Implement strategy instruction.
- Encourage students to employ self-assessment.
- Converse about strategy use.

Personalized Reading and Writing (PRW)

In personalized reading and writing (PRW), students are engaged in 10–15 minutes of personal reading and writing. This element offers students a time of quiet reflection to respond personally, using the language arts. Writing and reading influence each other and both develop from children's desire to communicate. In this phase, time is set aside for the students and teacher to read and write for their own purposes. Easing the structure of the teaching session and shifting the control to the students are crucial aspects of situating literacy. If the students do not experience "choosing to read and write," they may not define literate activities as a part of their lives. Personal reading and writing allows time for students to define their literacy interest, to read and write for their own purposes, and to read and write without failing because they establish their purposes and their responses. In this way, they are defining themselves as literate individuals.

For the silent reading time (see "Sustained Silent Reading" in Chapter 11), students select books, magazines, newspapers, or their own writing to read during the designated time period. Encouraging students to read books for their own enjoyment rather than instructional purposes develops the desire to read. They learn to ask themselves, "What do I want to read about?

What kind of stories do I find more interesting?" This facilitates habits of book selection and defining interests (Gambrell, 1997).

Students are taught to match the book to their reading levels by using the rule of thumb (Morrow & Walker, 1997). To determine whether it is a good match, they read a page from their selected book and put a finger on each unknown word starting with the little finger. If they reach their thumb before the end of the page, the book is too difficult and another should be selected. Therefore, personalized reading encourages students to select books they can successfully read and moves the control of the selection of reading material from the teacher to the students. In fact, during this element, the students are in control; they have no "have-to" reading. If the students want to skip pages, look at pictures, laugh or cry, they can read and think whatever they want. The students control what they learn from books.

For personal writing (see Modification #1 in "Journal Writing" in Chapter 11), the students and teacher communicate through writing. During each session, students write to the teacher about anything of interest or importance to them. Following the journal entry, the teacher comments with a brief, personal, and honest reaction to what was written.

The teacher responds during each session to what the students have written. The teacher's comments can be an empathetic response or can ask for more information. Such comments (e.g., "That sounds like fun, I would like to know more about . . ." or "Can you describe what it looked like?") allow the diagnostic teacher to encourage the fluent writing of ideas without evaluations. The focus is communication between students and teacher; therefore, the teacher should not correct any spelling or grammatical errors.

The teacher encourages the writing of ideas as he models correct writing forms in his responses to the student. This stream-of-consciousness communication is based on the students' personal, real-life experiences. The topics, length, and format are self-selected. As students compose text, they think about ways to express ideas. This thinking about how ideas are expressed sensitizes students to the visual aspects of text (how words are spelled and the order of words in sentences); consequently, students become more aware of how words are used.

In fact, personal reading and writing are both major sources of knowledge about word meaning and sentence and text structure. Both are major vehicles for self-reflection because they encourage students to think about what they want to read and learn as well as what they want to communicate in written form. Further, once students have written their thoughts on paper, they can reflect on their thinking, elaborating their personal ideas.

Thus, personal reading and writing develop within students an interest in reading and writing for their own enjoyment. It releases students from the "have-to" assignments made during direct and guided instruction, thus placing them in control of their interests, ideas, and emotions. By setting aside time for personal reading and writing, teachers are inviting these readers to be members of the literacy club. As problem readers continue to read and write for their own purposes, they set their own goals and thus control their

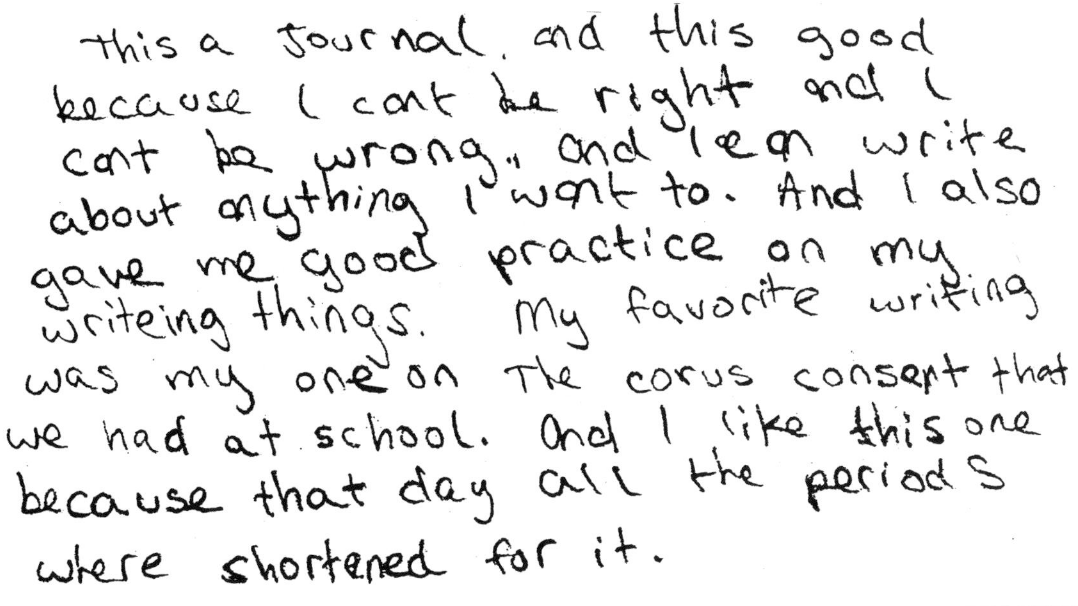

this a Journal, and this good
because I cant be right and I
cant be wrong., and I can write
about anything I want to. And I also
gave me good practice on my
writeing things.   My favorite writing
was my one on The corus consert that
we had at school. And I like this one
because that day all the periods
where shortened for it.

Figure 4-1   *Portfolio Reflection about Journal Writing*

responses. A student selects her journal writing to include in her portfolio (see Chapter 8). Figure 4–1 shows her reflection about why she selected the journal. This activity has no wrong answers; in fact, *no* answers; thus students cannot fail. This time gives students an opportunity to pursue their interests, responding personally to literacy.

FOCUS OF PERSONALIZED READING AND WRITING

- Encourage definition of interests.
- Evoke a personal response.
- Choose reading and writing purposes.

Summary

Reflecting on his roles as a diagnostic teacher and the variables of the reading event, the diagnostic teacher plans a teaching session that allows him to assess and instruct at the same time. *Familiar text time* begins each session with familiar activities that are chosen by the student. It provides time for easy, familiar reading allowing the student to use the strategies and skills that she has just learned. During *continuous diagnostic assessment,* the diagnostic teacher monitors the effects of his instruction by comparing unaided reading performance and mediated reading behavior. During *guided contextual reading,* he guides students' learning; therefore, he is constantly asking what will make this reading event successful for the students. As he teaches the planned lesson, he encourages students to read actively by focusing their attention on constructing meaning with text. He probes with leading questions: "What did the author mean when she said that? Does that (the answer) make sense in relation to the other ideas presented in the story?"

During *strategy and skill* instruction, the diagnostic teacher decides which strategies and skills would, if taught, result in higher reading achievement. Then he develops short demonstration activities to teach strategic reading and converses with students about using strategies. He uses charts to encourage self-assessment and continues the discussion about strategy use. Therefore, he builds responsibility within the students by gradually giving them the control to monitor their own reading behavior. During *personalized reading and writing,* the diagnostic teacher allows time for students to read and write for their own purposes, thus inviting them to participate in the literate community.

The format of the diagnostic teaching session allows the diagnostic teacher to develop instructional alternatives that fit the strengths and needs of problem readers. By systematically planning instruction, the diagnostic teacher provides learning opportunities that enable problem readers to become independent learners.

5

Gathering Diagnostic Data

Teachers gather data to formulate diagnostic hypotheses about the strategies a reader uses to construct meaning (see Figure 5–1). Diagnostic decisions are made based on data gathered before any instruction and also after instructional adjustments have been made. This chapter focuses on data acquired before the student has received instruction. Such data provide needed information about the independent problem-solving strategies of the learner.

In the decision-making cycle of diagnostic teaching, data are gathered to make initial decisions about instruction through informal reading inventories (a collection of graded passages). These passages are used to determine a level of instruction that is moderately difficult for the students. The diagnostic teacher also establishes the major instructional concern (presenting problem), whether it is print or meaning, by comparing performance when students read orally and silently. Using this information, the diagnostic teacher extends her diagnosis by conducting an on-level assessment using a story or passage that she is going to teach. The data gathered from it are later used to monitor the student's changes. This assessment can be taken from the first phase of the diagnostic lesson, which establishes baseline data (see "Establishing Baseline Data" in Chapter 7), or it can be the baseline information that is continuously gathered (see Chapter 4 for a discussion of the continuous diagnostic assessment element of the diagnostic teaching session). These procedures provide detailed information about the reader's strategies for constructing meaning with text. The diagnostic teacher uses these data to formulate hypotheses about a particular student's instructional needs. This chapter elaborates on these factors in the diagnostic process: the major presenting problem, an appropriate text level for instruction, and the reader's strategies.

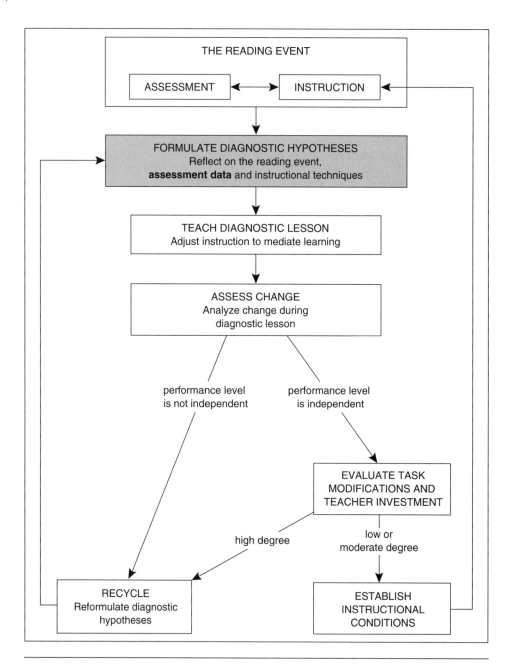

Figure 5–1   The Decision-Making Cycle of Diagnostic Teaching

Identifying The Major Presenting Problem

The ultimate goal of reading is to construct meaning with text. In this constructive process, both print and meaning processing occur simultaneously. Students combine sources of information and shift between the text, print knowledge, and personal knowledge to figure out what the text says. Meaning processing involves predicting, monitoring, and elaborating the author's intended meaning. Meaning is usually the predominant focus during reading instruction. In other words, when reading, students are constantly striving to construct meaning. On the other hand, print processing involves predicting, monitoring, and elaborating what the words on the page look like. When the meaning becomes unclear, the reader shifts his attention to a close examination of single words, that is, to print processing. When students read, they strategically combine all their resources to construct and reconstruct the author's message.

Based on an informal reading inventory, the diagnostic teacher decides whether print processing or meaning processing is the major inhibiting factor when reading becomes difficult for a student. As the diagnostic teacher works with a student, she asks herself, "What is inhibiting constructing meaning with text? Is the student having difficulty recognizing the words (print processing), or understanding the content (meaning processing), or both?" She knows that reading requires that the student use both print processing and meaning processing to construct meaning with text. She also realizes that oral reading is a different task from silent reading.

When reading orally, the reader must attend not only to meaning but also to the oral production of the text. According to Allington (1984b, p. 853), "the instructional setting for oral reading imposes different demands from that of silent reading (e.g., public vs. private performance, personal vs. external monitor of performance, emphasis on accuracy of production vs. accuracy of meaning construction)." If the diagnostic teacher needs information on print-processing ability, she uses an oral reading assessment. She observes how the student attends to print when reading breaks down. If reading is impaired by print processing, the diagnostic teacher listens to the student read orally and asks him questions to check comprehension, a process known as *oral reading analysis*. Some students call words fluently but need assistance in how to construct meaning with the words that they recognize (meaning processing). If the diagnostic teacher needs further information on meaning processing, she uses silent reading analysis and asks the student to think aloud at critical points in the story. She breaks a story into segments and discusses the story after each segment. These procedures are known as *silent reading analysis*.

By looking at the pattern in oral reading and silent reading on an informal reading inventory, the diagnostic teacher can decide which is the major presenting problem, print or meaning processing. For the diagnostic

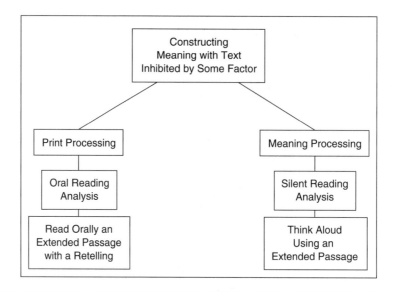

Figure 5–2   Assessment of Major Presenting Problem

teacher, this initial decision merely begins her analysis of how the student is approaching the reading task. Figure 5–2 illustrates the assessment of the presenting problem. The diagnostic teacher establishes the major presenting problem by thinking about how print processing and meaning processing affect the student's reading.

Establishing The Level of Student Performance

To begin gathering data, the diagnostic teacher samples reading behavior across levels of text difficulty to identify the student's level of performance. To make this assessment, the teacher uses a series of graded passages that range in difficulty from first grade to junior high. This procedure is known as *informal reading assessment.* A reader's responses on easy, moderate, and difficult texts can be used to determine a level at which the student will experience success in classroom instruction. In the initial assessment, the diagnostic teacher evaluates both oral and silent reading performance to establish appropriate instructional ranges for oral and silent reading.

Categories of Performance

To determine the level, the diagnostic teacher can administer passages from a standard informal reading inventory (IRI) such as the Basic Reading Inventory (Johns, 1993). Levels of performance can be established for both oral and silent reading, because the inventory has equivalent forms for both types of reading. Therefore, the diagnostic teacher administers one form for the oral reading analysis and another form for the silent reading analysis. Three estimates of reading performance are derived:

1. *The student's independent reading level* provides an estimate of the level at which the student can read fluently with a high level of comprehension. The student reads and understands enough of the text to monitor his own reading performance. He applies appropriate correction strategies when reading breaks down, using both reader-based and text-based processing; therefore, teacher-directed instruction is not necessary.

2. *The student's instructional reading level* provides an estimate of the level at which the student experiences a mild amount of stress between the text and his present reading strategies. It is assumed that classroom instruction would increase the student's understanding of the text and ability to obtain new information from a text.

3. *The student's frustration reading level* provides an estimate of the level at which the reader is not fluent and has little recall of textual information. It is projected that at this level, guided instruction would be extremely demanding and time-consuming because the reader does not know enough about what he is reading to make adequate connections between the new information and prior knowledge.

These levels are derived by having the student read passages from the informal reading inventory.

Scoring the Informal Reading Inventory

After each passage has been read, comprehension is evaluated by computing the percentage of correct answers to various types of comprehension questions, such as main idea, supporting details, inferences, and vocabulary. As the student reads orally, errors or miscues (deviations from the text) are recorded. These errors are used to compute an error rate, or percentage of word recognition. Although variation exists in what types of errors or miscues are used to compute a score, generally substitutions, mispronunciations, omissions, insertions, and unknown words are used to compute the error rate (see Table 5–1). Other reading behaviors such as repetitions and self-corrections are analyzed when a qualitative assessment of oral reading performance is conducted and indicate that the reader is constructing meaning. (Further directions for conducting informal reading assessments can be found in the Appendix.)

Establishing Instructional Level

From the information derived from the informal reading inventory, the diagnostic teacher identifies a level that would be moderately difficult for the student. She thinks again about the criteria for frustration and independent

Table 5–1   *Scoreable Errors (to be used in computing error rate)*

Substitutions or mispronunciations (the replacement of one word for another): Mark the mispronounced word by drawing a line through it and writing the substitution above the word.

want
"The man ~~went~~ to the store," said Ann.

Omissions (leaving out words): Circle the word omitted.

"The man went to (the) store," said Ann.

Insertions (adding extra words): Draw a carat and write the inserted word above it.

away
"The man went ^to the store," said Ann.

Transpositions (changing the word order): Mark with a ‿‿‿‿ .

"The man went to the store," said Ann.

Prompted words (words that have to be prompted or supplied by the teacher): Write the letter *P* above these words.

P
"The man went to the store," said Ann.

---

reading level and mentally pictures the ranges shown in Figure 5–3. Word recognition and comprehension criteria for *independent* reading are 1 miscue in 100 words ($\frac{1}{100}$ or 99 percent accuracy) and 90 percent comprehension accuracy. When readers know most of the words and concepts, they can then focus their attention on constructing meaning. In other words, they can independently read the text making a variety of connections between what they know and what's in the text. Other criteria are used to identify text that is extremely difficult for a reader. Word recognition and comprehension criteria for *frustration* reading are 1 miscue in 10 words ($\frac{1}{10}$ or 90 percent accuracy) and 50 percent comprehension accuracy. Clay (1993) believes that more than a 10% error rate represents a "hard" text for a young child. At this frustration level, readers have extreme difficulty constructing meaning for two general reasons. Either they don't recognize enough words to correct their miscues and thus regain meaning, or they don't understand enough of the concepts to relate what they are reading to what they know. In either case, readers struggle to regain meaning, but the attempt is futile because they don't have enough knowledge to engage in active processing of text.

The range of performance between frustration level reading and independent level reading is called the *instructional level,* or more appropriately the *instructional range.* The instructional level is an estimate of the level at

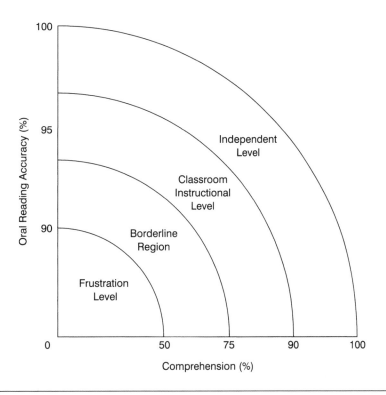

Figure 5–3   *Performance Ranges*

which the student would have some problems when reading classroom texts at sight, but most of these problems can be overcome after the student has a chance to read the same text silently (Johns, 1993). Therefore, the guidelines for regular classroom instruction are more in line with traditional scoring criteria in informal assessment. These criteria use 95 percent accuracy at word identification and 75 percent on comprehension as an estimate of instructional reading level. However, the range between independent and frustration level includes both (a) the acceptable instructional level used within a classroom setting and (b) a borderline range, which is often used in one-to-one tutoring or for extended diagnosis. In this borderline range, the reader typically uses active, constructive processes to regain meaning, which often reveal their strengths and strategies in meaning construction. As Barr, Blachowicz, & Wogman-Sadow (1995) have pointed out:

> *Students who perform in the borderline region between frustration level and acceptable instructional level may be helped by instruction that has been developed with their particular problem in mind. This borderline region is characterized by an accuracy of 90–94% on oral reading and 50–74% on comprehension questions (pp. 223–224).*

This borderline region represents a text level that is moderately difficult and is appropriate for one-to-one tutoring. The diagnostic teacher uses this information to select appropriate materials for instruction (see Chapter 4) and extended assessment.

Adding a Fluency Rating

While analyzing the student's performance using the traditional criteria on the informal reading inventory, the diagnostic teacher can also evaluate the student's fluency as she listens to him read orally. To do so, she asks herself three questions:

1. Is the student's reading fairly smooth?
2. Does the student read words in meaningful phrases?
3. Does the student's pitch, stress, and intonation convey the meaning of the text?

Using these questions, the diagnostic teacher rates the student's fluency on reading each paragraph and adds this information to that obtained from the traditional informal reading assessment. Sometimes the informal reading inventory does not reveal a problem with oral reading (few substitutions, omissions, or prompts), but the phrasing seems atypical. The student reads "as if print knowledge has not become sufficiently automatic to permit attention to phrasing . . ." (Barr, Blachowicz & Wogman-Sadow, 1995, p. 58). Thus, print processing must also be evaluated by rating fluency. The diagnostic teacher notes how the student's oral reading miscues and comprehension interact with his reading fluency on the informal reading assessment. Teachers have used a four-point fluency scale to evaluate upper elementary school children's reading fluency (Zutell, 1988). This scale is a valid and reliable measure of the student's fluent reading and correlates with overall reading ability (Zutell, 1988). The scale includes ratings to reveal patterns of oral reading fluency (see Table 5–2). Using this scale, a student's rating of 1 would indicate that the student is experiencing a great deal of stress and is reading at frustration level. A rating of 2 or 3 would indicate a mild amount of stress and that the student would profit from instruction at this level. A score of 4 would indicate fluent, independent reading. After listening to the students read, the diagnostic teacher uses the fluency rating in conjunction with the information obtained from the informal reading assessment to identify performance levels and major presenting problems.

Analyzing the Results from the Informal Reading Inventory

After administering the informal reading inventory, the diagnostic teacher analyzes the student's reading performance for both oral and silent reading by summarizing the data on a summary sheet (see Table A–8 in Appendix 1). For oral reading, she records the fluency rating, miscue rate, and compre-

Table 5–2   *Ratings for Oral Reading Fluency*

1. Clearly labored and disfluent reading, marked by very slow pace (less than 60 wpm), word-by-word reading, numerous pauses, sound-outs, repetitions, and/or lack of intonation and expression.
2. Slow and choppy reading, marked by slow pace (roughly 60–80 wpm), reading in two- and three-word phrases, many pauses, sound-outs, and/or repetitions, some difficulty with phrase, clause, and sentence boundaries and/or intonation problems at the ends of sentences.
3. Poor phrasing and intonation, marked by reasonable pace (roughly 80–105 wpm), but with some choppiness and possibly several repetitions, sound-outs, and/or run-ons.
4. Fairly fluent reading, marked by good pace (more than 110 wpm), longer phrases, and a good sense of expression and intonation. While there may be some difficulties with aspects of fluent reading behavior, this reader is aware of the need for appropriate phrasing and intonation; repetitions may be used to correct phrasing/expression errors.

From *Developing a Procedure for Assessing Oral Reading Fluency: Establishing Validity and Reliability,* by J. Zutell, May 1988. Paper presented at 33rd Annual Convention, International Reading Association, Toronto, Canada. Reprinted by permission.

hension percentage for each paragraph given. Likewise, she records comprehension percentages for the silent reading paragraphs given. When she has each paragraph recorded on the summary sheet, she reviews the data to establish an instructional level for both oral and silent reading. This level is indicated by the highest paragraph the student reads at the instructional level before reaching frustration. Using the criteria for performance on the chart in Table 5–3, or the charts in Appendix 1, the diagnostic teacher establishes independent, instructional, and frustration levels for oral and silent reading as she begins her analysis of oral and silent reading.

When the instructional level for both oral and silent reading have been established, the diagnostic teacher compares the performance on each set of paragraphs. She thinks about the instructional level for oral reading and silent reading realizing that she needs to establish a level at which the student will

Table 5–3   *Criteria for Determining Reading Instructional Reading Levels*

Grade Level of Paragraph	Fluency	Miscue Rate	Oral Comprehension	Silent Comprehension
1–2	2–3	$\frac{1}{10}$–$\frac{1}{16}$	65–80%	65–80%
3–5	2–3	$\frac{1}{13}$–$\frac{1}{26}$	65–80	65–80
6+	3–4	$\frac{1}{18}$–$\frac{1}{35}$	70–85	70–85

Adapted from W. R. Powell.

profit from instruction. In the following example, if she uses silent reading, she wonders whether Ricardo will read the words or just skip words and guess at the meaning. She knows that the overall instructional level at which the student will profit from instruction must be established in order to select material. Ricardo's scores were the following.

	Oral Reading	Silent Reading
Independent Level	1.25	2
Instructional Level	1.75	3
Frustration Level	2	4

Reviewing Ricardo's performance, the diagnostic teacher established the instructional level at the end of first grade because oral reading was lower than silent reading. Thus, Ricardo's major presenting problem is print processing. At the end of first grade, Ricardo will read at least 90 percent of the words correctly and use meaning and print clues to revise his miscues. To be sure that Ricardo is using both print and meaning processing to construct meaning with text, the diagnostic teacher looks for instructional material at the end of first grade to use during guided contextual reading. At this instructional level, Ricardo will be able to use both print processing and meaning processing. She selected *Marvin Redpost: Lost at Birth*, with a reading level estimated near the end of first grade. She hypothesized that at this level, Ricardo would be able to use both print and meaning processes as he reads. From the data, she can also conclude that Ricardo is more proficient at silent reading than oral reading. Using the chart at the beginning of the chapter, the diagnostic teacher hypothesizes that the student's strength is in meaning processing and that he needs support for print processing. She begins to build a program of instruction using his strength in meaning processing during guided contextual reading (see Chapter 4) and works on print processing during strategy and skill instruction.

As the diagnostic teacher gathers data about performance levels, she is also thinking about the strategies the student is using. However, the short paragraphs on the informal reading inventory are used for screening and are not long enough to reveal the student's pattern of use of reading strategies. The diagnostic teacher then conducts an extended assessment to analyze the readers' strategies when constructing meaning with text.

Conducting Extended Assessments

To formulate hypotheses about a reader's strategies, the diagnostic teacher selects a text that is expected to be in the borderline area, or moderately difficult (90 percent oral accuracy and 60 percent comprehension), for the student. She also decides whether the major inhibiting factor is print processing or meaning processing. Then she prepares an extended passage that is to be read either orally or silently. In either case, she constructs questions that require the student to understand the main idea or theme, identify supporting details or events, infer relationships between ideas, and explain how the key words are used in the text.

If print processing is inhibiting constructing meaning with text, the diagnostic teacher interprets oral reading behavior. She asks the student to read the selected text aloud while she records the errors or miscues (see "Scoring Criteria" in the Appendix). To cross-check oral reading behavior with comprehension, the oral reading is followed by an oral retelling. Then she asks the comprehension questions she constructed (those which have not already been answered in the retelling). Finally, the student's reading errors or miscues are analyzed to identify the cueing system used to repair the reading miscue (see Goodman & Marek, 1996, for detailed procedures) and the pattern of reading behavior employed.

If meaning processing is the major concern, however, the teacher conducts a *think-aloud* assessment. She divides the selected passage at strategic points. First, she asks the student to predict what the story is about and to read silently to strategic points in the story. Next she asks the student to respond to the information read. When the diagnostic teacher is uncertain whether the student can read the text silently, she asks the student to find support for the response in the text and read it out loud, which permits her to assess whether word identification is interfering with comprehension. Then she asks the student to predict what will happen in the next segment of the story and why he thinks it will happen. She asks him to evaluate his previous prediction in light of the new information read and to decide whether he wants to change the prediction, keep it, add to it, or discard it. When the student finishes reading the selected text, she asks any prepared questions that have not yet been answered. Each exchange during the think-aloud period is analyzed to identify patterns of reading behavior (see Glazer & Brown, 1993, for detailed procedures).

To assess the pattern of reading performance, the diagnostic teacher looks at the data collected when the student reads without assistance. When the student reads an extended passage that is moderately difficult, a pattern for constructing meaning emerges. The diagnostic teacher analyzes the miscues and miscomprehensions to evaluate both the student's patterns when reading breaks down and the strategies he uses to recover meaning while reading. Both oral reading analysis (of print processing) and silent reading analysis (of meaning processing) result in a more comprehensive understanding of the strategies that students use to interpret the text as they are reading. In the discussion that follows, the premises for each analytic process are laid out, together with the kinds of diagnostic data collected.

Analyzing Oral Reading

Premises

To interpret oral reading behavior, the diagnostic teacher evaluates how the reader miscalls words as he is reading. An error (or miscue) is an oral response that deviates from the printed text. The reader is viewed as an active interpreter of text. He creates expectations, using his background knowledge. Then he confirms or revises these expectations as he reads and checks the text to see whether his interpretation is making sense. A reader's miscues, therefore, are systematic attempts to construct meaning with text (Goodman, 1996).

Miscue analysis is a tool for evaluating the relative significance of miscues in the context of both the entire passage and the reader's experiences. Several frameworks for evaluating miscues have been developed; in this text, an adaptation of the procedures suggested by Goodman & Marek (1996) is used. This analysis is based on several theoretical assumptions:

1. Readers read to construct meaning.

2. Reading is not an exact process.

3. Some miscues or errors are more significant than others.

4. Miscues should be evaluated based on the degree to which they change meaning.

5. Readers use a consistent pattern of correction strategies that indicate their preferences for text processing.

In other words, miscues indicate the cue selected or the source of information the reader tends to use to construct meaning with text. Miscues that change meaning and remain uncorrected are viewed as diagnostically significant. They indicate what happens when a reader cannot regain meaning as he is reading. Miscues that change meaning but are subsequently corrected reveal self-monitoring strategies and are viewed as efficient strategies. They supply information about how readers construct meaning. Miscues that do not alter the meaning of the text are viewed as nonsignificant. Evaluating the nature of the information used to regain meaning reveals the student's approach to text interpretation.

The student may use various sources of information when he encounters an unknown word in his reading: (a) the context and his experience; (b) the way words sound in conversational speech, that is, whether the words make grammatical sense; (c) graphic information; and (d) phonic information. Using the context and his own experience, he might try various words to see if they make sense in the context of the sentence and the story.

Sentence: The girl hit the baseball.

Reader: The girl bit the baseball. *(Oops, that doesn't make sense. I'll try again.)* The girl hit the baseball. *(Yes, that makes sense because people hit baseballs, not bite them.)*

Sometimes, he might check to see whether the way he is reading the sentence sounds like a real sentence.

Sentence: The girl hit the baseball.

Reader: The girl hitted the baseball. *(Oops, that's not the way we talk. I'll try again.)* The girl hit the baseball. *(Yes, this sounds like the way we talk.)*

At other times, he might check the graphic information by asking himself how the word begins and how long it is.

Sentence: The girl hit the baseball.

Reader: The boy hit the baseball. *(Oops, the word is not* boy *because it starts with a* g *not a* b, *but it is the same length. It must be* girl *instead of* boy. *Yes, that looks right.)* The girl hit the baseball.

At still other times, he might check the phonic information to decipher unknown words by asking himself what sounds these letters make.

Sentence: The girl hit the baseball.

Reader: The girl hit the brassball. *(Oops, that doesn't sound right. Let's see* bbb-āāā-ss-bbb-all . . . *baseball. Yes, that sounds right.)* The girl hit the baseball.

Thus, analyzing oral reading involves watching how the student reads and what strategies he uses when combining information sources.

Diagnostic Questions

Using these premises, the teacher can develop diagnostic hypotheses. The diagnostic questions that follow are used to analyze oral reading behavior:

1. How close is the reader's interpretation (that is, how much meaning change results from the miscue)?

2. Does the reader monitor oral reading (that is, does he self-correct miscues that do not fit the context)?

3. Does the reader use reader-based or text-based strategies to regain meaning?

4. How has previous instruction influenced the student's miscue pattern?

5. Do the words in the text influence the miscue pattern?

The pattern of strategies revealed by these questions indicates the student's application of reading strategies. Each of the questions elicits data that contribute to a comprehensive analysis of the student's reading behavior.

1. How close is the reader's interpretation? Proficient readers' text interpretations maintain the basic intent of the author. Although they make miscues and continue reading, their miscues are insignificant in terms of the context of the entire selection. However, problem readers make miscues that change the meaning. Instead of correcting themselves, they continue reading, acting as if they did not anticipate the story to make sense.

The diagnostic teacher evaluates each miscue as to the degree it changed the author's intended meaning. She uses this information to determine the significance of the miscue. As she continues her evaluation, she thinks about what the student did when the miscue changed the meaning. Those miscues that did not change meaning are not evaluated.

2. Does the reader monitor oral reading? Proficient readers typically correct those miscues that change meaning but pay little attention to those oral reading miscues that do not change the meaning. Inefficient readers, however, do not distinguish between the miscues that affect meaning and those that do not. Little difference is observed in the frequencies with which they correct either type of miscue. Therefore, inefficient readers do not *consistently* read for meaning and do not monitor their oral reading behavior. As a result, inefficient readers make more miscues and correct them less often.

The diagnostic teacher summarizes the number of miscues that are corrected and those that are not corrected. She uses this information to decide which miscues to evaluate further. Miscues that change meaning and are corrected are closely evaluated to predict how the student combines sources of information when reading is efficient and to show how the student attempts to troubleshoot when reading problems occur. The miscues that are left uncorrected and change meaning are evaluated to look for reading problems that are ignored.

3. What source of information does the reader use to regain meaning? Proficient readers flexibly shift between sources of information when what they are reading does not make sense. They use what they already know (reader-based inferencing) as well as what the text says (text-based inferencing) to check and revise their miscues. However, inefficient readers use only one source of information to correct problems when reading orally (Allington, 1984b). Whether they rely too much on what they already know or how the text looks, they invariably limit their strategies to one source of information. This limitation leads to one of three diagnostic hypotheses.

The first hypothesis is that when reading breaks down, the student makes his miscues fit *his* interpretation and background information without referring to the information in the text. For example, a student who consistently substitutes a word that does not resemble the text but retains the meaning reflects a processing preference for a reader-based meaning search. He does not revise a miscue on the basis of the words in the text but relies solely on his background knowledge. If this is the pattern, the diagnostic teacher works with the student to encourage him to use how the words look as well as what he already knows. She chooses techniques that teach word identification as well as emphasize monitoring print processing.

The second hypothesis considered is that when reading breaks down, the student's miscues are similar to the graphic form of the text. For example, a student who depends on the graphic form for figuring out unknown words often produces a miscue that has the same initial letter and is approximately the same length as the word in the text and is a word that he has been taught. This reader is using what the text looks like but does not ask what the word would mean in this sentence. He needs to check not only the words he has been taught but also what word would fit in the meaning of the story. In this case, the diagnostic teacher chooses techniques that demonstrate using both text cues as well as meaning cues simultaneously.

The third hypothesis evaluated is that when reading breaks down, the student's miscues reflect an attempt to employ sound-symbol (phonic) associations. For example, a student who depends on grapho-phonic information produces miscues by sounding out a word one letter at a time, blending those sounds to form a nonword, and continuing to read. He often sacrifices meaning for inaccurate decoding. This reader is said to be bound by the text because he uses only letters in the words and not his own knowledge. In this case, the diagnostic teacher decides whether decoding is an efficient strategy. If it is, she uses techniques that incorporate strategy instruction for word identification. On the other hand, if decoding is an inefficient strategy for this reader, the diagnostic teacher looks for strategies that use overall meaning of the text rather than sounds of letters to decode unknown words.

Reviewing the data, the diagnostic teacher summarizes the information and looks for a consistent pattern of print processing. She makes a tentative hypothesis and continues her analysis with two more questions.

4. How has previous instruction influenced the reader's miscue pattern?   Young readers use the strategies they have been taught. Therefore, readers differ in their use of strategies to construct meaning because of the instructional emphasis in their initial reading programs (Barr, Blachowicz, & Wogman-Sadow, 1995). This emphasis affects a student's correction strategies through the third-grade reading level. Some reading programs emphasize using meaning and the initial letter of the word to remember words (meaning-emphasis programs). Other programs emphasize blending sounds together to remember words (phonics programs). Miscue patterns often reflect the type of initial reading instruction a student has received.

Sometimes the student is using a system he has been taught effectively. In a meaning-emphasis program, the student's attention is focused on the initial letter and word length along with context to figure out unknown words. As he reads for meaning, he develops fluent and appropriate phrasing while checking his guesses with the initial letter and word length. However, in a structured phonics program, the reader's attention is focused on the letter-sound relationships to identify words. Therefore, he sacrifices meaning for phonic decoding, reflecting less use of context and a higher tendency to focus on individual words to correct reading miscues.

The diagnostic teacher evaluates whether the student is effectively using the system he has been taught. If so, she plans a program to help him refine this system and integrate it with other cueing systems. In other words, if the student was taught phonics and is using it well, the diagnostic teacher continues to emphasize this cueing system while simultaneously asking the student to double-check his responses to see whether they make sense.

At other times, however, the student may try to use a system that he has been taught but reverts to using sources of information more in line with his cognitive abilities. When a mismatch occurs between the way a student has been taught to read and his cognitive abilities, often the student tries to use the cueing system that he has been taught but usually abandons it to rely on a source of information that seems more natural to him (Juel, 1984; Stanovich, 1981). For example, if a student has been taught to sound out words letter by letter but has no ability to synthesize sounds, he will *try* to sound out the word but abandon this strategy in favor of using meaning cues and the initial letter. Because he has been taught a system that he cannot use, he reverts to a strategy more in line with his cognitive abilities.

If the diagnostic teacher observes these phenomena, she can change her instruction to match the reader's strengths in print processing. She reinforces these strengths and plans a more integrative use of cueing systems. For example, a reader who was taught phonics continually miscues by substituting a word that makes sense in the context without regard for the letters in the word. The teacher notes that he is overriding his instruction and using his preference. Therefore, she chooses techniques that develop word recognition using the overall meaning of the text. As the student becomes more accurate with this system, she calls attention to the initial letter and word length.

5. Do the words in the text influence the miscue pattern?   The type of words in the text can affect the miscue pattern. If a text has predictable rhythmic sentence patterns, the student who has language facility can figure out words easily using the sentence patterns. Likewise, a text that contains many decodable words is easier to read for the student who has had phonics instruction. However, if the text contains high-frequency words with a mixture of regular and irregular decodable words, the student who uses initial-letter and word-length cues has more success in reading the text (Juel, 1984). Consequently, before making final decisions about the student's correction strategies, the diagnostic teacher checks the text to see whether it has caused an atypical error pattern.

In conclusion, oral reading patterns give insight into how the student is monitoring his reading behavior. The student's reading errors or miscues are analyzed to identify patterns of strategy use. The strategies that the student uses are affected by previous instruction, his cognitive abilities, and the text that is being read. The sensitive teacher considers all these influences when interpreting the student's oral reading behavior.

Analyzing Silent Reading

Premises

To analyze comprehension, the diagnostic teacher evaluates how the reader thinks through the comprehension of a passage. Using a *think-aloud* format of interrupted reading, the teacher observes how the student uses the text and what he knows to interpret the passage. A think-aloud analysis, therefore, is a tool for evaluating the reader's comprehension strategies in the context of the entire passage. Although several researchers have outlined think-aloud procedures, the approach discussed here has been drawn from the work of Glazer and Brown (1993).

A think-aloud analysis is based on three theoretical assumptions:

1. Reading is an active process (that is, a reader constructs a model of meaning as he reads).

2. To construct this model, the reader uses what he already knows (reader-based inferencing) and the information in the text (text-based inferencing).

3. Reading is a strategic process (that is, the reader checks his model of meaning to see whether it makes sense).

In other words, the reader is viewed as actively constructing meaning with text. He predicts what is going to happen. Then he confirms or revises these expectations, using both what he already knows (reader-based inferencing) and the important information from the text (text-based inferencing). Finally, he checks his interpretations to see whether they are making sense.

Asking the student to think aloud gives an indication of how the student is processing text. The think-aloud process shows the diagnostic teacher the strategies that the student uses to make sense of what he is reading (Glazer & Brown, 1993). As with the oral reading analysis, interpretations that change the author's intended meaning and that the reader does not revise are seen as diagnostically significant. They indicate what the reader does when he cannot interpret the text. Interpretations changing the author's intended meaning that the reader later revises are viewed as efficient strategies, revealing the comprehension strategies that the reader is using. They offer information about how the reader regains meaning. Interpretations that do not alter the author's intended meaning are viewed as nonsignificant. Basically, the student uses various sources of information for text interpretation: (a) what he already knows, (b) facts stated in the text, and (c) a combination of both the text and what he already knows.

Diagnostic Questions

Based upon these premises, the teacher can develop diagnostic hypotheses, using the following questions:

1. How close is the reader's interpretation (that is, how elaborate is the summary and are the important points covered)?

2. Does the reader monitor comprehension (that is, how does he use new information to predict and revise his model of meaning)?

3. What sources of information (reader-based, text-based, or both) does the reader use?

4. How has previous instruction influenced the think-aloud process?

5. Does the text influence the think-aloud process?

The diagnostic teacher uses these questions to analyze silent reading during the think-aloud experience. The pattern of answers indicates the student's application of reading strategies. When the student's interpretation changes the meaning, a careful analysis is needed to assess the strategies he uses to regain meaning. Each of these questions is designed to elicit the particular kinds of data necessary for a complete assessment of a student's silent reading behavior.

1. How close is the reader's interpretation?   During the think-aloud assessment, the student is asked to retell what he read silently. This retelling asks the student to select information important in illustrating the message as he perceived it. It reveals the student's ability to recall textual information and to make inferences using his own experiences. For narrative text, a good summary includes the important elements of story grammar: setting (characters and place), problem, key events, and resolution (see Roskos & Walker, 1994, for detailed procedures). For expository text, a good summary contains the main idea and key details. During the discussion, the diagnostic teacher evaluates how inclusive or narrow the summary is, the completeness of verbal responses, and the cohesiveness of the summary. After the student has finished his summary, the teacher uses questions to probe higher-level thinking, to focus on key ideas in the text, and to assess the student's knowledge of the meaning of the key words (Barr, Blachowicz, & Wogman-Sadow, 1995).

The diagnostic teacher uses this information to determine the significance of the miscomprehension. As she continues her evaluation, she thinks about how the reader's interpretation affects how he constructs meaning.

Summaries that do not change the intended meaning of the story are considered the result of effective strategies. However, summaries where the student changes the meaning of the text are evaluated to form hypotheses about the reader's strategies. Often poor readers do not organize textual information as they read (Paris & Oka, 1989). The details or events they include in their summaries become increasingly random and show a decreasing relationship to the text. Thus, summaries can alert the diagnostic teacher to problems in text processing that will be uncovered as she continues her analysis.

2. Does the reader monitor comprehension?　The diagnostic teacher uses this question to evaluate how the student uses new information to predict and revise his model of meaning. At each interruption, the teacher asks him to predict what will happen next in the story and why he thinks so. She asks him to evaluate his previous prediction in light of the new information read, and then she gives him the option of changing the prediction, keeping it, or discarding it. As the student makes predictions and evaluates them, the teacher observes his strategies for monitoring comprehension. She observes the inclusiveness of the prediction and the amount of textual information used up to the point of interruption.

Basically, inefficient readers have been found to be less active than more efficient readers. They change their predictions less often than more proficient readers. Some students rely too heavily on their initial prediction and make the entire story fit it. These readers do not use new textual information to revise predictions; rather they keep a prediction when it is no longer supported by the text. When they do revise their predictions, passive readers change only one part of their predictions. Less active readers hold onto previous predictions rather than become more tentative about their approach to text.

Active readers seem more comfortable keeping their models of meaning tentative. If the text provides no new information, they delay making a prediction (Dybdahl & Walker, 1996). Moreover, during a think-aloud experience, they change their predictions, adding and revising new information provided in the text as part of a continuous process.

This phase provides diagnostic information about how the student is monitoring his reading comprehension. The teacher notes the point at which the reader realizes that his model of meaning does not fit the stated information in the text. Since the story has been presented in segments, the diagnostic teacher can easily observe strategies such as rereading previous segments to check the text, modifying predictions, or remaining tentative until more information has been read. She uses this information to decide which summaries and predictions to evaluate further. Those interpretations that changed meaning but were subsequently revised are closely evaluated to predict how the student combines sources of information. The interpretations that were not revised and changed meaning are further analyzed to evaluate how the student attempts to make sense of what he is reading.

3. What sources of information (reader-based, text-based, or both) does the reader use? Beginning the think-aloud procedure by using the title of the text, the diagnostic teacher can assess the student's prior knowledge about the topic. Questioning the student about how he arrives at a prediction from just the title allows the diagnostic teacher to probe background knowledge and begin to assess how the student uses this background knowledge as he reads the text. As the student reads the text, the teacher can observe the student as he constructs a rationale to support his prediction, and evaluate whether the support is text-based or reader-based. This process leads to one of three diagnostic hypotheses.

The first hypothesis is that when reading breaks down, the student's interpretation fits something he can understand instead of what the whole text says. Some readers ignore information that they do not understand. (They actually do not *know* that they do not understand.) When this happens, their responses are marked with an elaborate interpretation of the one or two events that they were able to comprehend. No line of reasoning connects these students' responses to the story because they lack sufficient knowledge to interpret the text. If this pattern occurs, the diagnostic teacher needs to be cognizant of what the student knows about each topic. She then develops the necessary background knowledge for this particular student before he reads a story.

The second hypothesis suggests that when reading breaks down, the student's interpretations fit what he already knows and not what the text says. Some problem readers rely too heavily on their own knowledge and actually make their interpretations fit what they already know (McCormick, 1992). For example, some students consistently respond with information that they know, using it to explain a line of reasoning for their answers rather than using information provided by the author. In these cases, the student understands what he reads but relies too heavily on his own experiences to develop reasons that are close to, but not exactly like, what the author intended. When this pattern occurs, the diagnostic teacher uses techniques that show the student how to use what he knows in combination with what the text says.

The third hypothesis proposes that when reading breaks down, the student's interpretations fit what the text says without tying together information. Some problem readers rely too heavily on the text and fail to use their own knowledge to interpret or envision the text (Purcell-Gates, 1991). They have too narrow an interpretation because they view reading as simply restating the text and, thus, do not draw relationships between information in different parts of the text. If this pattern occurs, the diagnostic teacher uses techniques that first allow the student to discuss what the text says and then shows him how to use what he knows to elaborate on it.

During the think-aloud process, the diagnostic teacher evaluates the source of information used to construct responses as well as the accuracy of the interpretation.

4. How has previous instruction influenced the think-aloud procedure? Some students have participated in literature discussion groups where the teacher participated as a member encouraging students to discuss how they constructed an answer. However, other students have participated only in discussions where the teacher does the question asking. In latter instructional situations, the types of questions teachers ask students affect their comprehension (Almasi, 1996). Furthermore, studies indicate that when teacher-generated questions are posed prior to reading, comprehension narrows because students read to answer those specific questions rather than to construct meaning. Some students have learned to rely on the teacher's direction rather than to think independently. The diagnostic teacher analyzes the focus of previous instruction to find out how that focus has affected comprehension.

5. Does the text influence the think-aloud process? The diagnostic teacher evaluates whether textual characteristics affect the active reading process. She reviews the density of information as well as the elaboration used. Likewise, she double-checks the background knowledge required, the grammatical complexity, and word choices as well as the textual organization. Poor story construction affects the student's think-aloud process, and the choice of interruption points. When story plots are engaging enough to motivate readers to find out what happens, then the teacher-reader interactions during the analysis period are elaborate; however, bland and boring texts give the students no reason to read (Schallert & Reed, 1997). The diagnostic teacher needs to construct a story map of the selected story to determine whether the story actually lends itself to a think-aloud process and is engaging enough to elicit an elaborate interaction. Some initial ambiguity of the story plot allows the diagnostic teacher to observe the student's approach to problem solving when reading. The type of text also affects the think-aloud analysis. Narrative text lends itself to prediction, revision, and monitoring, while expository text lends itself to summarizing, clarifying, and discussing the line of argument used by the author.

In conclusion, having the student think aloud as he reads allows the teacher to assess the strategies that he uses to construct meaning. This procedure provides diagnostic data to help the diagnostic teacher formulate instructional hypotheses and subsequently to select appropriate techniques for improving reading comprehension.

Summary

The diagnostic teacher gathers data by asking questions that focus her evaluation of the strategies of the problem reader. First, she evaluates both oral and silent reading performance and determines the major presenting problem (print or meaning) using an informal reading inventory. Next, she evaluates the student's performance across levels of text difficulty using the informal reading inventory. From this information, she designates a level that is moderately difficult for the student. After she decides whether print processing or meaning processing is inhibiting constructing meaning with text and establishes a level of performance, then she selects an extended passage to continue her assessment. From the extended passage, she constructs an on-level assessment that is either an oral reading or a think-aloud experience. This assessment gives her more data about the student's strategies when reading is difficult. She then analyzes the data to formulate her diagnostic hypotheses.

6

Formulating Diagnostic Hypotheses

To formulate the diagnostic hypotheses, the diagnostic teacher analyzes the information he has gathered through the assessments in Chapter 5 and within the reading event (see Figure 6–1). He uses data from an informal reading inventory to assess the student's reading pattern in texts across a range of difficulty levels for both oral and silent reading. He performs an on-level reading analysis to assess the student's reading pattern when she reads a text that is moderately difficult either orally or silently. As the diagnostic teacher evaluates this information, he increases his specificity by reflecting on the diagnostic questions in Chapter 5. He reflects on the reading event and how it has influenced the data he has gathered. Then he reflects on instruction and predicts which technique(s) will help the reader make the desired change based on these data.

Reflecting on Diagnostic Questions

After collecting the data from the extended analysis of oral or silent reading, the diagnostic teacher reflects on the diagnostic questions (see Chapter 5). This analysis provides detailed information about the strategies the reader uses to recover from difficulties in processing print or meaning. The diagnostic teacher uses these data to formulate hypotheses about the most advantageous instructional design for the student. How a diagnostic teacher uses the data is described in this section within the framework of a case study of a hypothetical third-grader named Jenny, who is experiencing difficulty in fluent oral reading.

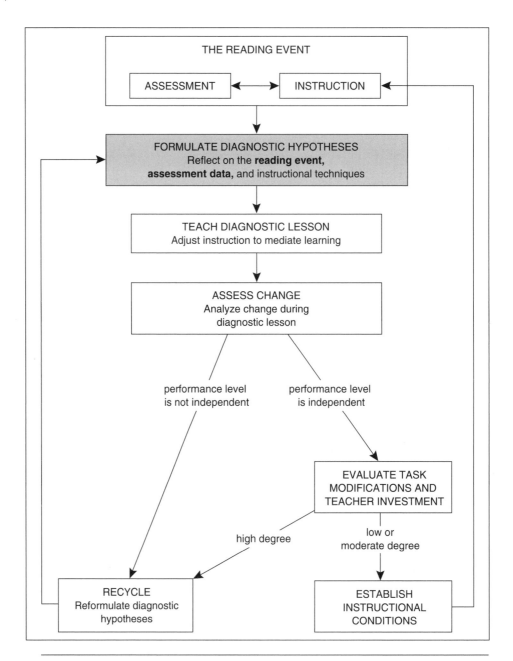

Figure 6–1   *The Decision-Making Cycle of Diagnostic Teaching*

Print Processing Questions

After analyzing the diagnostic questions in Chapter 5, the diagnostic teacher uses this information to identify patterns and suggest instructional frames. The following discussion delineates patterns representative of ineffective reading. The instructional techniques and major categories referred to in this section are explained in Chapter 10, "Selecting Techniques."

Meaning Change in the Reader's Interpretation

The diagnostic teacher analyzes the amount of meaning change that results from the student's miscues or errors. If the miscues do not significantly change the meaning of the passage, then the student is reading for meaning; however, if the meaning of the text is substantially changed because of the miscues, then the diagnostic teacher designs lessons that encourage sense making while reading.

1. First, the diagnostic teacher investigates whether the student is familiar with the concepts in the text. This requisite knowledge helps the student decode the words by asking what would make sense. If the student is not familiar with the concepts, the teacher carefully selects texts that include familiar topics that are easy to read, enabling the student to make sense of the story and use her understanding to correct miscues.

2. If the text is familiar, then as the student reads, the diagnostic teacher prompts the student using "sense-making" comments such as "Did that make sense?" or "Try that again, I didn't understand." or "Oops, what did you say?" These questions and nonverbal prompts can help students monitor their reading.

3. The diagnostic teacher selects techniques that naturally encourage students to predict and monitor their print processing (see the Print Processing column of Table 10–4 in Chapter 10). These teaching techniques are coupled with "sense-making prompts."

- *How Close Is Jenny's Print Processing?* When reading orally, Jenny reads to make sense of text as long as the topic is familiar. When Jenny makes a string of miscues, she misconstrues meaning and makes up the text. She ceases checking to see if what she is reading fits with the words in the text (monitoring print processing).

- *Diagnostic Hypothesis:* Jenny reads for meaning. However, if she reads a string of miscues, she reverts to word calling rather than sense making. Jenny needs to read interesting, familiar material so she can check her print processing by asking what makes sense.

Strategic Print Processing and Monitoring Oral Reading

The diagnostic teacher analyzes how students predict, monitor, and elaborate their model of meaning using the printed words in the text. She evaluates how actively students attend to what they read. Effective readers actively monitor their print processing, correcting miscues that significantly change meaning by rereading or predicting what comes next. In fact, effective readers have twice as many self-corrections as ineffective readers. Ineffective readers often exhibit one of the following patterns:

1. Some students simply call words and fail to correct miscues. They believe that reading is orally reading words without constructing meaning. They are unaware of the mistakes they make because they are not reading to make sense of text. When students exhibit this behavior, the diagnostic teacher constructs reading experiences in which the student will naturally make sense of text. Language experience is an excellent technique to help the student use prediction and to elaborate print processing strategies. Other techniques in the Print Processing column of Table 10–4 in Chapter 10 can also improve self-correction strategies.

2. Other students guess at words, but fail to check if the words they say match the words on the page. They continue to read, changing the story to fit the miscue rather than actively monitoring their print processing. When students exhibit this behavior, the diagnostic teacher constructs reading experiences that encourage the student to monitor and elaborate print processing. The use of repeated readings with conversations about strategic processing is an excellent technique for this purpose. Other techniques in the Print Processing column in Table 10–4 can also improve these strategies.

- *Does Jenny Use Strategic Print Processing?* Jenny predicts what words are by using overall textual meaning and her background knowledge. However, if she miscues, she does not check the print in the text to confirm her guesses. If her miscues don't make sense, she begins to decode every word and ceases to predict or recover meaning. Because this process has continued over a period of time, Jenny has not elaborated flexible strategies for print processing.

- *Diagnostic Hypothesis:* Jenny would profit from instruction that helps her monitor and elaborate strategies for processing print. Reading predictable books and then writing a new story using the same pattern would focus Jenny's attention on elaborating how print works.

Sources of Information

Through print processing analysis, the sources of information a student uses can be identified. The diagnostic teacher can then describe a consistent pattern of how the student uses information sources as well as how the student is processing information. From this pattern, the diagnostic teacher can make hypotheses about instruction. Although students vary in their use of the sources of information, three of the predominant patterns used by ineffective readers and appropriate instructional responses follow:

1. If the student uses her background knowledge at the expense of text-based information, the diagnostic teacher uses prompts that focus on "sense making" (a strength) and the letters in the text (a weakness) at the same time. Additionally, the diagnostic teacher selects techniques that emphasize monitoring print processing using reader-based information. The predictable language technique used in combination with repeated readings encourages combining sources of information. The diagnostic teacher selects other techniques that emphasize monitoring print processing using reader-based information by cross-checking selections from the Print Processing column in Table 10–4 with the information in Table 10–6.

2. If the student uses graphic clues from the text but fails to supply a word that makes sense, the diagnostic teacher prompts using "What word do you know that would make sense in this text?" Additionally, the diagnostic teacher selects techniques that emphasize predicting what would come next in the sentence. Predictable books coupled with cloze techniques would be useful for this type of reader. Other techniques can be found in Tables 10–4 and 10–6.

3. If the student overrelies on phonic information (a strength) without integrating this strength with sense-making strategies, the diagnostic teacher prompts using "What word has those same sounds (a strength) and would make sense in this story (a weakness)?" Repeated readings and charting miscues helps these students to combine text-based information with reader-based information as they reread the text. The diagnostic teacher selects other techniques that emphasize monitoring print processing using text-based information by cross-checking selections from the Print Processing column in Table 10–4 with the information in Table 10–6.

- *What Source of Information Does Jenny Use When Solving Print Problems?* Jenny predicts what the text will say using her own ideas about the story. When she is on the right track, reading progresses. However, when Jenny has misconceptions about the story content, she adds words to fit her understanding.

■ *Diagnostic Hypothesis:* Jenny would profit from instruction that shows her how to monitor her predictions using the words in the story. Repeated readings in interesting and predictable texts can encourage Jenny to monitor her print processing using her own knowledge.

Previous Instruction

As stated in Chapter 5, the instruction a student receives affects his reading pattern. However, the most significant effect occurs when the student overrides his previous instruction, reverting to his natural cognitive abilities. In these cases, reading problems often grow out of confusion about how to approach print processing and result in a disorganized set of strategies. The following patterns are most prevalent:

1. The student has been taught to sound out words, but often abandons this strategy in favor of using meaning cues (a strength). If the student is somewhat successful in using phonics, the diagnostic teacher focuses his prompting and instruction on first using meaning cues and then phonics when the student encounters difficulty in a text. The predictable language approach allows the student to easily combine these two sources of information. Predictable books such as *The Hungry Giant,* where many of the words are decodable, facilitate combining these cue systems.

2. The student has been taught to think about the meaning and how a word begins but guesses wildly using only the meaning. These students need to be encouraged to look at more of the letters in the word to regain meaning. The diagnostic teacher prompts using "What would make sense?" (a strength) and "Look closely at the letters" (a weakness). The language experience approach and message writing as well as other techniques that encourage monitoring and elaborating print processing are excellent techniques for this type of reader.

■ *How Has Previous Instruction Influenced Jenny's Print Processing?* Jenny has had three years of a structured synthetic phonics program. Thus, Jenny often tries to sound out words at the expense of using her natural cue system of meaning processing. Since sounding out is a laborious process for Jenny, she gives up using her strength and simply calls words, only half-heartedly searching for meaning.

■ *Diagnostic Hypothesis:* Jenny needs experiences where she can first use meaning cues and then use her learned strategy of sounding out words. Techniques that encourage the student to use reader-based processing while focusing on printed words are the most appropriate.

Textual Influence

Because the type of text can influence the miscue pattern, the diagnostic teacher thinks about the reading strategies that the problem reader uses and selects texts that will extend those strategies so they become more integrated and automatic (see Table 10–2 for a more complete analysis).

- *How Does the Text Influence Jenny's Print Processing?* Jenny has had numerous experiences reading decodable words in isolated word practice; however, she does not efficiently use phonic analysis when reading authentic texts.

- *Diagnostic Hypothesis:* Jenny would profit from reading many meaningful stories where she can use both reader-based inferencing and phonic knowledge at the same time. The diagnostic teacher needs to look for predictable stories that contain an abundance of decodable words.

Meaning Processing Questions

After analyzing the diagnostic questions for strategies for gaining meaning from text in Chapter 5, the diagnostic teacher uses this information to identify patterns and suggest instructional procedures. The following discussion portrays typical patterns of ineffective readers. The instructional techniques recommended are found in Chapter 10, "Selecting Techniques."

Meaning Change in the Reader's Interpretation

The diagnostic teacher analyzes the degree to which the students' summaries differ significantly from the author's intended meaning. Effective readers use the critical information when summarizing text, while ineffective readers fail to recount important information. If the student changes the meaning substantially, the diagnostic teacher designs lessons that encourage selecting important information when reading.

1. First, the diagnostic teacher makes sure that the student is familiar enough with the topic to construct summaries. If the student is not familiar with key vocabulary words or larger concepts, then the teacher carefully selects texts that include familiar topics and less challenging vocabulary.

2. If the text is familiar, then as the student reads, the diagnostic teacher prompts using leading questions that encourage students to integrate the major concepts within the framework of the story. Techniques such as story mapping, herringbone diagramming, retelling, and summarizing help students develop a textual framework for selecting important information and elaborating concepts (see the Meaning Processing column in Table 10–4).

- *How Close Is Jenny's Meaning Processing?* When Jenny was asked to retell the story section by section, her interpretation was extremely close, indicating that she strives to make sense of text. However, she omitted some information in her summaries. This information was later evaluated as containing words that were difficult for her to decipher.

- *Diagnostic Hypothesis:* Jenny's desire to make sense of text and ability to select important information are processing strengths and should be included in all instructional activities.

Strategic Meaning Processing and Monitoring Silent Reading

The diagnostic teacher analyzes how the student constructs a model of meaning by analyzing how students predict, monitor, and elaborate their model of meaning during the think-aloud procedure. Effective readers actively predict and revise their understanding, clarifying difficult areas by rereading and reading ahead. Ineffective readers passively read without revising or elaborating their understanding. These passive readers may demonstrate one of the following patterns:

1. Some students hang on to an initial incorrect prediction, or change it infrequently, by ignoring information that does not fit their interpretation. When a student fails to effectively revise predictions, the diagnostic teacher models her own predictions and how they change as the story progresses. Techniques such as self-questioning and prediction mapping show students how to monitor their comprehension (see the Meaning Processing column in Table 10–4). Ambiguous scary stories and mysteries where the plot twists near the middle and end of the story are excellent materials for these activities.

2. Some students refuse to predict because they don't want to be wrong. Often their instruction has focused on getting answers correct. These students need to learn how to guess, realizing they can change their predictions when they get new information. To help these students, the diagnostic teacher encourages them to predict more frequently and to make several guesses at a time. Techniques such as request and prediction logs aid them in predicting a model of meaning (see the Meaning Processing column in Table 10–4).

- *Does Jenny Use Strategic Meaning Processing?* During a think-aloud, Jenny was able to predict and revise her understanding, elaborating ideas using her personal knowledge. Sometimes, however, her elaborations included tangential information that had little to do with the theme or main idea.

- *Diagnostic Hypothesis:* Using Jenny's active processing strength, the diagnostic teacher needs to help Jenny focus her attention on key ideas and concepts. Although elaboration is a strength, Jenny should be encouraged to use her knowledge selectively.

Sources of Information

Through the think-aloud analysis, the sources of information a student uses can be identified. Effective readers combine information sources (text and background knowledge) while ineffective readers overrely on a single source of information. From the think-aloud, the diagnostic teacher can make hypotheses about instruction to help readers to strategically combine information sources. Two predominant patterns and suggestions for appropriate instruction follow:

1. If the student uses his background knowledge at the expense of text-based information, the diagnostic teacher uses prompts that focus on "sense making" (a strength) and uses the information in the text to verify guesses. A directed reading-thinking activity (see Chapter 11) would facilitate this type of instruction. The diagnostic teacher selects other techniques that emphasize predicting and monitoring meaning using reader-based information by cross-checking selections from the Meaning Processing column in Table 10–4 with the information in Table 10–6.

2. If students rely heavily on the text without thinking about what they know, the diagnostic teacher asks them to restate the text and then think about what they know that relates to the text. He selects techniques that emphasize predicting what the text might say and elaborating textual meaning. Using story mapping (see Chapter 11) during reading to encourage the student to predict using information from the map will facilitate combining sources. The diagnostic teacher selects other techniques that emphasize predicting and monitoring meaning using text-based information by cross-checking selections from the Meaning Processing column in Table 10–4 with the information in Table 10–6.

- *What Sources of Information Does Jenny Use for Meaning Processing?* When constructing meaning, Jenny relies heavily on her own knowledge about the topic. She does use the text to verify her response. Occasionally, however, she overrides the text by supplying information she already knew to support her interpretation. Most of the time this strategy is effective for Jenny.

- *Diagnostic Hypothesis:* Because meaning processing is a strength, Jenny is asked to explain her reasoning and then orally read sections of the text that support the explanation. This technique uses a strength to improve a weakness (print processing).

Previous Instruction

The instruction students receive affects how they strategically read text. Some students rely on the teacher's direction rather than constructing their own meaning. The diagnostic teacher decides whether previous instruction has affected the strategic application of meaning processes. The following may be found:

1. The student has been taught to answer questions literally using the text, and therefore fails to infer or elaborate meaning. In these cases, the diagnostic teacher uses text-based techniques such as story mapping and then asks the student to retell the story using what they know.

2. The student's use of extensive background knowledge when retelling or responding has been previously reinforced. Therefore, she tends to disregard the text. In these cases, the diagnostic teacher uses reader-based techniques such as the DRTA (see Chapter 11), but focuses on using the text to verify answers or completing a story map (see Chapter 11) after discussion.

■ *How Has Previous Instruction Influenced Jenny's Meaning Construction?* Previously, Jenny has been rewarded for embellishing the text with her own topic knowledge. This instruction, however, has caused Jenny to rely too heavily on her own topic knowledge when reading. She needs to learn to verify her answers using the text.

■ *Diagnostic Hypothesis:* Again Jenny is asked to verify her explanations using the text. She is also asked to write in new questions for other students to answer. This technique uses her strength of meaning processing to develop attention to text through writing.

Textual Influence

Because the type of text can influence meaning processing, the diagnostic teacher thinks about the reading strategies that problem readers use and their preference for narrative or expository texts. He selects texts that build on preferences, and then extends strategies so they become more integrated and automatic (see Table 10–1 for a more complete analysis).

■ *How Does the Text Influence Jenny's Meaning Processing?* Jenny enjoys reading information about science concepts. Her reading is more fluent, and her retellings are more elaborate in science text. Jenny also has a high need to read authentic text.

■ *Diagnostic Hypothesis:* Jenny would profit from reading science texts about familiar topics that are well constructed so that the information makes sense.

After the diagnostic teacher has reflected on print and meaning processing, he thinks about how the student has responded during an instructional event. He reflects on the reading event and how these factors have influenced the data.

Reflecting on the Reading Event

After collecting the data, the diagnostic teacher reflects on the reading event. He returns to the model of the reading event discussed in Chapter 2 and uses it to evaluate the influence of the variables on the student's reading behavior. He remembers that the information he has collected is a result of the interactions that occurred in the reading event. He systematically evaluates the influence of the task, the text, the reader, and the context of the reading event on the data. He looks for key factors by asking, for example, "What task did the student do? Is this task an important consideration in establishing this student's instructional program?" He considers the relative strengths of the student's oral and silent reading in constructing meaning with text. From this analysis, he formulates diagnostic hypotheses and selects teaching techniques to enhance reading growth.

How the diagnostic teacher uses the data from the initial assessments and relates them to the elements of the reading event is described in the pages that follow. The case study of the hypothetical third-grader named Jenny, who is experiencing difficulty in fluent oral reading is continued in this section. As the teacher reflects on the reading event, he makes observations about the student's performance, using the data he has collected. The asterisks (*) in the Task Analysis tables indicate key factors he has to consider when establishing Jenny's instructional program.

The Task

The diagnostic teacher analyzes the reading tasks that the student completes during the reading event. He carefully considers the range of possibilities related to the task and looks for key factors that might affect the student's reading behavior. During the informal reading assessment, he has already decided on the major presenting problem; now he uses this information to evaluate the effect that the question type is having on the reader's responses and to evaluate reasoning requirements. He compares the reader's performance on the informal reading inventory and the extended passage. From this comparison, he ascertains whether the task segment is affecting reading performance and whether production requirements are affecting reader response.

- *How Does Jenny Approach Reading Tasks?* Task analysis for Jenny is given in Table 6–1.

- *Diagnostic Hypothesis:* Jenny reads with moderate difficulty at the second-grade level ($1/11$ error rate and 75 percent comprehension) on an informal reading inventory. Oral reading presents the most difficulty for the student. Although she prefers silent reading, Jenny needs to read orally to improve fluency. Her informal comments ("I hate these stories") indicate that she prefers to choose her own stories.

Table 6–1   *Task Analysis for Jenny*

Purpose for the task: Teacher-directed reading was used for evaluation. Informal conversation revealed that Jenny liked to control her own learning.

Oral or silent reading: Both oral and silent reading behavior were evaluated, with the student comprehending all passages where she could decode the words. Oral reading was the difficult task. At the instructional level, silent reading comprehension was not a concern.

Question type: Literal and nonliteral responses were evaluated. Jenny performed equally well in both cases.

Production requirements: Retelling was used to assess comprehension, followed by inferential questions. Responses were elaborate in both cases.

Reasoning requirements of the task: Factual recall and applicative reasoning were required. Jenny did well in both types of tasks.

Availability of text: The text was not available for referral when responding; however, Jenny's responses were elaborate.

The Text

The type of text read during a reading evaluation can significantly influence the data being analyzed. The diagnostic teacher routinely assesses the text and its influence on reading behavior to identify which characteristics are affecting the student's reading. Again he seeks the key factors about the text that affect this student's reading behavior. To do so, he looks at the information from the informal reading inventory, the extended passage, and the final question of the oral/silent reading analysis (Does the text influence the results of this procedure?).

- *How Does the Type of Text Affect Jenny's Reading?* The text analysis for Jenny would contain the material covered in Table 6–2.

- *Diagnostic Hypothesis:* Jenny needs a text that is coherently organized, and she appears to prefer expository text. Increasing the complexity of the sentence structure seems to have a positive effect on miscues (that is, the longer the sentence, the more she is able to correct her miscues). Another possible influencing factor may be the word choices in the text. Since the student was taught with a synthetic phonic approach (see "Synthetic Phonics" in Chapter 11), words that are more decodable might improve performance.

The Reader

The reader is the major focus of traditional assessment. In diagnostic teaching, however, the reader is assessed in relation to herself as well as to the variables of the reading event. The teacher looks at the knowledge-

Table 6–2   *Text Analysis for Jenny*

Passage length: Short passages produced more oral reading miscues. The extended passage gave Jenny more opportunities to use overall context to self-correct miscues. Comprehension remained high on all passages.

Density of information: The high density of information did not affect understanding, but it did affect Jenny's miscue pattern. When too much information was presented, she could not self-correct.

Elaboration or use of examples: The various texts did not have examples or much elaboration; therefore, this aspect was not evaluated.

*Passage format: Both expository and narrative passages were read. Jenny made fewer miscues on expository text.

Organizational structure or coherence: When the story structure did not reflect the title of the passage, Jenny's miscues were affected because she tried to make the title fit the text. Jenny needs coherent text.

Engaging style: Jenny made fewer miscues on more engaging, predictable text.

Type of content: Jenny read various subject content. It did not seem to affect her responses because she always had extensive background knowledge.

Background knowledge required of reader: Various levels of background knowledge were needed, but Jenny knew about all the topics.

*Grammatical complexity: The more complex the sentence structure, the better Jenny read.

Word choices: Short words that fit the text were used. Elaborate word meanings were not required for comprehension. Decodable words were easier to read.

based requirements of the tasks and how the student responds to them. From the informal reading inventory, the diagnostic teacher evaluates general skill proficiencies and deficiencies. Returning to the extended passages, the diagnostic teacher uses the answer to the first question ("How close is the reader's interpretation?") to assess general knowledge. He must judge whether the reader changes the meaning of the selection because she has no similar experience. In addition, he uses data from the extended passage to evaluate the strategies the student employs as she reads. He specifically analyzes the data on self-corrections and revisions during oral and/or silent reading. Finally, he evaluates data on the sources of information used.

■ *How Does Jenny's Reading Performance Relate to Her Knowledge, Strategies, and Engagement?* Jenny's reader analysis is shown in Table 6–3.

Table 6–3   *Reader Analysis for Jenny*

Knowledge-Based Dimensions

*Reading level: On the informal reading inventory, Jenny read at the borderline level (moderate difficulty) on the second-grade paragraph.

*Skill knowledge: Answering comprehension questions and retelling a story were Jenny's strengths. However, she needed work on oral reading fluency. Phonic knowledge was inappropriately applied.

Language facility: The student used language well and often engaged in elaborate descriptions related to the story. She had a wealth of prior knowledge.

Strategy-Based Dimensions

*Source of information selected (text or background knowledge): As she constructed meaning, Jenny used an integration of both textual knowledge and reader knowledge; however, during oral reading, she used either textual knowledge or reader knowledge but not both when she encountered difficulty.

*Monitoring: Context of the story was used to help identify unknown words. Many miscues were semantically based (that is, she used reader-based inferencing more often than text-based knowledge). Jenny needs to self-correct during oral readings using *both* the semantic and graphic cueing systems.

Elaboration: All responses were elaborate except when Jenny encountered frustration-level reading. She used both literal and nonliteral responses when answering questions.

Engagement Dimensions

Value of literacy tasks: Jenny does not value literacy tasks. She does value her own knowledge, but it is not the same as reading and writing.

Ability beliefs: Jenny believes she is smart in world knowledge. But when it comes to literacy task, she believes she can't compete with her peers; therefore she often shuts down when she has to write as a response to reading.

*Attributions of success or failure: When reading aloud, Jenny attributes her failure to baby reading material and dumb stories rather than active strategies. When reading silently, she skips many words, but still believes she can construct some meaning from the discussion.

*Perception of available strategies: Jenny often gives up when reading orally, because she has a confused notion of the appropriate strategies to use. She continues to read silently skipping words she doesn't know and using only the single source of her background knowledge to construct meaning.

*Sensemaking: Jenny has a high need to learn from what she is reading. Thus, she expressed disdain for the second-grade stories. When she is learning from a story, she is more engaged, even when she miscues frequently.

Social interaction: Jenny learns while discussing information with her peers. She uses their text references to embellish her own understanding.

- *Diagnostic Hypothesis:* Using her meaning processing strength, Jenny would profit from instruction in word identification and fluency. She needs to be shown the effective strategies that she uses (e.g., self-correction from background knowledge). She tries to use phonic knowledge but is consistently unsuccessful in her attempts. Jenny, therefore, relies too much on her background knowledge and general story meaning. When she does, she reads a string of miscues that, however, make sense. Her unsuccessful attempts at self-correction reflect the use of either meaning cues or phonic cues without the integration of both cueing systems. She appears to like to direct her own learning rather than have the teacher tell her what to do. Because of her continual failure, Jenny needs to identify her strategy strengths and attribute her success to the combination of strategy use and effort.

The Context

The diagnostic teacher evaluates the instructional context in which the assessment occurs and how much influence he is having on the reader's response. At the same time, he evaluates how previous instructional experiences might have affected the student's responses. He reevaluates the patterns of performance, thinking about how the student's previous instructional experiences have influenced her reading patterns. He double-checks his data, focusing on the context of the reading event.

- *How Does the Instructional Context Affect Jenny's Reading?* An analysis for the context of Jenny's reading behavior is shown in Table 6–4.

- *Diagnostic Hypotheses:* Jenny's previous learning experiences in a one-to-one pull-out program and in the classroom focused on weaknesses and affect both her perception of reading and her miscue pattern. When she miscues, she tries to sound out unknown words because that is the way she has been taught (two years of instruction in synthetic phonics). This strategy usually fails, however, and Jenny becomes discouraged. Having forgotten the meaning of the story, Jenny creates a string of miscues that make sense for the sentence but not for the entire story. However, when Jenny participates in a group discussion, she circumvents her weakness and uses her extensive background knowledge to infer meaning from what she reads. This strategy allows her to discuss freely in an open-ended discussion.

Table 6–4   *Context Analysis for Jenny*

Format of Discussion

Shared meaning construction: Jenny participates in group discussions, using her extensive background knowledge. However, previous learning situations have focused on completing workbook pages and not discussing. The present classroom placement encourages collaboration in thinking.

Group composition: Jenny prefers group instruction where she can participate in the discussion, using her background knowledge. However, previous learning situations have included an extensive pull-out program with one-on-one instruction.

Point of assistance during the lesson: Before Jenny reads, she needs to review new words to facilitate print processing.

Responsiveness: Jenny profits when teachers and peers respond from a sense-making framework. She is easily annoyed if she makes a mistake and someone else corrects it.

Type of Assistance

Elicits responses: Although Jenny responds when asked questions, she prefers to create responses without teacher assistance. Jenny has had teachers who expected immediate responses to questions.

Prompts: Instruction needs to have minimal feedback from the teacher and maximal from the student. The teacher needs to prompt with this question: "What would make sense and start with a _____?"

Wait time: Wait time has been appropriate for Jenny, because she always has a response.

Nature of Teacher Expectations and Classroom Focus

*Focus on strengths: Jenny likes to use her extensive background knowledge, particularly in science activities. Previous learning situations, however, have focused on skill weakness, including a two-year program of intensive synthetic phonics instruction.

*Focus on strategy use: Jenny would profit from a classroom focus on strategies of monitoring oral reading, but present focus is only on constructing meaning. Previous instruction focused on grapho-phonic skill knowledge.

*Use collaborative assessments: Jenny has started keeping a portfolio so that she can evaluate her work. It has helped her focus on her effort and meaning construction. Previously, she was simply assessed on her skill weaknesses; therefore, she had not been engaged in literacy activities.

Summary

Formulating Hypotheses for Jenny

When cross-checking the elements of the reading event, the diagnostic teacher remembers that some of the factors may not be important in examining the particular reading event under scrutiny. Only the key factors affecting the student's reading performance are analyzed. For Jenny, the analysis resulted in the following key factors:

1. The type of text (expository) facilitates constructing meaning and heightens interest.

2. The student has a negative attribution to reading (she states that she hates reading).

3. The student uses only one cueing system at a time when reading breaks down. (She tries to use phonics, but when this strategy fails she uses sentence sense. She does not combine the sources.)

4. The more grammatically complex the sentence structure, the more the student can self-correct her miscues.

5. The student would rather direct her own learning than have the teacher tell her what to do. (This preference may be a function of the extremely structured program that was used during her initial reading instruction.)

6. The student overrelies on reader-based sources when constructing meaning when text becomes difficult.

7. The student has a well-developed background of information that she uses when responding to text.

Having identified these key factors, the teacher is then able to select an appropriate diagnostic teaching technique.

Reviewing the Steps

To formulate the diagnostic hypotheses, the diagnostic teacher reflects on the reading event, considering each variable and its relationship to the reader's performance. He looks at the interactions among the task, the text, the reader, and the context to establish patterns of reading performance.

After he has formulated hypotheses, he selects instructional techniques to advance the student's reading (see Chapter 10). To verify the hypotheses that have led to this selection, the teacher conducts a diagnostic lesson. The guidelines for conducting this lesson are found in Chapter 7, "Assessment Using Diagnostic Lessons."

7

Assessment Using Diagnostic Lessons

Although the diagnostic teacher uses informal assessment and extended assessment discussed in Chapter 5, she needs to constantly reinterpret the information in the light of student performance. She uses the informal reading inventory as a measure of what the student can do when he reads independently (without instruction). However, she also establishes how the student constructs meaning with text as she is teaching. Therefore, she continues her assessment and establishes a level at which the student profits from her instruction. From this knowledge, she derives her hypotheses for the student's instruction.

After the diagnostic teacher formulates her hypotheses, she teaches a lesson using techniques based on the hypotheses (see Figure 7–1). Diagnostic lessons provide a tool to assess the amount of growth that actually occurs as a result of the instructional adjustments. Through the *diagnostic lesson,* the teacher *assesses* the student's changes in reading behavior and establishes the student's optimal *learning conditions* (see Figure 7–1) including the student's mediated reading level.

Establishing Mediated Reading Level

The student's mediated reading level determines the level at which the student can efficiently be taught. This level is determined by evaluating the "distance between the actual developmental level as determined by independent problem solving and the level of potential development as determined through problem solving under adult guidance or in collaboration with more capable peers" (Vygotsky, 1978, p. 86). First, the diagnostic teacher identifies at what level the student can incorporate the targeted reading strategies as a result of specified instruction. This level is determined by calculating the "difference between the level of unaided performance a child can achieve, and the level he could achieve with aid" (Powell,

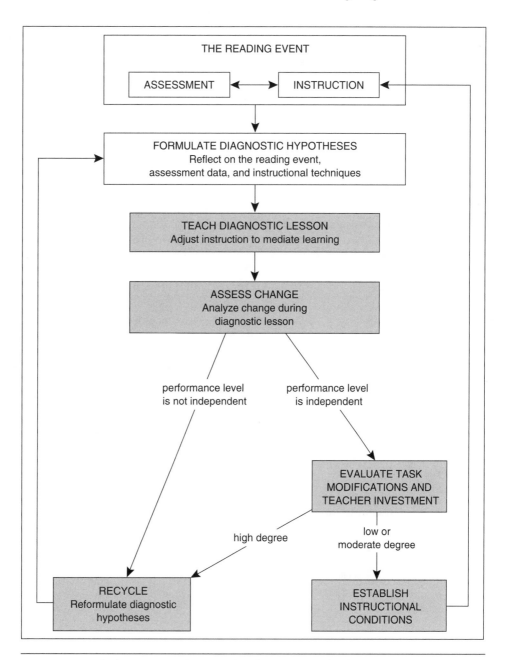

Figure 7–1   *The Decision-Making Cycle of Diagnostic Teaching*

1984, p. 248). Therefore, the diagnostic teacher establishes the highest difficulty level at which the student profits from instruction.

Because the goal is to determine how instruction improves reading performance, a text that is moderately difficult (90% oral accuracy and 60% comprehension) provides a more appropriate measuring tool. Using a moderately difficult text (within the borderline range in Figure 5–2) allows the teacher to assess the student's change in reading as a result of instruction. She wants to observe how the student learns from her instruction. After instruction, the selected text should be read at the independent level (98% accuracy and 90% comprehension). If this level is achieved, the diagnostic teacher selects a more difficult text and teaches another lesson. She continues this process of selecting more difficult texts until the student does not achieve an independent reading level after instruction. Placement is thus determined by identifying the highest difficulty level at which the student profits from instruction.

For example, a teacher took two short segments from a story in a text that was designated as moderately difficult for a student. Using the passages, she developed two assessments according to the constructs of informal reading assessment. Without teacher instruction, the student read the first segment with an error rate of $\frac{1}{11}$ words and 60 percent comprehension. After the targeted vocabulary words were introduced and a discussion about how these words related to the selection was conducted, the second segment was read with an error rate of $\frac{1}{50}$ and 90 percent comprehension. For this student, a text that was read near frustration without teacher direction could be read at independent reading level with instruction by the teacher.

The diagnostic teacher continued this procedure with a more difficult text. The highest level of text that the student read fluently after instruction was designated as the text to use during instruction. The level was then called the *mediated reading level*—the highest level of text that can be read meaningfully after instruction (Powell, 1986).

> The diagnostic teacher establishes the mediated reading level, the highest level of text that can be read fluently after instruction.

For the diagnostician, decisions about placement involve more than just establishing at what level the student will profit from instruction. Because she is actually teaching during her assessment, she also evaluates the amount of task modification necessary to create the desired reading change. Prior to instruction, the diagnostic teacher decides on certain task conditions that will enhance learning for a particular student. Some of these decisions include these questions:

Will I segment the selection? If so, how will I do it—sentence by sentence, or paragraph by paragraph? Will the instruction be entirely silent reading? Or will oral rereading be necessary? How many new vocabulary words will be introduced before reading the selection and how will instruction occur? Should part of the discussion be written down so it can be referred to later?

These decisions involve how she will modify the task so that learning will occur.

If a high degree of task modification is required, the diagnostic teacher needs to select either a less difficult text or a different teaching technique. If a low degree of task modification takes place during the lesson, a more difficult text can be selected. Therefore, placement can be determined by the amount of task modification needed to ensure constructing meaning with text.

> The diagnostic teacher evaluates the amount of task modification (changes in the reading task) that she makes during instruction—such as changing from oral to silent reading, or from one technique to another. `

A third consideration is the amount of teacher investment necessary to engage the student in an active interpretation of text. As she teaches, the diagnostic teacher adjusts her instruction to the needs of the student. She asks herself these questions: How can I elicit responses so that the student will understand the main idea? What does the student already know that will help him understand the story? How much time do I need to wait before I assist? What kind of assistance (prompting, questioning, or modeling) will be most helpful? These questions focus the teacher's involvement during instruction.

During instruction, the diagnostic teacher evaluates the amount of her investment. If the investment is extremely high, changes in instruction are needed that decrease complexity (an easier text or different teaching technique). If the investment is low, changes are needed that increase the complexity (a more difficult text or higher level questioning).

> The diagnostic teacher evaluates her investment or the changes she makes regarding her interaction with the student, which includes an array of interaction possibilities such as prompting, rephrasing, and feedback.

The diagnostic teacher uses three criteria to determine the mediated reading level, the highest level at which the student can profit from her instruction. She finds a reading level that is moderately difficult and teaches a lesson at this level. Then she evaluates the amount of change in reading behavior due to instruction as well as the amount of teacher investment and task modification needed to ensure active meaning construction.

After establishing a student's mediated reading level, the teacher continues her diagnostic lessons at this level. To begin, she chooses a reading passage that is at the student's mediated reading level.

Procedures For Diagnostic Lessons

The goal of conducting a diagnostic lesson is to establish the instructional conditions that promote active reading. As the lesson is conducted, the diagnostic teacher evaluates not only the success of the reader in terms of traditional criteria, such as miscues and comprehension, but also the degree of task modifications and teacher investment that were needed to produce the reading change. Two formats have been used to conduct diagnostic lessons. One format assesses the reader prior to instruction (at sight) and compares this information to an after-instruction assessment. This format is used when the student's reading level is near the end of first grade or above. The other format is used when students cannot read enough words fluently to successfully evaluate their reading prior to instruction. In these cases, the diagnostic teacher compares the reading change after several lessons using different techniques that have been taught. The procedures for both will be outlined in this section.

Diagnostic Lesson Using Baseline Data

The diagnostic teacher selects a story and divides it into three sections and uses the first section to assess students' reading performance without assistance. It is read *at sight*—either orally or silently—without any period of familiarization and without assistance to establish baseline data. The middle section of the passage is taught using the selected technique (see Chapters 10 and 11). This part of the lesson is the actual implementation of the hypotheses and requires keen observation of the changes that improve students' interpretation of text. To assess the degree of change in reading as a result of instruction, the student reads the third section of the text at sight and without assistance. As a result of the mediated instruction, changes in the students' reading should be apparent. If the instruction has been appropriate, the student should now be able to read the third section of the text at the independent reading level and exhibit patterns of performance that reflect a more integrated use of reader-based and text-based processing. Using the information from the diagnostic teaching lesson, the diagnostic teacher establishes the conditions that result in improved learning for the student. The following discussion delineates the purpose for each of the three sections of the diagnostic lesson.

Establishing Baseline Data

Having the student read the first section at sight and without assistance serves two functions: (a) to add information to the diagnostic hypotheses (see Chapter 6) and (b) to establish baseline behaviors so that the effectiveness of instruction can be evaluated. The section should be about 100 to 200 words long and may be read either orally to evaluate print processing or silently to evaluate meaning processing (see Chapters 5 and 6). The data are analyzed by computing the percentage of comprehension and error rate as well as evaluating the patterns of the reading performance.

   The diagnostic teacher reviews the data to expand her diagnostic hypotheses. However, her primary purpose for collecting baseline data is to measure growth as the result of instruction. Baseline data reflect the student's reading performance without aid and before adjusted instruction. During the instructional lesson, the teacher establishes the instructional conditions that mediate learning. To assess this change, the diagnostic teacher compares the student's reading without aid and his performance after specified instruction. During the third section of the diagnostic lesson, the baseline data are used to evaluate reading growth as the result of instruction.

Establishing the Conditions of Learning

After the baseline data have been established, the teacher designs a diagnostic lesson based on her hypotheses about the student's reading. She selects a technique (see Chapter 10) that matches the reader's profile. The second section is used to establish the optimal conditions for learning new reading strategies. As she teaches the lesson, her modifications are summarized and become part of the diagnostic data collection. Unlike the first section, where the teacher constructs diagnostic hypotheses based on a relatively static assessment of reading performance, during the instructional lesson, the teacher's assessments are dynamic. Modifications of hypotheses can occur as the teacher responds to the student's needs during instruction.

   When using repeated readings with Ted, a second-grader, for instance, the diagnostic teacher found that simply discussing the miscues did not result in decreased miscues, so she modeled her own self-correction process by saying, "Oops, that doesn't make sense; let's see what would make sense and start with a g. Oh, *girl* starts with a g. *The girl hit the home run.* Yes, that makes sense and sounds like it looks." Then Ted read the passage again, and the teacher recorded the miscues and evaluated the amount and kind of change evidenced in the reading performance. Because the number of miscues decreased and fluent reading increased, the teacher recommended the procedure with the modifications tried during the diagnostic lesson.

On another occasion, a fourth-grade student named John needed assistance in how to read silently and construct meaning with text. The diagnostic teacher formulated her hypotheses while she conducted a think-aloud assessment on the first section, which indicated John had difficulty making predictions (see Chapter 5). During the second section, the teacher used a directed reading activity. During the lesson, John could not answer an inferential question, so the diagnostic teacher rephrased the question to include some factual information to facilitate his response. John still had no clue about how to respond, so she asked him to find the part of the story that told about the factual information and to read it aloud. The ability of the student to perform this action indicates whether he understands the sequence of the story, as well as his ability to read the words without difficulty. He easily found the part of the text that contained the answer and read it without difficulty. Therefore, word identification did not present difficulty.

Again, the teacher began to elicit a response; however, this time she began with a factual question. Then she asked John to relate relevant personal experiences to the facts. After this discussion, the original inferential question was rephrased. John was able to respond to the inferential question, using the factual information and his personal experiences. Because this instructional sequence facilitated comprehension, the teacher hypothesized that John comprehends better when the instructional sequence begins with the facts and then develops an inferential understanding of the story.

During the diagnostic lesson, records of the instructional modifications are kept so that the amount and kinds of teacher intervention can be identified. When the teacher conducts a diagnostic lesson, however, her primary goal is to teach the student. Her second goal is to identify those instructional modifications that result in increased reading performance. In effect, the diagnostic teacher establishes the instructional conditions necessary to increase the reading.

Evaluating Change

To evaluate the effect the instructional adjustments have on the student's reading, the diagnostic teacher conducts a final assessment using the third section of the passage. She uses the same format as for the first section, either recording oral reading responses or a think-aloud experience. The final assessment, in which the students read at sight and without assistance, provides a systematic method for assessing the effects of instructional intervention on the student's reading. The teacher assesses reading change during the lesson as well as the amount of task modification and teacher investment needed to produce that change. These measures not only determine placement but also establish optimal instructional conditions.

Reading Growth as the Result of Instruction   First, the diagnostic teacher must establish the amount of growth that has occurred as a result of instruction. If the instruction was appropriate, the resulting scores should indicate an independent reading level (98% word identification and 90% comprehension).

Because the student received instruction adjusted to mediate learning, the number of questions answered correctly should increase and miscues decrease. Reading progress should be evident.

> Reading progress is indicated by a decrease in miscues and an increase in the number of questions answered correctly.

Next, the diagnostic teacher compares the student's patterns of reading behavior on the first section with those on the third section. The student's oral reading of the third section should reflect more semantically and syntactically appropriate miscues and an increase in self-corrections. This pattern indicates that the student is using his knowledge of the story theme to figure out unknown words. A student's think-aloud on the third section should reflect a more integrated use of textual and nontextual information as well as more elaborate responses to questions. Spontaneous self-monitoring and the student's awareness of the sources of information he uses to construct responses should also be increasingly evident.

> Reading progress is also indicated by an increasing use of both reader-based processing and text-based processing and by more self-monitoring for understanding.

Figure 7–1 highlights the final steps involved in assessing reading change using diagnostic lessons. When the diagnostic teacher analyzes change in this last phase of the decision-making cycle, two conclusions can result: a positive change in reading behavior (independent level obtained) or no change in reading behavior (independent level not obtained). These two outcomes necessitate different responses from the diagnostic teacher. If mediated instruction produces an independent reading level, the diagnostic teacher carefully evaluates the task modifications and teacher investment, or assistance, to establish the instructional modifications that produced the change. If mediated instruction does not produce reading progress, the diagnostic teacher eliminates those techniques and modifications that were used. She returns to her diagnostic hypotheses, adds any new information collected during the diagnostic lesson, and reformulates her hypotheses. Then she selects a new technique and conducts another diagnostic lesson.

Determining the Amount of Task Modification   Prior to instruction, the diagnostic teacher selects a technique to implement during the diagnostic lesson. She determines how she is going to work on active reading. She decides whether the reading task will be silent or oral and whether the story will be read as a whole or in segments. She decides whether she will introduce new vocabulary words and how to do it. As she teaches the lesson, the teacher modifies these original plans so that the student can construct meaning with text. It is these modifications that the teacher records and evaluates.

For example, the diagnostic teacher decided to use self-directed questioning (see "Self-Directed Questioning" in Chapter 11) with Luis, a third-grade student who was relatively passive when reading. He did not make guesses about the story or revise the few predictions he did make. The teacher began instruction by demonstrating the steps of self-directed questioning. As she silently read the text, she thought aloud when important information was presented. Next, she asked Luis to read silently and then to think aloud about the text. Luis readily began to talk about his interpretations. The teacher and student continued this process by alternately thinking aloud about the text. Luis began to make guesses and then to revise his thinking about the text.

In this example, the teacher needed to make relatively few task modifications. The student learned the new task and readily applied it. The teacher concluded that the passive reading behavior was due to a lack of experience with the task. It was evident that Luis had not transferred his active stance in other problem-solving situations to silent reading behavior before the instruction.

When evaluating Terry, another passive reader, the diagnostic teacher decided to use self-directed questioning again. As with the other student, the diagnostic teacher demonstrated the steps of self-directed questioning by thinking aloud about the text. Then she asked Terry to read silently and think aloud about the text when important information was presented. Terry read a long segment silently, then stopped and looked at the teacher for questions. However, he could not talk about the text. The teacher asked him to read the segment aloud and think out loud about the text. Again he read the words without stopping to think about their meaning. Therefore, the teacher demonstrated the same segment of the text, emphasizing how she thought about the text as she read out loud. Terry followed the teacher's example. However, he mainly recounted exactly what was stated in the text. He did not tie together events to make predictions or revise any previous thoughts.

The teacher demonstrated the next segment of the text. Terry was asked to follow the example, but he again read the words without thinking. The teacher, therefore, modified the task by segmenting the section into sentences. Reading sentence by sentence, she demonstrated her thinking about each sentence. Finally, Terry began to think aloud about the sentences and draw relationships among the sentences in the paragraph. During this segment, the teacher modified the procedures by asking questions such as: "What makes you say that? Was this character important? How do you know?"

To help this passive reader learn more active strategies for constructing meaning, the diagnostic teacher needed to modify a number of instructional areas. She changed the task from silent to oral reading when Terry could not talk about what he had read silently. She segmented the passage into sentences when he could not follow the paragraphs that she demonstrated. Moreover, she shifted from simply demonstrating to demonstrating with inquiry questions in order to help Terry see relationships among the ideas in the text.

The diagnostic teacher evaluates the amount of modification necessary to create a change in the student's reading performance. Luis required little task modification for the original task and learned the task readily. Terry, however, required substantial modification. The degree of task modification becomes a key factor in determining future instructional interactions. If a high degree of task modification is required, a less difficult text or a different technique should be selected. If a low degree of task modification is needed, however, a more difficult text or task can be employed.

> The degree of task modification is considered when establishing the conditions necessary to produce reading change.

Determining the Amount of Teacher Investment   During assessment, the diagnostic teacher becomes a powerful determiner of active reading. She thinks about how she set up instruction according to the procedures for the technique. Were these procedures sufficient for improving a student's text interpretation? Or did she have to change the procedures, draw out of the student his own knowledge, and then show him how to relate this information to what he was reading? She evaluates how many times she had to rephrase questions and how many clues she needed to provide for the student.

Sometimes relatively little teacher investment, or assistance, is needed. For instance, Bobby could not recognize the word *skated* in this sentence: "The girl skated around the rink." The teacher told him to read to the end of the sentence. Bobby did so, thought for a minute about the word, and then read, "The girl skated around the rink." In this case, very little teacher investment was needed to encourage self-correction. With the simple prompt "read to the end of the sentence," the student was able to figure out the word.

Another student had the same difficulty, but he needed more teacher investment. With the same prompt, Fred read to the end of the sentence but could not recognize the word *rink* either. In this case, the teacher had to probe further. She asked Fred to think about the story and what the girl might be doing. Still there was no response. The teacher then said, "In the picture, there is an ice rink. Now, what do you think the girl is doing?" "Skating" was his reply. The teacher instructed him to read the sentence again. Fred now read: "The girl . . . skated around the . . . rink."

The diagnostic teacher assesses modifications in terms of the amount of teacher investment necessary to create a change in the student's reading. Bobby required relatively little assistance, so there was minimal teacher investment. However, Fred required a great deal of assistance, so there was a higher degree of teacher investment.

> The amount and kind of teacher investment are evaluated to identify the conditions that produce reading change.

The diagnostic teacher assesses reading change as a result of instruction by selecting a reading passage that is moderately difficult. She follows the procedures for the diagnostic lesson: establishing baseline data on the first section through the student's reading at sight, instruction during the second section, and establishing postinstructional data on the third section through more reading at sight. She evaluates whether the third section was read at an independent level. When the third section does not produce reader change, she reformulates her hypotheses and conducts another lesson. When the student reads the final section at an independent level, the diagnostic teacher assesses the amount of task modification and teacher investment that produced that change.

Diagnostic Lessons Using After Instruction Assessments Only

When using techniques such as the collaborative reading procedure or language experience approach, the diagnostic teacher initially reads aloud to the student before the student is asked to read on his own. In these techniques, the diagnostic teacher does not have the student read without extensive support, so conducting an assessment before instruction would not be appropriate. In these cases the diagnostic teacher begins by teaching a lesson and *later* conducting an oral reading analysis of the student's reading. If the technique was effective, the passage should be read at the independent level even after a delayed period of time. These procedures are similar to the learning-methods tests developed by Mills (1956) and Ray (1970). After the lessons, the diagnostic teacher compares reading change under several different techniques as recommended in the preceding section.

A diagnostic teacher was working with Neil, a second-grader who was a nonreader (he knew only five words by sight). The diagnostic teacher began her diagnostic assessment with a language experience lesson (see "Language Experience" in Chapter 11). She created an experience, Neil dictated a story, and they read the story together numerous times. The story was chunked onto cards and the cards flashed in story order. Then Neil read the story on his own and performed at the independent level (error rate $\frac{1}{50}$). Later during the day, he read the story with an error rate of $\frac{1}{10}$. This technique could be used for Neil in future instruction, but it required a high degree of teacher investment to achieve the recorded growth, and he seemed to memorize the story without looking at the words. Neil could, however, correct many of his mistakes when the teacher repeated the preceding part of the sentence (moderate teacher investment). Therefore, the teacher wanted to explore another approach.

For this diagnostic lesson, the teacher used the predictable language approach (see "Predictable Language Approach" in Chapter 11). Neil and the teacher were supposed to read the story simultaneously; however, he did not look at the text. Neil did, however, begin to read the text as the teacher omitted words in the language pattern. As she omitted more words, Neil paid more attention to the words on the page and reread the text with an error rate of $\frac{1}{50}$. He also corrected many of his miscues by rereading sentences on his own. Later in the day, Neil still read the story with only 1 miscue every 50 words. The diagnostic teacher concluded that this technique was more effective than the language experience lesson because he was able to use the language pattern to self-correct his miscues.

To see whether another technique would require less teacher time but have similar results, the teacher conducted another diagnostic lesson. This time she used the talking books technique (see "Talking Books" in Chapter 11). Neil listened to a short story on a tape recorder until he had the story memorized. Then he read the story to the teacher, producing an error rate of $\frac{1}{15}$ and losing his place many times. Listening to the book repeated, Neil had memorized the words but not associated them with the printed words. Later that day, he read the book with an error rate of $\frac{1}{10}$. In this case, the diagnostic teacher continued using the predictable language technique and placed Neil in a small group, where he was still able to maintain the reader change that he exhibited in the one-to-one assessment.

Using a series of modified diagnostic teaching lessons, the diagnostic teacher selects the most appropriate technique to teach the beginning reader. These lessons use two readings of the text—one immediately after instruction and another several hours later—to establish a learning rate for that particular instructional technique. For the beginning reader, the diagnostic teacher pays special attention to the teacher investment and task modification needed to create reader change. This assessment determines under what conditions subsequent instruction will be conducted:

1. If little task modification and teacher investment were used to produce the desired change, the diagnostic teacher considers using a more difficult text for instruction.

2. If a moderate amount of task modification and teacher investment were needed, the diagnostic teacher continues to use those adjustments in the same level of text.

3. If there was a great deal of task modification and teacher invest-ment were required, the diagnostic teacher reformulates her hy-potheses and selects either another technique or an easier text.

Special Considerations

The procedures outlined are used when considering only one or two tech-niques or instructional modifications for the student. In many instances, however, the diagnostic teacher needs to consider several options before es-tablishing the optimal instructional conditions. Therefore, she compares growth under different techniques, uses several adapted lessons, and com-bines techniques to increase her effectiveness.

Comparing Reading Change Under Different Techniques

At times, the diagnostic teacher will conduct a series of diagnostic lessons so that she can identify the most efficient instructional procedure. After the final assessment with each technique, the diagnostic teacher compares how the reader constructs meaning under the different instructional conditions and evaluates the effectiveness of each technique. For example, Jason, a third-grade reader, was identified as having an oral reading fluency prob-lem. In working with the student, the diagnostic teacher first formulated her hypotheses. From the data collected, the teacher designed a program of re-peated readings (see "Repeated Readings" in Chapter 11), including a dis-cussion of the miscues after the first reading. She selected a text and con-ducted a reading-at-sight evaluation to establish baseline data. For the second section of the passage, she instructed Jason using a repeated read-ings format and discussed his errors with him. On the last section of the se-lected text, she conducted another reading at sight but without assistance. Jason decreased his error rate from $\frac{1}{10}$ on the first section to $\frac{1}{15}$ on the last section.

Because this technique resulted in only minimal change in reading per-formance, the diagnostic teacher designed another lesson. She decided to use the talking books technique (see "Talking Books" in Chapter 11) during the instructional phase of the diagnostic lesson. She followed the same pro-cedure: first establishing baseline data through unaided reading at sight, next instruction, and finally establishing postinstructional data through more unaided reading at sight. This time Jason decreased his error rate from $\frac{1}{10}$ on the first section to $\frac{1}{50}$ on the last section.

The diagnostic teacher compared the resulting changes from the two sets of readings to decide which technique was more effective. The talking books technique produced the most change; moreover, it required less teacher investment because the tape recording provided the words that would have needed the teacher's prompting under the repeated readings approach. As a result, the teacher used taped stories in the diagnostic teach-ing program. Whenever the diagnostic teacher can conduct a series of diagnostic lessons to compare the effectiveness of several techniques, she increases her ability to confirm the diagnostic hypotheses and select the best possible instructional approach for the reader.

Using More Than One Technique at the Same Time

Sometimes the diagnostic teacher needs to combine several techniques to produce the desired change. In these cases, the combined techniques are more effective than using either one of them alone. The decision-making process that results in combining techniques is illustrated in the case of Charles, a fourth-grade reader who had difficulty with silent reading comprehension. Initially, the diagnostic teacher designed a program using self-directed questioning (see "Self-Questioning" in Chapter 11). She selected a story, divided it into three sections, and conducted a think-aloud assessment that was unaided. She recorded her data. Next she instructed the lesson using self-directed questioning. She modeled the process, using the concepts missed during the first section. Charles had a great deal of difficulty remembering the steps in self-directed questioning, even after the diagnostic teacher had written them down (task modification). Charles was never able to do the task independently (without a high degree of teacher investment). The final section of the story was read like the first, as an unaided think-aloud assessment, but provided only minimal change (improvement from 55 percent to 65 percent in comprehension).

The diagnostic teacher decided to try the reciprocal teaching technique (see "Reciprocal Teaching" in Chapter 11), which is similar to self-directed questioning but is more structured. She again conducted an unaided think-aloud assessment on the first section of the selected text. Next she instructed the lesson using reciprocal teaching, returning to concepts missed during the first section of the text to model the process and to clear up misconceptions about the story. Charles was to follow her model and summarize, ask a good question, clarify difficult parts, and predict what the next segment would say. However, he had a great deal of difficulty learning this task, so the teacher used a high degree of modeling on each segment. Charles was not able to do the task independently. The final section of the story was read like the first, as an unaided think-aloud assessment. When this technique resulted in only minimal change in reading performance (improvement from 55 percent to 75 percent in comprehension) despite a high degree of teacher modeling, the diagnostic teacher decided to add another technique to her procedure.

The teacher selected another story and followed the same procedure: having the student read at sight to establish baseline data, instruction, and having the student read at sight again to establish postinstructional data. During the instructional phase of the diagnostic lesson, the diagnostic teacher introduced a story map (see "Story Map" in Chapter 11) along with reciprocal teaching. First, she modeled the combined sequence: add new information to the story map, summarize using the story map, use the story map to ask a good question, clarify any difficult parts that do not fit on the map, and finally, use the components of the story map to predict what will happen next.

Following instruction in this combined approach, Charles began to take over the teaching. He began to teach the lesson independently. For him, using the story map was more concrete than either self-directed questioning or reciprocal teaching alone. During the final third of the lesson, the diagnostic teacher conducted a think-aloud assessment, which revealed a change in his monitoring of understanding. Charles had begun to revise his predictions as he encountered new information. This new approach resulted in a growth from 55 percent to 90 percent in reading comprehension. As in this case, the diagnostic teacher may combine reading techniques to evaluate whether the new combination results in greater reading growth. If it does, she uses the combined, or piggy-back, approach rather than either technique alone.

Summary

The job of the diagnostic teacher is to identify appropriate techniques for instruction. By teaching a lesson using selected materials and techniques, the diagnostic teacher assesses the student's learning as she teaches and evaluates reading growth as the result of her instruction. She also measures the task modification and teacher investment needed to ensure reader change. Then she establishes the most appropriate instructional conditions for the student. Once these conditions are in place, the diagnostic teacher introduces more difficult tasks or texts and observes the student as he learns the task or reads the text. The diagnostic teacher becomes both teacher and evaluator. Her purpose during the diagnostic lesson is to record changes in reading behaviors and the instructional adjustments that produced them. She focuses on teaching rather than testing to reveal those instructional adjustments that produce reading change for a particular student.

8

Assessment Using Portfolios

The last three chapters focused on collecting observational data of students' reading behaviors. From these observations, the diagnostic teacher makes decisions about the readers' strategies for constructing meaning as well as the appropriateness of instructional techniques. These observations are in-process assessments. To be of use to teachers and students over time, diagnostic information must be collected in a convenient format. Although diagnostic teachers have always collected information in folders, the current use of portfolios has expanded the contents of such folders to include materials from both instruction and assessment. Portfolios document and evaluate literacy using multiple sources of information (oral reading recorded on tapes, written think-alouds, writing, retelling, and so on) and multiple contexts (alone, with a partner, with a teacher or parent, with a group, using the author's chair, and so on) in a collaborative fashion (Glazer & Brown, 1993; Stowell & Tierney, 1995). Both the diagnostic teacher and his students make decisions about what is included in the portfolio. Literacy portfolios, then, make connections among the contexts of literacy and document the unfolding of student learning over time, providing a dynamic record of the learning process.

Like diagnostic teaching lessons, which evaluate reading during actual learning experiences, portfolios assess literacy using artifacts from authentic activities in which students construct meaning. The contents of the portfolio are not items completed on a single day, but rather items collected over a period of time, which demonstrate the student's understanding during literacy activities. For example, a teacher included in a portfolio an example of students' story writing (See "Story Writing" in Chapter 11) from each of the months of October, February, and April. Then he analyzed each student's growth in writing over the year. This approach places the focus of portfolio assessment on the students' learning rather than a specific curriculum. In addition, artifacts can be drawn from many different aspects of the student's day. For instance, students might include a vocabulary map about China to excerpts from a response journal. Sometimes students include poetry they have written at home. In fact, teachers have found that placing nonschool items in the portfolio served to build a bridge between school and society, thus creating a more elaborate view of literacy learning (Hansen, 1995).

Consistent with the focus of diagnostic teaching, portfolios focus on strengths, rather than weaknesses (Glazer & Brown, 1993). As the diagnostic teacher and his students evaluate progress, they choose items that demonstrate what students know and can do. Thus, as they mutually discuss what to put into the portfolio, the students think about what they want to show about their literacy. Through deciding how to show strengths, the diagnostic teacher and his students begin to evaluate student strengths and see how to use them in literacy events. For example, Jenny decided to put a videotape of her oral science report, which was a demonstration about fossils into her portfolio. For her report, she had collected fossils with her father and labeled them. This activity showed that she did, in fact, have extensive background knowledge about the fossils even though she had difficulty reading about the topic in her textbook. As Jenny reflected on her science project, she began to understand that she could participate in many literacy activities as she developed as a reader. Likewise, her teacher could assess Jenny's science knowledge through the medium of the videotaped demonstration rather than a paper-and-pencil test.

Portfolios add to diagnostic assessment by interweaving instruction and assessment so that the learning does not stop in order to test. In portfolios, assessment is an authentic representation of what the student knows and can do. However, each piece includes a reflection (see "Reflecting" in this chapter) about what it shows or what was learned; by this means, both the students and teachers begin to describe the process of learning. Portfolios, then, paint a picture of the learning process for each student.

Procedures for Portfolios

Selecting Artifacts

Realizing that portfolios can easily become an overwhelming collection of student work, the diagnostic teacher often has both working portfolios and culminating portfolios. Working portfolios are where daily work is kept. When developing portfolios, the diagnostic teacher and his students set appropriate goals for learning and collect pieces that demonstrate progress toward these goals. By deciding what to include in the portfolio, both the diagnostic teacher and his students are setting and describing the goals of literacy.

As the diagnostic teacher thinks about the portfolio process, he decides what type of artifacts need to be selected to show the student's growth over time. Pieces that illustrate critical areas of strength and areas where the student is progressing are important, but not everything that the student produces needs to be included, even in the working portfolio. Being selective is important! Frequently the teacher wants the students to evaluate items in their working portfolio and select one piece that is an important piece and then tell why. Other times, however, the diagnostic teacher wants students to tell about their favorite books and copy excerpts that highlight what the book meant to them. These items demonstrate what the students view as important in their literacy development.

However, many times the diagnostic teacher wants to show progress on specific aspects of reading development. In these cases, he develops a series of questions to evaluate specific tasks related to the overall goals. For example, a diagnostic teacher developed a series of questions to help both himself and his students select summaries of expository text that they had produced to be included in their portfolios. Then the students evaluated each summary using these two questions: "Did the summary have important information and relevant content?" and "Did the summary demonstrate an attempt to make generalizations based on the textual information?" As they worked on summaries, the teacher and his students decided that showing they could select important information was a critical goal for them. They also decided to include lesson artifacts that demonstrated their knowledge of selecting important information. Some of the students selected webbing (see "Webbing" in Chapter 11) of key words, while others selected their K-W-L sheets (see "K-W-L" in Chapter 11) to put into the portfolio. One group of students selected entries from their science journals that depicted how their written analysis of a science experiment showed how they could summarize important information. Although students selected different items to illustrate summarization, all the entries showed how they could identify important information, a critical goal in literacy development.

The diagnostic teacher also uses questions related to the processes of reading and writing to help focus selecting artifacts. For diagnostic purposes, the teacher might include the in-process measures of reading such as a miscue analysis or a think-aloud in the portfolio. Also, he might include diagnostic lesson evaluations that highlight specific tasks such as nonliteral comprehension or oral retellings, the latter of which would give information about students' summarization abilities. Sometimes the diagnostic teacher includes the student's response to diagnostic teaching lessons because it shows critical information about how the reader constructs meaning with text.

Further, as artifacts are selected, it is important that the selection process be a collaborative experience between the diagnostic teacher and his students. The conversation about what to include provides an opportunity for problem readers to discuss their personal strategies for constructing meaning as well as how a particular text or the specific task influenced the deployment of these personal strategies. As problem readers engage in these types of discussions, they begin to view reading as a process that is influenced by many factors rather than simply their specific abilities. Thus, these discussions can be critical for readers who have experienced difficulty reading.

Artifacts, then, can be a mixture of in-process measures of reading and writing, lesson artifacts, and written drafts or vocabulary maps. They can also be final products such as written or oral research reports that demonstrate reading or writing development or other skills, such as the ability to summarize. However, what is important about the contents of the portfolio is that they demonstrate the students' reading strengths and strategies as well as their progress toward literacy goals.

Reflecting

A critical aspect of developing a portfolio is reflecting on what each artifact demonstrates about literacy development. This distinction separates a portfolio from simply a collection of work. Attached to each entry is a written reflection describing what this particular item demonstrates about the student's reading or writing. Either the teacher or the student completes the reflections and attaches one to each item placed into the portfolio. By illustrating the student's process of learning, the portfolio becomes a description of the student's personal literacy development. The description is developed collaboratively between the teacher and the student. Thus, the reflective analysis puts the decision making about reading development into the hands of the diagnostic teacher and his students rather than a test manual.

Once a piece of work is selected, a description of what it is and why it is included needs to be attached to it. Thus, the reflection answers the basic question: "Why was this piece selected, and what does it show about literacy?" For example, Jenny selected her repeated readings chart as one measure of her progress in print processing. Her reflection showed much more than the simple chart as she stated, "This chart shows that I am correcting my miscues more frequently by asking myself what makes sense and then looking at the letters in the word. I have to use these statements together. Before I would use one or the other but not both." This reflection revealed what Jenny understood about the self-correction process.

However, too often problem readers reflect on their reasons by saying simply, "I choose this because I like it" or "I think it is the best." These reflections fail to describe the process of learning. In these cases, the diagnostic teacher talks with students about how reading occurs.

As the diagnostic teacher begins using portfolios, he has the students list the characteristics of being a good reader or writer to help them focus on what they view as important during the specified period of time. The list identifies the integral aspects of reading and writing that the students will use to choose what is included in their portfolio and to write their assessment reflections. For example a student listed the following: predicting, understanding story parts, telling about the characters, telling about what happened in the story, etc. Using this list the student, along with the diagnostic teacher, asked herself, "What did I do that demonstrates my understanding of story parts or telling about the characters?" She selected a herringbone activity and wrote the assessment reflection found in Figure 8–1.

I Picked the Herring Bone aproach because
It shows how I Breakdown a story Into Sections
and came up with The Main Idea.

Figure 8-1   Portfolio Reflection on Herringbone Activity

Collaborating on portfolio reflections helps both the diagnostic teacher and the student review and evaluate what has been learned. Some students need the diagnostic teacher to model how to write an assessment reflection. In this case, he simply uses another artifact from the folder that illustrates a characteristic on the list and writes a reflection to describe how the artifact demonstrates that particular characteristic. Using a self-assessment prediction check-sheet during instruction can also facilitate writing reflections. (For an example of the self-assessment prediction check-sheet, see Table 8–5.) For instance, from a prediction check-sheet, one student wrote: "When I read, I use too much of the text. Although I have been working on using more of what I know, this story was extremely unfamiliar to me and I again relied more heavily on the text." This reflection described how the prediction check-sheet helped her think about the strategies she was using. She also began to realize that many factors influenced the implementation of her reading strategies. In her portfolio, she included her prediction log (see "Prediction Log" in Chapter 11), her check-sheet, and her reflection. These items were stapled together, with the short reflection on a half-sheet on top of the prediction log and check-sheet.

Sometimes the diagnostic teacher wants the students to review their work and select one piece for their culminating portfolio. In these cases, the students are asked to complete a more extensive reflection. In the New Hampshire portfolio project, students are asked to select a piece from their portfolio and complete a more elaborated reflection. Then these prompts are used to guide the students' reflection:

1. *Choose one item from your portfolio and write an explanation of what it shows about you as a person.*

2. *What does this information have to do with you as a reader or writer?*

3. *What would you like to learn next in order to become a better reader or writer?*

4. *What will you do to accomplish this goal?*

> 5. *When you accomplish this goal, how might you show it in your portfolio? (Hansen, 1994, pp. 30–31)*

These questions help the students think about their own literacy development and set new goals and means to accomplish these goals. As the students reflect on each piece, they restate their own definition of literacy, a critical aspect of the portfolio process.

Groups working with portfolios have used open-ended formats or a series of questions that elicit reflections about selections. Such reflections, however, require understanding the reading process, and many students have difficulty explaining their thinking. Some students profit from rubrics where specific aspects of literacy are rated. (Examples can be found in Table 8–1 and Table 8–3.) Self-assessment check-sheets (see Table 8–5) can also help focus students' thinking about portfolio artifacts and assist them in developing reflective statements. Other students, however, may need the diagnostic teacher to demonstrate his own thinking about what portfolio artifacts might show. Therefore, diagnostic teachers frequently demonstrate the reflective process that accompanies selecting a portfolio piece.

Demonstrating Reflections

When students are asked to write about their literacy, problem readers often are unclear about the strategies they use for constructing meaning. In fact, many remedial readers are so confused that they passively read without any knowledge of the strategies they are using. To help these readers participate in portfolio assessment, teachers need to reveal their own personal thinking about literacy artifacts. The students profit from demonstrations of the thinking process in order to understand how to write a reflection (Snider, Lima, & DeVito, 1994). Therefore, once goals for learners have been established, teachers need to demonstrate the strategies used to accomplish these goals as well as reflections about progress toward these goals.

For example, as one diagnostic teacher developed his own portfolio, he included how he read a passage from a book. He copied the passage from the book and wrote in the margins his self-talk. Then he wrote a reflection. Using this artifact, he talked aloud about his own reading process, using the portfolio artifact. He reread the text as well as his self-talk. Then he read aloud his reflection: "I am always connecting unusual experiences that help me remember and visualize what I am reading. Sometimes, however, I put too much of what I know into the text. I have to monitor myself continually to see whether I am on the right track." Talking to the students, he commented, "Can you believe I was so off track that I thought about reading development while I was reading Gary Paulsen's book, *The River?*" These kinds of demonstrations begin to show students how to describe their reading.

As teachers and students become evaluators, they must know the critical tasks at various grade levels. If students are to talk about strategies or how a piece evolved, then teachers must identify critical tasks and demonstrate the thinking behind these tasks. Thus, portfolios have shifted the emphasis from simply following the curriculum to being able to discuss the thinking needed to accomplish goals and describe the personal processes used when constructing meaning.

Using Portfolios

Specifying Goals

When the diagnostic teacher and his students set appropriate goals for learning, the teacher often develops a format or series of questions to evaluate specific tasks related to the overall goals. These formats help the diagnostic teacher evaluate the student's literacy behaviors in a consistent manner. Likewise, these formats help both the teacher and his students collectively evaluate what counts in a particular literacy task. Asking specific questions or filling out a check-sheet focuses the conversation on what counts. For example, a diagnostic teacher developed a series of questions similar to the one in Table 8–1 to evaluate written summaries of expository text.

Using these questions, the diagnostic teacher evaluated a student's work and was able to describe the student's written summaries. For example, he reflected on Sandy's summary saying, "Sandy included important information as well as relevant concepts about snakes in her summary. However, much of what Sandy included did not reveal her prior knowledge about snakes. However, Sandy's organization was exceptional since main ideas were supported by key facts revealing an overall theme in the summary." The questions about summaries helped both the diagnostic teacher and his students reflect on how the students were developing the summarization process and at the same time helped set new goals as they

Table 8–1   *Questions to Evaluate Summaries*

Did the summary have or show—

    important information?

    relevant content and concepts?

    information directly stated in the text?

    information inferred from the text?

    a connection to prior knowledge

    appropriate language?

    an organizational structure?

    a sense of purpose?

recognized areas of strength and need. Similarly, Sandy used a modified series of questions to aid her in analyzing her summaries. The questions were simply changed to the first person, such as "Did my summary have important information? Did my summary have relevant content and concepts?" Using consistent evaluation formats helps the diagnostic teacher and his students keep the goals of literacy in mind as they evaluate artifacts.

In schools, groups of teachers at a particular grade level often collaborate to develop a rubric to evaluate each student's work. For example, a group of second-grade teachers decided that story retelling was a critical task for their students. They developed a rubric similar to the one in Table 8–2 to evaluate students' retelling (Roskos & Walker, 1994). After they read stories, the teachers had their second-grade students write a summary as if they were telling the story to a friend. Then they took three pieces from their classes and each teacher rated the pieces based on the rubric.

After the teachers had individually rated each summary, they met to compare their ratings. The teachers discussed the differences and finally agreed on an adaptation of the rubric and designated "marker" pieces for each rating. Then they evaluated each student's retelling, attaching the retelling rubric and a written reflection to each. For example, a reflective analysis of Jerry's writing by a teacher included: "Jerry elaborates both the setting including the main characters in great detail; however, she only briefly mentions the problem but describes many events, some of which were not important. She does end her retelling so it makes sense but doesn't tell how the problem is solved. Jerry's strengths are in describing the setting and events; however, she needs to work on elaborating the problem and resolution."

The rubric not only provided a consistent form for evaluating retellings, but it also provided the language to write the reflection. Several things happened in the collaborative design of the rubric. First, the teachers were developing their understanding of what was important in a retelling. Second, they were developing a standard for what a second-grade retelling would include. Third, the teachers learned how to evaluate differences within a rubric. They realized that not every retelling had to be alike, but rather that a coherent and elaborate representation of the story was needed. Further, they began to use this evaluation as a way to inform instructional goals for individual students.

Finally, this group of teachers realized that this evaluation represented fairly text-based reading; therefore, they decided to add an affective response to the portfolio. As the students read during readers' workshop, they kept journals about their reactions to stories. From these journals, the teachers asked the students to select parts that demonstrated their emotional reactions to the stories. They constructed a different way to evaluate this affective response.

Table 8–2   *Retelling Assessment*

Setting

4   Has an elaborated explanation of setting, including introduction, names of major characters, important places and times

3   Has major character and other characters; briefly describes place and time

2   Has major character and mentions times or places

1   Contains only one idea, such as place, or names minor characters

0   Does not contain any ideas related to setting

Problem

4   Describes the major character's main goal or problem to be solved, including theme of the story; also describes the event that sets up the problem in the story

3   Describes main problem the major character needs to solve

2   Mentions briefly the problem

1   Has an insignificant problem

0   Does not describe any problem

Events

4   Elaborates key story events. Most events are related to working out the problem, are a consequence of this event, or are a character's reaction

3   Has key story events, some of which are related to working out the problem, a consequence of this event, or a character's reaction

2   Describes briefly some key story events

1   Has only a few insignificant events

0   Has no events

Resolution

4   Ends with a feeling of continuity and tells how the problem was solved

3   Ends with a feeling of continuity and briefly tells how the problem was solved

2   Ends with a feeling of continuity, but does not tell how the problem was solved

1   Ends abruptly

0   Ends in the middle of the story

Note: From *Interactive Handbook for Understanding Reading Diagnosis: A Problem-Solving Approach Using Case Studies* (p. 123) by K. Roskos and B. J. Walker, 1994, Englewood Cliffs, N.J.: Merrill/Prentice Hall. Copyright 1994 by Prentice Hall. Adapted by permission.

In portfolio assessment, setting goals for literacy is a constructive process among teachers and students. Research in the field of literacy directs teachers' thinking, but this research is adapted to the particular circumstances of the teaching and learning situation.

Evaluating Growth Over Time

The diagnostic teacher takes the information gathered from multiple sources (diagnostic teaching lessons, informal reading assessments, and authentic literacy activities) to target specific reading behaviors to monitor over time. For instance, a diagnostic teacher noticed that a student was overrelying on the text when predicting and retelling stories. He used a prediction rubric to evaluate the student's performance, further verifying his observations. These observations led to the development of techniques to improve the student's prediction strategies. Once a week the diagnostic teacher had the student read a short story and keep a prediction log (see "Prediction Logs" in Chapter 11) where the student wrote predictions and rationales at designated points in the story, thus creating a written think-aloud. These predictions and rationales were rated using a simple rubric (see Table 8–3) and placed in a working portfolio.

Using the prediction log, the diagnostic teacher talked with the student about the strategies she was using in this particular story and jotted a reflection at the bottom of the page. The check-sheet helped focus the conversations on the student's strategy use and how the text or her background knowledge might have affected her predictions. The prediction log, coupled

Table 8–3   *Prediction Rubric*

	Yes 3	Somewhat 2	No 1
Predicts			
makes predictions easily			
uses prior experiences			
uses textual information			
Monitors			
checks predictions			
revises predictions as needed			
justifies responses			
uses prior experiences			
uses text examples			

with the prediction check-sheet, allowed the diagnostic teacher to have a concrete representation of how the student was thinking. At the end of a month, the teacher and the student reviewed the prediction checksheets to ascertain growth as well as the change in specific strategies that the student used when predicting. This review allowed them to evaluate growth in a targeted strategy over time. Stapling the prediction logs and rubric together, the teacher wrote a reflection about the student's strategy development for that month. In this way, diagnostic teachers can use portfolios to monitor growth in reading development over time.

Comparing Reading Strategies Among Reading Tasks

The diagnostic teacher wanted to compare reading strategies among several reading tasks to evaluate a particular student. After completing a miscue analysis (see Chapter 6), the diagnostic teacher noticed that Jenny was mainly using the initial consonant as a cue and then was guessing what an unfamiliar word was. This miscue analysis was placed in the portfolio alongside a spelling assessment taken from a summary written by Jenny. Reviewing the written summary, the teacher evaluated each word using the spelling assessment rubric based on research by Gillet and Temple (1990) (see Table 8–4). Then he added the ratings together and divided by the number of words in the summary. He found that Jenny's average was 2.0, which indicated that she was just beginning the letter-naming stage, where many of the letters in the word were represented but their spelling resembled the way they sounded (invented spelling) rather than conventional spellings. Looking more closely, the diagnostic teacher noticed that more than half of the words simply had the initial part of the word with little resemblance to the final part of the word. This assessment was also consistent with Jenny's miscue analysis.

Next the diagnostic teacher evaluated the written summary, using the retelling assessment (see Table 8–2) to evaluate comprehension. This evaluation revealed that the student could retell a story but often embellished the story events with her own knowledge of similar situations rather than the actual events in the story. Additionally, the student had been keeping prediction logs so the teacher evaluated these logs using the prediction rubric (see Table 8–3) to assess active reading strategies. These assessments showed that Jenny actively predicted what might happen in a story, sometimes missing the point because she used too much of her background knowledge. By comparing assessments across these tasks, the diagnostic teacher observed a consistent pattern of overrelying on background knowledge when reading. Using this strength, the diagnostic teacher and the student discussed this strategy and developed a plan to help her monitor her reading, checking the text more frequently particularly to correct miscues that might have important clues to story meaning.

Portfolios are a way to collect information from a variety of reading tasks and look at them simultaneously. They help the diagnostic teacher

Table 8–4   *Spelling Assessment Rubric*

---

0 = Prephonemic Stage

Random letters depict a message and show some knowledge of top-bottom and left-to-right concept

No letter-sound relationship present

Uses and repeats known letters and numbers (prefers uppercase letters)

1 = Early Phonemic Stage

Words are depicted by one or more letters showing a left-to-right order

The letters represent some of the sounds in words, but not all

This letter naming strategy is erratic and restricted

2 = Letter Naming Stage

Entire words are present with a majority of the letters

The word has more than half the sounds in the word

Letters are based on sounds as student hears them (invented spelling)

3 = Transitional Stage

Conventional spellings are used properly but not accurately (e.g., *candel* for *candle*)

Spelling is based on standard spelling rather than invented spelling

Vowels appear in every syllable

4 = Correct Spelling

---

compare reading strategies in looking for a consistent pattern. Often these patterns indicate students' strengths and needs in literacy development.

Self-Assessment

As the portfolio movement gains momentum, it has become increasingly clear that student-centered portfolios are important aspects of instruction as well as assessment. They shift the control of learning from test makers and teacher's manuals to students and teachers collaborating on reading growth. When students evaluate their own work, they begin to establish goals for learning and to monitor their use of reading strategies. Thus, portfolios become tools for discussing with students the strategies that will advance their literacy.

Diagnostic teachers have used self-evaluation as instructional tools for many years. In fact, progress charts used in remedial programs for more than two decades are the forerunners of self-assessment. The power of flashing word cards was not in the rapid recognition of words, but the charting of progress so that the teachers and students could concretely discuss progress and establish new goals. Granted it was a very narrow perspective of literacy, but it put the students in charge of evaluating reading growth and establishing their own goals for learning. In portfolios, students began to evaluate their own literacy in broad rather than narrow terms. Thus, the power of student-centered portfolios lies in the reflective process by which students evaluate their strengths and strategies, thus making changes in how they orchestrate the reading process.

As students and teachers have conversations about what to put into their portfolios, students think about what they want to show about their literacy. Thus, portfolios provide a means to open the conversation about strengths and strategy use. In the portfolio process, students have to think about their reading strategies and how they constructed meaning with text. For instance, one student evaluated her own prediction strategies using a yes/no check-sheet (see Table 8–5). As she read a story, she completed a prediction log (see "Prediction Log" in Chapter 11). Then she reread her prediction log and used the self-assessment prediction check-sheet to evaluate how she predicted.

After evaluating her prediction logs, the student reviewed the self-assessment prediction check-sheet to complete a reflection sheet like the following: "Today my reading was _____ because _____. Next time I will work on _____." With this structure, this student wrote: "Today my reading was great because I actually read the words in the story and predicted what would come next. Next time I will work on using what I know and what's in the story." Using this type of self-assessment helped her identify her strategies for this particular story. It also helped her think about the targeted strategy (prediction) and how she used prediction. These types of check-sheets can be developed collaboratively among the diagnostic teacher and the students.

As students select and reflect on artifacts, they begin to describe their literacy. Whether the diagnostic teacher uses a check-sheet or simply con-

Table 8–5 *Self-Assessment Prediction Check-Sheet*

	Yes	No
I make predictions easily	X	
I use prior experiences		X
I use textual information	X	
I check predictions	X	
I change predictions as needed		X
I justify my responses	?	

verses with his students, the students write a reflection that helps them rethink their literacy. This self-assessment encourages students to monitor their own constructive processes as they engage in subsequent literacy activities. Portfolios serve as an instructional tool because they encourage students to monitor their own reading and writing, focusing on what they noticed in their artifacts. As their reflection includes strengths and needs, so this monitoring includes using their strengths to support development in areas of need. As a result of developing portfolios, students assess their own literacy, establish their own goals, and become more independent learners.

Summarizing (Cumulative Evaluation)

Periodically, the diagnostic teacher and his students select exemplar pieces to demonstrate literacy and put them along with their reflection into their cumulative portfolios. At the end of a session (semester or school year), students review their cumulative portfolio and write a summary illustrating what it demonstrates about their literacy development over the designated time period. Some schools have oral presentations describing the portfolios, while others use portfolios in parent conferences.

Glazer and Brown (1993) suggest periodic conferences with teachers, students, and parents to review work. Using the working portfolio, students select pieces that illustrate the progress they are making on their goals. The students, along with the teacher, spend time evaluating the contents of the working portfolio to answer specific questions about the students' progress during the designated time period. As the teacher and the student work together to decide what to include, they have conversations about how the student is progressing and the strategies the student is using during reading and writing activities. These conversations not only help the student evaluate her work, but they also help the student describe her understanding of literacy. During these conversations, the diagnostic teacher and the student fill out a summative check-sheet or an assessment letter explaining how each piece fits into the portfolio. The assessment letter describes the student's literacy and explains the student's goals (Marvuglio, 1994). Here is an example of an outline for an assessment letter:

When I read, I do _____ extremely well.

When I read, I usually _____. This helps me _____.

I think my best piece of writing is _____ because _____.

I am studying _____. It is interesting to me because _____.

My goals have been _____.

These pieces show that I can now _____ and that I am making progress toward my goals because _____.

The assessment letter provides the core for the student-led conferences, but other activities can be used during the conference, such as having the student read a favorite passage from a book or story, talk about the reading strategies she is working on, or even teach the parents a reading strategy. In any case, using either the assessment letter or an open-ended form, the students review their work with their parents and teacher. Here again they explain their literacy development. Such conferences serve to summarize a student's reading progress through a review of the portfolio contents. Older students can also respond to open-ended questions about their portfolio to help them review the contents of the portfolio. Some questions include the following:

1. *As you review your portfolio, what are your strengths and weaknesses?*

2. *Have you changed as a reader? If so, how?*

3. *Have you changed as a writer? If so, how?*

4. *Having looked at your work, what goals would you set for yourself as a reader and writer?*

5. *When you look at your portfolio, how do you feel about yourself as a writer? Tell why you feel that way.*

6. *When you look at your portfolio, how do you feel about yourself as a reader? Tell why you feel that way. (Valencia & Place, 1994, p. 146)*

These culminating experiences help students concretely see how they are progressing as a reader and a writer. They help students attribute their progress to the strategies they have learned and the effort they have expended.

Summary

The diagnostic teacher and his students select artifacts to illustrate how literacy is progressing in the classroom. These artifacts are organized into a portfolio. Attached to each piece is a reflective statement of what the artifact shows about literacy development. The portfolios provide an assessment of students' literacy over time and from multiple contexts, allowing the diagnostic teacher and student to evaluate growth. Portfolios, then, record the dynamic learning process that is embedded in instruction. To summarize the contents of a portfolio, the diagnostic teacher and students can write an assessment letter or culminating reflective analysis that involves reflecting over the entire contents of a portfolio. Thus, portfolios also become a tool for communicating with parents and teachers as well as putting the assessment in the hands of the student.

9

Selecting Materials

One of the decisions the diagnostic teacher makes is to select instructional materials that fit the students' reading performance. In fact, much of her initial diagnosis is directed toward finding an instructional range to inform decisions about instructional materials (see Chapter 5). Once this level is established, the diagnostic teacher selects material within this range that would be appropriate for the students she is teaching. As she plans instruction, the diagnostic teacher thinks about the various kinds of instructional materials and their influence on the students' learning (see Chapter 2, "Text"). Teachers have a myriad of materials available, including basal reader series, trade books, predictable books, magazines, skills books, computer software, Internet information, video tapes of classic stories/songs, and student-produced work. Teachers, however, often persist in using inappropriate materials because they lack the knowledge of how to make suitable selections. Knowledge about instructional materials allows teachers and students to make changes that can advance student reading performance.

Finding instructional materials that will improve the student's learning is an essential task of the diagnostic teacher. When the material is too difficult, students cannot construct meaning or flexibly use reading strategies. If too many words are unknown or the concepts too dense, students become flustered and decrease their attention. The students may instead worry about "how" to make sense with the text and develop negative emotions related to reading (Schallert & Reed, 1997). In fact, Roller (1998) found that as students read easier books, their word recognition accuracy increased and children began to discuss the meaning of the text more readily. When reading easier text at least at their instructional level, poor readers can flexibly use multiple strategies. Thus, finding the optimal match between the students' instructional level and the selected material can increase students' reading performance.

In the past many teachers, including diagnostic teachers, used materials organized by others. This approach is convenient and time-saving, but teachers need to make sure these materials align with the strengths and needs of the readers. The diagnostic teacher uses information about the reader to organize materials rather than a prescribed plan. Such an approach does not exclude the use of an organized sequence of materials published by others. It does, however, exclude the mindless completion of all units and tasks in the organized program. The diagnostic teacher asks, "How does the type of text affect the student's reading?" She is mindful of the individual progress of each student and selects material accordingly, constantly double-checking how successful the reader is.

Basic Types of Materials

Instructional materials often align with specific views of reading. Specifically, materials often are associated with either a text-based view or a reader-based view of instruction. However, the way the text is used is what makes the *instruction* text-based, reader-based, interactive, or socio-interactive. It is essential, however, that the diagnostic teacher find a text that fits the reader and will advance his reading using strengths rather than weaknesses. The basic types of materials offer options for the diagnostic teacher. No matter which type of material is selected, however, the key is to find material that is an instructional match for the reader.

Basal Readers

Basal readers are anthologies of stories arranged by grade level and packaged for each grade along with an instructional manual and workbooks. They are associated with more traditional methods that use a text-based approach to instruction. However, the most recent basal reader series include high-quality literature or excerpts from classic literature for their specific grade level. An advantage to using a basal reader is that the difficulty of the story has been calculated and will be approximately at the third-grade range if the basal reader is classified as a third-grade reader. However, these designations often don't include story-specific vocabulary such as difficult names and places. Nevertheless, using a basal reader at the expected grade level can reduce the problem of identifying a text that will fit a reader.

Chapter Books

Narrative books are more closely aligned with reader-based approaches to instruction; however, it depends on how the chapter book is used. Chapter books do not have an instructional manual nor are they designated to a specific grade level. Sometimes, publishers have indicated the reading level on the spine or back cover by using a readability formula (see "Readability formulas" in this chapter). Chapter books tell stories similar to everyday life events, but the author captivates the imagination by making these events larger than life (Schallert & Reed, 1997). Yet at the same time the reader engages with a text to see whether the stories the author tells ring true in her own life. This engagement becomes an inner conversation between the author and the reader. Thus, chapter books are often used in literature discussion groups so that students can share their experiences and interpretations, creating shared understanding of the world.

Focused Lesson Books

To work on specific strategies and skills, some publishers have produced material in workbook-type format that will help readers focus on a specific area of need. These books usually reflect a text-based theory of reading because the readers focus on a single part of the text in order to improve their overall reading. Sensible decisions must be made with this type of material because it has decontextualized the specific strategy or skill to be learned. Thus, the reader is not using the skill or strategy in naturally occurring text.

High-Interest, Low-Readability Books

Some publishers have designed books specifically for readers who are reading below grade level. These books are stories that would appeal to an older student but are written at an easier level to provide interesting stories that help improve literacy. Many of the classic stories, such as "To Build a Fire" by Jack London, have been rewritten so that these readers can experience the story without having to struggle with complex vocabulary and language structure. Basically, these materials are based on the text-based approach to reading in which the text is the driving force in comprehension. The topics of these books range from adventure and mystery to sports, history, and science fiction.

Picture Trade Books

Many trade books are well-illustrated books that are designed to be read aloud to young children. The difficulty of the vocabulary and concepts vary greatly; therefore, it is hard to estimate the reading level of these books. However, these books can be used to demonstrate minilessons to intermediate and middle school students or as an introduction or extension of a lesson. If the story is engaging as in "The Wretched Stone," students can learn sophisticated strategies when engaged in an authentic story. Typically reading aloud picture trade books is associated with the reader-based or interactive approaches to reading instruction.

Poetry Anthologies

Poetry is a type of material that is effective for developing readers. Many poems have rhyme and rhythm that invite students to read them again and again. An easy poem is a good way to begin tutoring sessions for older readers. When read chorally, the poems provide a successful experience that starts off a session well. Many anthologies of poetry can be used in classrooms and tutoring. Some of the favorite anthologies are those by Shel Silverstein and Jack Prelutsky. Many of their poems provide not only success, but also humor because of the absurd actions and ideas.

Predictable Books

These books have repeated language patterns that make them readable even for young children. Associated with reader-based approaches, predictable books have rhyme and rhythm that invite young children to read them again and again. The colorful illustrations are interesting and help children figure out words using their own interpretation of the pictures. These books have been so successful that many of them are set as Big Books to allow the whole class to read them together.

Technological Materials

Technology is another source for reading material. Most teachers have access to computers, computer programs, Internet, and video tapes. A variety of computer programs from various views of reading development can be used to promote reading growth. Some of the newer interactive predictable book programs can be a substantial assistance to teachers who work with more than one student at a time. On these CD-ROM programs, an entire predictable book appears with illustrations on disk. The student can listen to the book read aloud as the words are highlighted in the text. Elaborate, structured programs, such as *Wiggle Works,* offer computer-assisted learning within the total approach to literacy instruction including framed innovations on predictable books (see Chapter 11). They can add writing as a way to develop reading. Likewise, many computer programs help students with writing and word processing. These programs are also used by teachers when students dictate stories for language experience. The advent of technology is certainly a valuable aid in the teaching life of diagnostic teachers. See Appendix 2 for a listing of some quality computer programs.

Videos can offer another medium for understanding stories. Using sing-along videos can provide support for the beginning reader. Likewise, readers can benefit from watching a video of a book before reading it. Videos of many early reading books are available and can be shown to activate background knowledge. This approach helps readers predict what the words are and helps them elaborate the motives of characters. These newer technologies are motivational and provide another avenue for reading instruction.

Textbooks

These expository books are used for gaining information in the content areas. These books contain content-specific information and abstract concepts that make comprehension difficult. Students generally need some prior understanding of the concepts or at least an overview before they begin reading. As they read, they learn new information and study this information to be able to understand a topic. Textbooks are usually designated to a certain grade level because of the topic; however, textbooks often have a readability level more difficult than their designated grade level.

Selecting Material for a Particular Reader

The diagnostic teacher evaluates the type of material she is using and considers factors that will help her match the material to the instructional level, interests, and needs of the reader. A teacher may use numerous ways to investigate whether certain instructional material will be an instructional match. The first consideration is the level of difficulty of the text, which can be assessed by matching the text to the reader using a mini-IRI or a cloze text. Another way is to assess the reading ease of the text by using a readability formula or a leveling procedure. In addition to the level of difficulty, the diagnostic teacher considers how interesting the text is, whether to give the reader choice, what background knowledge is needed to understand the text, and how long the text is.

Matching the Text to the Reader

The diagnostic teacher realizes that having the student read the actual text under consideration is the most effective way to ensure an appropriate level of text. This assessment can be done using a sample informal reading passage or a cloze test.

Mini-IRI for Assessing a Match

As indicated in Chapter 4, the most effective way to match a story to a reader is to let the reader try it out. The diagnostic teacher collects a sample of reading behavior in the text she is going to teach. She selects about 50 to 120 words from the story and writes questions focusing on the main ideas and key facts or events. After the student reads the passage, the diagnostic teacher computes error or miscue rates and a percent of comprehension to decide whether the text is at the student's instructional level (see CDA in Chapter 4 and IRI in Chapter 5 for further details). If the text falls within the instructional range, then it is appropriate for that reader. However, if the text has too many unfamiliar words and concepts and falls at the frustration level, then this text is too difficult for most instructional formats. When using collaborative reading and language experience, the assessment is conducted after instruction (see CDA in Chapter 4). When using an assessment such as a mini-IRI, the diagnostic teacher has confidence that the material fits the student she is teaching.

Cloze Passage for Assessing the Match

Using a selected 300-word passage is another way to evaluate whether a text will match a reader. In a cloze passage 50 words of the selected text are deleted and replaced with blanks. The student reads the passage and fills in the blanks with an appropriate word. The passage fits the reader if he can replace at least 40 percent of the blanks accurately. This type of assessment is most appropriate for older readers and particularly useful in content area classes because it can be administered to an entire class at once. To construct a cloze test use the following guidelines (McKenna & Robinson, 1993).

1. Choose a passage that is typical of the text and free of references to illustrated information.

2. Do not delete words in the first sentence of the passage.

3. Retype the passage, replacing every fifth word with a blank of equal length.

4. For reliable results, use at least 50 blanks. Fifty blanks easily convert to percentages. Figure 9–1 provides an example of a cloze test using an excerpt from *Sam, Bangs, and Moonshine.*

Sam started to explain, but sobs choked her. She cried so hard
_____ it was a long _____ before her father understood
_____.

Finally, Sam's father said, "_____ to bed now. But
_____ you go to sleep, _____, tell yourself the difference
_____ REAL and MOONSHINE."

Sam _____ to her room and _____ into bed. With her
_____ wide open she thought _____ REAL and
MOONSHINE.

Figure 9–1   *Shortened Cloze Test from* Sam, Bangs, and Moonshine, *by Evaline Ness*

5. Before carrying out the assessment, have the students practice a cloze example to become familiar with the procedure.

6. Allow students to complete the text untimed.

The following guidelines are necessary for scoring.

1. Score only exact replacements as correct responses.

2. Convert score to a percentage by making a ratio of correct responses over total number of blanks (50). For example: 15/50 would equal 30 percent.

3. Use the following criteria to rate the match of the material to the student:
Independent Level	60% or higher
Instructional Level	40% to 59%
Frustration Level	39% or lower

Using the criteria, the diagnostic teacher decides whether the material is at an appropriate reading level for the student.

Evaluating the Text

To evaluate the reading ease of the text, the diagnostic teacher can use a readability formula for textbooks and chapter books or a leveling system for predictable books.

Readability Formulas

Using a readability formula is another way to help the diagnostic teacher select the material that would fit the student's instructional reading level. As mentioned in Chapter 2, text difficulty can be a result of various factors: grammatical complexity, vocabulary (word choices), structural organization, abstractness, density of ideas, background knowledge required, etc. Readability formulas are based on only two of the factors that affect text difficulty. Vocabulary and grammatical complexity are the most frequently used factors in a readability formula. Vocabulary difficulty is primarily measured by the number of syllables or letters in the word or how many words are more difficult than what an average fourth-grader could read. As the selected texts become more difficult, the words are more sophisticated and so is the complexity of the sentence structure. Thus, another indicator of text difficulty is its grammatical complexity, which is measured by the length of the sentence. The Fry readability graph is based on the number of syllables in a word and the number of words in a sentence. It is easy to use and provides an estimate of the reading level of the text (see graph in Figure 9–2).

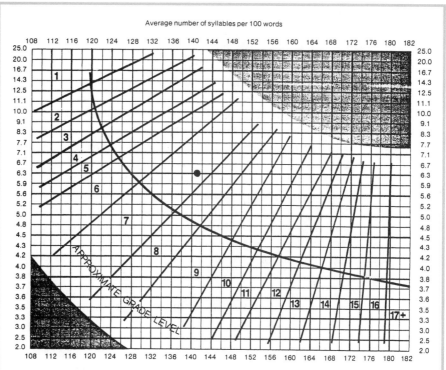

1. Randomly select three (3) sample passages and count out exactly 100 words each, beginning with the beginning of a sentence. Do count proper nouns, initializations, and numerals.
2. Count the number of sentences in the hundred words, estimating length of the fraction of the last sentence to the nearest one-tenth.
3. Count the total number of syllables in the 100 word passage. If you don't have a hand counter available, an easy way is to simply put a mark above every syllable over one in each word, then when you get to the end of the passage, count the number of marks and add 100. Small calculators can also be used as counters by pushing numeral 1, then push the sign for each word or syllable when counting.
4. Enter graph with *average* sentence length and *average* number of syllables; plot dot where the two lines intersect. Area where dot is plotted will give you the approximate grade level.
5. If a great deal of variability is found in syllable count or sentence count, putting more samples into the average is desirable.
6. A word is defined as a group of symbols with a space on either side; thus, *Joe, IRA, 1945,* and *&* are each one word.
7. A syllable is defined as a phonetic syllable. Generally, there are as many syllables as vowel sounds. For example, *stopped* is one syllable, and *wanted* is two syllables. When counting syllables for numerals and initializations, count one syllable for each symbol. For example, *1945* is four syllables, *IRA* is three syllables, and *&* is one syllable.

Figure 9–2 *The Fry Readability Scale. (Reproduced with permission from Fry, E. 1977. Elementary Reading Instruction. New York: McGraw Hill.)*

Leveling Predictable Books

Predictable books generally do not keep sentences short, therefore, the readability formula cannot be used to level this type of book. In predictable books the sentences may be long but repeated frequently creating a rhythmic effect. For example, the language pattern, "Little pig, little pig, let me come in," is repeated throughout the story of *The Three Little Pigs* with a sing-song effect. In even easier predictable books, these patterns are repeated every page. The repeated phrases and key pictures help make books easier to read (Peterson, 1991). If the picture depicts the key action or topic that is represented in the text, the page is easier to read because the student can use the picture to figure out the word. For instance, if the page has a picture of a house of straw and the text reads, "The first little pig [a repeated phrase] had a house made of straw," then the student can use the picture as a cue to figure out the word *straw* if it is forgotten. Along with repeated phrases and pictures, familiar experiences and characters such as a dog riding a tricycle or a family eating together also help young readers figure out words. In these cases, they associate a familiar experience with the words on the page. For instance if the text says, "I can hug my brother," the child can predict the next phrase might be "I can hug my sister." This prediction is based on their experiences with the composition of families and therefore is easier to read. To decide whether a predictable book is easier or harder to read, the diagnostic teacher evaluates the book by asking herself key questions. Let's use "Where can you put a dog?" to think about these questions. The sample book begins, "Where can you put a dog?" followed by a picture of a dog. The next phrase asks, "In a flower pot?" followed by the response, "Oh, no, no!" on the next page, as shown in Figure 9–3. This sequence is repeated throughout the book with different places to put a dog.

Where can you put a dog? | **In a flower pot?** | **Oh, no, no!!**

Figure 9–3   *Where can you put a dog?*

Reviewing the book, the diagnostic teacher asks and answers the following questions:

Question	*Answer*
1. Is the print in a consistent place?	Yes
2. Are phrases repeated?	Yes
3. If key words are changed can they be predicted easily from the pictures or prior experiences?	Yes
4. Do the phrases sound more like talking/singing?	They sound like talking.
5. Are familiar objects or experiences used?	Most objects are familiar.
6. Do the illustrations provide support for recognizing the words?	Yes
7. Are rhythm and rhyme evident?	The repeated nature of the phrases make the words easy.

These characteristics can be listed with a Lickert scale to estimate the level of difficulty for a predictable book, as shown in Figure 9–4. "Where can you put a dog?" has a familiar topic and commonly used language pattern. The common phrase "Where can you put a dog?" is repeated on almost every page. The pictures represent the words on the page and thus provide clues for the reader when a word is forgotten.

As predictable books become more difficult, the topics are not quite as familiar. The language patterns are less repetitive and include lines that are not repeated in the story. The pictures, however, still provide strong support for figuring out the words. For instance, *Five Little Monkeys Jumping on the Bed* by Eileen Christelow is easy to read, but the beginning of the book contains phrases that are more challenging than the repetition included in the rest of the book.

By the end of first grade through the middle of second grade, the familiar topics are maintained but the language pattern is varied, such as using a refrain after each new event as in *I Know a Lady Who Swallowed a Fly* by Charlotte Zolotow. These more difficult books still have fairly familiar topics, but sometimes the characters' actions are fanciful as an old lady who swallowed a fly. The language pattern often develops over several pages while the illustrations provide support for overall meaning but not specific words.

The predictable books are helpful in initiating reading and are appropriate for young children, but as children grow older, they also need a

1. **The print is in a consistent place:**

.5	1.0	1.5	2	2.5
all the time	almost all the time	most of the time	some of the time	none of the time

2. **Sentence pattern or phrases are repeated:**

.5	1.0	1.5	2	2.5
every page	every other page	every 2–3 pages	every 4–5 pages	every 6+ pages

3. **Key words are changed in the pattern but can be predicted easily (from pictures or prior experiences):**

.5	1.0	1.5	2	2.5
infrequently easy to predict	occasionally easy to predict	most of the time easy to predict	all the time not easy to predict	all the time unfamiliar

4. **Sentences sound like talking (oral language):**

.5	1.0	1.5	2	2.5
all the time	almost all the time	most of the time	blend of oral and written language	book language

5. **Familiar objects or experiences are used:**

.5	1.0	1.5	2	2.5
all the time	almost all the time	most of the time	sometimes	none

6. **Illustrations provide support for recognizing words and patterns:**

.5	1.0	1.5	2	2.5
all the time	almost all the time	most of the time	sometimes	none

7. **Rhythm and rhyme are evident:**

.5	1.0	1.5	2	2.5
in entire story	most of the story	on repeated phrases	sometimes	not included

Figure 9–4   *Predictable Books Evaluation Guide*

different kind of instructional material. (See Appendix 3 for listing of books for beginning reading.)

More to Consider When Selecting Material

Reading ease is not the only consideration when selecting material for students. Other key aspects, such as interest, topic familiarity, and book length, are important considerations as the diagnostic teacher selects material to use during the diagnostic lesson.

Interest

Interest is also a key in selecting books. If the topic and/or storyline is interesting and engaging, then the book is usually easier to read. Students can be drawn into a text when characters are interesting and readily befriended, words provoke strong images, and stories have unanticipated twists (Schallert & Reed, 1997). As mentioned in Chapter 2, expository text written in an engaging style is easier to read because students are more readily involved with prose-like vignettes than academic facts (Reed, Schallert, & Goetz, 1992).

Choice

One of the best ways to determine interest is by letting the student choose the book. When students believe they can make choices about the books they read, they are more likely to be interested in the books and the activities surrounding them (Deci et al., 1991). By presenting several books with mini-book talks, the diagnostic teacher can encourage the reader to choose the book that looks the most interesting. Having books accessible to young children encourages them to choose among multiple titles and allows them to define their interests and set their own purposes. Arranging books in tubs or displaying them on low-level shelves can assist readers in choosing books.

Background Knowledge of the Reader

Closely tied to both choice and interest is the background knowledge of the reader. A reader's interest in a particular textual selection may show a growing knowledge about the topic, "signaling an optimal match between interest and knowledge" (Schallert & Reed, 1997, p. 73). For example, a student who has hiked in the mountains will probably be more interested in reading *Beardance* by Will Hobbs than students who have spent most of their life in the city. Students' background knowledge helps them define their interests and inform their choices.

Length of the Book

The attention span of many struggling readers is relatively short; therefore as the diagnostic teacher selects books, she looks for texts such as chapter books that are short. Reading two short books instead of one long book will be more appealing to a struggling reader. The length of the text does influence readers' perceptions of their ability to read the text and, in turn, their attention and motivation during reading. Many readers believe they can read a short book and understand it as a whole, while a long book would be more difficult for them. The diagnostic teacher understands these aspects of student perception and their effect on the types of material selected.

Series Books

Series books are often easier for readers because the authors use the same characters and same language structures in each book. (See Appendix 4 for list of Series Books.) Students in the second- and third-grade ranges readily profit from series books because they provide predictable characters and actions. The chapters then provide the predictability that the patterned language did for the younger readers. In fact, many adults learned to read by reading Nancy Drew and Hardy Boys mysteries. Books written by the same author with the same characters can provide support for struggling readers. In fact, some of these series books appeal to older readers and can be used to develop fluency.

Summary

Finding instructional materials is an essential task of the diagnostic teacher. As she plans lessons, the diagnostic teacher thinks about materials and their influence on the student's learning. When material is too difficult, a student cannot construct meaning or flexibly use reading strategies; therefore, the diagnostic teacher selects instructional material that will allow the student to construct meaning and demonstrate his strengths. Knowledge about instructional materials facilitates the diagnostic teacher's decision making and enables teachers and students to adapt instruction.

10

Selecting Techniques

Knowing *how* instruction occurs allows the diagnostic teacher to modify his teaching effectively during the reading event. As he plans instruction, the diagnostic teacher thinks about the techniques he uses and their influence on learning. By classifying techniques according to several critical characteristics, the diagnostic teacher increases his specificity in matching instruction with the readers' patterns of constructing meaning. Therefore, this chapter classifies each teaching technique in the following ways:

1. The point at which the technique is implemented during the lesson

2. The type of text being read

3. The mode of response

4. The targeted reasoning strategy

5. The targeted reading skill

6. The information source

7. The type of structure (explicit or implicit teaching) embodied in implementing the technique

8. The cognitive process emphasized during implementation

This classification serves two functions for the diagnostic teacher: (1) to help select techniques that fit the readers' patterns, and (2) to help focus instructional modifications during the reading event.

Initially, the diagnostic teacher selects a technique and analyzes its underlying characteristics. This analysis increases his effectiveness in implementing a particular technique as well as broadening his knowledge of instructional alternatives. However, many teachers seem to be hesitant to change their routines even if they are not working well for individual students (Roskos & Walker, 1995). Another reason teachers resist change is a lack of knowledge about why one technique may be more effective in certain situations. Chapters 10 and 11 provide reasons why a given technique might be more effective under certain conditions. Knowledge about techniques allows teachers to make instructional changes that facilitate student learning.

The instructional techniques, which are described in detail in Chapter 11 can be used either as a part of the guided reading lesson to support authentic reading activities or as part of a specific strategy or skill lesson to focus on areas of concern. The orchestration of the techniques depends on the strengths and needs of a particular reader. Thus, the classification of the diagnostic teaching techniques is divided into three major categories. In the first, the techniques are classified according to their implementation within the instructional framework, and they fit appropriately during guided contextual reading (see Chapter 4). To select appropriate techniques for this part of the diagnostic teaching session, the teacher asks himself the following questions:

- Do I want to focus on print or meaning processing to advance student understanding of the entire passage?

- At what point during the guided reading lesson will the student need support in order to construct the entire message?

- What techniques will best suit the type of text I am using?

- Can using more writing or discussion during the lesson build on the strengths of the learner?

The second major category deals with the selection of techniques to encourage the students' use of weaker processing areas, and these techniques fit appropriately during the element of strategy and skill instruction (see Chapter 4) of the diagnostic teaching session. Here the diagnostic teacher selects techniques that work on learner needs by showing the students how to use their strengths when reading becomes difficult. To select appropriate techniques for this part of the diagnostic teaching session, the teacher asks himself the following questions:

- Would a strategy that the student is not using be helpful to her? If so, how should I approach instruction so that she can use the new strategy in combination with the strategies she already uses?

- Does the student have a skill that she is not using when she reads? If so, how should I mediate learning so that she incorporates this skill, using her strengths?

The third major category deals with the specificity of selection. In either of the first two categories, the diagnostic teacher may need to identify specific strengths to utilize during instruction. For instance, a reader might need a great deal of teacher direction. In this case, the diagnostic teacher uses Table 10–7 on explicit instruction and narrows his previous options, using this characteristic. To differentiate his selection of techniques, the teacher asks himself the following questions:

- If the student is overrelying on an information source, can I match this reliance with an instructional technique and show her how to integrate information sources?

- What kind of teacher support does the student need? Does she need to work on her own or does she need more teacher direction?

- If the student is compensating for deficits by using a strength in cognitive processing, can I match this strength in order to show her how to use her weaker processing style in combination with her strength?

Diagnostic teaching techniques from different views of reading have been classified according to these key questions so that the diagnostic teacher can match the students' strengths and needs and design lessons that mediate learning for each student. How a diagnostic teacher selects techniques according to the classifications is described in this chapter using the diagnostic hypotheses for Jenny (see Chapter 6), the third-grader who is experiencing difficulty in fluent oral reading.

Classifying Techniques For Guided Contextual Reading

When considering the instructional framework, the diagnostic teacher selects techniques that support reading an entire story. The diagnostic teacher thinks about the element of guided contextual reading and considers how instruction will occur as the student reads a particular selection so that the student constructs the meaning of the whole story. Selecting appropriate techniques facilitates a student's learning by providing instruction that assists the student when she can no longer learn independently. In other words, the instructional lesson is a planned exchange between independent student learning and teacher-guided learning. If the teacher intervenes with appropriate techniques, then he can move the students to more complex reading strategies.

First, the diagnostic teacher identifies the focus of instruction for the students. Most students read silently during guided contextual reading because the focus of this session element is constructing meaning. Thus, the diagnostic teacher uses meaning processing techniques. However, some students need to focus on print processing because once they can read the words, they will comprehend. In these cases, the diagnostic teacher uses print processing techniques but stresses meaning construction. Techniques can be classified, therefore, according to whether the instructional focus is on print processing or meaning processing. These techniques are then further classified by (a) instructional framework, (b) type of text, and (c) mode of response. Each of these variables is discussed in turn.

Classifying Techniques by Instructional Framework

The diagnostic teacher needs to analyze the instructional framework. Several critical points in the lesson influence decision making about the instructional framework for guided contextual reading. Techniques to increase story understanding can supplement instruction either before, during, or after reading the text. Sometimes it is most appropriate to provide instruction prior to reading so that the students readily construct meaning with text. For example, students might need instruction in word meanings or word identification as related to the story. Before reading, some students will need assistance to think about how what they already know will help them interpret text.

Another critical point in the instructional framework is during the reading of the text. During this part of the lesson, the teacher needs to encourage students' inferencing, elaboration, and monitoring of text comprehension. In these instances, she intervenes during reading to build reading strategies such as self-questioning, summarization, visualizing difficult parts, and organizing the information.

The final critical point in the instructional framework is after reading the selection. To mediate learning here, the diagnostic teacher provides instruction in integrating the text with personal experiences as well as organizing the information. He may also need to reinforce word recognition strategies or develop fluency. In any case, using appropriate diagnostic teaching techniques at the critical points in the instructional framework increases student learning.

Classifying Techniques by Type of Text

The selection of appropriate techniques also depends on the type of text (narrative or expository) that students will be reading. Techniques are often developed for a specific kind of text format. For example, story maps (see "Story Maps" in Chapter 11) are designed for narrative text and teach elements of story grammar, while reciprocal teaching (see "Reciprocal Teaching" in Chapter 11) is designed for expository text and teaches summarizing through the use of topic sentences. Techniques are most effective when used with the appropriate kind of text. The classification of techniques in Tables 10–1 and 10–2 is based on three instructional decisions: the instructional focus (meaning or print processing), the type of

Table 10–1   *Classifying Techniques by Instructional Framework*

	Meaning Processing	
	Narrative	*Expository*
Before	Direct Experience Approach Collaborative Reading Experience-Text-Relationship Imagery Instruction Motor Imaging Webbing	Contextual Processing Direct Experience Approach Experience-Text-Relationship Feature Analysis Grid Graphic Organizers Imagery Instruction K-W-L Motor Imaging Thematic Experience Approach Visualization Webbing
During	Directed Reading-Thinking Activity Prediction Logs Prediction Maps ReQuest Say Something Self-Directed Questioning Story Drama Story Maps	Herringbone Technique Reciprocal Teaching ReQuest SQ3R Triple Read Outline
After	Directed Reading-Thinking Activity Experience-Text-Relationship Framed Rhyming Innovations Journal Writing Literature Circles Retelling Story Drama Story Maps Summary Experience Approach Vocabulary Self-Collection Strategy	Cloze Instruction Experience-Text-Relationship Feature Analysis Grid Group Investigation Approach Journal Writing K-W-L Metaphors Opinion-Proof Approach Question-Answer Relationships Question-Generation Strategy Summarization Thematic Experience Approach Vocabulary Self-Collection Strategy Webbing

Note: Only the techniques that support meaning processing are classified. The lesson frameworks of strategy instruction, explicit teaching, implicit teaching, and sustained silent reading are not classified.

Table 10–2 *Classifying Techniques by Instructional Framework*

	Print Processing	
	Narrative	*Expository*
Before	Collaborative Reading Directed Reading Activity Language Experience Approach Sight Word Approach Synthetic Phonics Talking Books	Contextual Processing Language Experience Approach Webbing
During	Echo Reading Language Experience Approach Predictable Language Approach Talking Books	Collaborative Reading
After	Analytic Phonics Chunking Directed Reading Activity Framed Rhyming Innovations Multisensory Approaches Readers Theater	Cloze Instruction Multisensory Approaches Repeated Readings Word Sorts

Note: Only the techniques that support meaning construction are classified. The lesson frameworks of strategy instruction, explicit teaching, implicit teaching, and sustained silent reading are not classified.

text (expository or narrative), and the phase of instruction in which guided instruction is most appropriate (before, during, or after the lesson). The teacher thinks about the framework of the diagnostic teaching session. He must decide how to orchestrate instruction for guided contextual reading. Therefore, he evaluates the underlying strengths and needs of the student and predicts at which points within the guided reading lesson she will profit most from mediated instruction. Augmenting instruction at critical points during the lesson enhances text interpretation. He returns to his analysis of the extended passage to look at monitoring and summarization strategies and to his evaluation of the data from the student's informal reading inventory (see Chapter 5). Using his interpretation, he refers to Tables 10–1 and 10–2 to select an appropriate technique to support instruction.

> Within the guided reading lesson, which process (print or meaning processing) do I need to use for interpreting text?
> What type of text (narrative or expository) am I using?
> At what point during the guided reading lesson (before, during, or after) will the student need support?

Diagnostic Hypothesis

During guided contextual reading, Jenny needs to read silently. Prior to reading the story, she does need assistance in recognizing new vocabulary words. However, she does not need instruction during the story because she monitors comprehension. After instruction, the diagnostic teacher needs only to reinforce word recognition. The student also shows a preference for reading expository text.

Classifying Techniques by Mode of Response

An additional decision about the instructional framework is the kind of response mode that will be used. Readers' responses can be either oral or written. The diagnostic teacher considers the students' interaction patterns by asking himself. "Will discussing or writing advance this student's reading? Which mode is this student's strength?" Whether the response is in written format or discussion format changes the task. Some students prefer to write about what they read, while others prefer to discuss what they read. Both processes are constructive and facilitate reading growth.

Writing and Reading

Writing and reading are supportive processes that can enhance each other. Writing about what was read facilitates reading. First, writing requires learners to reconstruct their understanding and thus prompts a more thoughtful response. The students can later use this written record of their thoughts to reflect on and analyze their thinking, and it allows the diagnostic teacher to discuss students' interpretations with them. Writing brings inner thoughts into the open for verification and facilitates discussing personal interpretations.

Writing also facilitates reading because it reinforces the constructive process. Reading and writing require similar processes: both readers and writers make plans about how they are going to construct meaning; both monitor their understandings to see whether they are making sense; both revise their thinking by rereading, using what was written and comparing it to what they know; both elaborate what was written, making connections between what

was written and what is known to create new ideas. In these ways, both reading and writing are constructive processes in which one facilitates the other.

In addition, writing facilitates reading because both systems use the
same writing conventions. Both use letters grouped together to form words,
words grouped together to form sentences, and so on. The way the groups
are formed follows certain patterns or conventions. Writing heightens students' awareness of how to use these conventions when they read. For instance, a young writer trying to spell *mother* thinks about how that word
looked in the book *Are You My Mother?* Writing heightens an awareness of
the visual features of words. It accomplishes the same task as flashing word
cards. Writing facilitates reading through three avenues: reflective thinking,
constructing meaning, and using written conventions.

Discussion and Reading

Discussing what students read does facilitate reading growth. When students
verbalize their understanding of what they read, they reconstruct the text so
that they can communicate their understanding to others. This constructive
process is not simply a recall process. Readers think to themselves: "What is
important and how do I communicate it to the others in the group? What
did I learn that I want to share with this group? Did I think of something in
a new light that would help others understand?" In fact, the meaning of students' interpretations has been found to change during the discussion. As
students share their thinking, they co-construct meaning through social interaction (Almasi, 1994). In ongoing discussions, meaning seems to be negotiated moment by moment as students rethink and discuss their understanding.

Social interaction facilitates reading, therefore, because it provides a
vehicle for talking about the strategies, plans, and processes of meaning
construction (Vygotsky, 1978). In other words, thinking about what is read
is facilitated by conversations that encourage students to elaborate and explain their thinking. In this social situation, the teacher also explains and
elaborates his thinking. This process allows the student to use tools for
thinking (words, plans, strategies, ideas, and so on). The teacher responds,
encouraging a refinement of thinking (use of tools) and showing students
how he constructs his answer.

This interaction facilitates students' independent use of literacy
processes. As they discuss their thoughts and explain how they construct
their answers, the new ideas and strategies that they use become part of
their internal thought processes. Through social interaction, students verbalize their thinking, discussing their strategies as well as their ideas. Thus, the
verbalized strategies that come to the fore during discussion later become
individual mental processes. During discussion, the teacher facilitates reading by discussing interpretations, asking students to justify their interpretations, and sharing his own thought process. As a result, verbal discussion facilitates reading through three avenues: meaning construction, verbalizing

plans and strategies for meaning construction, and making social thinking an internal process.

Conclusions About Mode of Response

The diagnostic teacher thinks about the kind of responses that the student makes. He asks, "Will this student profit from discussing or writing about what she reads?" He realizes that both processes facilitate meaning construction. Writing provides a written record of thoughts so that the student can reflect on how she constructs meaning, while verbal discussion allows the reader to revise ideas on the spot. The diagnostic teacher selects a technique that matches the learner's strengths and needs. He thinks about the mode of response that the techniques demand and refers to Table 10–3 to select one that will assist the reader.

Table 10–3 *Classifying Techniques by Mode of Response*

	Meaning Processing	
	Discussion	*Written Response*
Before	Collaborative Reading	Feature Analysis Grid
	Contextual Processing	Imagery Instruction
	Direct Experience Approach	K-W-L
	Experience-Text-Relationship	Webbing
	Group Investigation Approach	
	Listening-Thinking Activity	
	Metaphors	
	Visualization	
	Webbing	
During	Directed Reading-Thinking Activity	Generative-Reciprocal Inference Procedure
	Group Investigation Approach	Herringbone Technique
	Reciprocal Teaching	Prediction Logs
	ReQuest	Prediction Maps
	Say Something	Story Maps
	Self-Directed Questioning	Triple Read Outline
	Story Drama	
After	Experience-Text-Relationship	Journal Writing
	Literature Circles	K-W-L
	Question-Answer Relationships	Opinion-Proof Approach
	Readers Theater	Question-Generation Strategy
	Retelling	Story Maps
	Story Drama	Story Writing Approach
		Summary Experience Approach
		Summarization
		Thematic Experience Approach

> Which mode of response (discussion or writing) will better assist this reader in advancing her reading?

Diagnostic Hypothesis

For Jenny, whose language comprehension is elaborate and whose verbal abilities are strong, discussion is most appropriate. During guided contextual reading, the diagnostic teacher allows ample time for discussion of the stories that Jenny reads, thus using her strength. Furthermore, for strategy and skill instruction, the diagnostic teacher selects a technique in which Jenny can practice and discuss her fluency.

Classifying Techniques For Strategy And Skill Instruction

The second major category is designed to help teachers select techniques that work on specific areas that are problematic for the students. Although techniques can be used either during guided contextual reading or strategy and skill instruction, the purpose and focus of instruction are different (see Chapter 4). During guided contextual reading, the focus is on reading entire stories and understanding the content. The techniques are selected to enhance story or passage understanding. However, during strategy and skill instruction, the diagnostic teacher creates activities that focus on areas of concern. Because no one likes to focus on what one can't do, these lessons are short and use engaging passages. The minilessons in this part of the diagnostic teaching session focus on strategy deployment during reading. Rather than mastery, the diagnostic teacher encourages the use of unfamiliar strategies and skills, showing the students how to use their strengths in combination with their weaknesses. With each lesson, he strives to promote conversations about strategy and skill use. These conversations lead to discussion about how literacy works and how to use strengths to construct meaning with text.

During strategy and skill instruction, the diagnostic teacher identifies students' strategy and skill needs and provides mediated instruction, showing students how a particular skill fits into their repertoire of reading strategies. In other words, the teacher creates an instructional context in which students can explore and talk about how strategies and skills are orchestrated. When selecting activities, the teacher must also remember that students might not use a particular strategy or skill as the result of a deficit. Instruction that begins with students' strengths is often more effective (see McCormick, 1995, for an elaboration of skill strengths and weaknesses).

For example, Student A uses background knowledge to identify unknown words; however, it is not always an effective strategy. She has a limited ability to manipulate the sounds of language (that is, she cannot segment sounds and then synthesize them to form words). In this case, the diagnostic teacher helps the student develop a large sight vocabulary, using the impress method (see "Impress Method" in Chapter 11). It allows the student to bypass word analysis and use background knowledge and sentence comprehension to identify unknown words.

Although use of phonic knowledge would increase this student's reading performance, instruction in word analysis is futile unless the student can synthesize and segment sounds. As the student's reading fluency increases, the diagnostic teacher then encourages decoding by analogy, using this prompt: "What would make sense (strength) and sounds like another word you know (weakness)?" This latter instructional task is accomplished easily using repeated readings (see "Repeated Readings" in Chapter 11) with a discussion of strategy deployment.

In the preceding example, the diagnostic teacher used the reader's strength to develop a successful reading program. Then he showed the student how to use her weaker skill area at times when using only her strength would not solve the reading problem. It is often necessary to try a variety of instructional techniques for problem readers. For example, Student B is having difficulty with sight word identification. She is a bilingual student and has limited language development with no skill in sound synthesis. Typical techniques to develop sight word identification (word cards, language experience, and so on) prove futile until the new words are tied to a conceptual base. In this case, vocabulary maps (see "Mapping" in Chapter 11) are used to tie background knowledge to the sight words so that the student can associate what the words mean with how the words look.

The following sections elaborate the reasoning strategies and reading skills used during reading. The techniques in Tables 10–4 and 10–5 have been identified according to the targeted reading task developed when the technique is implemented in a diagnostic program.

Classifying Techniques by Reasoning Strategies

Readers strategically reason about what they are reading, applying skills when necessary. As students read, they select, sort, and evaluate the text against what they know. In essence, readers are involved in an active problem-solving process. They predict what is going to be communicated. Then they select and sort important information from the text and relate it to their prior knowledge. Next, they confirm or revise their predictions based on new textual information. Finally, they elaborate their understanding as well as their strategy use. This reasoning process takes place automatically until readers cannot make sense of what they are reading.

When readers encounter difficulty, they consciously employ a variety of monitoring strategies to reconstruct meaning. They actively work to regain meaning.

Although students with reading problems exhibit individual variations in the strategies they employ, a body of research indicates that poor readers are not actively involved in constructing meaning (Paris & Oka, 1989). They view good reading as effortless; consequently, they do not make plans or vary their strategies as they read. Effective readers, however, are active. Before reading, "good readers use what they know about the topic, the type of text, the author's purposes and their own purposes to make predictions about the content of the text" (Duffy & Roehler, 1987, p. 416).

> Predicting requires guessing about what the author is going to say. It occurs before and during reading.

As they read, effective readers remain tentative and revise their predictions frequently, using a variety of reasons for their revisions. They intertwine the sources of information for revision (the text, background knowledge, or both) and the strategies for revisions (ignore the problem and read more, reread to check the facts, read ahead to clarify information, and consult an expert source if necessary) (Pearson, Roehler, Dole, & Duffy, 1992). Effective readers stop, reflect, and flexibly shift between reader-based processing ("Does that make sense?") and text-based processing ("What did the text say?"). This technique is called *monitoring reading*.

> Monitoring requires checking the text or one's experience to see whether what one is reading is making sense. Monitoring occurs during reading.

Finally, effective readers fit new information into what they know by elaborating relationships among information. In other words, active readers automatically embellish text by drawing unstated inferences and picturing scenes and information as they read. These elaborations help them draw connections among ideas in the text as well as their own knowledge. Furthermore, as they elaborate textual information, they also generate new thoughts, creating new connections among ideas. Thus, elaboration is a generative process in which text prompts readers to enhance their thinking and expand their understanding.

> Elaborating requires relating new information to what is known in order to remember it. Thus, the new information becomes part of what is known. Elaborating occurs during and after reading.

Some readers, however, are less active. Their reading can break down in the predicting, monitoring, or elaborating phases of the reasoning process. Some readers do not use what they know to think about what the author might say. They read exactly what the text says without thinking about what it might mean. They need instruction that helps them make predictions about what the text will mean. Other readers venture a guess but hold on to the initial prediction even when the text does not support it. Some readers revise their predictions but change only one part of it, such as the *who, when, where,* or *how* information (Dybdahl & Walker, 1996). Some readers rely too heavily on the text or their background knowledge when monitoring their reading. They do not shift between knowledge sources to check their reading. These students need instruction in how to monitor their understanding of text. Other students fail to elaborate the relationship between what they know and the text; therefore, they cannot remember what they read. These readers need instruction in how to reason while they are reading.

Demonstrating reasoning strategies can improve the reading performance of poor readers. However, the diagnostic teacher needs to evaluate the various instructional techniques. Some techniques lend themselves readily to talking about the different strategies of effective reading; others do not. Therefore, diagnostic techniques have been classified here according to the reading strategy that they develop: predicting, monitoring, or elaborating. In addition, techniques can teach the reasoning process related to print processing or meaning processing. Table 10–4 classifies techniques for reasoning while processing print and meaning.

The diagnostic teacher then looks for a strategy that, if learned, will increase this student's reading. He reflects on the strategies that the effective reader uses and evaluates how the student uses them. He returns to the data he has collected about the student's reading and looks at the hypotheses he formed when he analyzed the reading event. He considers whether the context or the text is affecting the strategies employed by this reader. If a strategy needs to be taught, the diagnostic teacher uses Table 10–4, "Classifying Techniques by Reasoning Strategy," to identify techniques that facilitate learning the strategy. Again, he remains tentative in selection until he completes all the diagnostic questions and evaluates several diagnostic lessons.

Table 10–4 *Classifying Techniques by Reasoning Strategy*

	Print Processing	Meaning Processing
Prediction	Collaborative Reading	Cloze Instruction
	Echo Reading	Directed Reading-Thinking Activity
	Framed Rhyming Innovations	Graphic Organizers
	Impress Method	Experience-Text-Relationship
	Language Experience Approach	Imagery Instruction
	Listening-Thinking Activity	K-W-L
	Message Writing	Listening-Thinking Activity
	Predictable Language Approach	Motor Imaging
	Summary Experience Approach	ReQuest
	Talking Books	Self-Directed Questioning
		SQ3R
		Thematic Experience Approach
Monitoring	Chunking	Directed Reading-Thinking Activity
	Collaborative Reading	Generative-Reciprocal Inference Procedure
	Language Experience Approach	Herringbone Technique
	Paired Reading	Prediction Logs
	Predictable Language Approach	Prediction Maps
	Readers Theater	Reciprocal Teaching
	Repeated Readings	Self-Directed Questioning
	Word Walls	Story Maps
		Triple Read Outline
		Visualization
Elaboration	Analytic Phonics	Experience-Text-Relationship
	Making Words	Group Investigation Approach
	Phonogram Approach	Herringbone Technique
	Readers Theater	Journal Writing
	Repeated Readings	K-W-L
	Retrospective Miscue Analysis	Literature Circles
	Synthetic Phonics	Opinion-Proof Approach
	Word Analogy Strategy	Prediction Maps
	Word Probe Strategy	Question-Answer Relationships
	Word Sorts	Question-Generation Strategy
		Reciprocal Teaching
		Retelling
		Story Drama
		Story Maps
		Summarization
		Thematic Experience Approach
		Triple Read Outline
		Vocabulary Self-Collection Strategy

Note: The techniques listed are the most effective; however, other techniques can be used. See individual techniques in Chapter 11.

Which strategy or strategies (predict, monitor, or elaborate), if learned, will increase this student's reading?

Diagnostic Hypothesis

For Jenny, the diagnostic teacher decides that she needs instruction in monitoring print processing in order to check both what makes sense and what the word looks like. The diagnostic teacher looks for a strategy that will facilitate combining print cueing systems when reading breaks down.

Classifying Techniques by Reading Skills

As readers strategically reason about what they are reading, they apply skills when necessary. Although meaningful interpretation of the text is the ultimate goal of reading instruction, certain tasks consume a major portion of children's thinking capacity as they develop as readers. The knowledge of particular skills is used as students reason about text; however, without the requisite skill knowledge, the reasoning process is hampered. The following explanation will provide a discussion first of the process of learning related to the overall reading task and then of the major skills involved at a given stage. Even though these skills have been associated with typical techniques, each skill can be developed through a variety of ways. The diagnostic teacher selects the technique that mediates learning for the particular student.

Stage One

For beginning readers, the major task is the association of oral language with its written equivalent. Young children have learned to communicate by using oral language within a social context. To read, however, they must infer the communicative intent of printed words. This new task places demands on learners. They must learn that printed words represent both a concept and spoken words. Therefore, the task of young readers is to develop this functional concept of printed language as well as the recognition of letters and sounds.

As these concepts of print develop, children begin to associate meaning with written words in stories. They automatically recognize a group of words at sight. They say, "I know a word that starts with *h* and is the same length, so this word must be *hat*." The development of a sight word vocabulary indicates that children are reasoning about the relationship between graphic symbols and meaning. Whether children use sounds, visual features, or background knowledge, their major task is to develop this sight word knowledge, which generally consumes a major portion of their thinking through the middle of first-grade reading level.

TARGETED SKILLS FOR STAGE ONE

Word Identification

Based on
- Association of prior knowledge with printed words
- Ability to remember the visual form (visual memory)
- Ability to use the initial letter and word length to remember words

Typical techniques
- Language experience approach
- Predictable language approach

Stage Two

As students can read more words and longer stories, reading changes from a predominately oral, shared experience to silent reading and discussion. Thus, the reader begins to focus on text-based information, particularly on the patterns in words and stories. Because the students can read longer stories, they encounter unfamiliar words that are not contained in their sight vocabularies. Therefore, emerging readers develop new ways to figure out unfamiliar words. In addition to experiential knowledge and sight word knowledge, they begin to use sound analogies to decode words (that is, "I know a sight word that looks similar to this new word; I will try substituting the sounds to see whether this new word makes sense in the story"). This stage of reading development is marked by the ability to use the alphabetic principle; namely, the understanding that words are made of sounds and letters that have a consistent pattern. Therefore, young readers match these patterns to known sight words.

As students begin to figure out many words independently, they are able to read longer stories; silent reading, therefore, becomes more efficient than oral reading. Thus, in order to communicate what they read, they retell the story, focusing on what the text said. This process places a high demand on literal comprehension because the learner's attention is focused on the logical development of a story line. Students begin to focus on the patterns of stories or how stories are organized (characters, problem, events, resolution) so that they can remember and retell more readily.

These skills occupy children's thinking capacity through the end of second grade, where techniques dealing with word analysis and literal comprehension are most appropriately employed.

TARGETED SKILLS FOR STAGE TWO

Word Analysis

Based on
- Ability to blend sounds (phonemic synthesis)
- Ability to divide words into their sounds (phonemic segmentation)
- Ability to use decoding analogies

Typical techniques
- Word analogy strategy
- Message writing

Literal Comprehension

Based on

- Understanding patterns in stories (story organization)
- Ability to determine what's important in the story to retell
- Use of background knowledge

Typical techniques
- Retelling
- Story maps

Stage Three

As learners encounter extended passages and chapter books where word meanings are embedded in complex sentence structures, the simple strategies of using known sight words, decoding by sound analogy, and thinking about the facts of a story are no longer sufficient. Because sentences are longer and more complex, students must focus on the forms of the sentences and match them with what they know about word and story meaning. This natural focus leads to increases in fluent word identification, which allows more thinking capacity for word, sentence, and idea meaning. Understanding sentence structure enhances fluent reading because the student breaks sentences into meaningful phrases. Likewise, students become more adept at using their background knowledge to predict sentence meaning. Sentence comprehension also enhances print processing: because words with multiple meanings are used in the text, students must use sentence context as well as decoding by analogy to figure out unknown words. Using sentence context to figure out unknown words and simultaneously associating appropriate word meanings becomes a major task for these readers. This stage occupies students' thinking capacity through the middle of the fifth-grade reading level, where techniques developing fluency and sentence comprehension are most appropriately employed along with the students' continuing development of the tasks involved in literal comprehension.

TARGETED SKILLS FOR STAGE THREE

Fluency

Based on
- Automatic association of how words look with what words mean
- Ability to break sentences into thought units
- Use of background knowledge to predict sentence meaning

Typical techniques
- Chunking method
- Readers theater

Sentence Comprehension

Based on
- Use of sentence structure to develop word meanings
- Use of sentence structure to decode words
- Prediction of sentence meaning to increase fluent reading

Typical techniques
- Cloze instruction
- Alternate writing

Stage Four

As students read more difficult text, they find the strategies that deal primarily with textual information are no longer sufficient. In texts at this level of difficulty, authors develop complex ideas that require an interpretation of text-based information within a reader's personal world view. Therefore, readers must be able to strategically shift between text-based and reader-based processing, synthesizing their understanding. One important area of this stage is the increasing need to develop and use a meaning vocabulary, or definitional word knowledge. Readers at this stage must think about what each new word might mean and how it is like other words and ideas that they already know. They must analyze what they know related to this new concept (word meaning) and integrate this knowledge with textbook usage. Likewise, they read for a variety of purposes and monitor their own understanding of text, questioning what is important to remember and how ideas and concepts fit together. This stage of development continues through the middle grades, where techniques emphasizing vocabulary knowledge and nonliteral comprehension are orchestrated with developing literal comprehension.

TARGETED SKILLS FOR STAGE FOUR

Meaning Vocabulary

Based on
- Integration of background knowledge with textual meaning
- Identification of likenesses and differences of word meanings
- Use of sentence and passage context to elaborate definitional knowledge

Typical techniques
- Webbing
- Contextual processing

Nonliteral Comprehension

Based on
- Synthesis of background knowledge with textual information
- Self-monitoring
- Self-questioning (I wonder what the author is going to say that is important to remember?)

Typical techniques
- Self-questioning
- Story drama

Stage Five

As readers develop, they begin to link information from a variety of sources into a cohesive point of view or a series of premises. This synthesis requires an increasing reflective stance that involves use of reasoning strategies as well as skill knowledge in an orchestrated and selective fashion. Traditionally it has been referred to as study skills. However, this stage is much more than studying: it is using information to construct personal points of view and increased reasoning about a particular topic.

TARGETED SKILLS FOR STAGE FIVE

Study Procedures

Based on
- Ability to summarize and organize information from multiple sources
- Ability to reorganize information to support a premise or point of view
- Ability to reflect and analyze others' point of view and one's own point of view

Typical techniques
- Group Investigation Approach
- Summarization

Thus, taking into account the appropriate stage for each reader, the diagnostic teacher looks for a skill that, if learned, will increase this student's reading. He reflects on the major skills of reading and evaluates their influence on this reader's performance. He looks at the level of performance that is at the borderline range and matches it with the targeted skills for that reading level. Then he checks previous instructional experiences to evaluate their influence on the targeted skill. Basically, he asks, "Has this student received instruction in this skill and is still not proficient?" If a skill needs to be taught, the diagnostic teacher uses Table 10–5, "Classifying Techniques by Reading Skills," (pp. 172–173) to identify techniques that facilitate learning that skill.

Which skills, if learned, would increase this student's reading?

The instructional techniques in this book have been analyzed as to the major skill developed. Within each major area, the techniques differ in the focus of instruction (reader-based/text-based; implicit/explicit; or simultaneous/successive), but each technique can increase the specific skill mentioned. The diagnostic teacher checks the chart to identify how to work with skill needs.

Diagnostic Hypothesis

For Jenny, whose borderline range is around the middle of second grade, the teacher decides that instruction in phonics is not appropriate because of her attempts and subsequent failures in using this cueing system. Jenny's literal comprehension is well developed and thus not the best choice for instruction now. Only when she reads text with just $\frac{1}{2}$ words correct did she ever miss a question. Therefore, the teacher decides to work on reading fluency, a skill that is at the third-grade level (that is, the next higher level).

Conclusions About Reading Strategies and Skills

After the diagnostic teacher evaluates the student's reading level and formulates hypotheses about how the student reads, he plans the strategy and skill lessons. Using the data collected, the diagnostic teacher identifies skills, strategies, or both that are inhibiting reading performance. He reviews the strategies employed by the reader as well as skill development. Then he selects an appropriate technique that will focus instruction on the targeted concern in order to improve the student's reading performance.

Classifying Techniques For Increased Specificity

The tables in this section are used in conjunction with the other tables. They increase the specificity of the previous selections. Readers demonstrate strengths and preferences that can be used to enhance active reading. Techniques that focus on critical areas for readers' progress are classified in this section in three ways: (a) by sources of information, (b) by type of structure, and (c) by strengths in cognitive processing.

Basically, reading is an interactive process in which readers use various sources of information (reader-based and text-based) at the same time to construct meaning with text. However, techniques differ according to which information sources are emphasized during instruction. Some techniques emphasize reader-based sources of information, while others stress text-based sources of information. Also, the type of structure needed during the diagnostic lesson varies depending on the strengths and preferences of the problem reader. Some students profit from a structured, direct approach to the material, while other students prefer to structure their own learning and discover rules. Techniques differ in how they structure the learning task. Finally, readers exhibit strengths in cognitive processing. Some readers use successive processing of information (a step-by-step analysis) while others prefer to use simultaneous processing (thinking about multiple relationships at the same time). These strengths can be matched with appropriate techniques, thus enhancing reading.

The techniques have been classified according to these characteristics, enabling the diagnostic teacher to select techniques that match the students' strengths as he is teaching a new task. As the task is learned, he can select techniques that have a more integrative instructional approach. The diagnostic teacher can thus use learner strengths to show students how to regain meaning when text interpretation breaks down. The following discussion and tables elaborate these areas.

Table 10–5 *Classifying Techniques by Reading Skills*

	Word Identification	Word Analysis	Fluency	Meaning Vocabulary	Sentence Comprehension	Literal Comprehension	Nonliteral Comprehension	Study Procedures
Alternate Writing					*	*	*	
Analytic Phonics		*						
Chunking			*		*			
Cloze Instruction				*	*	*		
Collaborative Reading	*		*					
Contextual Processing				*	*			
Direct Experience Approach				*			*	
Directed Reading Activity	*			*		*	*	
Directed Reading-Thinking Activity						*	*	
Echo Reading	*		*		*			
Experience-Text-Relationship				*		*	*	
Feature Analysis Grid				*				
Framed Rhyming Innovations		*		*	*			
Generative-Reciprocal Inference Procedure						*	*	
Graphic Organizers						*		*
Group Investigation Approach						*	*	*
Herringbone Technique						*		*
Imagery Instruction						*	*	*
Impress Method	*		*					
Journal Writing							*	
K-W-L						*	*	
Language Experience Approach	*		*					
Listening-Thinking Activity						*	*	
Literature Circles							*	
Making Words	*	*						
Message Writing		*						
Metaphors				*			*	*
Motor Imaging				*				
Multisensory Approaches	*	*						
Opinion-Proof Approach						*	*	
Paired Reading	*		*					
Phonogram Approach		*						

Table 10–5   Continued

	Word Identification	Word Analysis	Fluency	Meaning Vocabulary	Sentence Comprehension	Literal Comprehension	Nonliteral Comprehension	Study Procedures
Predictable Language Approach	*							
Prediction Logs						*	*	
Prediction Maps						*	*	
Question-Answer Relationships						*	*	*
Question-Generation Strategy						*	*	
Readers Theater			*			*	*	
Reciprocal Teaching						*	*	*
Repeated Readings	*	*	*					
ReQuest						*	*	
Retelling						*	*	
Retrospective Miscue Analysis	*				*			
Say Something						*	*	
Self-Directed Questioning						*	*	
Sentence Combining				*	*			
Sight Word Approach	*							
SQ3R						*		*
Story Drama						*	*	
Story Maps						*	*	
Story Writing Approach					*	*	*	
Summarization						*	*	*
Summary Experience Approach	*		*			*		
Synthetic Phonics		*						
Talking Books	*		*					
Thematic Experience Approach						*	*	*
Triple Read Outline						*		*
Visualization				*			*	
Vocabulary Self-Collection Strategy				*		*	*	
Webbing				*		*		
Word Analogy Strategy		*						
Word Probe Strategy		*						
Word Sorts	*	*						
Word Walls	*	*		*				

Note: 1) These classifications represent common uses for the techniques. Techniques can be adapted to accommodate the task demands of related skill areas; thus, word attack technique (synthetic phonics) might be used to establish a sight word vocabulary. 2) The lesson frameworks of strategy instruction, explicit teaching, implicit teaching, and sustained silent reading are not classified.

Classifying Techniques by Sources of Information

Students vary the use of information sources as they read, depending on the situation and their purposes for reading. Because active-constructive reading depends on combining all available sources of information, readers use reader-based sources (topic knowledge, rhetorical knowledge, phonological knowledge, and so on) and text-based sources (letters, pictures, words, and so on) as needed to construct meaning.

Sometimes readers employ reader-based processes to predict what the text will say, using their own knowledge. These predictions frame the text-based processing and are subsequently confirmed or revised. The degree to which the reader engages in reader-based processing depends on her purposes for the task of reading. For example, one Saturday afternoon a young teen was reading a novel. As she read, she embellished the story making inferences from her own life, rapidly predicting what the characters would do next. In this instance, the young teen used a great deal of reader-based information as she read. However, at other times, readers choose to engage in text-based processing where they defer evaluation until they have read enough textual information to form a conclusion (Garcia & Pearson, 1990). This kind of processing occurs when readers encounter unfamiliar information, when their previous predictions have been disproved, when they read new directions, or when text fails to make sense. For example, on the next Saturday afternoon, this same young teenager was taking a college entrance examination. As she read the test directions, she read and reread the printed page, focusing on the information exactly as it was stated in the text. In this case, she used the text predominantly as an information source.

Effective readers perpetually shift between information sources to select, combine, and restructure data from the text and their personal knowledge. However, problem readers often experience a deficit in either a skill or strategy that causes them to shift away from one information source. They compensate by using their strength and thus eliminate a need to use their deficient knowledge source (Stanovich, 1986). Therefore, ineffective readers circumvent, using their weaker information sources, and, as a result, often depend on a single source related to their strength.

Some readers have a wealth of general and topic knowledge, which they use continually to add to their general knowledge. They employ reader-based processes to predict what the text will say, using their topic knowledge and paying little attention to the text. This approach inhibits the development of knowledge sources dealing with the conventions of print. Because these readers overrely on reader-based processing of the content, they fail to develop knowledge sources dealing with the text (Walker, 1990b). For example, Sandy entered first grade with poor phonemic awareness, as many potentially poor readers do (Juel, 1998). This weakness in a knowledge source inhibited her understanding of the phonetic system, which hindered her progress in the basal reader program that was used in

the classroom. Therefore, Sandy used her strength of background knowledge to figure out words. When this strategy did not work, she made up the
text by looking at the pictures. Thus, Sandy began to overrely on her
reader-based strength, which inhibited her strategic meaning construction.

> Some problem readers overrely on reader-based information, making infer-
> ences from topic knowledge when a more careful reliance on the text is war-
> ranted.

Other problem readers, however, learn phonics easily and believe
reading is accurately calling a string of words. When asked comprehension
questions, they give answers using the exact words in the text even when
inferences from topic knowledge are more appropriate. They have come to
believe that meaning is found in the text. But as stories become more complex, they find that simply repeating sentences from the text does not result
in understanding (Walker, 1990b). For example, Dani rapidly reads words,
seldom needing to monitor her understanding. This strategy seemed to
work well when she read novels where the plot was similar to her own experiences. However, as she began reading content area texts, she became
lost. She could read the words, but she failed to check her understanding
and elaborate new word meaning. Dani continued to passively read words
and repeat text-based definitions (her strength) without relating ideas. This
approach inhibited her development of strategic reading.

> Some problem readers overrely on text-based information, repeating text seg-
> ments when inferences from background knowledge are more appropriate.

Instructional decision making is facilitated by knowing which information sources the problem reader is using and then matching those with particular techniques so that readers demonstrate their strength. After several
successful reading experiences, the diagnostic teacher chooses techniques
that encourage strategically combining information sources. The techniques
in this book have been classified by the source of information that is emphasized during instruction: (a) reader-based and (b) text-based. Some techniques initially ask students to use their prior knowledge, while other techniques ask students to use the information in the text.

Reader-Based Sources

When selecting approaches that focus on using reader-based information sources, the diagnostic teacher identifies techniques that initially have the students use their background knowledge in relation to the content of the story. In using these techniques, the diagnostic teacher continually asks students to think about what they know in order to create an expectation about what the text may say. For example, when using the directed reading-thinking activity (see Chapter 11), the teacher asks the students to predict what the story might be about. Then, after reading sections of the story, the teacher asks the students whether their predictions were on the right track or whether they would like to keep, add to, or change predictions. Thus, throughout the discussion, the teacher focuses on using reader-based inferencing to construct story understanding. Likewise, when the language experience approach is used (see Chapter 11), students are asked to tell a story, which is then recorded. This story constructed from the students' own words becomes the text, and the students are continually asked to refer to what they said (reader-based source) when they cannot figure out a word.

Text-Based Sources

When selecting approaches that focus on using text-based information sources, the diagnostic teacher identifies techniques that initially ask students to use text-based information. In using these techniques, the diagnostic teacher focuses on how the information in the text explains and describes major characters, events, and ideas. For example, in the story mapping approach (see Chapter 11), the diagnostic teacher asks students to identify the setting (characters and place), the problems, the events that lead to the problem's resolution, and the resolution, and then write this information on a visual framework (map) for the story. The focus is on putting the text-based information on the story map. Likewise, when the synthetic phonics approach is used (see Chapter 11), students are asked to look closely at words and sound them out letter by letter. The students are continually asked to refer to the text when problems in print processing occur.

Conclusions About Sources of Information

Effective readers do not operate using either reader-based information or text-based information sources exclusively, but rather strategically combine these sources of information. What is necessary when reading is a flexible interplay between these sources. To help students develop more efficient use of both sources of information, the diagnostic teacher begins by using the reader's strength (reader-based inferencing or text-based inferencing) and gradually introduces a merging of both sources of information by using scaffolding statements that prompt the student to combine sources. To expedite the selection of teaching techniques, Table 10–6 on the next page analyzes teaching techniques in terms of the major tasks and information sources. The teacher evaluates the students' use of information sources and analyzes the requisite task to be taught. He then selects a technique and constructs a diagnostic lesson to verify the appropriateness of the technique.

> What source of information (text-based, reader-based, or both) does the student tend to use?

Diagnostic Hypothesis

As she reads, Jenny uses reader-based sources of information, embellishing text with her wealth of knowledge. She predicts what the words are and the meaning is, using her background knowledge. She seldom checks the text to confirm or revise her interpretation, but continues to read, using what she knows, even though referring to the text would allow her to correct her miscues that affect her comprehension. This strategy has inhibited Jenny from developing print processing strategies that would facilitate her reading. Thus, Jenny overrelies on reader-based sources of information, particularly as reading becomes more difficult, failing to develop a flexible use of text-based and reader-based cues to figure out unfamiliar words in the text.

Classifying Techniques by Type of Structure

Instructional decision making also includes an analysis of how mediated instruction will occur. The diagnostic teacher thinks about how he will mediate learning. He asks what kind of structure (explicit or implicit) will be necessary for students to regulate their own learning. Learners differ in how they approach the reading event. Some readers are active, while others are passive.

Active Readers

Active readers automatically structure new learning situations by identifying key features, developing plausible solutions, and evaluating their effectiveness. These readers select key characteristics by sampling several alternatives and flexibly shifting among sources of information. As they solve these problems, they create their own rules for what they observe. This strategy may be an inherent way to process information, or it may be developed through the social interactions that students experience daily. Often the more active, independent learners have had numerous experiences with

Table 10–6 Classifying Techniques by Sources of Information

	Reader-Based	Text-Based
Word Identification	Collaborative Reading Language Experience Approach Listening-Thinking Activity Predictable Language Approach	Multisensory Approaches Echo Reading* Impress Method* Sight Words
Word Analysis	Framed Rhyming Innovations Language Experience Approach Message Writing Making Words Word Sorts	Analytic Phonics Multisensory Approaches Phonogram Approach Synthetic Phonics Word Analogy Strategy Word Probe Strategy
Fluency	Chunking* Language Experience Paired Reading Readers Theater Summary Experience Approach	Cloze Instruction Echo Reading* Impress Method* Repeated Readings
Vocabulary	Direct Experience Approach Feature Analysis Grid Metaphors Motor Imaging Visualization Vocabulary Self-Collection Strategy Webbing	Contextual Processing Cloze Instruction
Sentence Comprehension	Readers Theater Story Writing	Contextual Processing Cloze Instruction Framed Innovations Approach Sentence Combining

schoolbook language. To communicate socially, these students use a wide variety of words to describe events and elaborate descriptions to justify their actions. Through previous social interactions, they become more active and explicit when they solve verbal problems.

Passive Readers

Passive learners, however, learn by watching how other students and the teacher solve the problem. They have difficulty distinguishing between the context of learning (such as teacher praise and peer approval) and the task

Table 10–6 *Continued*

	Reader-Based	Text-Based
Literal Comprehension	Experience-Text-Relationship K-W-L Retelling Say Something Story Writing Summary Experience Approach Visualization Webbing	Herringbone Technique Question-Answer Relationships Reciprocal Teaching ReQuest* Story Maps Summarization
Nonliteral Comprehension	Experience-Text-Relationship Generative-Reciprocal Inference Procedure Group Investigation Approach Imagery Instruction Journal Writing Literature Circles Opinion-Proof Approach Prediction Maps* Prediction Logs Self-Directed Questioning* Story Drama	Question-Answer Relationships Reciprocal Teaching
Study Procedures	Imagery Instruction Question-Generation Strategy* Thematic Experience Approach Vocabulary Self-Collection Strategy	Graphic Organizers Herringbone Technique Question-Answer Relationships Summarization Triple Read Outline*

*These techniques utilize both reader-based and text-based sources of information but focus slightly more on one or the other.

Note: The lesson frameworks of strategy instruction, explicit teaching, implicit teaching, directed reading activity, directed reading-thinking activity, and sustained silent reading are not classified.

of learning. They approach problem solving as a spectator and remain passive toward their own process of learning, preferring to follow the teacher's model whenever possible. This passive stance may be an inherent way to process information, or it may be a result of the daily social interactions that the students experience.

Often the more passive students have relied on shared understandings during their social interactions. Communication is often limited to information that refers to events or ideas that are known to the listener; therefore, passive learners use less precise words and nonverbal language to communicate meaning. They rely on their listeners to infer meaning based on shared understandings rather than speaker explanations. When learning demands a more active verbal stance, these students are unfamiliar with the elaborate language that can be used to justify their actions. They remain passive, therefore, preferring to follow the teacher's model to solve problems.

Previous Experiences

For both active and passive students, previous experience with the task being taught affects the need for explicit instruction. If students have not had prior experiences related to the task, they might need some explicit instruction in the new task. If they have had prior experiences and *failed,* they might profit from explicit instruction that is different from the initial instructional context.

The diagnostic teacher analyzes the students' need for explicit instruction by evaluating how active they are when solving the reading problem. If the students are active and have positive experiences with the task, the diagnostic teacher chooses a task that focuses on implicit instruction (students read texts rich in language and figure out the underlying consistency as the teacher guides inquiry). However, if students are passive and have few positive experiences with the task, the diagnostic teacher chooses a technique that focuses on explicit instruction (students are directly informed of what they are learning, provided a model, and given directed practice).

Explicit Instruction

In explicit instruction (see "Explicit Teaching" in Chapter 11), the diagnostic teacher precisely states what is to be learned and models the thinking process that accompanies this new strategy or skill. Students are given reasons why this new strategy or skill will help them read better (Garcia & Pearson, 1990). Minilessons are constructed to show them how to use the reading strategy or skill, with the teacher modeling the steps of the task. Guided practice with a high level of teacher feedback is then provided. The feedback explicitly explains when and where students would use the strategy or skill. In the explicit teaching model, however, a gradual release of teacher-directed instruction allows students to direct their own learning. The diagnostic teacher identifies students who initially lack control of their own learning; then he explicitly teaches the new strategy. Finally, he plans for the independent use of the strategy.

EXPLICIT INSTRUCTION

Based on
- Reasons for learning
- Teacher modeling of how it works
- Collaborative practice
- Gradual release of control

Typical techniques
- Word Probe Strategy
- Question-answer relationships

Implicit Instruction

Implicit instruction (see "Implicit Teaching" in Chapter 11) is characterized by an emphasis on the text, the reading event, and the student as informant. Large quantities of text are read, which require students to use the targeted strategy or skill. Students apply the strategy or skill to make sense of what is read without consciously understanding the principle. Because the context has been carefully arranged, students can readily decide which mistakes make a difference in understanding. From these choices, they reason about text interpretation. The teacher plays the role of linguistic inquirer, asking students, "How did you know that . . . ?" This role allows students to generate their own rules for text interpretation.

IMPLICIT INSTRUCTION

Based on
- Immersion in reading
- Teacher as linguistic inquirer
- Scaffolding thinking, using student responses
- Student generation of rules and ideas

Typical techniques
- Language experience
- Literature circles

Conclusions About Type of Structures

The diagnostic teacher thinks about the student's reading performance and the information he has collected. He asks, "What kind of mediated instruction, implicit or explicit, will facilitate learning for this student?" In other words, does the student want direction on how to complete the tasks? Does she appear to need direct, explicit information before she attempts a reading task or does she want to control her own learning? The teacher theorizes about the kind of mediated instruction the student needs in order to change her reading behavior. The diagnostic teacher predicts whether implicit

Table 10–7 *Classifying Techniques by Type of Structure*

	Implicit	Explicit
Word Identification	Collaborative Reading Echo Reading Impress Method Language Experience Approach Listening-Thinking Activity Predictable Language Approach Summary Experience Approach Talking Books	Multisensory Approaches Sight Word Approach Word Walls
Word Analysis	Analytic Phonics Making Words Message Writing Repeated Readings Word Sorts	Framed Innovations Approach Phonogram Approach Synthetic Phonics Word Analogy Strategy Word Probe Strategy
Fluency	Echo Reading Impress Method Language Experience Approach Paired Reading Readers Theater Talking Books	Chunking Repeated Readings (with teacher mediation)
Meaning Vocabulary	Cloze Instruction Direct Experience Approach Motor Imaging Thematic Experience Approach Visualization Vocabulary Self-Collection Strategy Webbing	Contextual Processing Experience-Text-Relationship Metaphors Word Walls

(student-discovered strategies) or explicit (teacher-directed learning) instruction will result in a greater change in reading performance. The teacher matches this hypothesis with an appropriate technique using Table 10–7.

> In order to advance reading, what kind of mediated instruction (implicit or explicit) will be needed?

Table 10–7 *Continued*

	Implicit	Explicit
Sentence Comprehension	Alternate Writing Cloze Instruction Retrospective Miscue Analysis Story Writing	Contextual Processing Framed Innovations Approach Sentence Combining
Literal Comprehension	Alternate Writing Group Investigation Approach K-W-L Readers Theater ReQuest Retelling Say Something Story Writing	Herringbone Technique Opinion-Proof Approach Reciprocal Teaching Story Maps Summarization
Nonliteral Comprehension	Imagery Instruction Journal Writing Literature Circles Prediction Logs Readers Theater Story Drama Visualization	Experience-Text-Relationship Generative-Reciprocal Inference Procedure Prediction Maps Self-Directed Questioning
Study Procedures	Imagery Instruction Question-Generation Strategy SQ3R Thematic Experience Approach Vocabulary Self-Collection Strategy	Graphic Organizers Question-Answer Relationships Reciprocal Teaching Summarization Triple Read Outline

Note: (1) The lesson frameworks of strategy instruction, explicit teaching, implicit teaching, directed reading activity, directed reading-thinking activity, and sustained silent reading are not classified. Of these, explicit teaching and the directed reading activity are explicit techniques. (2) Teacher implementation can change any technique to make it more or less explicit or implicit.

Diagnostic Hypothesis

For Jenny, the decision is clear-cut. She prefers to control the decision making when she reads. During the retelling, for example, she stated, "I'm not saying this in order." She also made the self-evaluation about a statement that it "might not be right," which shows that she has control over her comprehension, although not over word recognition. Consequently, a more implicit technique to develop fluency is selected, which will allow Jenny to control her reading strategies and assess her progress.

Classifying Techniques by Strengths in Cognitive Processing

Individual differences in problem solving influence how students build their models of meaning as they read. A multitude of theoretical frameworks exist for studying individual differences; however, a model of dichotomous thinking referred to as simultaneous and successive cognitive processing seems to relate more appropriately to literacy interactions. This model refers to *how* students solve problems, recognizing and restructuring information in a problem-solving situation such as reading.

As students read, they vary their cognitive processing depending on the nature of the reading task (that is, they flexibly shift between simultaneous and successive processing). For example, when constructing a main idea from the text, readers organize important information (successive processing) while drawing relationships among the information (simultaneous processing).

When reading requires a step-by-step analysis of text, readers use successive processing and sequentially order the information to solve the problem. Reading tasks such as phonic decoding and sequencing story events require that readers recognize and structure information in a step-by-step sequence. This problem-solving process is referred to as successive processing.

On the other hand, when reading requires the analysis of several ideas at the same time, readers use simultaneous processing; they relate ideas according to a general category to solve the problem. Reading tasks such as predicting the author's purpose and interpreting character motives draw heavily on organizing many aspects of information around their most important characteristics. This process is referred to as simultaneous processing.

Students can be identified as having strengths in one of these ways of processing information. A *simultaneous* preference refers to the propensity to think about multiple relationships among ideas, relating the most important characteristics (Kaufman & Kaufman, 1983). Students who prefer simultaneous processing build their models of meaning using large, inclusive categories of meaning. A noticeable characteristic of these students is their well-developed ability to manipulate visual information. These readers often draw visual diagrams or pictures to organize information. Students with a strength in simultaneous processing look for the coherent patterns of text by tying together the underlying relationships implied by the author. They use a minimal amount of textual information and rely heavily on their background knowledge to interpret text. They often comment, "Oh, yeah, that's like a. . . ." Their language is noticeably less precise and characterized by a tendency to draw images with words rather than use specific definitional language.

At the word identification level, these readers prefer using the semantic cueing system over the grapho-phonic or syntactic cueing system because they have a high need to create meaning from what they read. This preference often precludes their making a careful analysis of the text.

> Simultaneous processing strength means that the student thinks first about the overall meaning and then organizes the parts as they relate to the entire meaning.

A *successive* preference refers to the propensity for developing sequential, logical relationships with words. Students who prefer successive processing tend to develop models of meaning by arranging information in a logical, hierarchical sequence. They develop meaning from precise words that are logically organized to form definitional language. Students with a successive processing strength look for the logical organization of the text to gain meaning. After reading a text, they can recall the sequence of story events but often cannot tie together events to form a main idea. Because they rely heavily on textual information to fill in unstated meanings, their models seldom reflect personal application of the text. They organize information according to its function; therefore, their comments are flooded with precise text-based references.

At the word identification level, successive readers prefer using the grapho-phonic or syntactic cueing system because they rely on the logical relationships among and within words. This preference often precludes using the overall meaning of the text to decode words, creating a word-bound reader. They forget to think about the overall meaning of the selection and to relate the textual information to their previous experiences.

> Successive processing strength means that the student thinks about the parts first and then orders the parts to form the general meaning.

Instructional decision making is facilitated by knowing which cognitive process is used in the various techniques. The techniques in this book have been classified by their simultaneous or successive framework. Some techniques initially ask students to consider the overall meaning before analyzing the parts. Other techniques ask readers to learn and use the parts before constructing the general meaning.

Simultaneous Framework

When selecting approaches that use a simultaneous framework, the diagnostic teacher identifies techniques that focus on the overall meaning of text. In using these techniques, the diagnostic teacher continually redirects attention by asking how things make sense within the entire passage. Specific facts are presented to show relationships to the overall meaning and to one another. These procedures require the synthesis of information, which is characteristic of simultaneous processing. For example, the predictable language approach (see "Predictable Language Approach" in Chapter 11) requires students to move from understanding the whole (memorizing the story) to identifying the parts (single words). Selecting techniques that focus on simultaneous processing, the diagnostic teacher also evaluates whether learning is mediated through a visual array of the relationships, through tactile/kinesthetic experiences, or through visualization. Techniques that have this focus ask students to look at multiple relationships simultaneously.

SIMULTANEOUS FRAMEWORK

Based on
- Multiple relationships among pieces of information
- Visual display of information
- Overall generalization

Typical techniques
- Predictable language
- Webbing
- Imagery instruction

Successive Framework

When selecting approaches that use a successive framework, the diagnostic teacher identifies techniques that focus on discrete parts that form meaning when grouped together. In these techniques, the diagnostic teacher gradually presents the sequential parts of the task, leading students to an overall understanding (see "Story Maps" in Chapter 11). These procedures require that new bits of information are evaluated individually and gradually arranged in a sequence that forms meaning. For example, the instructional emphasis of synthetic phonics (see "Synthetic (Explicit) Phonics" in Chapter 11) moves from knowing the parts (single letter sounds) to sequencing these sounds into words (sound synthesis) and finally to reading the words in stories. Selecting techniques that focus on successive processing, the diagnostic teacher also evaluates whether learning is mediated through auditory/verbal information, functional analysis, or analysis of small amounts of information. Each of these techniques requires a successive processing of individual sections within the text.

SUCCESSIVE FRAMEWORK

Based on
- Small, discrete parts
- Step-by-step arrangement
- Verbalizing function

Typical techniques
- Synthetic (explicit) phonics
- Question-answer relationships

Conclusions About Strengths in Cognitive Processing

Effective readers do not operate exclusively in either the simultaneous or the successive mode. What is necessary for fluent reading is a flexible interplay between simultaneous and successive processing of text. Efficient readers flexibly shift between a successive analysis of the textual elements and a simultaneous relating of textual and nontextual information to construct a model of meaning. However, inefficient readers often rely too much on their strength in cognitive processing, thus inhibiting fluent reading performance.

To develop a more flexible text processing, the diagnostic teacher begins instruction using readers' strengths in cognitive processing (teach new reading strategies using the strength) and gradually introduces a more integrated processing of text by showing them how to incorporate their weaknesses into their reading repertoires. Thus, the diagnostic teacher initially uses students' strengths in cognitive processing to mediate learning before introducing other strategies.

The sensitive teacher—understanding the problem-solving demands of the tasks of reading, readers' preferences, and the various ways to teach reading—can modify instruction to facilitate students' learning. In other words, if fluency is an identified inhibiting behavior in the initial assessment, a technique that develops fluency would be chosen. Furthermore, if the student's cognitive processing appears to proceed from the overall meaning to the isolated parts (simultaneous understanding), a technique that develops

Table 10–8 *Classifying Techniques by Sequence of Cognitive Processing*

	Simultaneous	Successive
Word Identification	Collaborative Reading Echo Reading Impress Method Language-Experience Approach Listening-Thinking Activity Predictable Language Summary Experience Approach Word Sorts	Making Words Multisensory Approaches Sight Words Word Walls
Word Analysis	Echo Reading Framed Rhyming Innovations Impress Method Language Experience Approach Repeated Readings	Analytic Phonics Making Words Message Writing Multisensory Approaches Phonogram Approach Synthetic Phonics Word Analogy Strategy Word Probe Strategy
Fluency	Echo Reading Impress Method Language Experience Approach Paired Reading Readers Theater Repeated Readings	Chunking Cloze Instruction Retrospective Miscue Analysis
Vocabulary	Direct Experience Approach Metaphors Motor Imaging Thematic Experience Approach Visualization Vocabulary Self-Collection Strategy Webbing	Cloze Instruction Contextual Processing Feature Analysis Grid Word Walls
Sentence Comprehension	Framed Rhyming Innovations Readers Theater Story Writing	Cloze Instruction Contextual Processing Sentence Combining

fluency from a simultaneous perspective would be selected. The teacher looks at the data he collected and asks, "Does the reader use simultaneous or successive strategies to regain meaning?" Using Table 10–8, he then selects a technique that matches the student's processing style and will remedy the inhibiting reading behaviors.

What processing sequence (simultaneous or successive emphasis) does the student seem to prefer?

Table 10–8 *Continued*

	Simultaneous	Successive
Literal Comprehension	Experience-Text-Relationship Question-Generation Strategy Story Maps* Story Writing Summary Experience Approach Visualization Webbing	Herringbone Technique Question-Answer Relationships Reciprocal Teaching ReQuest Summarization
Nonliteral Comprehension	Experience-Text-Relationship Imagery Instruction Journal Writing K-W-L Literature Circles Opinion-Proof Approach Prediction Logs Prediction Maps Story Drama	Generative-Reciprocal Inference Procedure Question-Answer Relationships Reciprocal Teaching Self-Directed Questioning
Study Procedures	Imagery Instruction Graphic Organizers Group Investigation Approach Question-Generation Strategy Thematic Experience Approach Triple Read Outline	Herringbone Technique Question-Answer Relationships Summarization

*These techniques are less simultaneous than the others in the list.

Note: (1) The lesson frameworks of strategy instruction, explicit teaching, implicit teaching, directed reading activity, directed reading-thinking activity, and sustained silent reading are not classified. Of these, explicit teaching and the directed reading activity are more successive than simultaneous. (2) Teacher implementation can change any technique to make it more or less simultaneous.

Diagnostic Hypothesis

Jenny appears to use simultaneous processing. She relates stories to what she already knows and often makes word substitutions that fit the overall meaning of the text. Although she has a successive strength in comprehension (excellent literal comprehension), she does not have these same successive strengths in word recognition. Her miscues often reflect letter and syllable reversals. Jenny needs techniques that encourage her to integrate simultaneous and successive processing rather than overrely on a single process.

Summary

Putting the Parts Together for Jenny

Reviewing Jenny's case, the teacher reaches the following conclusions. Jenny needs instruction in fluency (a skill) and self-correction (a strategy). Jenny also views her poor fluency as subject to forces outside her control, thus increasing her negative attribution of reading failure. She likes expository text and has a high need for stories to make sense. In fact, she overrelies on reader-based processing of text, often making her interpretation fit pictures or a miscue rather than referring back to the text. However, she prefers to control her own learning (implicit instruction) whenever she can. She also has a tendency to prefer material presented with the overall theme first (simultaneous), before learning the details.

When the diagnostic teacher looks at all the hypotheses, he selects a text that contains expository passages of interest to the student (predominately science stories) to use during guided contextual reading. Prior to instruction, he introduces key vocabulary words using mapping (see Chapter 11), which allows Jenny to elaborate her knowledge about the concepts. During the lesson, the teacher uses collaborative reading where he reads the story aloud and then has Jenny read it on her own (implicit instruction). After the lesson, Jenny presents science facts to the class. She is allowed to use the assigned reading or her own research efforts.

To help Jenny attribute her success to effective strategies and to lead her to more flexible strategies when reading errors occur, a program of repeated readings (see "Repeated Readings" in Chapter 11) is used in strategy and skill instruction. After Jenny reads a short informational passage for the first time, the teacher plans an intervention in which efficient strategies are discussed. The teacher demonstrates the following self-statement consistent with implicit instruction: "What would make sense and start with a _____ ?" This procedure allows Jenny to assume increasing responsibility for her own oral reading fluency, while permitting her to use the overall meaning (simultaneous processing) of the selection to correct her miscues, thus respecting her natural preference for using prior experience and context to self-correct. Charting the repeated readings also helps Jenny attribute her increasing fluency to her own efforts and ability, reversing her negative attribution in word recognition.

Reviewing Technique Selection

The teacher's selection of a technique reflects the diagnostic hypotheses about a student's learning at that particular time. To select the most appropriate technique, the diagnostic teacher analyzes each technique according to its instructional features. First, the diagnostic teacher thinks about the instructional framework during guided contextual reading and selects techniques that will lead the student to meaningfully interpret whole stories. He thinks about the students' print and meaning processing and how he will advance their overall reading by supporting reading before, during, or after instruction. He also thinks about the type of text students are reading and selects techniques that are appropriate for that type of text. He thinks about the students' preferences and decides whether more writing or discussing will advance story understanding.

Next, the diagnostic teacher selects techniques to encourage the students to use areas of weakness that are inhibiting the reading process. He thinks about the element of strategy and skill instruction and selects techniques that work on weaknesses by showing the students how to use their strengths to support their weaknesses.

Finally, the diagnostic teacher refines his selections by checking the selection against the students' strengths and needs so he can utilize these during instruction. He uses the following criteria: source of information, type of mediated instruction, and cognitive processing. He thinks about the sources of information the students rely upon: reader-based or text-based. He matches this assessment with instructional techniques that show them how to integrate information sources while at the same time use their strength. Then he decides on the type of structure that is needed: explicit or implicit. Providing the appropriate type of mediated instruction in the learning situation enhances students' reading performance. The diagnostic teacher decides which technique matches the students' strengths in cognitive processing. Some techniques incorporate a successive, serial approach to instruction, while others incorporate a global, simultaneous approach. For hard-to-teach students, instruction using their processing strength facilitates the learning of new information.

Throughout his instruction, the diagnostic teacher makes instructional modifications that increase each student's reading performance. To date, no single instructional sequence or instructional framework has proven effective for problem readers. However, teachers vary in their preferences for teaching, and these preferences often dictate how they conduct the diagnostic session. Effective teachers remember that student learning is not accomplished by a mindless implementation of instructional techniques, but by understanding the variables in the process of reading. Therefore, the diagnostic teacher needs to employ a variety of techniques to meet the individual needs of problem readers, identify the key features of these techniques, and evaluate how these features affect reading acquisition.

11

The Instructional Techniques

In this chapter, 68 instructional procedures are presented to help teachers design programs for problem readers. The instructional procedures, or techniques, include a variety of instructional formats, approaches, methods, and specialized remedial techniques. The techniques represent a variety of ways to encourage proficient reading. Each technique is discussed in two parts: (a) a simple procedural description followed by (b) an explanation of specific diagnostic applications.

In field use, this chapter may be used in the following manner. First, the diagnostic teacher consults the general description and its steps. In order to make instructional modifications, the teacher needs to evaluate how she instructs the lesson. As she instructs the lesson, she evaluates at what point she modified instruction to mediate learning. Consequently, this chapter describes the steps in implementing each technique, thus facilitating a comparison of how instruction occurs when using various techniques. The teacher may then wish to turn to the second part of the discussion; the knowledge of learner patterns in which the technique produces success will be of assistance when the teacher tries to match an appropriate instructional technique to the needs of an individual student. After she has selected a technique, the teacher uses a diagnostic lesson to evaluate her hypothesis (see Chapter 7).

The Information for Each Technique

Initially, the explanation is presented in simple terminology and is constructed to assist teacher-parent collaboration. The following topics are included:

- *Description.* In an effort to simplify communication, a two- or three-sentence description is presented. This description can be used in report writing or communicating with parents.

- *Targeted Reading Levels.* Many techniques were developed for use with students at a particular stage in reading development. This section will facilitate selecting a technique that matches the reading level of the student.

- *Predominant Focus of Instruction.* This section delineates the critical focus of each technique. Techniques can be placed on a continuum of various instructional features that are stressed during implementation. For example, most techniques have both an oral discussion and a written component; however, one of these aspects will predominate. It must be remembered that the significance of this emphasis depends on the learner's strategies, his task knowledge, and the situational context. In this section, the predominant focus is delineated according to the charts in Chapter 10. The following list represents the selected areas:
  1. Print or meaning processing
  2. Instructional phase (before, during, or after reading) in the lesson
  3. Response mode emphasized (oral or written)
  4. Strategy emphasized (prediction, monitoring, or elaboration)
  5. Skill emphasized (word identification, word analysis, fluency, sentence comprehension, word meaning, literal comprehension, nonliteral comprehension, or reflective procedures)
  6. Source of information (text-based or reader-based)
  7. Type of instruction (explicit or implicit)
  8. Type of cognitive processing (successive or simultaneous)

- *Procedures.* This section is a sequential enumeration of the process of instruction for each technique. This explanation serves two purposes. First, it facilitates implementation of the technique so that experimenting with new methods of instruction is not overwhelming. Second, using the steps of instruction, the diagnostic teacher can analyze in what part of the instruction the student has incorporated the desired reading behaviors. This knowledge facilitates modifying instruction to increase its effectiveness.

The next section specifies the diagnostic applications of each technique and includes the following elements:

- *Basic View of Reading.* Techniques have developed from various views of learning. As individuals formulate views of how learning occurs in young children, they propose teaching techniques that support their views. Therefore, instructional techniques reflect theories about how children learn. An assumption of this chapter is that the diagnostic teacher can match how a child is learning with a diagnostic technique that reflects that learning process. The major views are text-based, which focuses instruction on text-based processing; reader-based, in which instruction is focused on reader-based processing; interactive, with instruction focused on combining reader-based and text-based processing; and socio-interactive, in which instruction is focused on shared meaning construction (see Chapter 1).

■ *Patterns of Strengths and Strategies.* This section looks specifically at what the student is asked to do when the teacher implements the technique. The underlying strengths and strategies that are necessary for the student to profit from this instructional technique are then presented.

■ *Learner Patterns That Produce Increased Engagement.* Techniques can be used in different ways in order to engage students in literacy. This section analyzes the technique as it would be integrated into instruction with different learners. How the technique is implemented is matched to the corresponding learner patterns. Learner patterns (see Chapter 10 for further explanation) that are highlighted in this section include the following:

1. *Active readers,* who independently solve reading problems by reorganizing new information around its key features. They predict, monitor, and elaborate what they read, using both the text and what they know.
2. *Passive readers,* who rely heavily on cues from their environment to decide what is important to remember. They prefer to follow a teacher's model when predicting, monitoring, and elaborating what they read. When reading, they use either the text or what they know to solve the reading problem.
3. *Readers who have a simultaneous processing strength* and think first about the overall meaning, then organize the parts as they relate to the entire meaning.
4. *Readers who have a successive processing strength* and think about the parts first, then order the parts to form the general meaning.

Described first are the learner patterns that represent how the technique matches a learner strength. For these students, the technique can be used to modify the basic lesson during guided contextual reading or for strategy and skill instruction (see Chapter 4 for further explanation of these features of the diagnostic teaching session). The items designated by an asterisk, which appear second, represent how the technique would be used to remediate a weakness during strategy and skill instruction.

The last section is the following:

■ *Using the Technique as a Diagnostic Teaching Lesson.* This section provides a short checklist to focus the evaluation of a student's success when the technique is used. If the answers are "yes," the technique facilitates learning for this particular student.

Ways to Use This Chapter

The techniques in this chapter are arranged alphabetically so they can be used as a resource rather than procedures to be memorized. The alphabetical arrangement facilitates locating a technique that was selected in Chapter 10.

These pages have been used by preservice teachers, inservice teachers, and school psychologists in many different ways. Preservice teachers follow the procedures step by step as they learn how to teach in different ways. Then they read why they are doing what they are doing. When students do not succeed with a particular technique, these teachers analyze what they asked them to do by reading the second section. This assessment helps preservice teachers understand how children are different. Inservice teachers use Chapter 10 extensively to choose several techniques. They use each of these techniques to help them decide what the students' strengths are. As they identify what technique works best, they also identify their students' strengths. The school psychologist, on the other hand, uses Chapter 10 to match assessment data with particular techniques. Then she looks up each technique to verify which might be the most beneficial. She then recommends the procedures to the appropriate teacher.

Alternate Writing

Description   Alternate writing is the composition of a story among a group of students and a teacher. Writing for a specified amount of time, each person alternately continues the development of a cohesive story line. Each person's contribution to the story line must build upon prior information in the composition and must lead to the next event.

Targeted Reading Levels   4–8

Text   Students' and teacher's writing

Predominant Focus of Instruction

1. Processing focus: meaning
2. Instructional phase: during reading
3. Response mode emphasized: written discourse
4. Strategy emphasized: elaboration
5. Skill emphasized: sentence comprehension
6. Source of information: reader-based
7. Type of instruction: implicit
8. Type of cognitive processing: successive

Procedure

1. The teacher selects topics of interest to the students. As the procedure is used, an increasing variety of text types and subject areas needs to be included.

2. Using the story starter or topic selected, the teacher begins writing and continues developing the story line for two minutes. In a small group, an overhead can be used.

3. The story is passed to the next student. This student writes for two minutes.

4. In order to continue the story, each student must read the previous text and create text that maintains the story theme and moves the story to its conclusion.

5. When the story is completely written, the teacher reads the story as a whole.

6. The teacher revises her own parts of the story for coherence and grammatical clarity. As she is revising, she thinks out loud, "Will this make sense to my reader?"

7. The teacher encourages students to revise their writing for coherence and grammatical clarity.

Modifications

1. A story map can be developed prior to writing so that each student adds information that will fit the story map (see "Story Map" in this chapter).

2. A word processing program can be used, and students can write and revise the story on the computer.

3. Cartoons can be used as a framework for the story line.

4. This technique can be used in pairs, small groups, and tutoring situations.

5. This technique can be easily adapted to a writing center, where students add to the story when they attend that center. Students initial their additions.

Further Diagnostic Applications

Basic View of Reading   Reading and writing are socio-interactive processes in which the reader's ideas are shaped by group members. He uses prior knowledge to construct and monitor understanding, asking himself what would fit the story and be meaningful to group members. Through writing, the reader becomes sensitive to how stories are constructed so that they make sense.

Patterns of Strengths and Strategies   Alternate writing is most appropriate for students who have facility with writing and prefer to communicate through writing rather than discussing. This approach helps students develop a sense of the story line and approach text as a communication between reader and writer.

Learner Patterns That Produce Increased Engagement

1. For the successive learner who writes well but does not understand that reading is a communication process, this technique provides a tool for talking about the communicative intent of the author.

2. For the simultaneous learner who writes and reads for self-understanding and meaning but does not realize that the text is a contractual agreement between reader and writer, this technique provides a tool for talking about what needs to be in a text in order to make it understandable to a reader.

*3. For a learner who has verbal difficulty and who needs to participate in writing a story to understand story structure, this technique provides an experience in developing writing fluency in a group setting, which is less threatening.

Using the Technique as a Diagnostic Teaching Lesson   For alternate writing to be effective, a majority of the following statements must be answered in the affirmative:

Yes	No	
_____	_____	1. The student writes fluently and can construct text that makes sense.
_____	_____	2. The student prefers to write what he thinks rather than contribute to a discussion.
_____	_____	3. The student can retell a cohesive story and has an intuitive sense of story structure.

For Further Reading

Short, K. G., Harste, J. C., & Burke, C. (1996). *Creating classrooms for authors and inquirers.* Portsmouth, NH: Heinemann.

Analytic (Implicit) Phonics

Description   Analytic phonics (sometimes referred to as implicit phonics instruction) is an approach to teaching decoding that is based on drawing phonic relationships among words that have the same letter patterns. Using words already recognized "at sight," the student identifies the sounds of letter groups by making analogies to known words. In other words, the child says, "I already know a word that looks like this new word. I will match the sounds in that word with the sounds in the new word."

Targeted Reading Levels   1–2

---

*Indicates a technique that can be used to remediate a weakness.

Text   Known sight words and new words that have the same sound pattern

Predominant Focus of Instruction

1. Processing focus: print
2. Instructional phase: after reading
3. Response mode emphasized: oral discussion
4. Strategy emphasized: elaboration
5. Skill emphasized: word analysis
6. Source of information: text-based
7. Type of instruction: implicit
8. Type of cognitive processing: simultaneous to successive

Procedure

1. The teacher selects a text that contains an abundance of the letter sounds to be taught.

2. The teacher presents sight words that represent the targeted sound or sound cluster. For example, she places these words on the board: *green grass grow*

3. She asks the student to identify how these words are alike. The student responds, "They all have the letters *gr* at the beginning."

4. The teacher directs attention to the sounds by saying, "How does the *gr* sound in these words?"

5. If the student cannot figure out the sound, the teacher says, "Try the *gr-r-r* sound as in *green, grass, and grow.*"

6. The student reads a text with words that have the *gr* sound, such as the following:

   In the land of the gremlins, there were gobs of green grapes as big as Grandpa. One baby gremlin loved to eat the green grapes. He began to grow and grow and grow. So his mother said, "You cannot eat anymore. You have grown too big." This made the gremlin grumpy. He growled and growled. He grabbed a great big green grape and gobbled it up. Then he grabbed another green grape and gobbled it up. Then he grabbed another and another and another. He grew and grew and grew until he popped. That was the end of the gremlin.

7. The teacher draws attention to how the student used the strategy of decoding by analogy.

Further Diagnostic Applications

Basic View of Reading   Learning to read is a text-based process in which the learner makes inferences about the phonic relationships within words. When a student can read an abundance of words that contain a consistent phonic relationship, he will infer the phonic rule for the target words and similar words. This process is called implicit or analytic phonics.

Patterns of Strengths and Strategies   Analytic phonics is most appropriate for students who can segment words into their sounds and readily make phonic inferences about the consistency of sounds in words. This technique builds on their strengths and allows them to develop the strategy of decoding by analogy.

Learner Patterns That Produce Increased Engagement

1. For a simultaneous learner who can segment words into their sounds and has established a sight word vocabulary, this technique matches his strengths in knowing the whole word before the parts and finding the patterns between what he knows and what is new.

2. For an active reader who does not respond to the direct instruction of other decoding approaches, this technique allows him to develop his own rules for how phonics works.

3. For a learner who has an overriding need for meaning and purpose in his learning, minimal instruction in decoding by analogy makes sense and provides strategies for decoding.

Using the Technique as a Diagnostic Teaching Lesson   For analytic phonics to be effective, a majority of the following statements must be answered in the affirmative:

Yes   No

_____   _____   1. The student is effective at phonemic segmentation.

_____   _____   2. The student has a well-established sight vocabulary, which facilitates making phonic inferences to new words.

_____   _____   3. The student can draw sound analogies between known words and new words.

For Further Reading

Snow, C. E., Burn, M. S., & Griffin, P. (1998). *Preventing reading difficulties in young children.* Washington, DC: National Academy Press.

McCormick, S. (1995). *Instructing students who have literacy problems.* Englewood Cliffs, NJ: Merrill/Prentice Hall.

Chunking

Description   Chunking is a technique to encourage the student to read phrases of language that represent meaning rather than separate words. It focuses on reading phrases of text that represent a thought. Chunking facilitates comprehension and fluency by using thought units rather than word-by-word reading.

Targeted Reading Levels 4–8

Text All kinds

Predominant Focus of Instruction

1. Processing focus: print and meaning
2. Instructional phase: during reading
3. Response mode emphasized: oral production
4. Strategy emphasized: prediction
5. Skill emphasized: fluency and sentence comprehension
6. Source of information: text-based and reader-based
7. Type of instruction: explicit
8. Type of cognitive processing: successive to simultaneous

Procedure

1. The teacher chooses a passage at an instructional reading level that will take about three minutes to read.

2. The teacher tapes the student reading the passage.

3. The teacher and the student echo read (see "Echo Reading" in this chapter) the passage using meaningful phrases. In other words, the teacher reads a sentence modeling appropriate chunks of the sentence, and the student repeats the same sentence using the phrasing. The example that follows illustrates the sequence:

   Text: The bright girl liked to read stories about horses.

   Student reading: The/bright/girl/liked/to/read/stories/about/horses.

   Teacher modeling: The bright girl/liked to read/stories about horses.

   Student echoing: The bright girl/liked to/read stories/about horses.

   Teacher comment: I liked the way you chunked "read stories." Did it make more sense to you to read it that way?

4. The teacher and student continue reading the entire passage. When possible, the teacher increases the number of sentences chunked before the student repeats the model.

5. As the student's ability to chunk thought units increases, the teacher ceases to model the chunking, and the student reads the passage on her own.

6. The teacher tapes the reading of the passage again.

7. The teacher and the student compare fluency, intonation, and phrasing.

Modifications

1. For the extremely slow reader, the teacher may incorporate oral chunking experiences as an intervention with multiple timed, silent readings.

2. For the beginning reader, chunking a language experience story by writing phrases from the story on 3″ × 5″ cards is an effective technique.

Further Diagnostic Applications

Basic View of Reading   Reading is an interactive process whereby a reader thinks about how the words of the text are combined to form the ideas the author intended to convey.

Patterns of Strengths and Strategies   Chunking is most appropriate for students who have facility with word identification and reflect a sequential, text-based processing. Chunking of text encourages these students to connect the underlying thought with the text as they are reading.

Learner Patterns That Produce Increased Engagement

1. When chunking, a successive learner who has difficulty relating what is written in the text to his own thoughts must use understanding of the meaning to group the words together.

2. For the passive reader who reads words without thinking of their meaning, chunking uses recognizing the words (a strength) to understand how the words create meaning (a weakness).

*3. For a learner who is word-bound because of an overemphasis on phonics or oral accuracy, chunking increases her fluency and speed.

*4. For an extremely slow reader who thinks about every word, chunking encourages thinking about groups of words rather than individual words.

Using the Technique as a Diagnostic Teaching Lesson   For chunking to be effective, a majority of the following statements must be answered in the affirmative:

Yes   No
_____   _____   1. The student has accurate word identification skills.
_____   _____   2. The student can model the teacher's chunking of words.
_____   _____   3. The student transfers the chunking to new text.

For Further Reading
Rasinski, T. & Padak, N. (1996). *Holistic reading strategies: Teaching children who find reading difficult.* Englewood Cliffs, NJ: Merrill/Prentice Hall.
Samuels, S. J., Schermer, N., & Reinking, D. (1991). Reading fluency: Techniques for making decoding automatic. In S. J. Samuels & A. E. Farstrup (eds.), *What research has to say about reading instruction.* Newark, DE: International Reading Association.

Cloze Instruction

Description   The instructional cloze is a technique that develops comprehension by deleting target words from a text. It encourages the student to think about what word would make sense in the sentence and in the context of the entire story.

Targeted Reading Levels   4–12

Text   Paragraphs and stories that are coherent

Predominant Focus of Instruction

1. Processing focus: meaning
2. Instructional phase: after reading
3. Response mode emphasized: written
4. Strategy emphasized: prediction and monitoring
5. Skill emphasized: sentence comprehension and word meaning
6. Source of information: text-based with some reader-based
7. Type of instruction: implicit
8. Type of cognitive processing: successive

Procedure

1. The teacher selects a text of 200–400 words.

2. The teacher decides on the target words, such as nouns or verbs or targeted sight words.

3. The teacher systematically deletes the words from the paragraph and inserts a blank for the deleted word.

4. The student is instructed to read the entire passage to get a sense of the entire meaning.

5. The student is then instructed to fill in the blanks in the passage.

6. When the student finishes filling in the blanks, the answers are evaluated as to the similarity of meaning between the deleted word and the supplied word.

7. The student reviews his choices and talks about what strategies he used to decide on the word choices.

Modifications

1. An oral cloze can be used to develop predictive listening in the young child.

2. A cloze exercise can be constructed from language experience stories in order to develop the ability to predict a word by using prior knowledge (what I said) and the text (how I said it).

3. Cloze can be adapted so that pairs of students work together to decide what word fits in the text. This activity causes a discussion and justification of word choices.

Further Diagnostic Applications

Basic View of Reading   Reading is an interactive process of verifying text expectation by using knowledge of how language works (sentence structure) and what the passage means (overall contextual meaning).

Patterns of Strengths and Strategies   The cloze procedure relies on a well-developed sense of the redundancy of language and a manipulation of sentence structure. For students who have verbal fluency, this technique facilitates comprehension by encouraging the combination of text and meaning cues.

Learner Patterns That Produce Increased Engagement

1. For the successive learner who has become word-bound during the process of initial reading instruction and needs to increase the use of context to construct meaning, this technique increases the ability to guess what words are from context.

2. For the successive learner who tends to read isolated words rather than using the context and asking what would make sense, this technique helps the reader think about what groups of words mean.

*3. For the simultaneous learner who needs to use both sentence structure and overall meaning to read text effectively, this technique focuses attention on sentence meaning.

Using the Technique as a Diagnostic Teaching Lesson   For cloze instruction to be effective, a majority of the following statements must be answered in the affirmative:

Yes	No	
_____	_____	1. The student fills in the blanks with some degree of certainty.
_____	_____	2. The student has verbal facility, which supplements his performance on the cloze.
_____	_____	3. The student begins to use not only *word* knowledge but also *world* knowledge to complete the cloze.

For Further Reading
McKenna, M. C. & Robinson, R. D. (1993). *Teaching through text*. White Plains, NY: Longman.
Reutzel, D. R. & Cooter, R. B. (1996). *Teaching children to read: From basals to books* (2d ed.) Englewood Cliffs, NJ: Merrill/Prentice Hall.

Collaborative Reading

Description   In the collaborative reading technique, the challenge of unfamiliar selections is supported by reading together and sharing interpretations as with young children in shared reading. The teacher begins reading the story aloud and then invites the student to follow. They discuss what the story could be about as they read the story to develop an understanding of the story while reading together. Using his understanding of the story, the student reads the new selection on his own with only minimal support from the teacher.

Targeted Reading Levels   2–5

Text   Easy chapter books

Predominant Focus of Instruction

1. Processing focus: meaning and print
2. Instructional phase: before reading
3. Response mode emphasized: oral discussion
4. Strategy emphasized: prediction
5. Skill emphasized: literal comprehension and word identification
6. Source of information: reader-based
7. Type of instruction: implicit
8. Type of cognitive processing: simultaneous

Procedure

1. The teacher selects an easy chapter book to read.

2. The teacher and students discuss what they think the book will be about based on the title.

3. The teacher reads the story aloud modeling appropriate intonation. (If the student is reading well, then the first read is not necessary, but the teacher can ask the following questions as she and the student read together.) As the teacher reads, she stops and asks

   What do you think will happen next?

   Do you agree with what the main character did?

4. After the first reading the teacher asks open-ended questions that encourage a higher level of engagement in the selection, such as

   Which part of the story did you like best?

   What would you change in the story?

5. When reading the story a second time together, the teacher keeps a fluent pace and invites the student to join in the reading.

6. After the second reading, the student and teacher review the troublesome phrases and ideas.

7. On the third reading of the story, the student reads alone. The teacher prompts the student if he needs help.

Further Diagnostic Applications

Basic View of Reading   Reading is a socio-interactive process in which the reader's background knowledge and how he discusses the story with others help him understand the story and recognize the words. When the teacher reads the story aloud and discusses it with the child, she creates an expectation for the words in the text. The student then uses reader-based processing (i.e., what the text means) to figure out unfamiliar words. The ultimate goal is a reader who will simultaneously apply the decoding skills of reading while comprehending text.

Patterns of Strengths and Strategies   Collaborative reading is most appropriate for intermediate students who are simultaneous processers and have a high drive for meaning when reading. For these students, the approach uses their strengths of listening and thinking; then it asks them to use these strengths to recognize words.

Learner Patterns That Produce Increased Engagement

1. For a simultaneous learner with a high listening comprehension and minimal (second-grade) word identification skills, this technique uses his strength in listening and thinking to develop an anticipation of what the text will say, and facilitates word identification.

*2. For a passive learner with adequate listening comprehension skills and minimal word identification skills, the teacher needs to emphasize self-talk when revising miscues.

*3. For an extremely word-bound, successive reader who lacks fluency, this technique uses what the student hears to develop expectations for what words will be in the text.

Using the Technique as a Diagnostic Teaching Lesson   For collaborative reading to be effective, a majority of the following statements must be answered in the affirmative.

Yes   No

_____ _____   1. The student can listen to and remember stories read aloud.

_____ _____   2. The student follows the teacher's model during choral reading.

_____ _____   3. The student reads fluently after hearing the page or pages.

For Further Reading

Dowhower, S. (1987). Effects of repeated reading of second-grade transitional readers' fluency and comprehension. *Reading Research Quarterly, 22,* 389–406.

Rasinski, T. & Padak, N. (1996). *Holistic reading strategies: Teaching children who find reading difficult.* Englewood Cliffs, NJ: Merrill/Prentice Hall.

Contextual Processing

Description   Contextual processing is a technique used to develop new word meanings as they are found in the context of a selected story. This technique shows the student how to use context to figure out what new vocabulary words mean.

Targeted Reading Levels   2–12

Text   Paragraphs three to four sentences long, where the meaning of new vocabulary is apparent from the surrounding context

Predominant Focus of Instruction

1. Processing focus: meaning
2. Instructional phase: before or after reading
3. Response mode emphasized: oral discussion
4. Strategy emphasized: monitoring and elaboration
5. Skill emphasized: word meaning and sentence comprehension
6. Source of information: text-based
7. Type of instruction: explicit
8. Type of cognitive processing: successive

Procedure

1. The teacher selects unfamiliar key vocabulary words to teach.

2. The teacher finds a passage in the text where the meaning of the word is apparent from the surrounding context. If such texts are not available, she creates her own three-sentence paragraph.

3. She writes the paragraph on the overhead or chalkboard.

4. She reads the paragraph aloud to the students.

5. The students reread the paragraph silently.

6. The teacher asks the students about the meaning of the word found in the paragraph, asking, for example, "What does the paragraph tell you about the word . . .?"

7. The teacher uses the students' answers to probe further understanding, asking, "Why did you think that?"

8. The teacher asks students to write down what the new word might mean.

9. The teacher has students think of other similar situations in which they could use the word. She asks, "Who else might be . . .? Where else might you . . .?"

10. The students think of other words with similar meanings.

11. The students record target words and a personal definition in their vocabulary journals.

Modification   The teacher can increase the explicitness of the technique by modeling how to figure out the meaning of the word using the surrounding words in the paragraph. The teacher models step 6 (what the paragraph told her), step 7 (why she thought that), and step 8 (how she came up with the meaning).

Further Diagnostic Applications

Basic View of Reading   Reading is an interactive process in which the readers use what they know about the words in the story to elaborate word meaning.

Patterns of Strengths and Strategies   Contextual processing has students figure out unfamiliar word meanings from the context; therefore, it is most appropriate for students who have facility with sentence meaning but do not use this strategy to figure out what new words mean. This pattern is commonly used by successive learners who have facility with sentence structure but do not combine this technique with what they already know to expand their understanding of word meanings.

Learner Patterns That Produce Increased Engagement

1. For a successive learner who has the ability to use sentences to figure out how to pronounce new words but does not use his sentence knowledge to expand word meanings, this technique starts with his strength and then asks him to use sentence knowledge and background knowledge to elaborate word meaning.

2. For a passive learner who reads the words without actively thinking about what they mean in the new context or other contexts, this technique encourages him to think actively about what words mean. The modification of modeling may be needed.

*3. For a simultaneous learner who does not use the sentence context to figure out word meanings, this technique encourages him to use context as well as what he knows to figure out new word meanings.

Using the Technique as a Diagnostic Teaching Lesson   For contextual processing to be effective, a majority of the following statements must be answered in the affirmative:

Yes   No

____   ____   1. The student can use sentence comprehension to facilitate learning new word meanings.

____   ____   2. The student learns to use information from sentences to define the word easily.

____   ____   3. The student can use words to define new meanings and does not need a direct experience.

For Further Reading

Gipe, J. P. (1995). *Corrective reading techniques for the classroom teacher* (3rd ed.). Scottsdale, AZ: Gorsuch Scarisbrick.

Gunning, T. G. (1998). *Assessing and correcting reading and writing difficulties.* Boston: Allyn & Bacon.

Direct Experience Approach

Description   Direct experience is an approach where actual situations are used to develop word meanings. The actual object is manipulated or the event is enacted in order to develop an understanding of the concept. During the activity, the teacher and students use the new word (label) as they actually experience the concept. This approach associates the word label with the word concept.

Targeted Reading Levels   All levels; necessary for young children

Text   The object or event in a situational context

Predominant Focus of Instruction

1. Processing focus: meaning
2. Instructional phase: before reading
3. Response mode emphasized: oral discussion
4. Strategy emphasized: elaboration
5. Skill emphasized: word meaning
6. Source of information: reader-based
7. Type of instruction: implicit
8. Type of cognitive processing: simultaneous

Procedure

1. The teacher makes a list of target words that are not well developed in the students' meaning vocabularies.

2. She secures the objects that these words represent or plans an excursion where the student would use the words. To develop an understanding of the word *sour,* for example, the teacher brings lemons to the class.

3. The teacher constructs a situation in which to use the object. In the example, the students would taste the lemons.

4. The students use the objects in the situation and describe the experience. In the example, students could describe how the lemons tasted.

5. The students identify other objects that are similar and tell how they are alike and then how they are different. In the example, students could contrast the taste of the lemon with a pickle, a doughnut, and a hamburger.

6. The students identify other objects that are different and tell how they are different and then how they may be alike. In the example, the students would think of other fruits that are sour and those that are not sour.

7. The teacher writes the words on a card or the chalkboard so that meaning can be associated with what the words look like.

Modifications

1. Science experiments use activities to develop a concept and follow the activity with a labeling and recording of the information; therefore, they develop meaning through a direct experience.

2. Simulation of social studies concepts provides an activity in which words describing a concept are used in a socio-interactive context and, therefore, students develop meaning through a direct association between the concept and the label.

Further Diagnostic Applications

Basic View of Reading   Reading is a socio-interactive process in which a conceptual understanding of words is based on generalizations from specific events that the reader has encountered. Therefore, word meanings are based not only on categorical relationships but also on the knowledge of specific events each person has had. Definitions are developed as the student uses language in social situations.

Patterns of Strengths and Strategies   Direct experience is appropriate for students who learn through sensorimotor involvement in their learning. Concrete objects build a store of specific instances for the students to develop definitional language. For these students, the approach matches their underlying preference for developing meaning within the context of situations rather than by verbal descriptions devoid of actions.

Learner Patterns That Produce Increased Engagement

1. For a simultaneous learner who uses past experiences rather than specific definitional knowledge to construct meaning, direct experience shows him how to label his environment.

2. For a kinesthetic learner who needs to touch and feel concrete objects in order to develop word meanings, the direct experience helps him to develop verbal and concept meaning simultaneously.

*3. For a passive learner who uses word labels without understanding the underlying conceptual meaning of the words, direct experience makes the connections between the words he uses and their underlying conceptual meaning.

Using the Technique as a Diagnostic Teaching Lesson For the direct experience approach to be effective, a majority of the following statements must be answered in the affirmative:

Yes   No

_____ _____ 1. The student uses specific examples when defining words.
_____ _____ 2. The student uses *like a* statements rather than definitional language.
_____ _____ 3. The student finds manipulative activities meaningful and not boring.

For Further Reading

May, F. (1994). *Reading as communication: An interactive approach* (4th ed.). Englewood Cliffs, NJ: Merrill/Prentice Hall.

Directed Reading Activity

Description A directed reading activity (DRA) is an instructional format for teaching reading in which the teacher assumes the major instructional role. The teacher develops background knowledge, introduces new words, and gives the students a purpose for reading. Then she directs the discussion with questions to develop reading comprehension. Finally, she reinforces and extends the skills and knowledge developed in the story.

Targeted Reading Levels All levels

Text Graded stories in basal readers or content area textbooks

Predominant Focus of Instruction

1. Processing focus: print and meaning
2. Instructional phase: before and after reading
3. Response mode emphasized: oral discussion
4. Strategy emphasized: elaboration
5. Skill emphasized: word identification and literal comprehension
6. Source of information: text-based
7. Type of instruction: implicit
8. Type of cognitive processing: successive

Procedure

1. The teacher develops readiness for reading:
   a. The teacher presents new vocabulary words in oral and written context. Students are asked what these new words mean and directed to remember the words by their distinctive visual features.

   b. The teacher develops appropriate background knowledge so that students
      will understand the general setting of the story.
   c. The teacher gives the students a purpose for reading by telling them to read
      to find out a particular thing or concept. She develops purposes that require
      students to read the entire story before an answer is resolved.
2. The students read the story silently.
   a. If necessary, the teacher divides the story into sections. After the students read
      a section, the teacher asks a variety of questions emphasizing literal and
      nonliteral story understanding.
   b. The teacher asks the students to support their answers by reading the
      appropriate sections in the text.
3. The teacher reinforces and extends concepts introduced in the story.
   a. Activities to reinforce word recognition and word meanings are used to
      develop independence in reading.
   b. Activities that develop a creative response to the story are assigned.
   c. Activities that require students to relate the story to their own experiences and
      to other stories are used.

Further Diagnostic Applications

Basic View of Reading   Reading requires recognizing words and then associating
meaning with these new words. Initially, therefore, reading is a text-based process.
However, when new words have been learned and purposes have been set, students can read with comprehension.

Patterns of Strengths and Strategies   A directed reading activity is a flexible approach for instructing children to read. Following this format, the text can be narrative or expository, short or long, interrupted or read as a whole. However, it must
be remembered that the directed reading activity is just that, reading directed by the
teacher and not the student. Therefore, it is most appropriate when a substantial
amount of teacher direction is needed in order to construct meaning.

Learner Patterns That Produce Increased Engagement

1. For the active reader who needs new words presented before he reads so that
   word recognition does not interfere with story comprehension, this approach introduces new words to facilitate story comprehension.

2. For the passive reader who needs the teacher to direct his attention to important
   word recognition and comprehension cues, the teacher can begin with this format but should phase as quickly as possible to strategies that require a more active stance from the reader.

Using the Technique as a Diagnostic Teaching Lesson   For the directed reading activity to be effective, a majority of the following statements must be answered in the
affirmative:

Yes   No

____ ____ 1. The student comprehends the story and is fairly active when he reads.

____ ____ 2. The student needs his attention directed to recognizing words in isolation and context.

____ ____ 3. The student is more comfortable answering questions than retelling the story.

For Further Reading

Gunning, T. G. (1998). *Assessing and correcting reading and writing difficulties.* Boston: Allyn & Bacon.

Reutzel, D. R. & Cooter, R. B. (1996). *Teaching children to read: From basals to books* (2d ed.). Englewood Cliffs, N. J.: Merrill/Prentice Hall.

Tierney. R. J., Readence, J. E., & Dishner, E. K. (1995). *Reading strategies and practices: A compendium* (4th ed.). Boston: Allyn & Bacon.

Directed Reading-Thinking Activity

Description   A directed reading-thinking activity (DRTA) is an instructional format for teaching reading that includes predicting what the author will say, reading to confirm or revise those predictions, and elaborating responses. Teachers and students discuss both strategies and responses.

Targeted Reading Levels   All levels

Text   Can be applied to all narrative and expository texts

Predominant Focus of Instruction

1. Processing focus: meaning
2. Instructional phase: during and after reading
3. Response mode emphasized: oral discussion
4. Strategy emphasized: prediction and monitoring
5. Skill emphasized: nonliteral comprehension
6. Source of information: reader-based and text-based
7. Type of instruction: implicit
8. Type of cognitive processing: simultaneous

Procedure

1. The teacher asks the students to predict what will happen in the story by using the title and any available pictures.

2. She continues her questioning by asking the students why they made their predictions.

3. The students read to a turning point in the story.

4. The teacher asks the students whether their predictions were confirmed.

5. The teacher asks the students to support their answers, using the information in the text, and explain their reasoning.

6. The teacher then asks the following questions:

   *What do you think is going to happen next?

   *Why do you think that?

7. The students read to the next turning point in the story.

8. The teacher repeats steps 4, 5, 6, and 7.

9. When they are finished reading, the teacher and the students react to the story as a whole.

10. The teacher leads the students to analyze the story in relation to other stories, personal experiences, and the author's purpose.

11. The teacher discusses the strategies that were used to understand the story.

12. The teacher reviews the meaning of any key vocabulary words.

Further Diagnostic Applications

Basic View of Reading   Reading is an active thinking process in which a reader predicts, confirms, and revises her interpretation, using important textual information. The reflective thought process focuses on not only what was understood about the story but also how it was understood.

Patterns of Strengths and Strategies   A DRTA is appropriate for students who readily engage in constructing meaning as they read. They use what they already know to predict what will happen in the story and then select important information from the text to justify their answers. The teacher matches these active strategies by discussing not only what the students think but also how the students think.

Learner Patterns That Produce Increased Engagement

1. For the active reader who uses what he already knows and the text to construct meaning, a DRTA allows this reader to construct meaning with the guidance of the teacher.

2. For the simultaneous reader who uses what he already knows to understand stories but has difficulty justifying his answers with information from the text, this technique requires the reader to justify his thinking with information from the text.

Using the Technique as a Diagnostic Teaching Lesson   For a directed reading-thinking activity to be effective, a majority of the following statements must be answered in the affirmative:

Yes   No

___   ___   1. The student directs and monitors his own learning when reading.

___   ___   2. The student uses appropriate text-based and reader-based inferences when evaluating predictions.

___   ___   3. The student is more comfortable summarizing the story than answering questions.

For Further Reading

Tierney, R. J., Readence, J. E., & Dishner, E. K. (1995). *Reading strategies and practices: A compendium* (4th ed.). Boston: Allyn & Bacon.

Tompkins, G. E. (1998). *50 literacy strategies: Step by step.* Englewood Cliffs, NJ: Merrill/Prentice Hall.

Echo Reading

Description   Echo reading is a form of modeling oral reading in which the teacher reads a line of a story and the student echoes her model by reading the same line, imitating her intonation and phrasing.

Targeted Reading Levels   1–4

Text   Any text that is well written

Predominant Focus of Instruction

1. Processing focus: print
2. Instructional phase: during reading
3. Response mode emphasized: oral
4. Strategy emphasized: prediction
5. Skill emphasized: fluency
6. Source of information: reader-based
7. Type of instruction: implicit
8. Type of cognitive processing: successive

Procedure

1. The teacher selects a text approximately 200 words long that is near frustration level reading for the student.

2. The teacher reads the first line of the text, accentuating appropriate phrasing and intonation.

3. Immediately, the student reads the same line, modeling the teacher's example.

4. The teacher and the student read in echo fashion for the entire passage, increasing the amount of text when the student can imitate the model.

Modifications

1. Echo reading is an effective intervention with repeated readings (see "Repeated Readings" in this chapter). After the first reading, the teacher and student can echo read those sentences that prompted a string of miscues or errors.

2. Echo reading can also be used in conjunction with chunking (see "Chunking" in this chapter) so the student can hear the way the teacher chunks language into thoughts.

Further Diagnostic Applications

Basic View of Reading   Reading is a reader-based process in which a student matches what he hears with the text. The reader must read fluently to integrate the meaning with the text on the page.

Patterns of Strengths and Strategies   Echo reading is most appropriate for the student who needs the teacher to model fluent oral reading and needs to repeat that model immediately in order to remember how the text sounded.

Learner Patterns That Produce Increased Engagement

1. For an extremely slow reader who needs to hear language read fluently, the teacher reads each sentence in thought units so this reader can read fluently with intonation.

*2. For a passive and successive reader who has become word-bound and lost the flow of language, this technique allows him to hear fluent oral reading and immediately imitate the model.

*3. For a simultaneous learner who has become extremely word-bound by an overemphasis in decoding, echo reading shows him how to use sentence meaning as well as the model to increase oral reading fluency.

*4. For a learner who refuses to follow the teacher when using the impress method or simultaneous reading, echo reading provides a clear model for this student to follow.

Using the Technique as a Diagnostic Teaching Lesson   For echo reading to be effective, both of the following statements must be answered in the affirmative:

Yes   No
_____   _____   1. The student imitates the model of the teacher.
_____   _____   2. The student follows the line of print as the teacher reads the text.

For Further Reading

Cunningham, P. M. & Allington, R. L. (1999). *Classrooms that work: They can all read and write* (2d ed.). New York: Longman.

Tierney, R. J., Readence, J. E., & Dishner, E. K. (1995). *Reading strategies and practices: A compendium* (4th ed.). Boston: Allyn & Bacon.

Experience-Text-Relationship

Description   Experience-text-relationship (ETR) is specifically designed to use children's experiences to teach new concepts and new words in the story. In this technique, the teacher spends time showing students the relationships between what they know and what they are reading, both before and after reading the story. It is specifically designed for use with multicultural students (Au, 1993).

Targeted Reading Levels   All levels

Text   Stories with an interesting theme or plot that can sustain an in-depth discussion

Predominant Focus of Instruction

1. Processing focus: meaning
2. Instructional phase: before and after reading
3. Response mode emphasized: oral discussion
4. Strategy emphasized: elaboration
5. Skill emphasized: nonliteral and literal comprehension
6. Source of information: reader-based phasing to text-based
7. Type of instruction: implicit
8. Type of cognitive processing: simultaneous

Procedure

1. The teacher chooses an appropriate text.

2. The teacher reads the selected passage to decide the theme, topic, and important points.

3. The teacher thinks about what the students know related to the theme, topic, and important points.

4. The teacher formulates general questions that will initiate a discussion about what the students know.

5. The teacher begins the instruction with a general discussion of what the students know. (This step is the *experience phase* of the lesson and is student-initiated.)

6. The teacher uses the information that is generated to tie the students' experiences directly to the story. She uses pictures and information that come directly from the story. (This step is teacher-directed.)

7. She asks the students to make a prediction based on the discussion (student input).

8. Then, if necessary, the teacher sets other purposes for reading (teacher input).

9. The students read a portion of the story to see whether their predictions are right. This activity begins the *text phase* of the lesson.

10. The teacher returns to predictions and asks the students what they have learned so far about these predictions.

11. The teacher sets additional purposes.

12. The teacher calls attention to important information in the text if necessary.

13. The teacher alternates periods of silent reading and discussion until the entire story has been read.

14. When the entire story has been read, the teacher directs a discussion of the key ideas in the story.

15. She then compares the key ideas in the text to the key experiences of the students by returning to the information gained during the experience phase of the lesson. This process is called the *relationship phase* and is teacher-directed.

16. The teacher then contrasts the key ideas in the text with the students' experiences.

17. The teacher summarizes the main relationships after the discussion is complete.

18. Finally, the teacher recommends that the students use the ETR steps when they read on their own.

Further Diagnostic Applications

Basic View of Reading   Reading is an interactive process in which the learners use what they know to interpret what the text says. Readers need assistance learning how to figure out what they know that is useful to interpret the text. They also need assistance in making connections between this information and what the text says.

Patterns of Strengths and Strategies   The ETR technique is appropriate for students who need assistance in bringing their background knowledge to the text. It is especially useful for multicultural students who experience a gap between the way they talk about their experiences and the way an author describes those same experiences. This technique helps these students relate their own language and experiences to the text.

Learner Patterns That Produce Increased Engagement

1. For a passive learner who reads text without relating what he knows, ETR focuses on the student's experience during every step of the lesson.

2. For a passive learner who will not venture a guess while reading, ETR gives him the tools to make a guess.

Using the Technique as a Diagnostic Teaching Lesson   For experience-text-relationship to be effective, a majority of the following statements must be answered in the affirmative:

Yes   No

_____ _____   1. The student can orally express what he knows.

_____ _____   2. The student can make a prediction.

_____ _____   3. With teacher assistance, the student can see the relationship between his experience and what the text says.

For Further Reading

Au, K. (1993). *Literacy instruction in multicultural settings.* New York: Harcourt Brace Jovanovich.

Taylor, B., Harris, L., Pearson, P. D., & Garcia, G. (1995). *Reading difficulties: Instruction and assessment.* New York: McGraw-Hill.

Explicit Teaching

Description   Explicit teaching is a lesson framework that directly instructs a student in the strategies and skills of reading. The lesson framework is based on making the task relevant to the student and directly teaching the task through examples and modeling. The teacher systematically plans activities to increase independent application of the strategy or skill.

Targeted Reading Levels   Depends on the strategy or skill being taught

Text   Text chosen or constructed to teach the targeted task

Predominant Focus of Instruction

1. Processing focus: print or meaning
2. Instructional phase: before and during reading
3. Response mode emphasized: oral discussion
4. Strategy emphasized: monitoring
5. Skill emphasized: depends on task
6. Source of information: depends on task, most often the text
7. Type of instruction: explicit
8. Type of cognitive processing: successive

Procedure

1. The teacher selects the strategy or skill to be taught.

2. The teacher selects a series of texts to illustrate the strategy or skill.

3. The teacher introduces the strategy or skill. For example, she may choose finding the main idea in paragraphs.

4. She explains the reason why learning this strategy or skill will facilitate reading performance. In this example, she may say that finding the main idea is important because it helps us remember facts using one idea rather than many different facts.

5. She asks students how this strategy is like other strategies or skills that they have learned. This approach helps them understand the reasons for learning a particular skill. In this example, she may say, "We already studied how to identify key vocabulary words. How did this help us?" The students and teacher discuss how these words were often what the text was mainly about.

6. The teacher explains the process of the strategy or skill. For example, she may say, "When deciding on a main idea, you think to yourself, 'What does each sentence tell about and how is the information alike?' How the information is alike becomes the main idea."

7. The teacher demonstrates how to think when one uses the strategy or skill. A sample demonstration might include the steps that follow.
   a. The teacher puts a three- or four-sentence paragraph on an overhead or the chalkboard.
   b. She summarizes each sentence aloud.
   c. She tells how each sentence is related to the main idea.
   d. She explains that the way the sentences are alike is what the paragraph is mostly about, or the main idea.

8. The students and the teacher do the next example together. The students talk through the new example, explaining what they are doing, why they are doing it, and how they are doing it. The teacher explains her thinking to clarify any steps in the process.

9. The students do the next example by talking through how they complete the task. Then the students tell how this task will help them read.

10. The teacher provides feedback about what the students say by modeling how she would have completed the task.

11. The students read more paragraphs and use the newly learned task on their own.

Further Diagnostic Applications

Basic View of Reading   Reading is an interactive process in which the reader monitors his reading using both strategies and skills. Reading instruction, therefore, should explicitly teach the student to use reading strategies and skills independently.

Patterns of Strengths and Strategies Introducing the new strategy or skill, the approach systematically leads students through the reasoning process related to the strategy or skill. It takes the separate parts, explains them, and then integrates the parts into the whole task. It is most efficient for the passive or successive learner who profits from seeing how to fit the parts of reading into the whole process.

Learner Patterns That Produce Increased Engagement

1. For a simultaneous learner who needs to be shown how to control his own learning, mediation would be very short.

*2. For a passive learner who does not actively use a particular strategy or skill when reading stories independently, explicit instruction teaches the strategy or skill by showing him how to use it when he is reading.

*3. For a successive learner who needs to be shown exactly how the strategies of reading affect the entire reading process, explicit instruction shows him how the parts fit into the whole.

*4. For an inattentive learner who approaches reading in a trial-and-error fashion and doesn't understand the exact strategies and skills necessary for consistent reading performance, explicit instruction gives him a system for approaching learning.

Using the Technique as a Diagnostic Teaching Lesson For explicit teaching to be effective, a majority of the following statements must be answered in the affirmative:

Yes   No

_____ _____ 1. The student learns from the examples what the process is and how it works.

_____ _____ 2. The student improves his ability to do the strategy or skill.

_____ _____ 3. The student can explain how the process works in new situations.

For Further Reading

Garcia, G. E. & Pearson, P D. (1990). *Modifying reading instruction to maximize its effectiveness for all students* (Technical Report No. 489). Champaign, IL: University of Illinois, Center for the Study of Reading.

Tierney, R. J., Readence, J. E., & Dishner, E. K. (1995). *Reading strategies and practices: A compendium* (4th ed.). Boston: Allyn & Bacon.

Feature Analysis Grid

Description A feature analysis grid is a technique to develop word meanings by graphing the major characteristics of target words. Key words are compared as to how they are alike and how they are different.

Targeted Reading Levels   All levels

Text   Isolated words that are associated in categories

Predominant Focus of Instruction

1. Processing focus: meaning
2. Instructional phase: before and after reading
3. Response mode emphasized: oral discussion
4. Strategy emphasized: elaboration
5. Skill emphasized: word meaning
6. Source of information: reader-based
7. Type of instruction: explicit
8. Type of cognitive processing: successive

Procedure

1. The teacher selects categories and words to analyze.

2. The teacher makes a feature analysis grid with a column of words to analyze.

CATEGORY: LANDSCAPES

New and Known Words	Important Characteristics			
	Trees	Water	Rocks	Snow
Mountains	+	+	+	+

3. The teacher and the students discuss the characteristics of the first word.

4. The teacher adds the characteristics across the top of the grid, indicating the important characteristics with a plus in the respective squares of the grid.

5. The teacher and the students then discuss the second target word.

6. The teacher and the students evaluate this word according to the important features on the grid. The teacher puts a plus on those characteristics that the second target word has and a minus on those that it does not have.

CATEGORY: LANDSCAPES

New and Known Words	Important Characteristics				
	Trees	Water	Rocks	Snow	Sand
Mountains	+	+	+	+	−
Deserts	−	+	−	?	+

7. The teacher adds any new important characteristics, indicating those with a plus in the appropriate square on the grid. The teacher and the students discuss any uncertain responses. In the example, deserts consist mainly of sand, but there are some snow deserts.

8. The teacher and the students discuss how the two words are alike and how they are different.

9. The procedure is repeated for other words. The teacher adds important characteristics as needed.

10. The teacher adds other words that are prevalent in the students' oral vocabularies to make comparisons between what is new and what is already known.

Modifications

1. A rating scale (1–3) can be used to show the relative importance that each characteristic contributes to the meaning of the words.

2. The technique can be used as a prewriting activity for a comparison paragraph among words and concepts.

Further Diagnostic Applications

Basic View of Reading   Reading is an interactive process that is based on what the reader already knows about the words used in the text. Comprehension is facilitated by understanding the specific attributes of the words used in a passage.

Patterns of Strengths and Strategies   The feature analysis grid is most appropriate for students who have a well-developed background of experiences but who overgeneralize word meanings, failing to see the likenesses and differences between specific definitional meanings. For these students, the graphic representation of important characteristics organizes the prior knowledge into specific linguistic categories.

Learner Patterns That Produce Increased Engagement

1. For a successive learner who has difficulty drawing comparisons among word meanings but has verbal fluency and analyzes individual words by their major features, this technique allows him to compare and contrast the major features of words at the same time.

2. For a divergent thinker who notices features other than the major characteristics but easily understands the grid and the relationships among word meanings, this technique focuses his attention on the key features of the words.

*3. For a passive learner who does not think about the differences among words, this technique helps him think and talk about how words are alike and different.

Using the Technique as a Diagnostic Teaching Lesson   For a feature analysis grid to be effective, a majority of the following statements must be answered in the affirmative:

Yes   *No*

___   ___   1. The student understands the purpose of the grid and can visualize the negative and positive aspects of the important characteristics.

___   ___   2. Using the grid, the student develops a clear understanding of the attributes of the target words.

___   ___   3. The student understands likenesses and differences.

For Further Reading

Gunning, T. G. (1998). *Assessing and correcting reading and writing difficulties.* Boston: Allyn & Bacon.

Johns, J. L., & Lenski, S. (1997). *Improving reading: A handbook of strategies* (2d ed.) Dubuque, IA: Kendall/Hunt.

Framed Rhyming Innovations

Description   The framed innovations approach is the rewriting of a predictable book using a structured frame. The teacher and student rewrite the predictable book using the predictable frame but changing key words.

Targeted Reading Levels   K–3

Text   Predictable books

Predominant Focus of Instruction

1. Processing focus: print
2. Instructional phase: after reading
3. Response mode emphasized: writing
4. Strategy emphasized: prediction
5. Skill emphasized: word identification and word analysis
6. Source of information: reader-based and text-based
7. Type of instruction: explicit
8. Type of cognitive processing: simultaneous

Procedure

1. The teacher selects a familiar predictable book that can be easily rewritten and has rhyme. For instance, *I Was Walking Down the Road* by Sarah Barchas can easily be rewritten and has rhyming phrases.

2. The teacher prepares a frame for rewriting the predictable book. For *I Was Walking Down the Road,* she would write

Complete frame

I was walking down the road.

I saw a little toad.

I caught it.

I picked it up.

I put it in the cage.

Frame for innovation

I was walking down the _____.

I saw a little _____.

I caught it.

I picked it up.

I put it in the cage.

3. The teacher and the student read the predictable book.

4. The teacher presents the frame for the innovation.

5. The teacher and student reread the complete frame first.

6. The teacher prompts the student for each blank in the frame. She might say, "What are you going to pick up?" The student suggests a frog and writes the word in the blank. "I saw a little frog."

7. After the student decides what is going to be picked up, then he generates a rhyming word to go with it that makes sense in the first sentence.

frog

dog

log

8. The student rewrites the first line. In this case he thinks of something that fits with "I saw a little frog." The student said, "I was running with my dog." He writes this line below the frame and rewrites the rest of the phrase.

9. This procedure is repeated several times so that the student can make his own book.

10. The student and teacher make a book based on the rewriting of the framed predictable book.

Modification

1. *Reviewing writing for misspellings.* One of the best ways to learn about print is to look at the students' own writing. The teacher and the student look at the story to find those words that are misspelled, and then the teacher helps the student figure out the spelling by using message writing (see "Message Writing" in this chapter).

2. *Reviewing writing for word families.* When the teacher asks the student to generate words that rhyme with a particular word, the teacher can extend these patterns by showing how the spelling pattern is part of longer words. For the *og* sound cluster, these words could be initially suggested: *frog, dog, log, jog, hog.* Then, the teacher shows how these little words are also in longer words such as: *doggy, froggy, logging, hogging, jogger, hotdog, underdog.*

Further Diagnostic Applications

Basic View of Reading   Reading is an interactive process. By using story patterns that rhyme, students have to use their own knowledge about rhymes in words and synthesize sounds to make that rhyme. But they also have to make sure the word fits with the story pattern. This approach will facilitate word analysis and sentence comprehension.

Patterns of Strengths and Strategies   The framed rhyming innovations approach is most appropriate for students who have facility with language and phonemic awareness. If the student uses his own language and sense of phonic analogies, then this approach matches his own way for figuring out words.

Learning Patterns That Produce Increased Engagement

1. For a simultaneous processor who readily thinks of the rhymes in words and sees the analogous relationship among words, this approach uses the strength of seeing patterns to develop print processing.

2. For an extremely creative verbal student who easily thinks of words that will fit the story, this approach increases the knowledge of word patterns and phonic analogies.

Using the Technique as a Diagnostic Teaching Lesson   For the framed innovations approach to be effective, a majority of the following statements must be answered in the affirmative:

Yes   No

____   ____   1. The student can segment sounds.

____   ____   2. The student applies analogies to both known and unknown words.

____   ____   3. The student can easily think of rhyming words that fit in the predictable frame.

For Further Reading

Morrow, L. & Walker, B. (1997). *The reading team: A handbook for volunteer tutors K–3.* Newark, DE: International Reading Association.

Rasinski, T. & Padak, N. (1996). *Holistic reading strategies: Teaching children who find reading difficult.* Englewood Cliffs, NJ: Merrill/Prentice Hall.

Generative-Reciprocal Inference Procedure

Description   The generative-reciprocal inference procedure (GRIP) is an instructional procedure for teaching children how to make inferences in both reading and writing. It involves reading and writing short paragraphs that require making an inference. After the teacher models the inferencing procedure, students, in pairs, write and exchange paragraphs that require an inference.

Targeted Reading Levels   2–8

Text   Constructed by students and teacher

Predominant Focus of Instruction

1. Processing focus: meaning
2. Instructional phase: during reading
3. Response mode emphasized: written
4. Strategy emphasized: prediction and monitoring
5. Skill emphasized: nonliteral comprehension
6. Source of information: reader-based
7. Type of instruction: explicit
8. Type of cognitive processing: successive phasing to simultaneous

Procedure

1. The teacher selects a short paragraph to model how to make an inference.

2. The teacher puts the paragraph on the board or an overhead projector and highlights key words as the paragraph is read aloud. For example,

   Dennis *looked* surprised. *He had not intended it to happen. It was just that getting the* dog food *was difficult because it was* behind the table. *"It was my* new lamp," *said* Mrs. Wilson. *"I just purchased it yesterday."*

   What had Dennis done?

3. The teacher explains that an inference is figuring out the key idea that is not in the text by using the key words that are in the text.

4. The teacher justifies how she figured out the inference by explaining how she used the text clues together with what she knew.

5. The teacher uses several more example paragraphs, letting the students make and justify the inference until they understand the procedure. The suggested sequence is the following:

   a. The teacher marks key words, the students make the inference, and the teacher explains the justification.

   b. The students mark the key words; the teacher makes the inference and explains the reasons.

   c. The students mark the key words and make the inference; the teacher explains the reasons.

   d. The students mark the key words, make the inference, and explain their reasoning.

6. Students write their own inference paragraphs in pairs, starting by creating a list of five or more key words.

7. The students write the paragraph without telling the inference.

8. In groups of four (two pairs), the students exchange paragraphs.

9. The students mark key words, make an inference, and explain their thinking to one another.

10. The students discuss their thinking, giving each other feedback about the inferencing process.

Further Diagnostic Applications

Basic View of Reading   Reading is a socially constructed process in which learners use what they know to interpret what is written in the text. Readers need assistance learning how to identify key words in the text that can be used to predict unstated information and meaning. They also need assistance justifying how the text information and what they know support the inference.

Patterns of Strengths and Strategies   The GRIP technique is appropriate for students who need assistance in identifying key words that can be used in making inferences by using these words and what they already know.

Learner Patterns That Produce Increased Engagement

1. For a passive learner who reads text without figuring out the unstated ideas needed to interpret text, GRIP helps focus how information in the text can suggest ideas not directly stated in the text.

2. For a passive learner who does not identify important textual information to make inferences, GRIP shows him how selecting key information can facilitate thinking.

Using the Technique as a Diagnostic Teaching Lesson   For GRIP to be effective, a majority of the following statements must be answered in the affirmative:

Yes   No

____ ____ 1. The student has facility with written communication.

____ ____ 2. The student can work collaboratively.

____ ____ 3. With teacher assistance, the student can select important information and see how it supports an inference.

For Further Reading

Reutzel, D. R. & Cooter, R. B. (1996). *Teaching children to read: From basals to books* (2d ed.). Englewood Cliffs, NJ: Merrill/Prentice Hall.

Reutzel, D. R. & Hollingsworth, P. M. (1988). Highlighting key vocabulary: A generative-reciprocal procedure for teaching selected inference types. *Reading Research Quarterly, 23,* 358–378.

Graphic Organizers

Description   The graphic organizer technique is designed to provide a visual representation of the main concepts in content area readings. By conceptually arranging the key words in a chapter, the teacher and students develop an idea framework for relating unfamiliar vocabulary words and concepts.

Targeted Reading Levels   3–12

Text   Expository text

Predominant Focus of Instruction

1. Processing focus: meaning
2. Instructional phase: before reading
3. Response mode emphasized: oral discussion with graphic information
4. Strategy emphasized: elaboration
5. Skill emphasized: word meaning and literal comprehension
6. Source of information: text-based
7. Type of instruction: explicit
8. Type of cognitive processing: simultaneous

Procedure

1. The teacher chooses a chapter from a textbook.

2. The teacher selects key vocabulary words and concepts.

3. The teacher arranges the key words into a diagram that shows how the key words interrelate.

4. The teacher adds a few familiar words to the diagram so students can connect their prior knowledge with the new information.

5. The teacher presents the graphic organizer on the chalkboard or an overhead transparency. As she presents the organizer, she explains the relationships.

6. Students are encouraged to explain how they think the information is related.

7. The students read the chapter referring as needed to the graphic organizer.

8. After reading the selection, the students may return to the graphic organizer to clarify and elaborate concepts.

Modifications

1. Students can generate their own graphic organizers after they read the chapter. In this situation, graphic organizers are an implicit instructional technique.

2. Students can work in cooperative learning groups to construct a graphic organizer after they read. This adds a socio-interactive aspect to the technique.

Further Diagnostic Applications

Basic View of Reading   Reading is an active process in which learners use what they know to elaborate and extend what the text says. By constructing a visual map of word relationships, the teacher helps create an idea framework prior to reading the information.

Patterns of Strengths and Strategies   The graphic organizer technique is appropriate for students who profit from a visual framework relating unfamiliar words and ideas to known information. It is especially useful for the highly visual students who profit from seeing relationships in order to tie them to what they are reading.

Learner Patterns That Produce Increased Engagement

1. For a simultaneous reader who thinks in visual images by relating patterns of information, graphic organizers help relate and elaborate topic knowledge.

*2. For a reader who reads without relating what he knows to the text, graphic organizers help him relate what he knows to unfamiliar concepts.

*3. For the passive reader who reads words without defining their meaning or conceptualizing how words relate, graphic organizers help such readers focus on new word meanings and concepts.

Using the Technique as a Diagnostic Teaching Lesson   For graphic organizers to be effective, a majority of the following statements must be answered in the affirmative:

Yes   No

_____ _____   1. The student can easily see the visual pattern.

_____ _____   2. The student refers to the organizer as he reads.

_____ _____   3. The student can organize the information learned.

For Further Reading

McKenna, M. C. & Robinson, R. D. (1993). *Teaching through text: A content literacy approach to content reading.* New York: Longman.

Tierney, R. J., Readence, J. E., & Dishner, E. K. (1995). *Reading strategies and practices: A compendium* (4th ed.). Boston: Allyn & Bacon.

Group Investigation Approach

Description   Group investigation uses cooperative groups to plan and execute extended projects. By focusing their questions, investigations, and responses within the project group, the students use their interests to focus their learning and assist one another in learning the content information.

Targeted Reading Levels   4–12

Predominant Focus of Instruction

1. Processing focus: meaning
2. Instructional phase: before, during, and after reading
3. Response mode emphasized: oral discussion
4. Strategy emphasized: elaboration
5. Skill emphasized: literal and nonliteral comprehension
6. Sources of information: reader-based with some text-based
7. Type of instruction: implicit
8. Type of cognitive processing: simultaneous

Procedure

1. The teacher provides an overview of the topic, framing the topic with various interesting questions (Ex: What can we learn from Native American cultures in Montana?) and suggestions about avenues to explore.

2. The students and teacher scan various information sources: speakers, films, texts, magazines, TV specials, and so on.

3. The students meet in buzz groups to generate what they would like to investigate.

4. The groups compare their lists, eliminating repetitions and finally creating a common list of questions to investigate.

5. This common list is classified into several key categories with subtopics.

6. Research groups are organized around the subtopics. Students join groups according to interest.

7. The groups plan the investigation recording the topic, group members, roles (coordinator, resource persons, recorder, and so on), and the subquestions each member or pair are investigating.

8. The groups clarify the scope of investigation and list possible resources.

9. The groups carry out the investigation by summarizing information and sharing this information in reporting sessions during class work times.

10. The groups prepare a final response, focusing on what is most important to present to the whole class and how to present this information.

11. If needed, the teacher and students prepare summary questions to be used as an evaluation of student learning.

12. Students reflect on what they learned by writing or discussing the important aspects of their learning.

Further Diagnostic Applications

Basic View of Reading   Reading, thinking, and composing are sociointeractive processes in which the social context influences what students view as important and interesting to learn about a topic. Through sharing their investigations in small groups, students focus and elaborate their understanding of a subject area.

Patterns of Strengths and Strategies   The group investigation approach is appropriate for students who can discuss their ideas in a group, which encourages them to seek more information to clarify uncertainties, thus giving them more control over their learning. The conversations help these students connect new learning to their experiences.

Learner Patterns That Produce Increased Engagement

1. For a self-directed reader who profits from sharing his ideas in a group, group investigation helps this student clarify and elaborate his ideas.

2. For a reader who profits from pursuing individual interests but also needs a group to focus personal interests as well as to complete ideas, group investigation uses interests and group interaction to encourage elaboration.

3. For a reader who tends to focus on irrelevant textual information and narrow personal experiences, group investigation helps these students focus on important information and to verbalize important ideas in a group.

Using the Technique as a Diagnostic Teaching Lesson   For group investigation to be effective, a majority of the following statements must be answered in the affirmative:

Yes   No

_____   _____   1. The student can share information in a group.

_____   _____   2. The student likes expository text so that he finds it engaging enough to pursue answers to questions.

_____   _____   3. The student can generate questions to investigate.

For Further Reading
Ruddell, M. R. (1997). *Teaching content reading and writing* (2d ed.) Boston: Allyn & Bacon.
Sharan, S. & Schacher, H. (1988). *Language and learning in the cooperative classroom.*
   New York: Springer Publishing Co.

Herringbone Technique

Description   The herringbone technique develops comprehension of the main idea by plotting the *who, what, when, where, how,* and *why* questions on a visual diagram of a fish skeleton. Using the answers to the *wh* questions, the student writes the main idea across the backbone of the fish diagram.

Targeted Reading Levels   5–12

Text   Particularly suited for expository text; can be used for narrative text

Predominant Focus of Instruction

1. Processing focus: meaning
2. Instructional phase: during and after reading
3. Response mode emphasized: written response and oral discussion
4. Strategy emphasized: elaboration
5. Skill emphasized: literal comprehension
6. Source of information: text-based
7. Type of instruction: implicit with some explicit
8. Type of cognitive processing: successive, but is written in a visual display (simultaneous)

Procedure

1. The teacher selects a text at the appropriate reading level.

2. The teacher constructs a visual diagram of the herringbone.

3. The teacher tells the student to record the answers to the questions on the diagram (see Figure 11–1).
   a. Who is the author talking about?
   b. What did they do?
   c. When did they do it?
   d. Where did they do it?
   e. How did they do it?
   f. Why did they do it?

4. The student reads to find the answers and records the answers on the diagram.

5. After the information is recorded, the teacher shows the student how each answer fits into a slot in a main idea sentence.

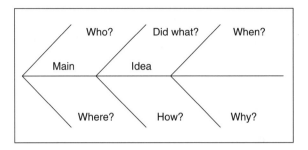

Figure 11–1   *Herringbone Technique*

Note: From *Reading Strategies and Practices: A Compendium* (3rd ed.) by Robert J. Tierney, John E. Readence, and Ernest K. Dishner, 1990, Boston: Allyn & Bacon, Copyright 1990 by Allyn & Bacon, Inc. Reprinted with permission.

6. The student writes a main idea, using the information from the herringbone diagram.

7. The teacher duplicates sheets with the herringbone diagram, and students complete the diagram on their own.

8. The diagram becomes a tool for discussion of readings. During the discussion, the teacher and students compare their answers and their rationales.

Modification   The implementation of the herringbone can be changed from finding the facts first to writing the main idea and then looking for the facts that support this main idea.

Further Diagnostic Applications

Basic View of Reading   Reading is a text-based process in which the reader uses the facts in the text to construct a main idea.

Patterns of Strengths and Strategies   The herringbone technique is most appropriate for students who need a visual structure to draw relationships between the facts in a text and the main idea. For these students, the technique records the information so that it can be organized into a whole.

Learner Patterns That Produce Increased Engagement

1. For a successive learner who has difficulty organizing factual information to form a main idea, this technique shows him how the facts fit together to form the main idea.

2. For a passive learner who has difficulty identifying the important facts that are used to form a main idea, this technique helps him identify important information.

*3. For a simultaneous learner who has difficulty identifying the factual information that he used to construct a main idea, this technique can be modified so that first the student writes the main idea and then rereads the text to find the facts that support the main idea.

Using the Technique as a Diagnostic Teaching Lesson For the herringbone technique to be effective, a majority of the following statements must be answered in the affirmative:

Yes   No

_____ _____ 1. The student can find the facts in the text and record them on the diagram.

_____ _____ 2. The student can construct a main idea from the facts.

_____ _____ 3. The student is more active in a group discussion after using the herringbone diagram.

For Further Reading

Rasinski, T. & Padak, N. (1996). *Holistic reading strategies: Teaching children who find reading difficult.* Englewood Cliffs, NJ: Merrill/Prentice Hall.

Tierney, R. J., Readence, J. E., & Dishner, E. K. (1995). *Reading strategies and practices: A compendium* (4th ed.). Boston: Allyn & Bacon.

Imagery Instruction

Description Imagery instruction uses sensory images related to the story line to increase active comprehension and activate background knowledge about (a) situations and characters in a story or (b) key concepts in expository text.

Targeted Reading Levels K–Adult

Text Narrative text or concepts in expository text

Predominant Focus of Instruction

1. Processing focus: meaning
2. Instructional phase: before reading
3. Response mode emphasized: oral discussion
4. Strategy emphasized: prediction and monitoring
5. Skill emphasized: nonliteral comprehension
6. Source of information: reader-based
7. Type of instruction: implicit (can be adapted to explicit)
8. Type of cognitive processing: simultaneous

Procedure

1. The teacher selects a text.

2. The teacher identifies key events and characters or key concepts, depending on the type of text.

3. The teacher writes a guided journey that uses these key items. In the journey, the teacher intersperses calming statements with the story events and character descriptions or the key concepts. The following is an example that might be used prior to reading:

   "Close your eyes . . . and relax in your chair . . . Now listen to the noises in the room . . . Can you hear them? Feel the temperature of the room . . . Now turn the noises of this room into the sounds of a meadow . . . What kind of day is it? You can hear a river . . . Begin walking toward the river. . . . You are closer . . . closer . . . closer to the river . . . As you reach the river . . . you see a boat. . . . Walk toward the boat. . . . Notice the water as it rushes around the boat. . . . You get in the boat and begin to float . . . down . . . down . . . down the river you float. . . . The current or waves begin to rush faster . . . faster . . . faster . . . You see rocks and boulders ahead. . . . You are steering the boat through the rapids. . . . I will leave you now . . . When you have finished your journey . . . you may return to this room . . . and open your eyes."

4. For narrative text, the teacher uses the key events to develop the guided imagery, but she leaves the problem in the story unresolved. The students are to finish the story in their minds.

5. For expository text, the teacher develops a guided imagery that illustrates the attributes of the key concepts.

6. To begin the lesson, the teacher has the students relax in their chairs and think of sounds and smells relating to the setting. Then she reads the prompt or the journey in a calm, serene voice, interspersing action statements with calming statements.

7. The teacher tells the students to return to the classroom when they have completed their journeys in the mind.

8. The students can share their images with a partner.

9. Students read the selection to compare their journeys with the text.

Modifications

1. The teacher uses imagery prompts such as "When you read this story, I want you to make pictures or scenes about the story."

2. The guided imagery can form the basis for a dictated language experience story. The teacher uses targeted sight words to compose the guided imagery (see "Language Experience Approach").

3. In narrative text, the use of images facilitates comprehension by activating what students already know (images) so they can use this information to understand how the author resolved the problem.

4. In expository text, the use of images helps students remember the key concepts in the text so they can elaborate or compare those images with the text as they read.

Further Diagnostic Applications

Basic View of Reading Reading is an active process that uses personal images (reader-based inferencing) to create meaning. As the student reads, he forms an expectation for meaning that is represented by images of specific events. The student refines his model of meaning (basically images) when he reads.

Patterns of Strengths and Strategies Imagery instruction is a technique for students who prefer to create images while they read. It is appropriate for the reflective, simultaneous thinker who refers to specific events and images when discussing text. Using guided imagery helps this learner translate images into a verbal response.

Learner Patterns That Produce Increased Engagement

1. For the simultaneous thinker who uses images to construct meaning that often results in changing the story line to fit his model of meaning, this technique helps him see how his own ideas and images affect his comprehension.

2. For an extremely imaginative thinker who enjoys sharing his images and comparing them to the text, this technique allows him to use this strength when comprehending.

3. For a simultaneous reflective thinker who uses images instead of words when thinking, this technique allows images to be connected with words.

*4. For the passive reader who does not check what he knows while he reads, learning to image can increase his elaboration and monitoring of what he is reading.

*5. For the extremely literal thinker who seldom constructs images, imagery instruction provides a support for him to construct images before reading, thus increasing his understanding.

Using the Technique as a Diagnostic Teaching Lesson For imagery instruction to be effective, a majority of the following statements must be answered in the affirmative:

Yes	No	
____	____	1. The student constructs a coherent and logical ending to the guided journey.
____	____	2. The student reads with increased involvement, comparing his images with the text.
____	____	3. The student does not overly rely on the images and make the text fit his predictions.

For Further Reading

Gambrell, L. B. & Jawitz, P. B. (1993). Mental imagery, text illustrations, and children's story comprehension and recall. *Reading Research Quarterly, 28,* 264–276.

McNeil, J. D. (1992). *Reading comprehension: New directions for classroom practice* (3rd ed.). New York: HarperCollins.

Implicit Teaching

Description   Implicit teaching is a nondirective approach to instruction in which the teacher creates an instructional environment that stimulates thinking about specific reading tasks. The teacher participates only as a cognitive inquirer, asking the student, "How did you know that?" The student makes generalizations because he is immersed in a literate environment.

Target Reading Levels   All levels

Text   Authentic texts selected to demonstrate the strategy or skill that is targeted for instruction

Predominant Focus of Instruction

1. Processing focus: print or meaning
2. Instructional phase: after reading
3. Response mode emphasized: oral discussion
4. Strategy emphasized: elaboration
5. Skill emphasized: depends on child, environment, and scaffolds (prompts)
6. Source of information: reader-based phasing to text-based
7. Type of instruction: implicit
8. Type of cognitive processing: depends on child and task

Procedure

1. The teacher decides on the targeted learning outcome.

2. The teacher strategically arranges the physical environment so that students can discuss with the teacher what they read in a relaxed atmosphere.

3. In prominent places in the room, the teacher arranges attractive books or printed materials that incorporate the strategy or skill.

4. The teacher creates a social activity that causes the students to use the targeted strategy or skill in a meaningful way.

5. When the students use print to make sense of their environment, the teacher asks, "How did you know that?"

6. The teacher creates the expectation of the learning outcome by discussing the learning outcome informally. She says, "Did you notice . . .?"

7. When appropriate, the teacher demonstrates reading the text for meaning and enjoyment. She says, "When I read that I thought . . ."

8. The teacher creates a similar experience that causes the students again to use the targeted strategy or skill in a meaningful way.

Comment: Implicit instruction is an instructional format in which the teacher assumes an indirect role in mediating learning. This type of instruction is associated with a whole language environment in which the children are more actively involved in directing their own learning. Techniques fall along a continuum, ranging from *less teacher intervention* to *more teacher intervention*. Implicit instruction has less teacher intervention and more student participation in the learning activity.

Further Diagnostic Applications

Basic View of Reading   Reading is a socio-interactive process in which the reader uses what he knows to make sense of his environment. Reading instruction, therefore, should consist of creating a literate environment in which a child can use and discuss print to make sense of his environment.

Patterns of Strengths and Strategies   This format engages students in literate activities in which they construct meaning with text. The teacher asks a student what he did to make sense of his environment. The student who actively restructures his environment so that it makes sense learns easily through this method.

Learner Patterns That Produce Increased Engagement

1. For an active learner who needs learning activities to make sense, this method allows him to use his thinking strategies in natural learning environments.

2. For an active learner who prefers to learn without teacher direction, this method allows him to direct his own learning.

3. For a simultaneous learner who needs to experience the whole before understanding the parts, this method allows him to use the socio-interactive experience to understand the parts of reading.

Using the Technique as a Diagnostic Teaching Lesson   For implicit teaching to be effective, both of the following statements must be answered in the affirmative:

Yes   No

_____ _____   1. The student actively explores the context to make sense of his reading.

_____ _____   2. The student can explain his reasons for the way language works.

For Further Reading

Short, K. G., Harste, J. C., & Burke, C. (1996). *Creating classrooms for authors and inquirers*. Portsmouth, NH: Heinemann.

Impress Method

Description   The impress method uses unison oral reading between the teacher and the student. The teacher and student sit side by side, with the teacher reading out loud slightly louder and ahead of the student, modeling fluent and expressive oral reading.

Targeted Reading Levels   K–5

Text   Self-selected text is recommended

Predominant Focus of Instruction

1. Processing focus: print
2. Instructional phase: during reading
3. Response mode emphasized: oral production
4. Strategy emphasized: prediction
5. Skill emphasized: fluency and word identification
6. Source of information: reader-based
7. Type of instruction: implicit
8. Type of cognitive processing: simultaneous

Procedure

1. The student and the teacher select a text that is near the student's frustration-level reading and about 200 words long.

2. The teacher and the student read the text in unison. The teacher reads slightly ahead of, and slightly louder than, the student.

3. The teacher sits on the right side of the student and reads with the student.

4. The teacher moves her finger along the line of print so that the student's eyes can follow the reading.

5. The student's eyes follow the line of print as he reads.

6. As the student gains success through understanding the context, the teacher gradually lets him take the lead.

7. At this time, the teacher releases her lead in reading; however, she supplies difficult words when needed.

Modifications

1. Unison choral reading can be used with a group of students.

2. The textual characteristics seem to influence the effectiveness of impress reading. Rhythmic and repetitive texts seem to increase the student's participation. A good source is Shel Silverstein's *Where the Sidewalk Ends*.

Further Diagnostic Applications

Basic View of Reading   Reading is a process of accurate word identification in which automatic word identification precedes understanding. Therefore, reading is a text-based process. An abundance of reading errors contributes to an incorrect visual form being imprinted in memory. Therefore, accurate word identification is increased by unison reading, with the teacher modeling fluent oral reading.

Patterns of Strengths and Strategies   The impress method is most appropriate for students who make a series of miscues without using passage meaning to self-correct the miscues, which is often the result of reading at frustration level for an extended period of time. In the impress method, the student follows the teacher's model and imitates her fluent, accurate oral reading.

Learner Patterns That Produce Increased Engagement

1. For a simultaneous learner who relies heavily on background knowledge when reading orally and who does not attend to the graphic cues, the impress method establishes accurate identification of words through use of the overall textual meaning.

2. For a nonfluent reader who is word-bound because of a heavy emphasis on phonic instruction, this method can rapidly increase oral reading fluency by providing a model of fluent reading.

*3. For a nonreader who has not established a sight vocabulary, this technique can develop the student's sight vocabulary, particularly when high-interest material is used.

Using the Technique as a Diagnostic Teaching Lesson   For the impress method to be effective, a majority of the following statements must be answered in the affirmative:

Yes   No

_____ _____   1. The student is sufficiently motivated to read along with the teacher.

_____ _____   2. The student begins to track with the teacher and follows the model.

_____ _____   3. An increase in sight word accuracy is a result of using the method.

For Further Reading

Rasinski, T. & Padak, N. (1996). *Holistic reading strategies: Teaching children who find reading difficult.* Englewood Cliffs, NJ: Merrill/Prentice Hall.

McCormick, S. (1995). *Instructing students who have literacy problems.* Englewood Cliffs, NJ: Merrill/Prentice Hall.

Journal Writing

Description   Journal writing is a written response from students of their understanding and exploration of ideas related to reading or a particular unit of study. In notebooks, students write about their reactions to new information, ask questions, elaborate new understandings, and so on. The teacher responds to these ideas with questions, comments, and personal reactions. Through multiple journal entries, the students and the teacher carry on a written conversation.

Targeted Reading Levels   All levels

Text   Self-generated written responses

Predominant Focus of Instruction

1. Processing focus: meaning
2. Instructional phase: after reading
3. Response mode emphasized: written discourse
4. Strategy emphasized: elaboration
5. Skill emphasized: nonliteral comprehension
6. Source of information: reader-based
7. Type of instruction: implicit
8. Type of cognitive processing: simultaneous

Procedures

1. The teacher secures writing notebooks. She can use bound composition notebooks, student-made books of stapled pages, or loose-leaf notebooks.

2. The teacher explains that a journal is a written explanation of the student's thinking about a topic. It is like writing a letter to the teacher about the topic.

3. She tells the students she will comment personally on what is written.

4. The teacher shows the students an example from a journal. (The teacher first secures permission from the writer.)

5. She tells the students that they are to write about the focus topic.

6. The teacher designates a time for writing and then sets the timer.

7. The students and teacher write in their journals.

8. The teacher reads what the students write.

9. The teacher responds with questions or comments that encourage elaboration of the topic.

10. The students read the teacher's comments.

11. The students write a response or elaborate new information.

12. The writing cycle continues.

Modifications

Many modifications can be made in the focus of journal writing. Some common ones are described in the following list:

1. Dialogue journals are a personal communication between the teacher and the student. It has no designated topic, but rather is a personal exchange, like writing a letter to a friend. With it, students write important things about their life to their teacher. Although this kind of dialogue journal is more effective for some students than others, it is recommended as part of the diagnostic teaching session because it releases the structured format of directed and guided instruction.

2. Learning logs are specific journals about a unit of study. The teacher comments are to focus the students on aspects of their study, such as selecting and narrowing a topic, gathering information, organizing the information, elaborating and integrating concepts as well as evaluating the information learned.

3. In double-entry journals, notebook pages are divided in half. On the left-hand page, the student makes notes, diagrams, clusters, and observations while on the right-hand page, the student integrates this information into a coherent understanding.

Further Diagnostic Applications

Basic View of Reading   Reading is an active, reader-based process in which readers' personal understanding focuses thinking. Both reading and writing are constructive processes that are influenced by the desire to communicate ideas.

Patterns of Strengths and Strategies   Journal writing is most appropriate for simultaneous, high imagery students who enjoy communicating ideas through writing rather than talking. In this technique, ideas and understandings are communicated without an oral explanation or eye contact.

Learner Patterns That Produce Increased Engagement

1. For a simultaneous learner who needs time to express his ideas in words, writing allows him to think through ideas without noticeably lengthy pauses.

2. For a visually orientated reader who prefers to communicate his ideas through writing rather than talking, journal writing allows him to put his thoughts into words without talking.

*3. For a passive reader who does not realize that reading and writing are constructive processes, this technique allows him to experience reading and writing as communicating learning.

*4. For a text-bound reader who does not use his personal understanding of the world to interpret information, journals show him how a writer uses personal understanding to compose text.

Using the Technique as a Diagnostic Lesson   For journal writing to be effective, a majority of the following statements must be answered in the affirmative:

Yes   No
____ ____   1. The student can write (produce letters) fairly easily.
____ ____   2. The student likes to communicate his ideas in writing.
____ ____   3. The student uses the teacher's model to correct his own writing errors.

For Further Reading
Short, K. G., Harste, J. C., & Burke, C. (1996). *Creating classrooms for authors and inquirers.* Portsmouth, NH: Heinemann.
Ruddell, M. R. (1997). *Teaching content reading and writing* (2d ed.). Boston: Allyn & Bacon.

K-W-L

Description   K-W-L is a technique used to direct students' reading and learning of content area text. Before the text is read, students write what they already know about the topic as well as questions that they would like to explore. After the text is read, students write what they learned about the topic.

Targeted Reading Levels   3–12

Text   Especially suited for expository text, but can be applied to all text

Predominant Focus of Instruction

1. Processing focus: meaning
2. Instructional phase: before and after reading
3. Response mode emphasized: written with some discussion
4. Strategy emphasized: prediction and elaboration
5. Skill emphasized: literal and nonliteral comprehension
6. Source of information: reader-based phasing to text-based
7. Type of instruction: implicit
8. Type of cognitive processing: simultaneous

Procedure

1. The teacher chooses an appropriate topic and text.

2. The teacher introduces the K-W-L worksheet (see Figure 11–2).

3. The students brainstorm ideas about the topic.

4. The teacher writes this information on a chart or chalkboard.

5. Students write what they know under the K ("What I Know") column.

6. Together, the teacher and students categorize the K column.

7. Students generate questions they would like answered about the topic and write them in the W ("What I Want to Learn") column.

8. Students silently read the text and add new questions to the W column.

9. After reading the selection, the students complete the L ("What I Learned Section").

10. The students and teacher review the K-W-L sheet to tie together what students knew and the questions they had with what they learned.

Modifications

1. The K-W-L Plus technique extends the after-reading phase to include organizing the learned information through mapping (a graphic outline) and then writing a summary.

What I Know	What I Want to Learn	What I Learned

Figure 11–2 *K-W-L Technique*

Note: Adapted from "K-W-L: A Teaching Model That Develops Active Reading of Expository Text" by Donna Ogle, 1986, *The Reading Teacher, 39,* pp. 564–570. Copyright 1986 by International Reading Association. Adapted by permission.

2. The information known and learned can be combined to form a book about the topic.

3. The technique can be modified to include a column for students to discuss "How" they learned new information.

Further Diagnostic Applications

Basic View of Reading   Reading is a socio-interactive process in which learners share what they know to elaborate and extend what the text says. Readers need experience relating what they know, the questions they have, and what they have learned from text in order to actively construct meaning.

Patterns of Strengths and Strategies   The K-W-L technique is appropriate for students who need to talk and write about the topic prior to reading. It is especially useful for students who need to see concretely what they know in order to tie it to what they are reading.

Learner Patterns That Produce Increased Engagement

1. For a self-directed reader who does not readily elaborate what he learns as he reads, K-W-L helps this student expand and elaborate topic knowledge.

*2. For a reader who reads without relating what he knows to the text, K-W-L helps tie together what he knows and the text.

*3. For a passive reader who needs to see what he has learned in relation to what he knows, the K-W-L helps him assess the understanding he has developed through reading.

Using the Technique as a Diagnostic Teaching Lesson
For K-W-L to be effective, a majority of the following statements must be answered in the affirmative:

Yes   No
_____ _____   1. The student easily writes what he knows.
_____ _____   2. The student develops at least one question that he wants
                  answered.
_____ _____   3. The student can organize the information learned.

For Further Reading
Johns, J. L., & Lenski, S. (1997). *Improving reading: A handbook of strategies* (2d ed.) Dubuque, IA: Kendall/Hunt.
Ogle, D. (1989). The know, want to know, learn strategy. In K. D. Muth (ed.), *Children's comprehension of text* (pp. 205–223). Newark, DE: International Reading Association.

Language Experience Approach

Description   The language experience approach (LEA) is a technique used for beginning reading instruction in which the child dictates a story to the teacher. The story becomes the text for instruction and a collection of the stories becomes the child's first reader.

Targeted Reading Levels   K–3

Text   The child's own language

Predominant Focus of Instruction

1. Processing focus: print
2. Instructional phase: before and during reading
3. Response mode emphasized: oral discussion
4. Strategy emphasized: prediction and monitoring
5. Skill emphasized: word identification
6. Source of information: reader-based
7. Type of instruction: implicit
8. Type of cognitive processing: simultaneous

Procedure

1. The teacher engages students in dialogue about a particular topic. A stimulating, engaging, and concrete topic tends to elicit more language from the students.

2. The students dictate a story while the teacher serves as secretary for the class.

3. Using leading questions, the teacher guides the students to develop a story line by using questions such as these: "What happened next? Is this what you wanted to say? How can you make a story using this information?"

4. The students and the teacher read the story simultaneously to revise any statements or phrases that are unclear to the students. The story is to follow the natural language patterns of the students.

5. Then the teacher and the students read the story *repeatedly* because repetition of the entire story will encourage a predictive set for the story.

6. The students are asked to read the story independently.

7. Activities to reinforce word identification are constructed from the story.

8. Chunk cards are developed using the words in the story. These cards are made by dividing the entire story into meaningful phrases, which are written on cards.

9. Initially, these chunk cards are flashed in the order in which they appear in the story. Later, they are mixed up. This activity maintains the sense of the whole while the whole is being broken into parts.

10. Stories are collated into anthologies that create the initial reading material for the student.

11. As words are repeatedly read in context, the teacher checks them off a word list, but does not assess this knowledge in isolation.

Modification   The teacher can design a guided imagery journey that incorporates targeted sight words. For instance, if the targeted sight words are *balloon, climb, sky,* and *wind,* the journey might contain the events that follow.

> *Close your eyes and imagine that you are walking on a narrow pathway. . . . The wind is blowing gently as you walk softly down the path. . . . You come to an open meadow, and you see a hot-air balloon. . . . A wise teacher offers to take you for a ride in the sky. . . . You climb into the basket. . . . You soar up . . . up . . . up . . . in the sky. I will leave you now. . . . You can finish the journey in your mind. . . . When you have finished your journey . . . you may return to the classroom and open your eyes.*

Then follow these steps:

1. When all the students have opened their eyes, they share their journeys in pairs. This activity allows them to verbalize the images.

2. The students dictate the journey while the teacher serves as secretary for the class (or individual student).

3. The students are reminded that the stories represent what happened in their imaginations. Their stories represent their images, just like a published story represents an author's images.

Further Diagnostic Applications

Basic View of Reading   Reading is an active, reader-based process. By reading his own story, the student will infer the consistency of printed language patterns. Because the story is based on his own experience, he continually uses this experience to remember the words in the story.

Patterns of Strengths and Strategies   Language experience is most appropriate for students who have facility with language and are simultaneous, reader-based thinkers. If a student predicts from his own experiences rather than the words in the text, then language experience matches his strategies (using what he knows); therefore, this technique facilitates word learning by asking the student to identify words using his own experiences.

Learner Patterns That Produce Increased Engagement

1. For a simultaneous thinker who uses prior knowledge to construct meaning, often resulting in overpredicting or guessing without identifying words by how they are written, LEA uses the student's strength (using prior knowledge) to facilitate word identification.

2. For an extremely verbal, creative student whose verbalization interferes with the mundane task of looking at words, LEA uses the strength (verbalization) to facilitate word identification.

3. For a student who is unwilling to take a guess unless he is certain the response will be correct, LEA provides a text that allows the student to make a safe guess, using both what is on the page and what he remembers was written.

4. For a learner who has had an overemphasis on phonics, language experience can increase his fluency and the predictive set.

Modifications

1. The extremely imaginative, creative learner can use guided imagery as a medium for creating stories.

2. The extremely concrete learner can use field trips and science activities as a medium for creating stories.

3. The student who deals most effectively in visual-spatial relationships can use mapping (see Modifications in "Vocabulary Mapping") as a medium for developing a story.

4. The learner who has difficulty developing a coherent story can use wordless picture books to boost his confidence in developing a story.

Using the Technique as a Diagnostic Teaching Lesson For LEA to be effective, a majority of the following statements must be answered in the affirmative:

Yes *No*

_____ _____ 1. The student can remember the story he told.

_____ _____ 2. The student tells a fairly coherent story.

_____ _____ 3. The student remembers the story well enough to predict the words she does not remember.

_____ _____ 4. The student responds correctly when prompted, using the preceding context and story theme.

For Further Reading

Stauffer, R. G. (1970). *The language experience approach to the teaching of reading.* New York: Harper & Row.

Tompkins, G. E. (1998). *50 literacy strategies: Step by step.* Englewood Cliffs, NJ: Merrill/Prentice Hall.

Listening-Thinking Activity

Description A listening-thinking activity (LTA) is an instructional format for developing predictive listening and comprehension. It involves predicting what will happen, talking about what happened, and talking about how you know what is happening.

As the teacher reads aloud, she communicates the message by adding intonation and gestures to facilitate understanding.

Targeted Reading Levels   All levels

Text   An interesting, well-written text; picture storybooks are excellent

Predominant Focus of Instruction

1. Processing focus: meaning
2. Instructional phase: before and during reading
3. Response mode emphasized: oral discussion
4. Strategy emphasized: prediction and monitoring
5. Skill emphasized: listening comprehension
6. Source of information: reader-based
7. Type of instruction: implicit
8. Type of cognitive processing: simultaneous

Procedure

1. Using the title of the story, the teacher has the students brainstorm what the story might be about.

2. She reads to a turning point.

3. She asks the students to talk about what they are thinking, using "I wonder" statements. The teacher can also demonstrate her thinking.

4. The teacher asks the students to tell what has happened so far to make them curious. The teacher adds her own interpretation.

5. The teacher and the students review previous predictions. Then they decide whether they still want to keep all the predictions.

6. The students revise predictions or make new predictions.

7. The teacher alternates reading and discussing until the end of the story.

8. The teacher uses nonverbal cues from the students (such as their facial expressions and attentiveness) to check their understanding. When students are confused, the teacher stops to discuss the story line and how they arrived at their interpretations.

9. The teacher and the students discuss the story as a whole, relating various interpretations.

Modification   The teacher can demonstrate predicting using the first several stopping points. She uses the following steps:

1. The teacher models her questions about what is happening thus far in the story: "I wonder why the author said . . .?"

2. The teacher summarizes what she has read so far, relating it to the *I wonder* statements.

3. From the summary, she develops a prediction or bet. She says, "Oh, I know, I bet . . ."

Further Diagnostic Applications

Basic View of Reading   Reading is a socio-interactive process in which the student thinks about what he reads, using what he knows and the text. Then he shares his predictions and thinking with class members. Listening is also an active process in which the student interprets the story as he listens. In a listening activity, the interpersonal communication occurs during reading when the teacher can use nonverbal cues such as gestures and intonation to convey the author's message.

Patterns of Strengths and Strategies   A listening-thinking activity is appropriate for developing readers who need the added input of social interaction to learn either the strategy of predicting or monitoring comprehension. This technique allows the teacher to demonstrate these active reasoning strategies and to check students' understanding.

Learner Patterns That Produce Increased Engagement

1. For a passive reader who likes group work and needs to learn how to make predictions, LTA provides a short lesson in which the student can be involved in making predictions and discussing his thinking.

2. For a passive reader who needs to check his understanding, LTA provides a short lesson in which the teacher can demonstrate comprehension monitoring.

*3. For the student with a severe reading disability, this technique allows the student to practice active thinking strategies without having to read the words. LTA leads the student to more active thinking strategies that he can use when he can read the words.

*4. For a simultaneous reader who needs to experience the steps of active thinking to clarify his thinking, LTA provides such an opportunity.

Using the Technique as a Diagnostic Teaching Lesson   For LTA to be effective, a majority of the following statements must be answered in the affirmative:

Yes	No	
_____	_____	1. The student listens to stories and can remember what was read.
_____	_____	2. The student can construct an oral response after listening.
_____	_____	3. The student likes listening to stories that are read orally.

For Further Reading

Gillet, J. W. & Temple, C. (1994). *Understanding reading problems* (4th ed.). Boston: Little, Brown.

Literature Circles

Description   Literature circles are used to develop personal responses to literature by having students share their interpretations in a discussion group. By talking about the literature, students integrate the author's ideas and concepts with their own.

Targeted Reading Levels   K–12

Text   Authentic children's literature

Predominant Focus of Instruction

1. Processing focus: meaning
2. Instructional phase: after reading
3. Response mode emphasized: oral discussion
4. Strategy emphasized: elaboration
5. Skill emphasized: nonliteral comprehension
6. Source of information: reader-based phasing into text-based
7. Type of instruction: implicit
8. Type of cognitive processing: simultaneous

Procedure

1. The teacher introduces several books by giving short summaries or book talks.

2. The students choose a book to read over the next two days or week.

3. After the books are read, the students reading the same book gather into a literature circle.

4. The discussion is open-ended, with the teacher beginning with an invitation such as "Tell me about this book" or "What was your favorite part?"

5. At the end of the discussion time, the group decides what they will talk about the next day.

6. As the students become familiar with this format, the teacher becomes less involved in the discussion and lets the students take the lead.

7. The teacher's role in discussion includes these activities:
   a. Listening closely and focusing on students' ideas
   b. Supporting thinking and reflection by saying "Let's think more about that"
   c. Keeping the discussion focused on a theme
   d. Pointing out literary elements (characters, setting, and so on) and strategies (using background knowledge) and encouraging students to discuss them

8. At the conclusion of the discussion, group members can present their interpretation to the class as a "book talk."

Modifications

1. To add a writing component, students can keep a literature log (see "Journal Writing" in this chapter) so they can more easily share their ideas.

2. For some groups, the teacher may continue in the literature circle as a group member.

Further Diagnostic Applications

Basic View of Reading   Reading is a socio-interactive process in which the social context affects individual interpretation of text. Through sharing ideas in a peer group, students define and elaborate their ideas.

Patterns of Strengths and Strategy   The literature circle technique is appropriate for students who can discuss their ideas freely in a group. The dialogue helps these students elaborate their understanding of literature and connect that understanding to their experiences.

Learner Patterns That Produce Increased Engagement

1. For a self-directed reader who profits from sharing his ideas in a group, literature circles help this student verify and create interpretations.

2. For a self-directed reader who likes to share personal feelings about text but needs time to reflect on ideas before discussing, literature circles help this student connect his personal feelings with the text.

*3. For a reader who is bound by the text and believes that reading means getting right answers, literature circles allow this student to verbalize ideas in a safe environment and see how his peers think about a story.

Using the Technique as a Diagnostic Teaching Lesson   For literature circles to be effective, both of the following statements must be answered in the affirmative:

Yes	No	
____	____	1. The student can share interpretations in a group.
____	____	2. The student likes narrative text so that he finds it engaging enough to make a response.

For Further Reading

Short, K. G., Harste, J. C., & Burke, C. (1996). *Creating classrooms for authors and inquirers.* Portsmouth, NH: Heinemann.

Fountas, I. C. & Pinnell, G. S. (1996). *Guided reading: Good first teaching for all children.* Portsmouth, NH: Heinemann.

Making Words

Description   Making words is used to help readers develop their ability to spell words and apply this knowledge when decoding. In this procedure, children learn to make a six- or seven-letter word as they make smaller words. This activity is used along with regular writing activities to increase the children's decoding ability.

Targeted Reading Levels   1–4

Text   Letter cards

Predominant Focus of Instruction

1. Processing focus: print
2. Instructional phase: skill instruction
3. Response mode emphasized: oral
4. Strategy emphasized: monitoring
5. Skill emphasized: word identification and word analysis
6. Source of information: text-based
7. Type of instruction: implicit
8. Type of cognitive processing: successive

Procedure

1. Before beginning, the teacher decides on the final word in the lesson and makes a list of the shorter words that can be made from its letters. She picks 10–15 words that include: (a) words that can be sorted for the patterns, (b) words of different lengths to provide challenging and easy work, (c) a proper name so they can be reminded to use capital letters, and (d) words with familiar meanings. She writes all the words on cards and orders them from shortest to longest so the order emphasizes letter patterns.

2. The teacher places the larger letter cards in a pocket chart or along the chalk ledge and gives the student a set of letters.

3. The teacher and student review the letter cards.

4. She tells the student to take two letters and make the first word. She says the word and uses it in a sentence.

5. The teacher has the student make the other words indicating the number of letters needed and cues the student as to whether to change one letter, change letters around, or use all the letters.

6. The teacher reviews all the words in the lesson, saying and spelling each word and putting it on an index card.

7. The words are then sorted (see "Word Sort" in this chapter) for phonic patterns. For example, all the words beginning with the same letter would be one sort; rhyming words are another sort, etc.

Further Diagnostic Applications

Basic View of Reading   Learning to read means understanding how letters work within a word. Readers need to use their knowledge of letter patterns to figure out new words; therefore, reading is an interactive process. By listening closely to a word pronounced, the student can match the letters to the sounds in the words.

Patterns of Strengths and Strategies   The making words approach is most appropriate for students who can segment words into their sounds and match those sounds to the letters in the word. This technique builds on their strength and allows them to develop a system for decoding by analogy to key words.

Learning Patterns That Produce Increased Engagement

1. For a simultaneous thinker who readily uses what he knows and manipulates visual information, this technique promotes understanding the sound relationships in words.

*2. For a passive learner who is phonetically aware but needs help focusing on the letters in words, this technique uses his strength of sound knowledge to enhance the decoding process.

*3. For a successive learner who can match sounds to letters, this technique helps them develop a system for using what he knows to figure out words.

Using the Technique as a Diagnostic Teaching Lesson   For the making words approach to be effective, a majority of the following statements must be answered in the affirmative:

Yes   No

1. The student can segment sounds.
2. The student can match sounds to letters.
3. The student applies decoding analogies to both known and unknown words.

For Further Reading

Cunningham, P. M. & Cunningham, J. W. (1992). Making words: Enhancing the invented spelling-decoding connection. *The Reading Teacher, 46,* 106–107.

Snow, C. E., Burn, M. S., & Griffin, P. (1998). *Preventing reading difficulties in young children.* Washington, DC: National Academy Press.

Message Writing

Description   Message writing is a technique to develop prediction and monitoring of print processing. The student writes a message, usually a sentence, by slowly saying the words. The student predicts and then writes the letters in the words.

Targeted Reading Levels   1–4

Text   Student-generated

Predominant Focus of Instruction

1. Processing focus: print
2. Instructional phase: after reading
3. Response mode emphasized: written and oral production
4. Strategy emphasized: prediction and monitoring
5. Skill emphasized: word identification
6. Source of information: reader-based information
7. Type of instruction: implicit
8. Type of cognitive processing: simultaneous phasing to successive

Procedure

1. The teacher provides a blank writing book with each page divided in half. The top half is for practice writing, and the bottom half is for sentence writing.

2. Assisted by the teacher, the student composes a brief message (one or two sentences).

3. The sentence is written word by word.

4. If the student is unfamiliar with the printed form of a word, he uses the practice section of the page.

5. The teacher assists by drawing boxes for each letter of the unfamiliar word. For example, the word *dog* would look like this:

```
┌─────┐ ┌─────┐ ┌─────┐
│     │ │     │ │     │
└─────┘ └─────┘ └─────┘
```

6. The student slowly says the sounds and places the letters he knows in the appropriate boxes.

7. The teacher supplies any unknown letters in the appropriate boxes, slowly saying the sounds in the word. In the example, the teacher places an *o* in the middle box and says, "d-d-o-o-g-g."

8. The teacher asks, "Does this look right?"

9. The student evaluates the word and writes it in his sentence.

10. After the sentence is written, the teacher writes it on a sentence strip and then cuts it apart into words.

11. The student reconstructs the sentence, matching the words in his writing book.

12. The sentence is always read in its entirety.

Modifications

1. When a word is unfamiliar to the student, the teacher may want to use magnetic letters before having the student use the writing book. In that case, the student constructs a familiar part and then the teacher supplies other letters.

2. The teacher may use this technique when editing writing during classroom activities.

Further Diagnostic Applications

Basic View of Reading   Reading is an active, reader-based process in which the reader predicts what words will look like by using his understanding of the grapho-phonic system (sound segmentation and sound synthesis).

Patterns of Strengths and Strategies   The message writing approach is most appropriate for students who write with facility and can predict some letters in a word. By predicting and writing the letters, the student creates his own system for recognizing words.

Learner Patterns That Produce Increased Engagement

1. For a simultaneous learner who uses only what he knows when comprehending text and therefore guesses wildly when he comes to an unknown word, message writing helps this student focus on the details of printed words as he writes a sentence.

*2. For the passive learner who does not attempt to figure out unknown words, the student actively predicts letters in words by writing a message.

Using the Technique as a Diagnostic Teaching Lesson   For message writing to be effective, a majority of the following statements must be answered in the affirmative:

Yes   No
____ ____   1. The student can form letters.
____ ____   2. The student can predict some letter sounds in words.
____ ____   3. The student wants to communicate a message.

For Further Reading

Fountas, I. C. & Pinnell, G. S. (1996). *Guided reading: Good first teaching for all children.* Portsmouth, NH: Heinemann.

Gunning, T. G. (1998). *Assessing and correcting reading and writing difficulties.* Boston: Allyn & Bacon.

Metaphors

Description   Metaphors are used to relate words and concepts to already known objects by identifying their likenesses and differences. For young children, common concrete objects can be used to develop metaphors.

Targeted Reading Levels   4–8

Text   Isolated words or concepts

Predominant Focus of Instruction

1. Processing focus: meaning
2. Instructional phase: after reading
3. Response mode emphasized: oral discussion
4. Strategy emphasized: elaboration
5. Skill emphasized: word meaning
6. Source of information: reader-based
7. Type of instruction: implicit
8. Type of cognitive processing: simultaneous

Procedure

1. The teacher selects a key word or concept from the assigned text.

2. The teacher creates a metaphor that describes the key attributes of the word or concept.

3. The teacher describes how the metaphor is like the key word and how it is different from the key word. For example, "A cloud is a puddle in the sky. It is like a puddle because a cloud is made of water droplets. A cloud is not like a puddle because the water droplets have become water vapor. It is not like a puddle because it is in the sky and not on the ground."

4. Then the students create a metaphor within a particular class. For example, "What can you think of that is like a volcano? What animal is like a volcano?"

5. The students decide on a metaphor. For example, "A dragon is like a volcano."

6. The students explain the similarity. For example, "A dragon is like a volcano because they are both hot and spit fire."

7. The students explain how it is different from the metaphor. For example, "A dragon is not like a volcano because it is a make-believe animal. It has four legs, and can run very, very fast."

8. The students discuss the meaning of the words.

Modification   A brainstorming or listing of options in group situations can facilitate understanding of metaphors. In this situation, students would justify their metaphors and decide on one or two metaphors to use as the concept is developed in class.

Further Diagnostic Applications

Basic View of Reading   Reading is an interactive process in which a reader's prior knowledge influences his comprehension of the text. Word knowledge is based on conceptual knowledge that is related by analogous relationships among prior experiences.

Patterns of Strengths and Strategies   Metaphors are most appropriate for students who have facility with verbal language but draw unspecific relationships among concepts. The words *like a* are often prevalent in their conversations. For these students, creating metaphors elaborates the relationships they draw between what they already know and the new information.

Learner Patterns That Produce Increased Engagement

1. For a simultaneous learner who relates many concepts at once but is often unaware of the relationship or the precise words used to associate them, this technique helps him label and categorize word relationships.

2. For a highly verbal student whose facility with words needs to elaborate the analogous relationships between what he already knows and new words, this technique helps him relate what he knows into more inclusive categories.

*3. For a successive learner who uses words without drawing relationships between the word concepts and the word labels, this technique helps him explain relationships among words and experiences.

Using the Technique as a Diagnostic Teaching Lesson   For metaphors to be effective, a majority of the following statements must be answered in the affirmative:

Yes   No

____ ____ 1. The student understands how a metaphor is constructed and can readily draw analogous relationships.

____ ____ 2. The student can rationally explain the similarities and differences of the metaphors he creates.

____ ____ 3. The student creates more elaborate definitions of words as a result of explaining the relationships.

For Further Reading

McNeil, J. D. (1992). *Reading comprehension: New directions for classroom practice* (3rd ed.). New York: HarperCollins.

Wood, K. D., Lapp, D., & Flood, J. (1992). *Guiding readers through text: A review of study guides*. Newark, DE: International Reading Association.

Motor Imaging

Description   The motor imaging technique is specifically designed to develop word meanings by using images of movements related to the key attributes of a word. This technique ties together actions, images, and words.

Targeted Reading Levels   All levels

Text   Any kind, but especially helpful in content areas

Predominant Focus of Instruction

1. Processing focus: meaning
2. Instructional phase: before reading
3. Response mode emphasized: oral and kinesthetic
4. Strategy emphasized: elaboration
5. Skill emphasized: word meaning
6. Source of information: reader-based
7. Type of instruction: implicit
8. Type of cognitive processing: simultaneous

Procedure

1. The teacher selects target words from the passage to be read.

2. One of the words is written on the chalkboard.

3. The teacher explains what the word means.

4. Then the teacher asks the students to visualize a pantomime for the word meaning ("How could you demonstrate without words what this word means?").

5. At the teacher's indication, the students do their "pantomimes" all at the same time.

6. The teacher selects the most frequent, sensible pantomime.

7. The teacher demonstrates this action to the class.

8. Then the students say the word and make the same gesture.

9. This procedure is continued with each new and difficult vocabulary word.

10. The students read the assigned text.

Further Diagnostic Application

Basic View of Reading   Reading is an active, reader-based process in which the reader uses his own understanding of words to predict and confirm textual meaning. Word meaning is developed through concrete experiences, and revisiting those experiences connects new meanings to written words.

Patterns of Strengths and Strategies   The motor imaging technique is most appropriate for less verbal students who rely on their prior experiences when interpreting text. By acting out word meanings, they can tie their experiences to verbal information.

Learner Patterns That Produce Increased Engagement

1. For a simultaneous thinker who draws patterns from experiences, motor imaging uses this strength to develop word meanings.

2. This technique has been used with bilingual students to increase their understanding of English as a second language. Through their actions, they code the experience in both languages.

*3. For a text-based reader who needs to connect what he reads with his own experiences, motor imaging helps the student make these connections.

Using the Technique as a Diagnostic Teaching Lesson   For the motor imaging technique to be effective, a majority of the following statements must be answered in the affirmative:

Yes   No

_____   _____   1. The student can act out images.
_____   _____   2. The student can readily imagine actions.
_____   _____   3. The student ties actions, images, and words together.

For Further Reading

Manzo, A. & Manzo, U. (1995). *Teaching children to be literate: A reflective approach.* Fort Worth, TX: Harcourt Brace.

Multisensory Approaches

Description   Multisensory approaches or VAKT (visual/auditory/kinesthetic-tactile) techniques reinforce learning by having students trace letters and words to develop mastery. Relying on tactile-kinesthetic reinforcement, these techniques provide a multisensory stimulation for word learning.

Targeted Reading Levels   K–3

Text   Varies with approach; however, a generic VAKT can be used to reinforce any word that is difficult to learn

Predominant Focus of Instruction

1. Processing focus: print
2. Instructional phase: before reading
3. Response mode emphasized: written production

4. Strategy emphasized: elaboration
5. Skill emphasized: word identification
6. Source of information: text-based
7. Type of instruction: explicit
8. Type of cognitive processing: successive

Procedure

1. The teacher selects the key words to be learned and writes them with a crayon on cardboard or large paper. (A rough surface is better for the tactile reinforcement.)

2. The teacher models writing the word one letter at a time, saying the letter name, syllable, or letter sound.

3. The student traces each word letter by letter, saying either the letter name or letter sound. Then the student says the entire word.

4. The procedure is repeated with each word until the word can be written (not copied) from memory.

5. At any point that an error is made, the procedure is stopped and the teacher models the correct form of writing and saying the word.

6. This structured presentation continues until the student has mastered a sight vocabulary sufficient to read the stories.

Modifications   Many variations of the generic VAKT exist. The following approaches are a few examples of how the variations can be used to differentiate instruction.

1. The Fernald Technique moves from self-selected word learning to creating personal stories from individual word banks. Words are presented by syllables, maintaining more of a sense of the whole than other VAKT procedures. Therefore, the technique is highly personalized and motivational for students who like to structure their own language.

2. The Orton-Gillingham-Stillman Method, the Herman Method, the Cooper Method, and the Spaulding Method use the generic VAKT to reinforce the sounds of letters and require the student to blend sounds of letters to form words. Therefore, words are selected that are decodable and follow an extremely structured presentation of phonic generalizations. This variation is most appropriate for a student who guesses at words and has poor visual memory but can blend sounds to form words. Thus, if he can't remember a word, he can sound it out in order to recognize it.

Further Diagnostic Applications

Basic View of Reading   Reading is a text-based process in which the reader learns a basic sight vocabulary through repetitious, multisensory reinforcement of letters in words before reading complete stories.

Patterns of Strengths and Strategies Multisensory approaches are most appropriate for students who have strong tactile-kinesthetic preferences for learning and exhibit difficulty in initial word learning. This approach focuses the attention of the learner to the key features of each word.

Learner Patterns That Produce Increased Engagement

1. For a successive learner with tactile-kinesthetic preferences who has difficulty remembering sight words that have been taught, this technique reinforces those words that are difficult to learn.

2. For an extremely passive learner with tactile-kinesthetic preferences who does not attend to the key features of words but instead makes wild guesses, this technique draws attention to what words look like and the key features of the words.

3. For the simultaneous learner who has difficulty remembering key sight words, multisensory techniques reinforce words that are difficult for him to remember.

Using the Technique as a Diagnostic Teaching Lesson For multisensory techniques to be effective, a majority of the following statements must be answered in the affirmative:

Yes   No

____ ____ 1. The student guesses at words without using their graphic or phonic cues.

____ ____ 2. Tracing the word facilitates recognition of sight words or sounds.

____ ____ 3. Tracing the words focuses the student's attention on the key features of words.

For Further Reading

McCormick, S. (1999). *Instructing students who have literacy problems* (3rd ed.). Englewood Cliffs, NJ: Merrill/Prentice Hall.

Opinion-Proof Approach

Description The opinion-proof approach is a technique designed to engage students in higher-level thinking skills by asking them to write opinions and supporting evidence about a selection. This technique emphasizes evaluative thinking, verification, and persuasive argument.

Targeted Reading Levels 4–12

Text Any kind that supports various points of view

Predominant Focus of Instruction

1. Processing focus: meaning
2. Instructional phase: after reading
3. Response mode emphasized: written discourse to oral discussion
4. Strategy emphasized: monitoring and elaboration
5. Skill emphasized: nonliteral comprehension
6. Source of information: reader-based information supported by text-based
7. Type of instruction: implicit
8. Type of cognitive processing: simultaneous

Procedure

1. The students read a selected text usually in the content area.

2. The teacher guides the silent reading using an appropriate technique (see Table 10–2).

3. After the text is read, the teacher provides the students with an "Opinion-Proof" guide either on the chalkboard or a handout.

4. She explains that on the left side of the page the students are to write opinions about characters or events.

5. The teacher further explains that on the right side of the page, the students are to write proof for their opinions. This proof is to be derived directly from the text.

6. When students have completed their Opinion-Proof guide, they are to write an essay using their opinions with the supporting evidence they collected.

7. The teacher and students develop specific criteria for evaluating the essay. Some examples are "Is the evidence found in the text?" and "Does this evidence support my opinion?"

8. The teacher divides the class into groups or pairs.

9. The students share their essays and revise unclear ideas.

Modification   If writing an essay is difficult, the teacher may provide "framed paragraphs" with leading lines that introduce the opinion followed by the support. For example, "In this story, I believe . . . The reason I think this is . . ."

Further Diagnostic Applications

Basic View of Reading   Reading is a socio-interactive process in which the reader predicts and interprets information, using his own ideas based on information in the text. This interactive process begins with the reader using his own knowledge and then finding support in the text. Finally, the reader's understanding is shared and revised with classmates.

Patterns of Strengths and Strategies The opinion-proof approach is most appropriate for students who need time to write and think about their ideas prior to discussion. The writing helps them elaborate their ideas, integrating both the text and background knowledge.

Learner Patterns That Produce Increased Engagement

1. For readers who use reader-based inferencing and are quiet and reflective, the opinion-proof allows them to have time to think through their ideas before discussion.

*2. For readers who are highly verbal and can write with ease but who are text-based, this approach uses their writing strength to lead them to tie the text to reader-based inferencing.

*3. For readers who use reader-based inferencing when comprehending text, the opinion-proof approach helps them return to the text to support, revise, and modify their thinking based on textual information.

Using the Technique as a Diagnostic Teaching Lesson For the opinion-proof approach to be effective, a majority of the following statements must be answered in the affirmative:

Yes	No	
___	___	1. The student readily writes information.
___	___	2. The student can generate at least one opinion.
___	___	3. The student listens to ideas from his peers and refines his thinking.

For Further Reading
Manzo, A. & Manzo, U. (1990). *Content area reading: A heuristic approach.* Englewood Cliffs, NJ: Merrill/Prentice Hall.

Paired Reading

Description The paired reading technique uses joint reading aloud between two individuals. They sit together and read a story aloud simultaneously. One individual (another adult or child) serves as a model of fluent reading.

Targeted Reading Levels K–5

Text Stories and poems

Predominant Focus of Instruction

1. Processing focus: print
2. Instructional phase: during reading

3. Response mode emphasized: oral reading
4. Strategy emphasized: prediction
5. Skill emphasized: fluency
6. Source of information: reader-based
7. Type of instruction: implicit
8. Type of cognitive processing: simultaneous

Procedure

1. The student and the teacher select a text that is interesting and not too long. The paired reading needs to be short.

2. Before beginning, the teacher and the student decide on a sign for the student to give when he is ready to read on his own and one for when he needs help.

3. The teacher and the student read the text in unison.

4. The teacher sets a pace that is appropriate for the text, modeling intonation and phrasing.

5. The teacher can move her finger along the line of print if necessary.

6. As the student gains success, he signals the teacher to stop reading aloud.

7. The student continues on his own.

Modification

1. This technique is effective with peer tutoring when the teacher can divide the class into two groups and establish pairs for reading. Some teachers call this approach *partner reading*.

2. The pairs or partners can rate each other's fluency using a modified fluency scale (see Chapter 5 for fluency scale).

Further Diagnostic Applications

Basic View of Reading   Reading is a socio-interactive process in which fluency is developed as students read along with others. Using a model of a more fluent reader, the student readily integrates word recognition and comprehension as he reads.

Patterns of Strengths and Strategies   Paired reading is most appropriate for students who read slowly but accurately. The paired reading provides a model of fluent reading and increases the student's reading rate at the same time.

Learner Patterns That Produce Increased Engagement

1. For a simultaneous learner who relies heavily on background knowledge when reading orally, paired reading allows him to attend to letters and meaning simultaneously.

2. For a highly social student who likes to interact with others and follow their model, this technique lets him use his preferences while practicing reading.

*3. For a nonfluent reader who is word-bound because of a heavy emphasis on phonic instruction, this method can increase reading fluency.

Using the Technique as a Diagnostic Teaching Lesson

For the paired reading technique to be effective, a majority of the following statements must be answered in the affirmative.

Yes   No
___   ___   1. The student likes to read along with someone.
___   ___   2. The student begins to take over the reading.
___   ___   3. The student becomes more fluent and expressive.

For Further Reading

Topping, K. (1987). Paired reading: A powerful technique for parent use. *The Reading Teacher, 40,* 608–614.

Topping, K. (1989). Peer tutoring and paired reading: Combining two powerful techniques. *The Reading Teacher, 42,* 488–494.

Phonogram Approach

Description   The phonogram approach is a structured program to introduce phonic principles by use of sound clusters within words. As whole words are introduced, the student is directed to look at the sound clusters in the words. Then the student finds similar letter clusters in new words and associates them with the known cluster words.

Targeted Reading Levels   1–3

Text   Isolated words that have the same word patterns and text that contains these patterns

Predominant Focus of Instruction

1. Processing focus: print
2. Instructional phase: after reading
3. Response mode emphasized: oral discussion
4. Strategy emphasized: elaboration
5. Skill emphasized: word analysis
6. Source of information: text-based
7. Type of instruction: explicit
8. Type of cognitive processing: generally successive, but does look at patterns (simultaneous)

Procedure

1. The teacher presents isolated words that contain the letter cluster. For the *an* sound cluster, these words could be presented:

fan	can	candy
man	pan	fancy
ran	Stan	candle

2. The teacher pronounces the whole word and identifies letter names and letter sounds of that target cluster. For example:

   "In the word *fan*, the letter *f* goes '*f-f-f*' and the letters *a-n* go '*an.*'"

3. The teacher pronounces the letter sound or cluster sounds and asks the student for its name. For example:

   "In the word *fan*, what letter goes '*f-f-f*' ?"

   "In the word *fan*, what letters go '*an*' ?"

4. The teacher pronounces the letter name or cluster and asks the student for its sound. For example:

   "In the word *fan*, what sound does the *f* make?"

   "In the word *fan*, what sounds do *a-n* make?"

5. The teacher asks the student, "What is the word?"

6. Steps 2, 3, 4, and 5 are continued until the pattern is learned.

7. The teacher presents the words in sentences, and the student reads the sentences. For example:

   The man canned the fancy candy.

   Stan ran to fan the candle.

8. If a word cannot be decoded, the teacher directs the student to the letter cluster and asks for its name and sound. For example:

   "Look at the word. Where is the a-n? What sounds do they make?

   What's the first letter? What sound does it make?"

9. The teacher returns to the list of words and asks the student, "How are *can*, *candy*, and *canopy* alike, and how are they different?"

Modifications

1. Similar to the phonogram approach is the linguistic method, an approach for instructing a beginning reader, which is also based on word patterns. The word families introduced have a minimal contrast in the word patterns *(cat, mat, fat)*. Therefore, this approach emphasizes decoding by visual analogy and does not emphasize sound analogies. The teacher introduces the words before the story

by having the students spell each new word and then asking how the word patterns are alike and how they are different. Then the students read the text that uses the word pattern.

The cat is fat.

The cat is on the mat.

The fat cat is on the mat.

Therefore, this approach is more implicit than the phonogram approach.

2. The target words can be selected to teach the word patterns that are causing the student difficulty.

3. The target words can be selected to teach a particular letter sound. For example, if short *a* words are difficult for the student, the teacher can choose the patterns of *an, at, am, ab,* and *ap* so the student can generalize the concept of short *a* without separating the individual letter sound from its pattern.

Further Diagnostic Applications

Basic View of Reading   Reading is a text-based, process in which the student must learn to decode printed words before he can read for meaning. As such, the learner is explicitly taught the analogous sound relationships to enhance decoding.

Patterns of Strengths and Strategies   Looking for sound clusters in whole words is most appropriate for a simultaneous learner. For this student, the approach facilitates word identification by using the similarity among sounds in already known words.

Learner Patterns That Produce Increased Engagement

1. For a simultaneous learner who needs direct instruction in forming phonic analogies among the words he already knows and new words he encounters, this technique uses his strength in identifying patterns.

2. For an older student who needs to add a decoding strategy to supplement contextual analysis, this technique helps him use what he knows about context and word identification.

Using the Technique as a Diagnostic Teaching Lesson   For the phonogram approach to be effective, a majority of the following statements must be answered in the affirmative:

Yes   *No*

_____   _____   1. The student can segment sounds.

_____   _____   2. The student applies the analogies to both known and unknown words.

_____   _____   3. The student applies the strategy when reading connected text and encountering an unknown word.

For Further Reading
Cunningham, P. M. & Allington, R. L. (1999). *Classrooms that work: They can all read and write* (2d ed.). New York: Longman.
McCormick, S. (1999). *Instructing students who have literacy problems* (3rd ed.) Englewood Cliffs, NJ: Merrill/Prentice Hall.

Predictable Language Approach

Description   The predictable language approach is an approach for beginning reading instruction that uses the rhythmic, repetitive sentence patterns in young children's stories. The teacher and children read the story together, which creates a predictive set for the words in the story. Then the students read the story by themselves.

Targeted Reading Levels   K–2

Text   Predictable books with patterned language, such as

Run, run, as fast as you can

You can't catch me; I'm the Gingerbread Man.

Predominant Focus of Instruction

1. Processing focus: print
2. Instructional phase: during reading
3. Response mode emphasized: oral
4. Strategy emphasized: prediction and monitoring
5. Skill emphasized: word identification
6. Source of information: reader-based and text-based
7. Type of instruction: implicit
8. Type of cognitive processing: simultaneous

Procedure

1. The teacher chooses a predictable book or story.

2. The teacher and the students talk about the story to develop a predictive set.

3. The students tell what they think happens in the story by telling the story page by page, using the pictures. This progression creates a predictive set for the story.

4. The teacher reads the story, letting the students confirm or revise their thinking about what the story is about.

5. The teacher reads the story aloud a second time, inviting the student to read along. She moves her finger above the line of print to mark the flow of language.

6. The teacher continues to read using an oral cloze. The student supplies the missing word in the language pattern.

7. When the student knows the language pattern, he reads the rest of the story on his own.

8. The student reads the whole story again on his own. The teacher assists him when necessary.

9. Using the predictable pattern, the student writes his own story, changing the characters and the setting.

Modification   When the student can predict easily and follows the teacher as she reads, then the teacher can omit steps 3 and 4.

Further Diagnostic Applications

Basic View of Reading   Reading is a socio-interactive process in which the readers use their shared understanding as well as language sense to figure out words. Through rhythmic, repetitious language patterns, the student recognizes the printed forms of words and infers the grapho-phonic rule system.

Patterns of Strengths and Strategies   The predictable language approach encourages the student to associate printed words with the predictive patterns of language; therefore, it is most appropriate for students who laboriously try to decode words to derive meaning from text. Because a repetitive sentence pattern is used in this technique, the student can easily predict both what the words are and what they mean at the same time.

Learner Patterns That Produce Increased Engagement

1. For a reader who has facility with verbal language but does not attend to the key features of short similar words found in basal readers, this technique allows him to identify words using the language pattern.

2. For a learner who needs a sense of the whole story before reading, the predictable language approach provides him with a brisk, paced reading of the entire story prior to word identification.

*3. For an extremely slow, laborious letter-by-letter reader, the predictable language approach can restore his sense of the whole and illustrate the predictive nature of reading.

*4. For the learner who reads in a monotone, this approach can restore his sense of rhythm and cadence in reading.

Using the Technique as a Diagnostic Teaching Lesson   For the predictable language approach to be effective, a majority of the following statements must be answered in the affirmative:

Yes	No
____	____	1. The student identifies the language patterns easily and can complete the oral cloze.
____	____	2. The student models the teacher's fluent reading and intonations readily.
____	____	3. The student enjoys repetitive language and does not find it boring.

For Further Reading

Short, K. G., Harste, J. C., & Burke, C. (1996). *Creating classrooms for authors and inquirers.* Portsmouth, NH: Heinemann.

Tompkins, G. E. (1998). *50 literacy strategies: Step by step.* Englewood Cliffs, NJ: Merrill/Prentice Hall.

Prediction Logs

Description   Prediction logs are written accounts of students' active reading. At designated points, the students write a prediction and a reason for their prediction. As they read and write, they evaluate new information in relation to their previous predictions. The written record of their previous thoughts allows the students to analyze how they construct meaning.

Targeted Reading Levels   4–12

Text   Narrative text

Predominant Focus of Instruction

1. Processing focus: meaning
2. Instructional phase: during reading
3. Response mode emphasized: written discourse
4. Strategy emphasized: prediction and monitoring
5. Skill emphasized: nonliteral comprehension
6. Source of information: reader-based
7. Type of instruction: implicit
8. Type of cognitive processing: simultaneous

Procedure

1. The teacher selects interesting stories so that the readers can make predictions.

2. She decides on key turning points in the story and marks them for the students.

3. The teacher prepares sheets with the following information:

```
Name of story:
Author:
                              Prediction              Reason for Prediction
Section #1:


Section #2:
```

4. After the story is read, the prediction logs are used as a basis for discussing the story.

5. The students discuss how their interpretation developed through the story.

6. The students discuss the influence of personal understanding on comprehension.

7. The students write a reaction to the discussion, telling how their comprehension developed.

Further Diagnostic Applications

Basic View of Reading   Reading is a socio-interactive process in which the reader builds a model of meaning based on textual and nontextual information and then revises this model during a discussion. As a result of predicting and revising and the subsequent discussion, the reader builds his model of meaning, he predicts, monitors, and evaluates his interpretation in relation to the context of the situation.

Patterns of Strengths and Strategies   Prediction logs are most appropriate for the reflective student who needs to evaluate how he forms his model of meaning. He often does not realize what information he uses from the text and what he already knows. Furthermore, he has difficulty thinking about how he forms his ideas as well as discussing them in a group. Prediction logs provide a method for analyzing how he constructs meaning before he participates in a group setting.

Learner Patterns That Produce Increased Engagement

1. For a simultaneous, reflective learner who understands the story but does not understand how he constructs a response, prediction logs provide a record of his thoughts so that he can analyze them.

*2. For a passive learner who needs actively to engage in forming and revising his model of meaning, reading logs have the student elaborate his understanding during the reading of the story.

Using the Technique as a Diagnostic Teaching Lesson   For prediction logs to be effective, a majority of the following statements must be answered in the affirmative:

Yes   No
_____   _____   1. The student can write a prediction.
_____   _____   2. The student can write a rationale for predictions.
_____   _____   3. The student will discuss his thinking in a group.

For Further Reading

Macon, J. M., Bewell, D., & Vogt, M. (1991). *Responses to literature: Grades K–8*. Newark, DE: International Reading Association.

Short, K. G., Harste, J. C., & Burke, C. (1996). *Creating classrooms for authors and inquirers*. Portsmouth, NH: Heinemann.

Prediction Maps

Description   The prediction map uses a conceptual flowchart to visually map the comprehension process of prediction and revision. In using the map, teacher questioning focuses on what the reader is understanding about the text and the sources of information he is using. The teacher suggests that he can revise or expand his prediction according to what he has read and what he already knows.

Targeted Reading Levels   4–8

Text   Short narrative stories

Predominant Focus of Instruction

1. Processing focus: meaning
2. Instructional phase: during reading
3. Response mode emphasized: written
4. Strategy emphasized: prediction and monitoring
5. Skill emphasized: literal and nonliteral comprehension
6. Source of information: reader-based with some text-based
7. Type of instruction: explicit
8. Type of cognitive processing: simultaneous, but is an interrupted story (successive)

Procedure

1. The teacher selects a narrative text at the appropriate reading level.

2. The teacher identifies the key turning points in the story. (A story map can help.)

3. The teacher designates the story intervals that reveal enough of the story line to encourage logical inferences, but not enough to draw exact conclusions.

4. Using the title, the student and teacher make a prediction and place it in the center of the oval on the left side of the page (see Figure 11–3).

5. The teacher and the student select important information from the text and what the reader already knows as illustrated.

6. The student reads to a designated point in the story.

7. The teacher demonstrates her thinking by saying, "I predict _____ is going to happen next."

8. The teacher adds her prediction to the map as well as the textual information and what she knows to support her prediction.

9. The student is asked if he wants to revise, change, or add to his prediction. The new ideas are written in the center oval.

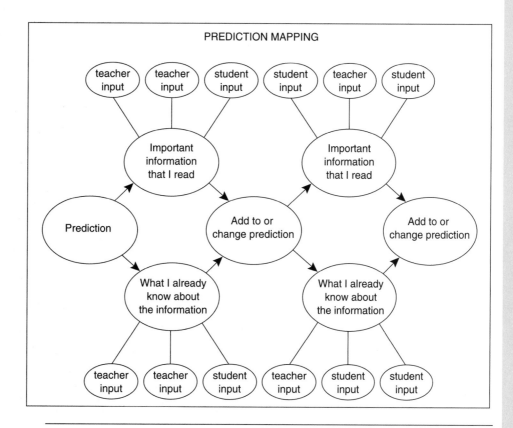

Figure 11–3 Prediction Mapping

Note. From "Right-Brained Strategies for Teaching Comprehension" by Barbara J. Walker, 1985, *Academic Therapy, 21,* p. 137. Copyright 1985 by PRO-ED, Inc. Reprinted by permission.

10. The teacher asks, "What did the text say that made you think that?" The student adds textual information to support or revise the prediction.

11. The teacher asks, "What do you know about the information that made you think that?" The student writes what he knows on the map to support his prediction.

12. The prediction/revision process is mapped at predetermined points in the story. Important information from the text and what is already known about the important information are used to make predictions.

13. Initially, the teacher takes an active role by mapping her own process of comprehending as the story is read.

14. The predictions, important textual information, and personal interpretations are mapped in the flowchart, with the teacher modeling how the comprehending process is restructured during the reading of a story.

15. The teacher phases out her modeling as the student becomes more active in predicting and revising.

Further Diagnostic Applications

Basic View of Reading   Reading is an interactive process in which a reader uses both textual and nontextual information to build a model of meaning. The reader actively builds his model of meaning by predicting what the author is going to say, selecting important information from the text, and evaluating his interpretation using prior knowledge (reader-based inferencing) and the text (text-based inferencing).

Patterns of Strengths and Strategies   Prediction mapping is most appropriate for the simultaneous nonverbal student who tends to overrely on what he already knows about the text rather than the textual information. In this technique, the information is displayed in a spatial orientation and offers the reader more flexibility of options, revisions, and additions during the reading of a story.

Learner Patterns That Produce Increased Engagement

1. For a student who has difficulty expressing ideas in words and who needs to see a map of how to use the information he knows and the text, the map provides a tool for verbalizing how he is thinking.

*2. For a passive reader who maintains his initial prediction without revising it even when conflicts develop between the prediction and important new information from the text and what he already knows, the map helps him see when he needs to revise a prediction because of new information presented in the text.

*3. For a text-bound reader who does not use background knowledge when reading a story, the map helps him see how he can use what he knows to interpret what he is reading.

Using the Technique as a Diagnostic Teaching Lesson   For prediction maps to be effective, a majority of the following statements must be answered in the affirmative:

Yes   No

_____ _____ 1. The student can make a prediction and fill in the oval.
_____ _____ 2. The student responds to the teacher model and adds information of his own.
_____ _____ 3. The student retells the story in greater detail, relating important information and background knowledge.

For Further Reading

Johns, J. L., & Lenski, S. (1997). *Improving reading: A handbook of strategies* (2d ed.) Dubuque, IA: Kendall/Hunt.

Question-Answer Relationships

Description   The question-answer relationships (QAR) technique is used to identify the type of response necessary to answer a question. Questions are the most prevalent means of evaluating reading comprehension; therefore, knowledge about sources of information required to answer questions facilitates comprehension and increases a student's ability to participate in teacher-directed discussion and answer questions in textbook exercises.

Targeted Reading Levels   4–8

Text   Any text on which questions can be based

Predominant Focus of Instruction

1. Processing focus: meaning
2. Instructional phase: after reading
3. Response mode emphasized: oral discussion
4. Strategy emphasized: monitoring and elaboration
5. Skill emphasized: literal and nonliteral comprehension
6. Source of information: text-based with some reader-based
7. Type of instruction: explicit
8. Type of cognitive processing: successive

Procedure

1. The teacher selects a text that can be the basis of different kinds of questions.

2. She introduces "right there" and "on my own" sources of information:
   a. "Right there" means that the answers are "right there" on the page, and the words from the text can be used to answer the question. The teacher points out that this source must often be used in answering a teacher's questions and in completing textbook exercises.

b. "On my own" means that the students must fill in missing information, using what they know about what is in the text to answer the question. In this instance, the students must realize that they are "on their own" and use their own experience when they answer the question.

3. The teacher completes an example lesson identifying the kind of answer that is required by the question as well as giving the answer itself. She models the strategy of finding answers to questions and identifying the sources of information used.

4. The teacher introduces the "think and search" question-answer relationship. Here the student must read the text carefully and then "think and search" different parts of the text to find the answers that fit together to answer the question.

5. Then the teacher introduces "author and you" sources of information. In this response, the students need to think about what they know, what the author tells them, and how this information fits together.

6. The teacher completes an example lesson, identifying the kind of answer that is required by the questions as well as the answer. She models by using all four sources of information (right there, think and search, author and you, and on my own) and telling why and how the answers were obtained.

7. The students complete a third example lesson using a paragraph, the questions, and the answers. The students as a group identify the question-answer relationships. The students talk about reasons for a particular answer and the strategy used to obtain the answer.

8. The students complete a fourth example lesson using a paragraph, the questions, and the answers. Individually, the students identify the question-answer relationship. Then the students tell why they chose an answer, based on textual and nontextual information and the strategy used to obtain the answer.

9. Steps 5, 6, and 7 are extended to longer passages in progressive steps until the procedure can be used with basal readers or content area texts.

Further Diagnostic Applications

Basic View of Reading   Reading is a socio-interactive process where a reader's interpretation of text is based on textual and nontextual information. As they share their thinking, readers construct answers to questions, shifting between the text and what they know. Therefore, not only do students figure out answers to questions, but they also know the source of information they are using to construct the answer.

Patterns of Strengths and Strategies   QAR is most appropriate for students who rely heavily on one source of information to answer questions or who cannot answer questions. For these students, the technique requires them to distinguish when it is appropriate to use their background knowledge and/or textual information to answer questions.

Learner Patterns That Produce Increased Engagement

1. For a passive learner who is unaware of the various sources of information used to answer questions, this technique increases his active reading by asking him to evaluate how he got an answer.

2. For a learner who relies heavily on background knowledge about the subject to answer questions, this technique shows him when and how he can use background knowledge effectively and when he needs to use the text.

3. For a successive text-bound learner who does not use what he already knows to answer questions, this technique shows him how to fill in missing information using what he knows.

Using the Technique as a Diagnostic Teaching Lesson

For QAR to be effective, a majority of the following statements must be answered in the affirmative:

Yes   No

_____ _____ 1. The student can understand the differences between reader-based answers and text-based answers.

_____ _____ 2. The student can explain which source of information was used when he answered the question.

_____ _____ 3. The student elaborates his responses to questions.

For Further Reading

Alvermann, D. E. & Phelps, S. E. (1994). *Content reading and literacy.* Boston: Allyn & Bacon.

Barr, R., Blachowicz, C., & Wogman-Sadow, M. (1995). *Reading diagnosis for teachers: An instructional approach* (3rd ed.). White Plains, NY: Longman.

Question-Generation Strategy

Description   Writing postreading questions uses student-generated questions to develop an understanding of the important information in the text. By deciding what to ask in their questions, students think about what is important in the text.

Targeted Reading Levels   4–12

Text   Narrative or expository

Predominant Focus of Instruction

1. Processing focus: meaning
2. Instructional phase: after reading
3. Response mode emphasized: written
4. Strategy emphasized: elaboration
5. Skill emphasized: literal and nonliteral comprehension
6. Source of information: reader-based because the student writes the question, but can be text-based if the student uses only the text

7. Type of instruction: initially explicit, then rapidly moves to implicit
8. Type of cognitive processing: simultaneous

Procedure

1. The teacher selects a text at the appropriate level.

2. She discusses how to write questions:
   a. A question has an answer.
   b. A good question begins with a question word like *who, what, when, where,* or *why.*
   c. A good question can be answered using information in the story.
   d. A good question asks about important information in the story.

3. The teacher selects a short paragraph and models writing questions about the important information in the text.

4. The students write questions after they read a short paragraph.

5. The students answer their questions.

6. The students compare their questions and answers with the teacher's questions and answers.

7. The teacher gives feedback about the importance of the questions.

8. The students write questions about the important information in their assigned text.

9. The students answer their questions.

10. The students compare their questions and answers with the teacher's questions and answers.

Modifications

1. Instead of step 2, the teacher uses story grammar questions (e.g., "Who was the leading character?"). Then she has the students make story-specific questions (see "Story Map" in this chapter).

2. Instead of step 10, the teacher allows the students to share their questions and answers in small groups, which makes the technique more socio-interactive.

3. The teacher uses postgenerated questioning with book reports. After reading a book, the student writes his questions on cards. Then other students who have read the same book can use the cards to answer questions about the book.

Further Diagnostic Applications

Basic View of Reading   Reading is an interactive process in which the reader selects important textual information by constructing questions using his background knowledge and selected information.

Patterns of Strengths and Strategies Postgenerated questioning is most appropriate for students who have facility with word identification and word meaning but have difficulty studying for tests. For these students, this approach requires them to read text in order to formulate questions about the important information in the text.

Learner Patterns That Produce Increased Engagement

1. For a successive learner who knows the meanings of words but depends on teacher questioning to interpret the important information, this technique helps the student become more independent by having him write the questions before comparing them with the teacher's questions.

2. For a simultaneous learner who has not learned to ask himself questions to monitor what he needs to remember when he reads, this technique encourages him to monitor his understanding by asking himself questions.

*3. For a passive learner who tries to remember all the details rather than focusing on the important facts, by writing and comparing questions he thinks about what is important to remember.

Using the Technique as a Diagnostic Teaching Lesson For the question-generation strategy to be effective, a majority of the following statements must be answered in the affirmative:

Yes	No	
___	___	1. The student can recognize and understand the individual words in the text.
___	___	2. The student begins to ask himself what information is important enough to remember.
___	___	3. The student rehearses important information.

For Further Reading

Alvermann, D. E. & Phelps, S. E. (1994). *Content reading and literacy.* Boston: Allyn & Bacon.

Barr, R., Blachowicz, C., & Wogman-Sadow, M. (1995). *Reading diagnosis for teachers: An instructional approach* (3rd ed.). White Plains, NY: Longman.

Readers Theater

Description Readers theater is a dramatic interpretation of a play script through oral interpretive reading. The story theme and character development are conveyed through intonation, inflection, and fluency of oral reading.

Targeted Reading Levels 2–5

Text Scripts designed for the appropriate number of readers

Predominant Focus of Instruction

1. Processing focus: print and meaning
2. Instructional phase: after reading
3. Response mode emphasized: oral
4. Strategy emphasized: elaboration
5. Skill emphasized: nonliteral comprehension and fluency
6. Source of information: reader-based and text-based
7. Type of instruction: implicit
8. Type of cognitive processing: simultaneous

Procedure

1. The teacher selects a narrative text at the appropriate reading level and constructs a play script.

2. The teacher presents a brief description of the characters, setting, events, and problem.

3. The students select or are assigned appropriate parts to read.

4. The students preview the scripts silently.

5. Standing in a line in front of a seated audience, the students read the scripts orally.

6. No props or costumes are used.

7. The students convey the story line by their intonation and phrasing.

8. Listeners must use their imaginations to interpret the story line.

Modifications

1. A readers theater can be developed from the text that the students are reading. It provides additional reinforcement for word recognition. For example, when deciding how to write a script from a preprimer, the students and teacher reread parts of the text numerous times as they write the scripts on chart tablets.

2. Having the students write a readers theater script from a story can also improve comprehension. The students must decide what important dialogue and narration are necessary to understand the story.

3. Different reading levels can be included in a script to allow readers of varying reading abilities to participate in the same activity.

Further Diagnostic Applications

Basic View of Reading   Reading is an active, reader-based process in which the reader interprets the author's intended meaning through oral interpretative reading.

Patterns of Strengths and Strategies   Readers theater is most appropriate for students who have a dramatic flair and when given the stage will perform. Often a quiet, less verbal student will perform in a readers theater because the expectation is performance.

Learner Patterns That Produce Increased Engagement

1. For a simultaneous learner who communicates through drama and needs to develop oral reading fluency, this technique is a natural way to develop fluency for this reader.

*2. The highly efficient decoder who is word-bound and does not identify with characters benefits from the naturalness of character identification forced by the readers theater script.

*3. A student who has difficulty tracking develops a purposeful reason to track when reading *short* readers theater scripts.

Using the Technique as a Diagnostic Teaching Lesson   For readers theater to be effective, a majority of the following statements must be answered in the affirmative:

Yes   No

____   ____   1. The student has enough oral reading fluency to convey the message.

____   ____   2. The student likes to perform.

____   ____   3. The student becomes more fluent as he identifies with the character.

For Further Reading

Bagert, B. (1991). Act it out: Making poetry come alive. In B. Cullinan (ed.), *Invitation to read: More children's literature in the reading program* (pp. 14–23). Newark, DE: International Reading Association.

Tompkins, G. E. (1998). *50 literacy strategies: Step by step.* Englewood Cliffs, NJ: Merrill/Prentice Hall.

Walker, B. J. (1999). *Supporting struggling readers* (2d ed.). Markham, Ontario: Pippin Publishing Limited.

Reciprocal Teaching

Description   Reciprocal teaching is a technique to develop comprehension of expository text by modeling and practicing how to read and understand the text. The teacher and students take turns leading a discussion about sections of the text. The teacher provides the initial model by thinking aloud about *how* she constructs a summary, makes up questions, clarifies what is difficult, and predicts what else the text will discuss.

Targeted Reading Levels   5–12

Text   Expository text is preferred.

Predominant Focus of Instruction

1. Processing focus: meaning
2. Instructional phase: during reading
3. Response mode emphasized: oral discussion
4. Strategy emphasized: elaboration
5. Skill emphasized: literal comprehension
6. Source of information: text-based
7. Type of instruction: explicit
8. Type of cognitive processing: successive

Procedure

1. The teacher selects a text from a content area.

2. The teacher explains the four tasks: (a) question generating, (b) summarizing, (c) clarifying the difficult parts, and (d) predicting what the next section will discuss.

3. Both the students and the teacher silently read the first section of the text.

4. The teacher talks about the four tasks of reading for that section.
   a. She constructs several good questions.
   b. She constructs a summary of the section, using the main idea and supporting details.
   c. She clarifies difficult parts by stressing vocabulary and organization.
   d. She predicts what the next section will discuss by using the title and headings.

5. The students help revise the summary, answer the questions, clarify unclear parts of the summary and the text, and evaluate the prediction (agree or disagree and add a rationale for doing so).

6. After a few models by the teacher, a student takes the turn of teacher. He thinks aloud, using the four steps.

7. The teacher becomes a student and assumes the student's role.

8. Students take turns playing "teacher."

9. Periodically the teacher reviews the four activities with the student.
   a. Rule for good questions: They should be clear and stand by themselves.
   b. Rule for summaries: Look for the topic sentences, make up a topic sentence if there is none, make lists, and delete what is unimportant.
   c. Rule for clarifying: Look for difficult vocabulary, incomplete information, unclear references, and unusual expressions.
   d. Rule for predictions: Use the title and headings, use questions in the text if present, and use text structures (references to *two kinds, four levels,* and so on).

10. As the students play "teacher," the teacher does the following:
    a. She provides feedback about the quality of summaries or questions. When necessary, she models her thinking for the student. For example, she might comment, "That was a start on a summary, but I would summarize by adding . . ."
    b. She provides encouragement to the student playing "teacher." For example, she may say, "I liked the way you identified the important information."

Further Diagnostic Applications

Basic View of Reading   Reading is a socio-interactive process in which a reader's interpretation of the text is shaped by discussing ideas with others as well as by the use of the textual and nontextual information. By thinking aloud, the student becomes more aware of how to integrate knowledge sources when reading.

Patterns of Strengths and Strategies   Reciprocal teaching is most appropriate for students who have verbal fluency and experiential knowledge of the topics but need to focus their understanding. These students read and retain information, but the complexities of content area reading often produce an overload of unorganized facts rather than important related information.

Learner Patterns That Produce Increased Engagement

1. A passive yet verbally fluent learner who needs to organize the information thinks about his section of the text by leading the discussion. He also can follow the teacher's model.

2. For a sequential learner who tries to memorize a string of unrelated facts rather than focus on the important points and how the facts relate to these points, this technique encourages him to use only the important information in his summary.

*3. For a passive reader who does not monitor information learned and relate it to an organized whole, this technique helps him actively summarize text and clarify the difficult parts.

Using the Technique as a Diagnostic Teaching Lesson   For reciprocal teaching to be effective, a majority of the following statements must be answered in the affirmative:

Yes	No	
_____	_____	1. The student has enough expressive language so that constructing a summary is not terribly time-consuming.
_____	_____	2. The student can ask good questions.
_____	_____	3. The student can summarize information and convey this information to the group.

For Further Reading

Gipe, J. P. (1995). *Corrective reading techniques for the classroom teacher* (3rd. ed.). Scottsdale, AZ: Gorsuch Scarisbrick.

Palincsar, A. S. & Brown, A. L. (1989). Instruction for self-regulated reading. In L. B. Resnick & L. E. Klopfer (eds.), *Toward the thinking curriculum: Current cognitive research* (pp. 19–40). Alexandria, VA: Association for Supervision and Curriculum Development.

Repeated Readings

Description   The repeated readings technique is the oral rereading of a student-selected passage until accuracy and speed are fluent and represent the natural flow of language. Students must be able to read the selection with some degree of accuracy at the beginning of instruction.

Targeted Reading Levels   1–4

Text   Self-selected

Predominant Focus of Instruction

1. Processing focus: print
2. Instructional phase: after reading
3. Response mode emphasized: oral production
4. Strategy emphasized: monitoring
5. Skill emphasized: fluency and word identification
6. Source of information: text-based phasing to reader-based
7. Type of instruction: implicit, but can be adapted to explicit
8. Type of cognitive processing: initially successive, but rapidly moves to simultaneous

Procedure

1. The student selects a text that he wants to read. The teacher segments the text into manageable passages for oral reading.

2. The teacher makes a copy of the text so she can mark errors as the student reads.

3. The teacher explains that rereading a passage is like practicing a musical instrument or practicing a football play. The repetition helps students read more smoothly and automatically.

4. The student reads the passage orally while the teacher records errors and speed.

5. The errors and speed are charted on a graph.

6. The student practices silently rereading the passage while the teacher listens to other students.

7. The student rereads the passage to the teacher while she records errors with a different-colored pen.

8. The errors and speed are charted on a graph for the second reading. Progress toward the reading goals is discussed.

9. The procedure is continued until a speed of 85 words per minute is reached.

10. Steps 6, 7, and 8 are repeated as needed.

Modifications

1. The teacher can select a text that corresponds to instructional needs.

2. Instead of step 4, the following interventions have been successfully used:
   a. Discussion of the miscues and process of self-correction. The teacher suggests that the student say to himself, "Did that make sense? Can we say it that way?"
   b. Echo reading (see "Echo Reading") of sentences where the most miscues occur
   c. Discussion of the author's use of language and intended meaning of the paragraph
   d. Tape-recording the readings. Then the student listens to the recording, marks errors, and records his time.
   e. Chunking (see "Chunking") the selection to improve fluency and the interaction of thought and language

3. Only one or two rereadings are used. All readings are charted.

Further Diagnostic Applications

Basic View of Reading   Reading is both a text-based, decoding process as well as an interactive comprehension process. Comprehension is dependent on the automatic decoding of printed language. Therefore, fluent and accurate decoding are necessary for efficient comprehension. Thus initially, reading is a text-based process.

Patterns of Strengths and Strategies   Repeated readings are most appropriate for students who read word by word and do not use contextual clues to confirm anticipated words as they read. For this learner, the repeated readings encourage the use of overall contextual meaning and sentence structure to predict words and correct mistakes.

Learner Patterns That Produce Increased Engagement

1. For a learner who has a great deal of difficulty with word recognition because of an overemphasis on isolated word drill, this technique uses the overall textual meaning to increase word recognition accuracy.

2. For a simultaneous learner who cannot blend sounds and must rely, therefore, on the context for word recognition accuracy, this technique, if progressively difficult text is used, allows the student to read more complex text, where words can be recognized by using context rather than what the word looks or sounds like.

*3. For a successive learner who has become word-bound with a heavy phonics instruction and needs to develop fluency and use of contextual cues for word identification, this technique emphasizes using context to identify words rather than sounding out individual words.

Using the Technique as a Diagnostic Teaching Lesson   For repeated readings to be effective, a majority of the following statements must be answered in the affirmative:

Yes   No

_____   _____   1. The student's errors decrease on a second reading.
_____   _____   2. The student's speed increases on a second reading.
_____   _____   3. The student's pattern of errors includes more self-corrections as fluency increases.
_____   _____   4. Over several interventions, the student decreases the number of errors on an initial at-sight reading.

For Further Reading
Dowhower, S. (1989). Repeated reading: Research into practice. *The Reading Teacher, 42,* 502–507.

ReQuest

Description   The ReQuest (reciprocal questioning) technique develops comprehension by having the teacher and the student take turns asking and answering questions. At turning points in the text, the teacher models effective question-asking strategies. The student, in turn, asks appropriate questions by following the model. The goal is to develop self-questioning strategies for the student.

Targeted Reading Levels   4–12

Text   Particularly suited for narrative text but can be used with expository text

Predominant Focus of Instruction

1. Processing focus: meaning
2. Instructional phase: during reading
3. Response mode emphasized: oral discussion
4. Strategy emphasized: prediction and elaboration
5. Skill emphasized: literal and nonliteral comprehension

6. Source of information: reader-based
7. Type of instruction: implicit
8. Type of cognitive processing: successive

Procedure

1. The teacher selects a text that is at the student's reading level and that is predictive in nature.

2. The teacher identifies appropriate points for asking questions.

3. The teacher introduces the ReQuest procedure in terms the student will understand. She tells him that they will be taking turns asking questions about the sentence or paragraph and what it means. The student is to ask questions that a teacher might ask. Then the teacher emphasizes that questions must be answered fully and that they sometimes require support from the text.

4. The student and teacher read the first sentence silently.

5. When the teacher closes her book, the student asks questions. The teacher answers the question, integrating background knowledge and textual information. She also tells how she decided on her answer.

6. Then, the teacher asks questions about any important points not mentioned, modeling integrating information and the predictive nature of the reading by using questions such as "What do you think will happen next? Why do you think so?"

7. The teacher provides feedback about the student's questioning behavior during the procedure.

8. The procedure is used to develop purposes for reading and employs only the first three or four paragraphs.

9. The student reads the rest of the story silently to see whether he answers his questions.

10. Follow-up discussion and activities can be used.

Further Diagnostic Applications

Basic View of Reading   Reading is a socio-interactive process in which readers' questioning strategies are shaped by discussing questions with others. This shared thinking requires the reader to monitor his behavior by asking himself questions about the important information in the text and answering these questions, using both textual and nontextual information.

Patterns of Strengths and Strategies   The ReQuest procedure is most appropriate for the sequential learner who likes to ask questions but does not always attend to the text for answers. For these students, the approach matches their desire to ask questions, but it focuses on the relevant information in a story and develops an active question-asking role rather than a passive role.

Learner Patterns That Produce Increased Engagement

1. For a successive learner who asks questions and enjoys breaking a story into parts, reading only sections at a time, this technique uses his strength to show him how to elaborate his understanding using the text and what he knows.

2. For a successive learner who asks irrelevant questions when reading and fails to comprehend the main points of the story, this technique focuses his attention on asking important questions and justifying answers.

*3. For a passive learner who reads words fluently but does not ask himself what the passage means, this technique develops self-questioning and monitoring of comprehension.

*4. For a passive reader who reads words fluently but does not use his prior knowledge to interpret text, this technique asks the student to use both textual and nontextual information to ask and answer questions.

Using the Technique as a Diagnostic Teaching Lesson   For the ReQuest technique to be effective, a majority of the following statements must be answered in the affirmative:

Yes   No
____   ____   1. The student likes to ask questions.
____   ____   2. The student can answer questions.
____   ____   3. The student can follow the teacher's model in question-answering behavior.

For Further Reading

Manzo, A. V. & Manzo, U. C. (1995). *Teaching children to be literate: A reflective approach.* Fort Worth, TX: Harcourt Brace.

Tompkins, G. E. (1998). *50 literacy strategies: Step by step.* Englewood Cliffs, NJ: Merrill/Prentice Hall.

Retelling

Description   Retelling is a technique in which a reader makes a mental representation of the story and uses it to orally retell the story. The student tells about the characters, setting, problem, main episodes, and resolution.

Targeted Reading Levels   1–5

Text   Narrative, but can be applied to all kinds

Predominant Focus of Instruction

1. Processing focus: meaning
2. Instructional phase: after reading
3. Response mode emphasized: oral production
4. Strategy emphasized: elaboration
5. Skill emphasized: literal comprehension
6. Source of information: both reader-based and text-based
7. Type of instruction: implicit
8. Type of cognitive processing: simultaneous

Procedure

1. Before reading, the teacher explains to the students that she is going to ask them to retell the story when they have finished reading.

2. If the teacher is expecting the students to include specific information, then she should tell the students before reading.

3. The teacher asks the students to retell the story as if they were telling it to a friend who has never heard it before.

4. The students tell the story, noting the important parts: story setting, theme, plot, sequence, and resolution.

5. If the student is hesitant, the teacher uses prompts at the beginning, middle, and end (see step 6).

6. If the student is unable to tell the story, the retelling is prompted step by step: "Once there was . . . who did . . . in the. . . . (The character) had a problem. . . . To solve the problem, (the character) . . . first . . . second . . . third. . . . Finally, the problem was solved by . . . and then. . . ."

7. When the retelling is complete, the teacher can ask direct questions about important information omitted.

8. The teacher can also refer the student to the text to reread omitted important information.

Modifications

1. Retelling can be enhanced through the use of feltboards, role playing, and puppets.

2. Retelling can be easily adapted to small group or partner activities in the classroom.

Further Diagnostic Applications

Basic View of Reading   Reading is a socio-interactive process in which the reader reconstructs the story, thinking about what he wants to communicate to the instructional group. His interpretation includes his own perceptions of what is important to remember as well as what he needs to communicate.

Patterns of Strengths and Strategies   The retelling approach is most appropriate for students who have verbal strengths and remember the story long enough to internalize it and retell it. Retelling uses their strength to elaborate textual information.

Learner Patterns That Produce Increased Engagement

1. For readers who like to tell stories but fail to recount the most important events in the passage, retelling uses their strength to draw attention to important textual information.

*2. For readers who are hesitant to communicate their ideas, retelling increases the students' confidence by having them practice reformulating the information they read.

*3. For bilingual readers who become confused because they represent text in two language codes, retelling helps these learners use the text and classroom language to express their ideas.

Using the Technique as a Diagnostic Teaching Lesson   For retelling to be effective, both of the following statements must be answered in the affirmative:

Yes	*No*	
_____	_____	1. The student can verbalize some ideas about the story.
_____	_____	2. The student organizes a response that includes some of the story elements.

For Further Reading

Glazer, S. M. (1992). *Reading comprehension: Self-monitoring strategies to develop independent readers.* New York: Scholastic.

Morrow, L. & Walker, B. (1997). *The reading team: A handbook for volunteer tutors K–3.* Newark, DE: International Reading Association.

Retrospective Miscue Analysis

Description   The retrospective miscue analysis technique asks the student to listen to his miscues and evaluate the strategies he used as well as the strategies he might have used. In the discussion, the student and teacher discuss what good readers do when they encounter problems when reading.

Targeted Reading Levels   K–5

Text   Stories

Predominant Focus of Instruction

1. Processing focus: print and meaning
2. Instructional phase: during reading

3. Response mode emphasized: oral reading
4. Strategy emphasized: monitoring
5. Skill emphasized: word identification
6. Source of information: reader-based
7. Type of instruction: implicit
8. Type of cognitive processing: simultaneous

Procedure

1. The teacher selects an interesting text that is near the student's instructional level.

2. Before beginning, the teacher conducts a reading interview.

3. The teacher tapes the student reading the selected text.

4. After initial session, the teacher codes miscues on a printed version of text and preselects miscues to discuss during retrospective miscue analysis.

5. Sometimes, the teacher may want the student to listen to the tape and stop when he hears a miscue.

6. The teacher and student listen to the tape and mark miscues on a printed version of text.

7. The teacher and student discuss miscues using the following questions taken from Goodman and Marek (1996, p. 45):

---

1. Does the miscue make sense?
2. Does the miscue sound like language?
3. a. Was the miscue corrected?
   b. Should it have been?
If the answers to Questions 1 and 3a were "No," then ask:
4. Does the miscue look like what was on the page?
5. Does the miscue sound like what was on the page?
For all miscues, ask:
6. Why do think you made this miscue?
7. Did that miscue affect your understanding of the text?

---

8. As they discuss, the teacher expands the student's responses by asking, "Why do you think that?" or "How do you know?"

Further Diagnostic Applications

Basic View of Reading   Reading is a socio-interactive process in which understanding the process of reading is developed as students explain their thinking about how reading occurs. As students develop an understanding of the reading process, they begin to revalue themselves as readers.

Patterns of Strengths and Strategies   Retrospective miscue analysis is most appropriate for students who do not integrate the cueing systems; instead, they rely on a single system for figuring out words. As they evaluate their miscues using the structured questions, they explain how to correct miscues based on more than one cueing system.

Learner Patterns That Produce Increased Engagement

1. For a highly social student who likes to interact with others and discuss his thinking, this technique lets him discuss his strategies for figuring out words.

2. For a simultaneous learner who relies heavily on background knowledge when reading without attending to text cues, retrospective miscue analysis encourages him to attend to letters and meaning simultaneously.

*3. For a word-bound reader who does not use his understanding of the passage to correct miscues, this technique helps him talk about how the meaning and words can be used together to read fluently.

Using the Technique as a Diagnostic Teaching Lesson   For the retrospective miscue analysis technique to be effective, a majority of the following statements must be answered in the affirmative.

Yes	No	
_____	_____	1. The student understands how his miscue occurred.
_____	_____	2. The student begins to value his strategy use.
_____	_____	3. The student becomes more strategic.

For Further Reading

Goodman, Y. M. & Marek, A. M. (1996). Retrospective miscue analysis. In Y. M. Goodman & A. M. Marek (eds.), *Retrospective Miscue Analysis: Revaluing Readers and Reading*, pp. 39–49. Katonah, NY: Richard C. Owen Publishers, Inc.

Watson, D. & Hoge, S. (1996). Reader-selected miscues. In Y. M. Goodman & A. M. Marek (eds.), *Retrospective Miscue Analysis: Revaluing Readers and Reading*, pp. 157–164. Katonah, NY: Richard C. Owen Publishers, Inc.

Say Something

Description   Say something is a technique to develop personal response to literature by having students take turns saying something at intervals during the reading of the story.

Targeted Reading Levels   2–12

Text   Especially suited for engaging, narrative text but can be applied to all text

Predominant Focus of Instruction

1. Processing focus: meaning
2. Instructional phase: during reading
3. Response mode emphasized: oral discussion
4. Strategy emphasized: elaboration
5. Skill emphasized: nonliteral comprehension
6. Source of information: reader-based
7. Type of instruction: implicit
8. Type of cognitive processing: successive because story sections are used initially

Procedure

1. The teacher and students choose an engaging text.

2. The teacher demonstrates reading with a partner and making a personal response about the text read.

3. The teacher encourages students to challenge and extend the ideas of their partner.

4. The students choose partners for reading.

5. The partners decide whether the reading will be oral or silent.

6. The partners take turns reading and saying something about what they have read.

7. After the students have finished, the teacher leads a group discussion.

8. The teacher puts a central topic in the middle of an overhead or on the chalkboard.

9. The students generate ideas about the topic and discuss how they fit with the author's ideas.

10. After reading several selections in this fashion, the teacher engages students in a discussion of how they use this strategy as they read.

Further Diagnostic Applications

Basic View of Reading Reading is a socio-interactive process in which interpretations develop through communicating ideas to others. This sharing enhances and extends text understanding.

Patterns of Strengths and Strategies The say something technique is appropriate for students who like to talk about what they read as they are reading the text. This dialogue helps social students refine their ideas using their strength.

Learner Patterns That Produce Increased Engagement

1. For a self-directed reader who needs to talk aloud about his personal feelings related to the story, say something allows him to talk about his personal responses to the story.

*2. For a quiet student who needs to verbalize ideas in a safe environment before discussing those ideas in a large group, the say something technique gives him a chance to try out ideas with a partner.

Using the Technique as a Diagnostic Teaching Lesson   For the say something technique to be effective, a majority of the following statements must be answered in the affirmative:

Yes   No

_____   _____   1. The student can talk about the text read.

_____   _____   2. The student can attend to the meaning while reading so that he can make a response.

_____   _____   3. The student can relate personally to his partner.

For Further Reading

Short, K. G., Harste, J. C., & Burke, C. (1996). *Creating classrooms for authors and inquirers*. Portsmouth, NH: Heinemann.

Walker, B. J. (1999). *Supporting struggling readers* (2d ed.). Markham, Ontario: Pippin Publishing Limited.

Self-Directed Questioning

Description   Self-directed questioning uses student-generated questions to develop active reading. By following the sequence of self-directed questions, the student learns to monitor his understanding as he reads.

Targeted Reading Levels   All levels but most appropriate for 4–12

Text   Narrative text is most appropriate.

Predominant Focus of Instruction

1. Processing focus: meaning
2. Instructional phase: during reading
3. Response mode emphasized: oral discussion
4. Strategy emphasized: prediction and monitoring
5. Skill emphasized: nonliteral comprehension
6. Source of information: reader-based
7. Type of instruction: initially explicit, but moves rapidly to implicit
8. Type of cognitive processing: simultaneous, but is an interrupted story (successive)

Procedure

1. The teacher selects a text that is at the appropriate level and that has a fairly cohesive story line.

2. She decides on key prediction points. A story map (see "Story Map" in this chapter) can facilitate this process.

3. The teacher models the following steps with a short passage.

   STEP 1: Problem Definition

   "What must I do? . . . I must guess what the author is going to say. . . . A good strategy is to use the title. . . . From the title, I bet that . . ."

   STEP 2: Plan of Action

   Using another section of the story, the teacher models her plan for betting, placing her self-statements on the chalkboard.

   "Now, let's see what's my plan for betting. . . . To make my bet, I already know that . . . To prove my bet, I must look for hints in the text . . ."

   The teacher presents these two aspects on a chalkboard:

   I already know . . . Hints from the text are . . .

   STEP 3: Self-Instruction in the Form of Self-Questioning

   "I wonder how it fits? . . . The _____ must be important because the author keeps talking about it. . . . It fits because _____."

   STEP 4: Ways of Coping with Frustration and Failure

   Using other sections of the story, the teacher models her correction strategies by saying:

   "Oops, that doesn't make sense. . . . I need to check my thinking. . . . So far, I'm right about . . . but wrong about . . ."

   As she models this strategy, she writes on the chalkboard:

   Oops!

   Then she models the self-statement:

   "It's okay to make a mistake. . . . I can change my bet as I get more information. From the new information, I bet that . . . or I wonder whether . . ."

   The student then recycles to step 1.

   Using another section, she models her tentative thinking by saying, "Hmmmm" and writing it on the chalkboard:

   "Hmmm. Sometimes, I am just not sure . . . Maybe it's . . . or maybe it's . . ."

STEP 5: Self-Reinforcement

As she finishes the story, she models confirming her predictions by saying, "I knew it, that sure fits. . . . So far I'm right!"

She writes, "I knew it" on the chalkboard and says, "Now I bet the author . . ." The student then returns to step 1.*

4. The teacher emphasizes self-correcting behavior and self-reinforcement.

5. The student reads another example passage, talking aloud and using the steps.

6. When comprehension breaks down, the teacher models her own thinking rather than asking questions. She says, "When I read that I thought . . ."

7. The teacher phases in and out of the story discussion as necessary, using questions such as "Have you defined your problem? What is your plan? Does that make sense?"

8. At the end of the story, the student and the teacher discuss the story content and how they constructed meaning.

Modification   A chart of active reading behaviors can be kept by the teacher or student. In the chart, they assess how many predictions or bets were revised and what sources of information were used.

Further Diagnostic Applications

Basic View of Reading   Reading is an interactive process in which the reader builds a model of meaning based on textual and nontextual information. As the reader builds his model of meaning, he predicts, monitors, and reinforces his learning.

Patterns of Strengths and Strategies   Self-directed questioning is most appropriate for students who overrely on what they know, failing to monitor reading comprehension and to relate textual information to prior knowledge. For these students, the approach matches their strength of prior knowledge and helps them revise their understanding based on textual information.

Learner Patterns That Produce Increased Engagement

1. For a simultaneous learner who understands the story but cannot recall the textual information used to construct his answer, the technique has him check the text, which will help facilitate memory.

---

*The procedure in step 3 is adapted from *The Effects of Self-Questioning on Reading Comprehension* (pp. 9–10) by B. J. Walker and T. Mohr (1985). Paper presented at the Washington Organization for Reading Development—Research Conference, Seattle, WA. (ERIC Document Reproduction Service No. ED 262 392). Adapted by permission.

2. For a simultaneous learner who does not use self-talk to monitor the sources of information used to construct his answers, this technique encourages the internal dialogue that accompanies effective comprehension.

*3. For a passive learner who needs to actively engage in forming and revising his interpretations of the text, this technique gives him a plan for thinking and checking his understanding.

*4. For a successive learner who knows the meanings of words but depends on teacher questioning to interpret the important information in the text, this technique gives him the steps to develop his own questions.

*5. For a successive learner who cannot tie story events together, using what he already knows and these events, this technique asks the student to check both the text and what he knows to see whether they fit together.

Using the Technique as a Diagnostic Teaching Lesson   For self-directed questioning to be effective, a majority of the following statements must be answered in the affirmative:

Yes   No
_____   _____   1. The student can make a prediction.
_____   _____   2. The student can follow the oral discussion of strategic reading.
_____   _____   3. The student does not use background knowledge when reading.
_____   _____   4. The student does not use key events to predict outcomes.

For Further Reading
Roskos, K. & Walker, B. J. (1994). *Interactive handbook for understanding reading diagnosis*. Englewood Cliffs, NJ: Merrill/Prentice Hall.

Sentence Combining

Description   Sentence combining is a technique designed to help students write and understand complex sentences. The student is shown how to combine short sentences to make increasingly more complex sentences.

Targeted Reading Levels   3–7

Text   Structured programs of short sentences, the student's own writing, or short sentences from the text

Predominant Focus of Instruction

1. Processing focus: meaning
2. Instructional phase: after reading

3. Response mode emphasized: oral discussion and written discourse
4. Strategy emphasized: elaboration
5. Skill emphasized: sentence comprehension
6. Source of information: text-based
7. Type of instruction: implicit
8. Type of cognitive processing: successive, but using manipulatives adds a simultaneous aspect

Procedure

1. The teacher introduces the concept of combining sentences by using short sentences that the student can read.

2. The teacher explains that simple sentences can be combined and still have the same meaning.

3. She begins by writing sentences on the board, such as these:

   The dog is brown.

   The dog is in the park.

   The dog bit the man.

4. Then she shows the students how to delete repeated words or phrases. For the example in step 3, the following process would take place.
   a. The teacher might say, "If the dog is brown, we can call it a brown dog." On the board, the teacher would write this:

      brown + dog = brown dog

   b. The teacher explains that the sentence can be expanded by adding a phrase to tell where the dog is: "in the park." The teacher then shows the change:

      brown dog + in the park = the brown dog in the park

   c. She also explains that sentences can be further combined by telling what the dog did as the action in the sentence. Therefore, she adds *bit the man* as the action. The teacher writes this:

      The brown dog in the park + bit the man = The brown dog in the park bit the man.

   d. The teacher states that the combined sentences would be "The brown dog in the park bit the man."

5. The teacher points out to the student that by combining ideas into one sentence, reading and writing become more interesting.

Modifications

1. Phrases can be placed on cards and then combined and recombined to form new sentences.

2. Closed sentence combining, where cued words are provided to indicate how the sentence is combined, can be used to increase sensitivity to a particular sentence structure. For example, the following two sentences might be combined.

I know_____.

Chris stole the cookie.

The teacher supplies the cue word *that,* and the sentences are combined with the following result.

I know that Chris stole the cookie.

Further Diagnostic Applications

Basic View of Reading   Reading is a text-based process that involves the action of constructing meaning with words in sentences. The sequence of how words are linked in sentences affects reading comprehension; therefore, learning how the words are related in sentences facilitates both reading and writing.

Patterns of Strengths and Strategies   Sentence combining is most appropriate for students who can read short sentences but have difficulty following sentence order in longer sentences. Usually these students have verbal skills but lack the ability to link information in more complex frameworks.

Learner Patterns That Produce Increased Engagement

1. For a successive learner who speaks in short choppy sentences without using signal words to combine ideas, the technique shows him how short sentences are combined to form longer sentences.

*2. If a simultaneous learner has difficulty with sentence order as exhibited by continued failure with a cloze activity, using sentence cards helps this student because he can visually manipulate the words in the sentence.

Using the Technique as a Diagnostic Teaching Lesson   For sentence combining to be effective, both of the following statements must be answered in the affirmative:

Yes   No

_____ _____   1. The student can easily see the connection between the short sentences and the complex sentences.

_____ _____   2. The student likes to manipulate words and phrases.

For Further Reading

McNeil, J. D. (1992). *Reading comprehension: New directions for classroom practice.* New York: HarperCollins.

Wilkinson, P. A. & Patty, D. (1993). The effects of sentence combining on the reading comprehension of fourth grade students. *Research in the Teaching of English, 27,* 104–125.

Sight Word Approach

Description   The sight word approach is a technique for beginning reading instruction that uses what words mean to develop what the word looks like. Through the use of pictures and oral context, students associate meaning with isolated sight words. Then the teacher can place sight words on individual cards so that they may be used to review and reinforce a recognition vocabulary. Also, decoding by analogy is taught to expand reading acquisition.

Targeted Reading Levels   K–2

Text   The basic preprimers and primers of published reading series, which contain a regular and controlled introduction of sight words in simple text. Decoding by analogy is taught through known sight words.

Predominant Focus of Instruction

1. Processing focus: print
2. Instructional phase: before reading
3. Response mode emphasized: oral discussion
4. Strategy emphasized: prediction
5. Skill emphasized: word identification
6. Source of information: text-based
7. Type of instruction: implicit
8. Type of cognitive processing: successive, but has a simultaneous quality

Procedure

1. The teacher selects a text that has a controlled sight word vocabulary.

2. She introduces sight words for the story by presenting them in isolation, supplemented by oral context and/or pictures.

3. The teacher reviews the words by placing words on cards and flashing the words in various orders. If the student cannot recall the words, a meaning or semantic prompt is used. If the student cannot recall the word *dog*, the teacher might prompt him by saying, "It rained cats and _____."

4. The student reads the story that contains the words. (The teacher uses the format for directed reading activity or directed reading-thinking activity to direct discussion.)

5. The teacher reinforces sight words by using cloze exercises, games with the word cards, and repetitive reading of stories with the controlled vocabulary.

6. After the student can recognize selected words at sight, the teacher uses analytic phonics (see "Analytic Phonics" in this chapter) to introduce how to decode new words by using analogies to known sight words. For example, the teacher might write *green*, *grass*, and *grow* on the board. She might then ask the students the following series of questions (the appropriate student answers are supplied in

parentheses): "How are they alike? (They have *gr* letters.) What can we say about the *gr* sound? (It goes *gr-r-r.*) The next time you see *gr*, what sound are you going to try? *(gr-r-r.)*"

Modifications

1. The teacher can make a word bank by selecting target sight words (including easy words and concrete words) from each lesson and writing them on 3" × 5" cards. On the back of the card, she places the word in a sentence taken from the child's own vocabulary or the story.

2. To reinforce sight word recognition, the teacher can flash the word cards, adding a semantic cue from the story. For example, when the target word *play* is forgotten, the teacher uses the semantic cue, "We like to run and _____."

3. The teacher can chart the number of word cards recognized by recording the student's responses on a graph so that the student can monitor his progress.

4. The teacher uses the word cards to form a word bank that can be used to write and combine sentences. This bank becomes a spelling dictionary of known words for writing during uninterrupted sustained silent writing.

5. The teacher uses word cards to construct games to reinforce learning.

6. Students classify the word cards according to categories and make a feature analysis grid (see "Feature Analysis Grid" in this chapter).

7. The teacher constructs word sorts (see "Word Sorts" in this chapter).

Further Diagnostic Applications

Basic View of Reading   Reading is a text-based process in which the reader learns the words in the text before he reads the story. As he learns the words, he associates their meaning in oral context. Therefore, learning to read is a process of accumulating enough words recognized at sight that a student can decode new words in a story by using the written context and decoding analogies to known words. Initially, this approach places a high demand on visual feature analysis and phonemic segmentation.

Patterns of Strengths and Strategies   The sight word approach is most appropriate for students who have developed a systematic way of analyzing the key visual features of words. At the readiness level, this strength is often indicated by letter naming.

Learner Patterns That Produce Increased Engagement

1. A simultaneous learner who attends to the key features of words notices what visual features are alike and what visual features are different. Presenting the word with a semantic cue helps the student focus on meaning and visual cues at the same time.

2. For an inattentive learner who attends more to the pictures and context when reading stories than the important features of the words, the sight word approach isolates the word so the student can identify and remember the key visual features.

*3. For a passive learner who needs direct instruction in how to select the key features so he can remember what the words look like, the sight word approach provides a tool for the teacher to talk about what words look like.

Using the Technique as a Diagnostic Teaching Lesson   For sight word approach to be effective, a majority of the following statements must be answered in the affirmative:

Yes   No

_____ _____   1. The student easily remembers the sight words taught.
_____ _____   2. The student analyzes the words, noticing visual differences among words.
_____ _____   3. The student can segment sounds so that applying decoding analogies is easy.

For Further Reading

Gipe, J. P. (1995). *Corrective reading techniques for the classroom teacher* (3rd ed.). Scottsdale, AZ: Gorsuch Scarisbrick.

Taylor, B., Harris, L., Pearson, P. D., & Garcia, G. (1995). *Reading difficulties: instruction and assessment.* New York: McGraw-Hill.

SQ3R

Description   SQ3R is a procedure for studying content area text that includes the five steps of *survey, question, read, recite,* and *review.* It is designed as a procedure for students to use to monitor their comprehension and learning as they read and study expository text.

Targeted Reading Levels   5–12

Text   Expository

Predominant Focus of Instruction

1. Processing focus: meaning
2. Instructional phase: before, during, and after reading
3. Response mode emphasized: oral discussion
4. Strategy emphasized: elaboration and prediction
5. Skill emphasized: study skills
6. Source of information: text-based

7. Type of instruction: explicit, but lacks modeling
8. Type of cognitive processing: successive

Procedure

1. The teacher selects a content-area text at an appropriate reading level.

2. She introduces the five steps in a short minilesson.

3. *S—Survey.* The teacher explains how to skim (briefly read) the entire passage to construct an overall framework for the information. She directs the student to use the paragraph headings as key information in understanding the overall framework.

4. *Q—Question.* After the text is surveyed, the teacher directs the student to develop questions that he thinks will be answered in the passage. The teacher helps the student focus on the key concepts of the text as he develops the questions. She directs the student to use paragraph headings and italics to form the questions for each *section*.

5. *R—Read.* The student reads the text section by section to answer the questions posed at the beginning of each section. After a section has been read, the student proceeds to the next step.

6. *R—Recite.* The teacher explains that the student now is to answer the questions he posed for the section just read. The teacher encourages the student to construct an answer rather than read word for word from the text. At this point, the student may need to write down his answer to facilitate recall.

7. The three steps (question, read, and recite) are repeated for each section.

8. *R—Review.* After the last section is read, the student reviews the questions and answers for the entire text. At this time, the student tries to relate the information into an overall framework that will facilitate recall.

Further Diagnostic Applications

Basic View of Reading   Reading comprehension is a text-based process in which information from the text forms the framework for recalling facts and elaborating concepts in content-area texts.

Patterns of Strengths and Strategies   SQ3R is most appropriate for students who have facility with word recognition and comprehension but lack an overall method for organizing factual information in a content-area text. For these students, the approach provides a systematic method for studying the information.

Learner Patterns That Produce Increased Engagement

1. For the student who develops self-control easily, this technique gives him the steps to manage his own learning.

2. For a successive learner who questions and recalls facts without using an organizational framework so that facts can be conceptually related, the survey and review steps provide a means for relating information into an overall framework.

*3. For a passive learner who can use the steps to develop a procedure for studying and remembering text, this technique gives him a tool for active reading.

*4. For a successive learner who asks questions but forgets to look for the answers, SQ3R gives him a tool for finding answers to the important questions in the text.

Using the Technique as a Diagnostic Teaching Lesson   For SQ3R to be effective, a majority of the following statements must be answered in the affirmative:

Yes   No
____ ____   1. The student identifies important textual information.
____ ____   2. The student can construct questions from the subtopics.
____ ____   3. The student follows the procedures and easily incorporates the steps.

For Further Reading
McKenna, M. C. & Robinson, R. D. (1993). *Teaching through text: A content literacy approach to content area reading.* New York: Longman.
Pauk, W. (1993). *How to study in college* (5th ed.). Boston: Houghton Mifflin.

Story Drama

Description   Story drama is a method for developing reading comprehension by using the natural dramatic abilities of students. The students think about how a story will end by role-playing scenes from a story that they have read up to a certain point. By taking the roles of the various characters, the students use their knowledge of similar experiences, their affective response to the characters, and key information to act out their interpretation of the story.

Targeted Reading Levels   2–6

Text   Various kinds of literature. Picture storybooks and adventure stories with an intriguing plot lend themselves to dramatic interpretation.

Predominant Focus of Instruction

1. Processing focus: meaning
2. Instructional phase: during reading
3. Response mode emphasized: oral and kinesthetic

4. Strategy emphasized: prediction and monitoring
5. Skill emphasized: nonliteral comprehension
6. Source of information: reader-based
7. Type of instruction: implicit
8. Type of cognitive processing: simultaneous

Procedure

1. The teacher selects a story with an intriguing plot.

2. The teacher or the students read until they have enough information about the characters to role-play the story.

3. The teacher assigns the students the character roles from the story.

4. The teacher uses key props to engage the students in the drama in a concrete way.

5. The teacher and the students begin the drama at the point of interruption.

6. The students dramatize their predictions through role playing.

7. In the process of the dramatization, the teacher may stop the drama and have students exchange roles.

8. The students discuss their predictions and the information used to make the predictions.

9. After the dramatization, the students write an ending for the story.

10. Finally, the students finish reading the story.

11. The students discuss and compare both the drama and the story ending.

12. The teacher and the students discuss their personal interpretations evidenced in the drama and how their individual viewpoints influence those interpretations.

Further Diagnostic Applications

Basic View of Reading   Reading is a socio-interactive process in which the roles students play in the drama shape their personal interpretation and the group interaction focuses their comprehension. Reading requires a personal identification with the story's characters, problems, and events; therefore, the affective purposes of the reader and situational variables influence his model of meaning.

Patterns of Strengths and Strategies   Story drama is most appropriate for students who are extremely expressive, divergent, and simultaneous when thinking. For these students, the powerful influence of personal, kinesthetic imagery is used to analyze the constructive process. This strategy encourages active involvement in analyzing not only the story line and character development but also the effect that personal identification with story characters has on comprehension.

Learner Patterns That Produce Increased Engagement

1. For a student who prefers to use dramatic expression and body language to communicate, instead of words, story drama uses this strength to aid the student in verbally communicating his ideas about the story.

2. For the dramatic, impulsive learner who needs to attend to the important information in the text, story drama focuses his attention on character traits and story theme in order to portray a character.

*3. For a simultaneous learner who relies too heavily on personal identification with story characters and has difficulty establishing a sense of distance when reading, story drama helps him analyze how his personal identification affects his interpretation.

*4. For a passive learner who needs to engage in active interpretation of the story line, story drama concretely demonstrates how to be actively involved in a story.

Using the Technique as a Diagnostic Teaching Lesson   For story drama to be effective, a majority of the following statements must be answered in the affirmative:

Yes   No

_____ _____   1. The student enjoys a dramatic presentation and can easily portray characters.

_____ _____   2. The student makes predictions as a result of the drama.

_____ _____   3. The student analyzes his personal identification with characters more objectively.

For Further Reading

Cunningham, P. M. & Allington, R. L. (1999). *Classrooms that work: They can all read and write* (2d ed.). New York: Longman.

Short, K. G., Harste, J. C., & Burke, C. (1996). *Creating classrooms for authors and inquirers*. Portsmouth, NH: Heinemann.

Story Maps

Description   Story maps are visual representations of the logical sequence of events in a narrative text. The elements of setting, problem, goal, events, and resolution are recorded visually on a sheet of paper.

Targeted Reading Level   1–8

Text   Any narrative text with a fairly coherent story line

Predominant Focus of Instruction

1. Processing focus: meaning
2. Instructional phase: during or after reading

3. Response mode emphasized: written
4. Strategy emphasized: monitoring and elaboration
5. Skill emphasized: literal comprehension
6. Source of information: text-based
7. Type of instruction: explicit
8. Type of cognitive processing: successive, but has a visual arrangement (simultaneous)

Procedure

1. The teacher selects a narrative passage of sufficient length so that it has a cohesive story line.

2. The teacher prepares questions to lead students through the story map.

3. The teacher discusses the organization of a story by explaining that every story has a beginning, middle, and an end.
   a. The beginning tells the place and who the characters are.
   b. During the middle of the story, the central character has a problem and makes a plan to solve it. Certain events in the story lead to solving the problem.
   c. The end of the story tells how the character(s) solved the problem.

4. The teacher explains the visual story map (see Figure 11–4) and relates it to story organization.

5. The students read the story.

6. The teacher and the students fill out the map together. The teacher uses the prepared questions to guide the completion of the map.

7. The teacher and the students compare this story with other stories they have read.

Further Diagnostic Applications

Basic View of Reading   Reading is an interactive process in which the reader's understanding of the elements of a story affects interpretation of the story.

Patterns of Strengths and Strategies   Story mapping is most appropriate for the learner who profits from a visual representation of story organization in order to develop adequate comprehension. Often the abundance of facts overwhelms the young reader, who needs a simple structure such as a story map to apply to stories to help him organize and remember events.

Learner Patterns That Produce Increased Engagement

1. For a simultaneous learner who has difficulty organizing sequential events of the story and remembering factual detail, the story map uses his visual strengths to develop the text-based skill of story development.

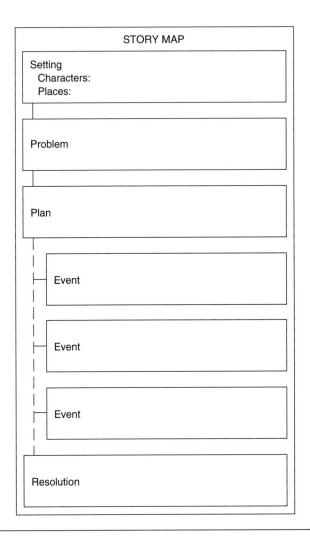

STORY MAP

Setting
   Characters:
   Places:

Problem

Plan

Event

Event

Event

Resolution

Figure 11–4   Story Map

Note. Adapted from *Asking Questions About Stories* by P. David Pearson, Number 15 of the *Ginn Occasional Papers,*© Copyright, 1982, by Ginn and Company. Used by permission of Silver Burdett Ginn Inc.

*2. For the passive learner who has difficulty retelling the story and often leaves out key events or characters in the retelling, the story map gives a structure to the retelling and reasons for the facts to be remembered.

*3. For the fact-bound learner who lacks a cohesive sense of story, the map provides him with an overall view of the story.

Using the Technique as a Diagnostic Teaching Lesson   For story maps to be effective, a majority of the following statements must be answered in the affirmative:

Yes   No

_____ _____ 1. The student understands the story map elements.
_____ _____ 2. The student improves his ability to retell the story.
_____ _____ 3. The student improves the number of questions about story
             events he can answer.

For Further Reading

Macon, J. M., Bewell, D., & Vogt, M. (1991). *Responses to literature: Grades K–8*. Newark, DE: International Reading Association.

Story Writing Approach

Description   Story writing is an instructional format for teaching narrative writing that includes three stages: prewriting, writing, and evaluating. By writing their own stories, students increase their awareness of story parts.

Targeted Reading Levels   3–6, but can be used at all levels

Text   Student's own writing

Predominant Focus of Instruction

1. Processing focus: meaning
2. Instructional phase: after reading
3. Response mode emphasized: written discourse
4. Strategy emphasized: elaboration
5. Skill emphasized: nonliteral comprehension
6. Source of information: reader-based
7. Type of instruction: implicit
8. Type of cognitive processing: simultaneous

Procedure

1. The teacher introduces the structure of a story. Stories have a beginning (the characters and place), middle (problems and the events), and an end (solution of the problem).

2. The teacher and the students brainstorm ideas to select a topic and information that might go into the story.

3. Using the information collected, the students write their stories. The teacher emphasizes that the story needs to flow from one idea to the next and make sense.

4. The teacher has the students reread their stories to see whether they make sense. She uses the following questions:
   a. Does the story make sense?
   b. Do I have all the story parts?

    c. Have I left out any information that the reader might need to know in order to understand my story?

5. The students revise any unclear information.

6. The students make a final copy of their stories.

Modifications

1. In prewriting, students can use a visual story map to form the outline of the story.

2. For the student who has a great deal of difficulty, the teacher might use a story frame with only minimal ideas deleted.

3. Guided imagery journeys may be used as a prewriting activity.

4. A story can be composed by a small group of students. Each person writes a segment of the story and then passes the text to the next person. Each student's contribution to the story line must build upon prior information and make sense.

5. Pairs of students can read and edit each other's stories.

6. Instead of step 4, the students can take their stories to the author's circle where students provide input on the three questions.

Further Diagnostic Applications

Basic View of Reading   Reading is an active, reader-based process in which the reader interprets the author's intended meaning. An author writes a text that allows a clear interpretation by the reader but assumes that a certain amount of inferencing will occur on the part of the reader.

Patterns of Strengths and Strategies   The story writing approach is most appropriate for students who need to write in order to experience how a story is organized so that it makes sense. This approach emphasizes the constructive nature of reading and that the text needs to "make sense."

Learner Patterns That Produce Increased Engagement

1. For the simultaneous learner who writes and reads for self-understanding and meaning but does not realize that a story is a contractual agreement between reader and writer, this technique helps him think about what the author wants him to understand.

*2. The passive learner who does not understand story organization learns to attend to story features when he reads by writing his own parts of a story.

*3. The reader who relies on his own background knowledge to interpret text and does not attend to sentence meaning becomes more sensitive to the function that text structure has in developing meaning by writing his own stories and listening to others interpret them.

Using the Technique as a Diagnostic Teaching Lesson   For story writing to be effective, a majority of the following statements must be answered in the affirmative:

Yes   No

____ ____ 1. The student prefers to write what he thinks rather than contribute to a discussion.

____ ____ 2. The student writes fluently and can construct text that makes sense.

____ ____ 3. The student understands the parts of a story well enough to be able to construct a coherent story.

For Further Reading

DeCarlo, J. E. (1995). *Perspectives in whole language.* Boston: Allyn & Bacon.

Short, K. G., Harste, J. C., & Burke, C. (1996). *Creating classrooms for authors and inquirers.* Portsmouth, NH: Heinemann.

Strategy Instruction

Description   Strategy instruction is an instructional format designed to teach procedures related to print and meaning processing. In such lessons, teachers model their own thinking related to an unfamiliar task, and then ask students to think out loud about how they are completing the task. This instruction is followed by coaching students to ensure self-regulated learning.

Targeted Reading Levels   All levels

Text   Authentic text

Predominant Focus of Instruction

1. Processing focus: print or meaning
2. Instructional phase: before, during, and after reading
3. Response mode emphasized: oral discussion
4. Strategy emphasized: monitoring and elaboration
5. Skill emphasized: depends on focus
6. Source of information: text-based and reader-based
7. Type of instruction: explicit phasing to self-directed learning
8. Type of cognitive processing: successive, quickly phasing to simultaneous

Procedure

1. The teacher selects the new procedure to be learned.
2. The teacher talks about what the strategy is, what it is like, and gives some examples.

3. The teacher explains why the strategy works when reading.

4. The teacher models the new strategy in authentic texts by talking out loud about how she reads the text, paying particular attention to the targeted strategy.

5. The students use the targeted strategy in authentic texts. They talk out loud about their problem-solving strategies.

6. The teacher supports the "strategic thinking" of the readers. She phases in to coach thinking and phases out to let students use strategies independently.

7. After reading, the students and teacher discuss the strategies they used for text interpretation.

8. Students are asked to assess their strategy deployment and how it affected their text interpretation.

9. The teacher explains when to use the strategy and what to do if its use is not effective.

Further Diagnostic Applications

Basic View of Reading   Reading is an interactive process in which the reader strategically implements the strategies and skills he knows to solve problems when interpreting texts.

Patterns of Strengths and Strategies   The strategy instruction format is most appropriate when teaching unfamiliar reading procedures or when students lack particular reading strategies.

Learner Patterns That Produce Increased Engagement

1. This format can be used to teach unfamiliar strategies to active readers. It helps them consolidate strategies.

2. This format is designed for the student who needs a teacher to model strategic reading. By following the teacher's model, the student develops active reading strategies.

*3. This format has been used with passive readers who read words without constructing meaning. The modeling and coaching help passive readers use active reading strategies.

Using the Technique as a Diagnostic Teaching Lesson   For strategy instruction to be effective, a majority of the following statements must be answered in the affirmative:

Yes   No

_____ _____   1. The student can imitate the teacher's model.
_____ _____   2. The student profits from oral discussion of strategic reading.
_____ _____   3. The student can assess his own strategy use.

For Further Reading

Duffy, G. G. (1993). Rethinking strategy instruction: Four teachers' development and their low achievers' understanding. *Elementary School Journal, 93,* 231–247.

Walker, B. J. (1996). Discussions that focus on strategies and self-assessment. In L. B. Gambrell & J. F. Almasi (eds.), *Lively Discussions! Fostering Engaged Reading.* pp. 286–296. Newark, DE: International Reading Association.

Summary Experience Approach

Description   The student and teacher talk about the story the class is currently reading. Based on the classroom reading material, the student is asked to retell the classroom story while the teacher records or writes down the retelling. This summary (dictated retelling) becomes material that is read by the student.

Targeted Reading Levels   K–3

Text   Classroom stories

Predominant Focus of Instruction

1. Processing focus: print and meaning
2. Instructional phase: after listening
3. Response mode emphasized: oral retelling
4. Strategy emphasized: prediction and monitoring
5. Skill emphasized: word identification and literal comprehension
6. Source of information: reader-based and text-based
7. Type of instruction: implicit
8. Type of cognitive processing: simultaneous

Procedure

1. The teacher checks with the classroom teacher to find out what story is being studied and obtains a copy of the story, book, or book chapter.

2. The teacher engages the student in dialogue about the selection being read in the classroom, asking the student to relate the key ideas.

3. The student is asked to retell the classroom selection while the teacher serves as a secretary and writes down what the student says, which becomes a written summary that the student reads.

4. Using leading questions, the teacher guides the student to retell the selection by using questions such as: What happened next? Who are the characters? How does the story end? (For additional prompts, see "Retelling" in this chapter.)

5. The students and teacher read the summary together to revise any statements or phrases that are unclear. The summary follows the natural language patterns of the student.

6. The teacher and the students read the summary repeatedly so that the repetition of the summary helps the student recognize the words in the summary and the words in the classroom story.

7. Retype the summary and make several copies. Let the students take one copy home to practice.

8. Create a book of story summaries.

Modification

1. The teacher can use a story map before the retelling to help the students dictate the summary.

2. The teacher can use a story self-assessment (see Chapter 8) evaluation to help the student revise and edit the story summary.

Further Diagnostic Applications

Basic View of Reading   Reading is an active, reader-based process. By reading his own summary, the student will learn the key vocabulary words. Because the summary is short and uses his own language structure, the student will be able to remember the words in the summary, which will in turn facilitate understanding the classroom story.

Patterns of Strengths and Strategies   The summary experience approach is most appropriate for students who have facility with language and are simultaneous reader-based thinkers. If the student uses his own language to retell the story rather than the exact words in the text, then the summary experience matches his own way of expressing and interpreting meaning; therefore, this technique facilitates word learning by asking the student to identify words using his own interpretation of the story.

Learning Patterns That Produce Increased Engagement

1. For a simultaneous thinker who readily thinks of the main ideas in the story and can retell a story with ease, the summary experience approach uses the student's strength (thinking of the main actions) to facilitate word identification.

2. For an extremely verbal student whose verbalization, at times, interferes with focusing on the words in the text, the summary experience approach uses this strength to facilitate recognizing individual words.

*3. A student who needs to improve comprehension will be able to use his own language to understand the story rather than answer direct questions posed by the teacher.

Using the Technique as a Diagnostic Teaching Lesson   For the summary experience approach to be effective, a majority of the following statements must be answered in the affirmative:

Yes   No
___ ___ 1. The student can retell the main actions of the classroom story.
___ ___ 2. The student can remember how he retold the story well enough to predict the words he does not remember as he rereads his summary.
___ ___ 3. The student responds when prompted, using the summary and the story theme.

For Further Reading

Walker, B. (1999). *Supporting Struggling Readers* (2d ed.). Markham, Ontario: Pippin Publishing Limited.

Summarization

Description   Summarization teaches the student how to write summaries of what he reads. He is shown how to delete unimportant information, group similar ideas, decide on or invent topic sentences, and list supporting details. These procedures culminate in a short paragraph that reflects the most important information.

Targeted Reading Levels   6–12

Text   Most appropriate for expository text

Predominant Focus of Instruction

1. Processing focus: meaning
2. Instructional phase: after reading
3. Response mode emphasized: written discourse
4. Strategy emphasized: elaboration
5. Skill emphasized: literal comprehension and study skills
6. Source of information: text-based to reader-based
7. Type of instruction: explicit
8. Type of cognitive processing: simultaneous

Procedure

1. The teacher selects an expository text.

2. She describes a summary as a short version of the text that contains all the important information.

3. The teacher explains that the purpose of writing summaries is to put all the important information together so it can be remembered better.

4. The students read a short selection.

5. The students reread the selection and ask themselves, "What is this mainly about?"

6. The teacher reads her summary of the selection and presents it on the overhead.

7. In the original text, the student marks the information the teacher used in the summary.

8. The teacher talks about the rules for writing summaries by telling the students how she wrote her summary.

9. The teacher demonstrates the rule of deleting trivial information. She points out that many writers tell us interesting information that is not a key idea. She tells them to ignore this information when writing a summary.

10. The teacher demonstrates the rule for deleting repeated information. She explains that many writers repeat information to make their point. When writing a summary, students should use an idea only once and ignore repeated information.

11. The teacher demonstrates the rule for combining details into a generalization. When possible, students should combine details that fit into the same category and rename that category with a bigger category. For example, *pigs, horses, cows,* and *chickens* can be renamed to *farm animals.*

12. The teacher demonstrates how to select the topic sentence. She points out that the topic sentence is the author's one sentence summary. It usually comes at the beginning or the end of the paragraph.

13. The teacher demonstrates how to invent a topic sentence when a paragraph has no summary sentence. In this case, she shows how to organize all the important information into one category. Then she writes a sentence that tells what the paragraph is mainly about. She shows how to think about the important information and relate it.

14. The students write a summary for the demonstration selection and check their summaries individually against the rules.

15. The students compare their summaries in small groups.

16. The students write a summary for another selection.

17. When they have finished, the students describe how they constructed their summaries.

18. The teacher shows them her summary for the same selection and talks about how she constructed it.

19. The students write summaries for several more selections on their own.

Further Diagnostic Applications

Basic View of Reading   Reading is an interactive process in which the reader decides what is important about the text in order to summarize and remember what it says.

Patterns of Strengths and Strategies   Summarization is most appropriate for students who like to think about what a text says but have difficulty remembering the facts that support this main point. The approach helps this student focus on relating all the textual information that is important to the key idea.

Learner Patterns That Produce Increased Engagement

1. For a simultaneous reader who quickly reduces information to the main ideas but needs to write out some important details to support the main idea, this technique helps the reader understand how details relate to main points.

*2. For a successive reader who cannot tie important information together in order to remember information, summarization helps him decide on general categories that relate details.

*3. For a successive reader who thinks everything in the text is important to remember, summarization helps him learn to delete unimportant and repeated information.

Using the Technique as a Diagnostic Teaching Lesson   For summarization to be effective, a majority of the following statements must be answered in the affirmative:

Yes   No

_____   _____   1. The student can write fairly fluently; therefore, writing the words on paper does not interfere with the task.

_____   _____   2. The student learns to distinguish what is important and what is unimportant fairly easily.

_____   _____   3. The student learns to group individual information of like categories easily.

For Further Reading

John, J. L., & Lenski, S. (1997). *Improving reading: A handbook of strategies* (2d ed.) Dubuque, IA: Kendall/Hunt.

Malone, L. D. & Mastropieri, M. A. (1991–1992). Reading comprehension instruction: Summarization and self-monitoring training for students with learning disabilities. *Exceptional Children, 58,* 270–279.

Sustained Silent Reading

Description   Sustained silent reading (SSR) is the designation of an uninterrupted time period where both the students and the teacher read self-selected reading materials for their own purposes. The teacher models her own engagement during reading. In turn, the students begin to define their interests and read for their engagement in literacy.

Targeted Reading Levels   All levels

Text   Self-selected

Predominant Focus of Instruction

1. Processing focus: meaning
2. Instructional phase: during reading
3. Response mode emphasized: some oral discussion
4. Strategy emphasized: depends on student
5. Skill emphasized: fluency and nonliteral comprehension
6. Source of information: reader-based
7. Type of instruction: implicit
8. Type of cognitive processing: depends on student

Procedures

1. Before beginning SSR, the teacher collects a variety of reading materials that represent a wide range of reading levels and text types (magazines, newspapers, novels, and informational texts).

2. Next, the teacher reads aloud favorite parts of books or talks about books other students have enjoyed in order to stimulate interest.

3. The teacher designates a specific time for reading each day. (After lunch is a good time; students select their books before lunch so they can be ready to read as soon as lunch is over. Another good time is at the end of the day.)

4. The students select their books prior to the designated reading time.

5. The teacher explains the "rule of thumb," which aids in book selection. According to this rule, the student selects a book and reads a page at random. When he reaches the first word he does not know, he places his little finger on it. On the next difficult word, he places the next finger, and so on. If he reaches his thumb before the end of the page, the book is too difficult and he must find another book.

6. The students do not browse and select books during the designated time span.

7. Initially, the teacher sets aside a short time period (5 to 10 minutes) for silent reading and then increases the amount of time each day.

8. The teacher uses a timer to monitor the time so everyone is free to concentrate on reading.

9. The students read silently for the time period.

10. The teacher and anyone else in the room read silently for the time period.

11. The teacher does not keep records or have students make reports on what they read. The students are in control of what and how much they read.

12. Initially, the teacher allows pretend reading, browsing through books, and looking at pictures. She also initially provides a narrow range of selection choices.

13. The teacher reiterates some key principles of sustained silent reading:
    a. Read what you want.
    b. Getting all the words right is not necessary.
    c. If it meets your needs, skipping pages is okay.

Comment: Although this technique is more effective for some children than others, it is recommended as part of the diagnostic teaching session because it allows students to read for their own purpose and therefore provides them with an experience in which they cannot fail.

Further Diagnostic Applications

Basic View of Reading   Reading is an engaging, reader-based process in which the readers' personal interpretations and engagement are the focus. By the teacher's modeling her own engagement in literate activities, she shares "wanting to read."

Patterns of Strengths and Strategies   Sustained silent reading is most appropriate for the active, independent reader who enjoys reading for his own purposes rather than the teacher's purposes. In this technique, personal enjoyment is gained while reading for individual purposes.

Learner Patterns That Produce Increased Engagement

1. For a successive learner who needs to identify his own reasons for reading, sustained silent reading allows him to identify his own interests and reasons for reading.

*2. For an inattentive reader who cannot read long sections of text silently, this technique allows him to increase his attention during silent reading.

*3. For a passive reader who views himself as a failure when reading, this technique allows him to feel success when reading because he controls the reasons for reading.

Using the Technique as a Diagnostic Teaching Lesson   For SSR to be effective, a majority of the following statements must be answered in the affirmative:

Yes   No
_____ _____ 1. The student selects books he wants to read.
_____ _____ 2. The student observes the rules of silent reading and is not disruptive during that time.
_____ _____ 3. The student increases his own task reading time and asks for longer time for sustained silent reading.

Caution: Be persistent in expecting success. Even though some students will pretend to be reading, it is the model and message that they can read what they like that are important.

For Further Reading

Morrow, L. & Walker, B. (1997). *The reading team: A handbook for volunteer tutors K–3.* Newark, DE: International Reading Association.

Rasinski, T. & Padak, N. (1996). *Holistic reading strategies: Teaching children who find reading difficult.* Englewood Cliffs, NJ: Merrill/Prentice Hall.

Synthetic (Explicit) Phonics

Description   Synthetic phonics teaches sound-symbol relationships (rules) in words to facilitate word identification. The student is systematically instructed to say the letter sounds in words and then blend the sounds together to decode the unknown word. The rapid transfer of decoding principles to new words is expected as the text includes many words that follow the rule but were not presented before reading.

Targeted Reading Levels   1–2

Text   Decodable words and some isolated drill

Predominant Focus of Instruction

1. Processing focus: print
2. Instructional phase: before reading
3. Response mode emphasized: oral discussion
4. Strategy emphasized: elaboration
5. Skill emphasized: word analysis
6. Source of information: text-based
7. Type of instruction: explicit
8. Type of cognitive processing: successive

Procedure

1. The teacher selects phonic rules to be taught.

2. She selects texts and words to illustrate the rule.

3. The teacher directly teaches the letter sounds.

    The letter *s* goes *"s-s-s."*

    The letter *t* goes *"t-t-t."*

    The letter *n* goes *"n-n-n."*

    The letter *m* goes *"m-m-m."*

In short words that have a consonant at the beginning and the end and an *a* in the middle, the letter *a* says *"a-a-a."*

4. The student blends the sounds together to form words.

   S-a-m says *"Sam."*

   S-a-t says *"sat."*

5. The student reads the words in a text that uses the sound-symbol relationships that the teacher has introduced.

   Sam is on the mat.

   The man is on the mat.

   Sam sat on the man on the mat.

6. The teacher facilitates the transfer of rules to new words. In the example, she teaches the sounds for *d, h,* and *c.* Then she asks the student to read the following story:

   The man has a hat. The hat is in the sand.

   Sam is a cat. Sam ran in the sand.

   Sam ran to the man.

   Sam sat on the man's hat.

   The man is mad at Sam. Sam ran.

Further Diagnostic Applications

Basic View of Reading Reading is a text-based process in which effective reading is based on accurate decoding of words. Learning sounds of letters and sounding out words precedes reading stories; therefore, decoding precedes comprehension.

Patterns of Strengths and Strategies Synthetic phonics is a process of successive blending of sounds, requiring the child to hold a sequence of sounds in her memory while synthesizing them to form a word. Young children who have facility with sound blending and can hold oral sequences in memory will have the greatest success with this method.

Learner Patterns That Produce Increased Engagement

1. For a successive learner who has facility with language so that the systematic decoding of words becomes a tool rather than an end by itself, the phonics approach facilitates word identification without interfering with fluency.

*2. For a passive learner who can blend sounds and profits from direct instruction in the sound system, this technique directly shows him how to decode new words as well as directs his attention to individual letters.

*3. The successive learner who can blend sounds but has no visual memory can always decode the word he has forgotten. The Distar reading program allows for this approach because more than 99 percent of the words in the stories are decodable.

Using the Technique as a Diagnostic Teaching Lesson   For synthetic phonics to be effective, a majority of the following statements must be answered in the affirmative:

Yes	No	
____	____	1. The student can blend sounds.
____	____	2. The student can segment sounds.
____	____	3. The student can hold a sequence of letter sounds in memory long enough to blend the sounds to form a word.

For Further Reading

McCormick, S. (1995). *Instructing students who have literacy problems*. Englewood Cliffs, NJ: Merrill/Prentice Hall.

Snow, C. E., Burn, M. S., & Griffin, P. (1998). *Preventing reading difficulties in young children*. Washington, DC: National Academy Press.

Talking Books

Description   The talking books method uses tape-recorded readings of selected stories to increase word recognition and reading fluency. The student repeatedly reads along with a tape until he can read the text fluently with comprehension.

Targeted Reading Levels   K–5

Text   Stories with specially prepared tape recordings

Predominant Focus of Instruction

1. Processing focus: print
2. Instructional phase: during reading
3. Response mode emphasized: oral
4. Strategy emphasized: prediction
5. Skill emphasized: word identification and fluency
6. Source of information: reader-based
7. Type of instruction: implicit
8. Type of cognitive processing: simultaneous

Procedure

1. The student selects a text that is interesting to him.

2. The teacher secures or makes a tape recording of the story.

3. If she makes a tape, she includes the following:
   a. She segments the story so that the student can easily finish a tape in one sitting.
   b. She cues the page numbers so the student can easily find the page.
   c. She records the text, using the natural phrases of language.
4. The student follows the line of print with his finger.
5. The student listens to the tape recording to develop an overall understanding of the story.
6. Then the student listens and reads along with the tape as many times as necessary until he can read the text fluently.
7. The student rehearses the text by himself.
8. The student reads the text to the teacher.
9. The teacher evaluates fluency and comprehension.
10. If the student reads the passage fluently with comprehension, he listens and reads the next segment of the story or another story.

Further Diagnostic Applications

Basic View of Reading   Reading is a reader-based process in which the reader's personal understanding of the story drives the word recognition process. By repeatedly listening to the story, the reader gains an understanding of the story meaning, story structure, and sentence structure. He uses this understanding to facilitate word recognition in the story.

Patterns of Strengths and Strategies   The talking books technique is most appropriate for the beginning reader or the nonfluent reader who easily memorizes stories. This memorization facilitates fluent reading of text and allows the student to attend to both meaning and print simultaneously. By memorizing stories, the student is exposed to lots of words in context, enabling him to apply phonic knowledge, recognize sight words, and self-correct as he meaningfully reads text.

Learner Patterns That Produce Increased Engagement

1. A simultaneous learner who relies too heavily on background knowledge when orally reading does not self-correct using graphic cues. This technique develops word identification by using the overall textual meaning (a strength) to identify words.
2. For a passive reader who reads word by word without attention to meaning, this technique restores reading for meaning by having the student learn to read whole stories with expression and by allowing the student to experience success.

*3. A nonfluent reader who has had an overemphasis of synthetic or explicit phonic instruction has become word-bound. This technique develops reading in meaningful phrases.

*4. For a slow reader who has not developed either decoding skills or a recognition vocabulary, talking books use memorizing whole stories so that the student can read lots of words before developing either phonic knowledge or a sight word vocabulary.

Using the Technique as a Diagnostic Teaching Lesson   For talking books to be effective, a majority of the following statements must be answered in the affirmative:

Yes   No

_____ _____ 1. The student is sufficiently interested in the text to listen and read the story repeatedly.

_____ _____ 2. The student memorizes the story fairly easily, requiring only a minimal number of listen-and-read sessions. (More than a week on the same story is too long.)

_____ _____ 3. As the story is read, the student follows the text and associates the words he hears with the words on the page.

For Further Reading

Rasinski, T. & Padak, N. (1996). *Holistic reading strategies: Teaching children who find reading difficult.* Englewood Cliffs, NJ: Merrill/Prentice Hall.

Walker, B. J. (1999). *Supporting struggling readers* (2d ed.). Markham, Ontario: Pippin Publishing Limited.

Thematic Experience Approach

Description   The thematic experience approach is a technique to develop an in-depth knowledge of a particular topic through integrating reading and writing activities.

Targeted Reading Levels   4–12

Text   Particularly suited for expository text, but can be used with all types

Predominant Focus of Instruction

1. Processing focus: meaning
2. Instructional phase: before and after reading
3. Response mode emphasized: oral discussion and written responses
4. Strategy emphasized: elaboration
5. Skill emphasized: literal and nonliteral comprehension
6. Source of information: text-based leading to reader-based

7. Type of instruction: implicit
8. Type of cognitive processing: simultaneous

Procedure

1. The teacher and students select a topic to be studied.

2. The teacher creates experiences to engage students in a general understanding of the topic.

3. The teacher and students then discuss what they are learning and already know about the topic.

4. The teacher and students brainstorm possible research topics while the teacher records these on a chart or chalkboard.

5. The students select a possible research topic and discuss this topic in a small group.

6. The teacher discusses research focus with each student elaborating ideas and suggesting possible reference sources.

7. Each student independently researches his special focus related to the topic.

8. Each student takes notes on his special focus area.

9. Each student prepares a presentation on his special focus to share with the class. This presentation can take many response modes: graphic organizer, video, written report, and so on.

10. The teacher and students evaluate their learning.

Further Diagnostic Applications

Basic View of Reading   Reading is an active, reader-based process in which students build topic knowledge, using what they know. What they know is usually related to their individual interests.

Patterns of Strengths and Strategies   The thematic experience approach is appropriate for students who build a background of experiences by pursuing their own interests. In researching their interests, these students build a network of new concepts.

Learner Patterns That Produce Increased Engagement

1. For simultaneous readers who prefer to independently research topics to expand their knowledge, the thematic experience approach allows them to build their own theories and concepts.

*2. For readers who have little prior knowledge about a topic, the thematic experience approach begins by using interest to build a network of ideas on an unknown topic.

*3. For bilingual readers who need to build a network of language to express concepts, the thematic experience approach allows them to make connections in both language codes during the experience.

Using the Technique as a Diagnostic Teaching Lesson   For the thematic experience approach to be effective, a majority of the following statements must be answered in the affirmative:

Yes   No

____ ____ 1. The student can easily decide what interests him.

____ ____ 2. The student likes to work independently, researching information about a particular topic.

____ ____ 3. The student can share the information with a group of students.

For Further Reading

Davis, S. J. (1990). Breaking the cycle of failure through thematic experience approach. *Journal of Reading, 33*(6), 420–423.

Short, K. G., Harste, J. C., & Burke, C. (1996). *Creating classrooms for authors and inquirers.* Portsmouth, NH: Heinemann.

Triple Read Outline

Description   Triple read outline is the rereading of expository text to develop an organizational framework of main ideas and supporting details. By reading the information three times, the student focuses on different purposes for organizing information during each reading.

Targeted Reading Levels   7–12

Text   Expository

Predominant Focus of Instruction

1. Processing focus: meaning
2. Instructional phase: during reading
3. Response mode emphasized: written discourse
4. Strategy emphasized: monitoring and elaboration
5. Skill emphasized: study skills
6. Source of information: reader-based and text-based
7. Type of instruction: explicit
8. Type of cognitive processing: simultaneous, but interrupted reading (successive)

Procedure

1. The teacher selects a short expository passage to demonstrate the triple read outline.

2. She makes an overhead of the passage and copies for the students.

3. The teacher states the purpose for the first reading—identify the main idea—and models the step by reading a paragraph out loud and identifying the main idea. Then she writes or illustrates the main idea in the paragraph margins. She continues the procedure for the entire passage, identifying the main idea of each paragraph in the passage.

4. The teacher models the second procedure—identify supporting details—by talking out loud as she rereads the entire passage and underlining the key details that support the main idea for the first paragraph. She continues the procedure for each paragraph in the entire passage.

5. On the third reading, the teacher models the third step—organize the information into an outline. She puts the notes that she wrote in the margins and the key details into an outline of the passage. Some of the key ideas will not fit into the overall outline. She writes those on a separate page.

6. The teacher writes a summary of the passage. She uses the main idea as the topic sentence and puts in the details that support the main idea. She leaves out information that is not important.

7. Next the teacher distributes copies of a passage from the textbook to be read.

8. This time the students read the passage, looking for the main idea of each paragraph and writing the main idea in the margin. She tells them that some paragraphs will not have a main idea.

9. The students compare their margin "main ideas" with the teacher's margin "main ideas."

10. The students revise the information as necessary.

11. The students read the passage again, looking for and underlining the supporting details for the main ideas in the margin.

12. The students compare the facts they underlined with the facts the teacher underlined.

13. The students revise the underlining as necessary.

14. The students read the passage a third time to organize the information into an outline of main ideas and supporting details. Unimportant information is not to be included.

15. The students compare their outlines with the teacher's outline. They discuss the differences and similarities.

16. If the students have left out important information, the teacher models her thinking about why something is important enough to leave in the outline.

17. Using the outline, the students write a three- to four-sentence summary of passage.*

---

*Source: From *The Triple Read Method for Expository Text* by P. D. Pearson (1985). Seminar presentation, Eastern Montana College, Billings, MT. Adapted by permission.

Further Diagnostic Applications

Basic View of Reading   Reading is an interactive process that requires the reader to select information and organize this information so it can be remembered. Organizing the information into a logical structure facilitates recall, as does rereading the text with different purposes for selecting information.

Patterns of Strengths and Strategies   The triple read outline is most appropriate for students who read expository text rapidly and fluently but remember very little of the information when they have finished. Frequently these students do not understand how the author organized the information, so they passively read the words without a reason for gaining information. They think that good readers read the text once rapidly and are somehow able to remember an enormous amount of facts with this simple strategy.

Learner Patterns That Produce Increased Engagement

1. For the simultaneous reader who remembers main ideas but forgets the facts, this technique gives the student a strategy for remembering facts within an overall framework.

2. For the passive reader who lacks the strategy to read for different purposes as he is reading, this technique shows him how to read information for different purposes and the results of these rereadings.

*3. For the successive reader who verbalizes the words, remembers some facts, but does not organize the facts by relating them to the key ideas, triple read outline gives him a tool for organizing information.

Using the Technique as a Diagnostic Teaching Lesson   For the triple read outline to be effective, a majority of the following statements must be answered in the affirmative:

Yes   No

_____ _____   1. The student is able to read the passage rapidly enough that the technique is not too time-consuming.
_____ _____   2. The student learns how to find a main idea rather easily.
_____ _____   3. The student learns how to find the supporting details for each main idea without much difficulty.

For Further Reading

Taylor, B., Harris, L., Pearson, P. D., & Garcia, G., (1995). *Reading difficulties: Instruction and assessment.* New York: McGraw-Hill, Inc.

Visualization

Description   Visualization is an approach for improving word meaning by suggesting to children that they form mental images of words, relating descriptors with the new word.

Targeted Reading Levels   All levels

Text   Key vocabulary words in narrative text or expository text

Predominant Focus of Instruction

1. Processing focus: meaning
2. Instructional phase: before reading
3. Response mode emphasized: nonverbal responses and oral discussion
4. Strategy emphasized: elaboration
5. Skill emphasized: word meaning
6. Source of information: reader-based
7. Type of instruction: implicit
8. Type of cognitive processing: simultaneous

Procedure

1. The teacher selects target words for which to develop meanings.

2. The students look at a word and then close their eyes.

3. The teacher reads a definition and *like a* statements and asks the students to form a mental picture of the word. For example, if the target word is *geyser,* the teacher could say, "Think about a geyser like a large whistling teapot just about to boil. The water is bubbling and the pressure is mounting. When enough pressure builds up, the teapot begins to whistle and blow steam into the air. The geyser is a large teapot in the ground."

4. The teacher and the students discuss their mental pictures.

5. In some cases, the students draw their images.

6. The students read text that uses and elaborates the targeted words.

Further Diagnostic Applications

Basic View of Reading   Reading is an interactive process in which information is stored in images as well as words. Reading involves inferencing from the text by using words and images that are stored in memory.

Patterns of Strengths and Strategies   Visualization is most appropriate for the highly visual, simultaneous learner who initially searches visual images to develop word meanings. This approach activates these students' strength in representing knowledge in its visual-spatial relationships and encourages them to relate this information to definitional knowledge.

Learner Patterns That Produce Increased Engagement

1. For the student who has difficulty verbalizing ideas and who codes information in images rather than words, visualization links his visual images to verbal descriptions.

*2. For the passive reader who does not check his past experiences to develop word meanings, visualization enhances his active thinking as he learns to elaborate his understanding with his images.

*3. For the text-based learner who needs to relate information to past experiences, visualization offers him a tool to connect textual information with prior knowledge.

Using the Technique as a Diagnostic Teaching Lesson   For visualization to be effective, both of the following statements must be answered in the affirmative:

Yes   No

____   ____   1. The student sees pictures in his mind and uses these to elaborate his interpretation.

____   ____   2. The student has difficulty verbalizing ideas and the visualization helps him connect words and images.

For Further Reading
McNeil, J. D. (1992). *Reading comprehension: New directions for classroom practice* (3rd ed.). New York: HarperCollins.

Vocabulary Self-Collection Strategy

Description   The vocabulary self-collection strategy (VSS) is a technique for developing word meanings by having small groups of students select words they would like to study and tell why they are important to a topic of study.

Target Reading Levels   All levels

Text   Selected vocabulary words from a text that has been read by all students

Predominant Focus of Instruction

1. Processing focus: meaning
2. Instructional phase: after reading
3. Response mode emphasized: oral discussion
4. Strategy emphasized: elaboration
5. Skill emphasized: word meaning
6. Source of information: reader-based and text-based
7. Type of instruction: implicit
8. Type of cognitive processing: simultaneous

Procedure

1. After reading a selected passage, the teacher organizes students into groups of four or five students each.

2. The student groups are to find at least two words they would like to study.

3. In their groups, the students describe the following about words each member would like to study:
   a. Demonstrate where they found the words in the passage.
   b. Discuss what they think the word might mean.
   c. Discuss why the word is important to them.

4. The small groups prioritize the words they would like to study.

5. Each group nominates a word that has not been previously listed with the reasons for learning in a total class discussion.

6. The total class refines definitions and, if necessary, selects words for further study.

7. Students record the final word list along with personalized definitions in their vocabulary journals (see "Journal Writing" in this chapter).

8. Students revisit their new words, using extension activities such as a feature analysis grid (see "Feature Analysis Grid" in this chapter).

9. If needed, incorporate vocabulary item into unit tests.

Further Diagnostic Applications

Basic View of Reading   Reading is a socio-interactive process in which readers' definitional knowledge is shaped by group members' understanding as well as their personal understanding.

Patterns of Strengths and Strategies   The vocabulary self-collection strategy encourages the student to use not only his experiences but also the experiences of his peers to expand his definitional knowledge; therefore, it is most appropriate for students who share and rely on their social interactions for learning. This strategy facilitates learning for these students because it allows students to converse about what and how they are learning.

Learner Patterns That Produce Increased Engagement

1. For a highly verbal learner who likes learning through incidental learning, this technique allows him to use the nuances of personal language to develop definitional knowledge.

2. For a highly social learner who likes to learn from his peers in the classroom, this technique allows him to learn word meanings as he talks with others in the classroom.

*3. For a learner who needs to use his personal interest to develop word meanings because previous word learning experiences resulted in negative attributions toward vocabulary development, vocabulary self-collection offers a group setting to share interests.

Using the Technique as a Diagnostic Teaching Lesson   For the vocabulary self-collection strategy to be effective, both of the following statements must be answered in the affirmative:

Yes   No

____   ____   1. The student converses readily in instructional settings.

____   ____   2. The student readily identifies words that interest him.

For Further Reading

Ruddell, M. R. (1997). *Teaching content reading and writing* (2d ed.). Boston: Allyn & Bacon.

Webbing

Description   This technique develops word meanings by visually mapping the relationships among words. The target concept is placed in the center of the web. Related concepts are arranged around this concept to show relationships between what the student already knows and the new concept.

Targeted Reading Levels   All levels

Text   Key concepts; often used to introduce vocabulary words for a story

Predominant Focus of Instruction

1. Processing focus: meaning
2. Instructional phase: before or after reading
3. Response mode emphasized: oral discussion and written responses
4. Strategy emphasized: elaboration
5. Skill emphasized: nonliteral comprehension
6. Source of information: reader-based
7. Type of instruction: implicit
8. Type of cognitive processing: simultaneous

Procedure

1. The teacher chooses a concept that is a key element of what is to be read.

2. She places the word inside a circle in the middle of a blank page or chalkboard.

3. The students and the teacher brainstorm what is already known about this concept and place the information in conceptual relationships, making a visual array of the relationships.

4. The teacher adds each new concept or word that describes the central concept to the web by drawing lines and new circles that indicate their relationships (see Figure 11–5). For the concept *image*, for example, some relationships involve

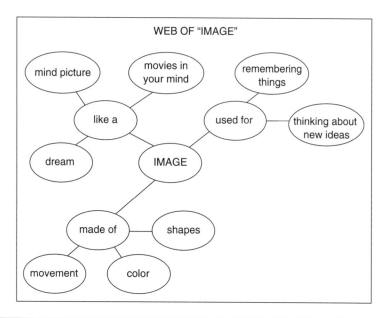

Figure 11–5   *Web*

similes of what an image is like, some suggest the composition of an image, and others look at how an image might be useful.

5. The students read the story.

6. The students and the teacher add additional story information to the web.

7. The students and the teacher discuss new understandings to known concepts and new relationships that were gained by reading.

Modifications

1. For narrative text, character webs can be developed where the attributes of the main character is webbed. This technique is especially useful when reading chapter books.

2. For the student who needs to build a meaning vocabulary, vocabulary cards can be made with webs on one side of the card and the words in sentences on the reverse side. These words are then reviewed periodically for comprehension.

Further Diagnostic Applications

Basic View of Reading   Reading is an interactive process in which readers use their background knowledge to create web relationships between word knowledge (verbal labels) and world knowledge (concepts).

Patterns of Strengths and Strategies   Webbing encourages the student to use his experiential knowledge to expand his definitional knowledge; therefore, it is most appropriate for the student who tends to think visually about the relationship of information without describing these relationships in words. This strategy facilitates learning for this student because it begins by showing the visual relationships and then uses words to explain that relationship.

Learner Patterns That Produce Increased Engagement

1. For a simultaneous thinker who perceives visual-spatial relationships rather than definitional relationships, this technique helps the student use his visual understanding of relationships to increase his understanding of what concepts mean.

2. For a bilingual student who has a well-developed conceptual base but needs development of word knowledge, the visual webbing of relationships helps him make specific comparisons between the events of his life and the words that are commonly used to express them.

*3. For a student with verbal weaknesses who needs to develop word conceptual knowledge in order to read and understand, this technique helps him develop conceptual relationships among words as well as the verbal labels used to express those relationships.

Using the Technique as a Diagnostic Teaching Lesson   For webbing to be effective, a majority of the following statements must be answered in the affirmative:

Yes   No
____   ____   1. The student has a sound experiential base, and webbing helps to express it.
____   ____   2. The student often has a general understanding but does not know specific words, and webbing helps to express that understanding.
____   ____   3. The student's elaboration of ideas is marked with the word *thing* instead of a specific word.

For Further Reading
Bromley, K. D. (1996). *Webbing with literature: Creating story maps with children's books* (2d ed.). Boston: Allyn & Bacon.
Tompkins, G. E. (1998). *50 literacy strategies: Step by step.* Englewood Cliffs, NJ: Merrill/Prentice Hall.

Word Analogy Strategy

Description   Word analogy strategy is an approach to teaching phonics in which children are taught a strategic process of using word patterns they know to figure out unfamiliar words.

Targeted Reading Levels   1–4

Text: Individual words

Predominant Focus of Instruction

1. Processing focus: print
2. Instructional phase: skill lesson
3. Response mode emphasized: oral
4. Strategy emphasized: monitoring
5. Skill emphasized: word identification and word analysis
6. Source of information: text-based
7. Type of instruction: explicit
8. Type of cognitive processing: successive

Procedure

1. The teacher explains that sometimes individuals use words they know to figure out unfamiliar words.

2. The teacher models how to find familiar letter patterns in unfamiliar words. For instance when reading the word *stain,* the student could identify *ain* as a pattern in *rain,* a familiar word.

3. Next, she models the self-talk that she uses to try out the sounds from *rain* in the unfamiliar *stain.*

4. Then, she has the student try out the strategy on a series of unknown preselected words. These words share letter patterns with familiar words.

5. The teacher posts a set of model words that have common word patterns such as the *at* in *cat, ay* in *hay.* She uses picture clues next to the words to help readers remember the model word.

6. Thirty-three common word patterns are listed in the following box (Stahl, 1998).

ack	ain	ake	ale	all	ame	an	ank
ap	ash	at	ate	aw	ay		
eat	ell	est					
ice	ing	ink	ip	ir	ick	ide	
ight	ill	in	ine				
op	or	ore	ock	oke			
uck	ug	ump					

7. On a regular basis, the children read texts that contained words with familiar spelling patterns.

Further Diagnostic Applications

Basic View of Reading   Learning to read is an interactive process. By developing procedures to figure out words, the student uses the text first to sound out the word and then relates the new word to familiar words with the same language pattern.

Patterns of Strengths and Strategies   The word analogy strategy is most appropriate for students who can segment words into their sounds and match those sounds to the letters in the word. This technique builds on their strength and allows them to develop a system for decoding by analogy to key words.

Learning Patterns that Produce Increased Engagement

1. For a successive learner who can match sounds to letters, this technique helps develop a system for using what he knows to figure out new words.

*2. For a simultaneous thinker who readily uses what he knows but needs help focusing on letter pattern cues to figure out words, this technique matches the familiar with the unfamiliar in decoding words.

*3. For a passive learner who needs explanations to understand how to decode unfamiliar words, this technique provides a tool to build word recognition.

Using the Technique as a Diagnostic Teaching Lesson   For the word analogy strategy to be effective, a majority of the following statements must be answered in the affirmative:

Yes   No

_____ _____   1. The student knows initial consonants and blends.

_____ _____   2. The student can match sounds to letter clusters.

_____ _____   3. The student applies analogies to both known and unknown words.

For Further Reading

Cunningham, P. M. & Allington, R. L. (1999). *Classrooms that work: They can all read and write* (2d ed.). New York: Longman.

Gunning, T. G. (1998). *Assessing and correcting reading and writing difficulties.* Boston: Allyn & Bacon.

Word Probe Strategy

Description   Word probe strategy is a structured phonics approach in which children are taught a strategic process of using key words to figure out unfamiliar words. The key words are displayed so the students can refer to them as they decode by analogy.

Targeted Reading Levels 1–4

Text Single words on word walls

Predominant Focus of Instruction

1. Processing focus: print
2. Instructional phase: skill lesson
3. Response mode emphasized: oral
4. Strategy emphasized: monitoring
5. Skill emphasized: word identification and word analysis
6. Source of information: text-based
7. Type of instruction: explicit
8. Type of cognitive processing: successive

Procedure

1. The teacher explains reasons for learning about individual words such as:
   a. Using a picture of a cat to figure out the word *cat*.
   b. Using two cues such as a picture of a cat and the initial letter *k* to figure out the word *kitten*.
   c. Using all the letters and sounds to figure out a word, such as using *k-a-t* for *cat*.

2. The teacher models how to talk about the letters and sounds of the key words as they are introduced by saying, "I stretch out the word so I can hear all the sounds."

3. Next, she models holding up a finger for each sound in the word and counting the sounds in the word.

4. Then, the teacher models counting the letters in the word and matching the number of letters to the sounds.

5. The student repeats her model using the same self-talk with a key word or words and fills out the self-talk chart (Gaskins, et al., 1996-1997).

Talk to Yourself Chart
1. The word is _____.
2. Stretch the word. I hear _____ sounds.
3. I see _____ letters because _____.
4. The spelling pattern is _____.
5. This is what I know about the vowel _____.
6. Another word in the key word list with the same vowel sound is _____.

---

6. Each day the children read texts that contain words with familiar spelling patterns. They use the partner sharing chart or the making words chart as they work with partners in the classroom.

7. At the conclusion of each reading session, the student restates what he learned about language.

8. At home, the student tells his parents about the key word and talks aloud about how decoding works.

9. The parents write notes in the child's "What I Know About My Language" journal.

Further Diagnostic Applications

Basic View of Reading   Learning to read is an interactive process. By developing procedures to figure out words, the student uses the text first to sound out the word and then relates the new word to familiar words with the same language pattern.

Patterns of Strengths and Strategies   The word probe strategy is most appropriate for students who can segment words into their sounds and match those sounds to the letters in the word. This technique builds on their strengths and allows them to develop a system for decoding by analogy to key words.

Learning Patterns That Produce Increased Engagement

1. For a successive learner who can match some sounds to letters, this technique helps them develop a system for using what they know to figure out new words.

*2. For a simultaneous thinker who readily uses what he knows but needs help focusing on letter and sound cues to figure out words, this technique reinforces decoding words into sounds to increase recognition.

*3. For a passive learner who needs explicit explanations to understand the decoding process and how to use phonic knowledge when reading an unfamiliar word, this technique provides a tool for building word recognition.

Using the Technique as a Diagnostic Teaching Lesson   For the word probe strategy to be effective, a majority of the following statements must be answered in the affirmative:

Yes   No

_____ _____ 1. The student can segment sounds.

_____ _____ 2. The student can match sounds to letter clusters.

_____ _____ 3. The student applies analogies to both known and unknown words.

For Further Reading

Gaskins, I. W., Ehri, L. C., Cress, C., O'Hara, C., & Donnelly, K. (1996–1997). Procedures for word learning: Making discoveries about words. *The Reading Teacher, 50,* 312–327.

Word Sorts

Description   Word sorts are ways to sort word cards that enable the readers to share how they categorize words: for example, on the basis of similar letter patterns, word meanings, or grammatical functions. This technique uses target words to help students review and remember words by categorizing like characteristics.

Targeted Reading Levels   1–4

Text   Isolated words

Predominant Focus of Instruction

1. Processing focus: print or meaning
2. Instructional phase: after reading
3. Response mode emphasized: oral
4. Strategy emphasized: elaboration
5. Skill emphasized: word identification or word meaning
6. Source of information: reader-based
7. Type of instruction: implicit
8. Type of cognitive processing: simultaneous

Procedure

1. The teacher or students select target words and write them on word cards (3" × 5" cards).

2. Each student collects a box of personalized word cards drawn from language experience stories, basal readers, and/or trade books to form a word bank.

3. To start a lesson, the teacher asks the students to get out their word banks and form small groups or pairs.

4. The teacher demonstrates how to do a word sort by showing the words *one, two, six,* and *ten* and saying, "Why do you think these words go together?"

5. The students respond by saying, "They are numbers."

6. Then the teacher shows them three more word cards *(hat, rat, sat)* and asks, "Why so you think these words go together?"

7. The students respond that all the words have the letters *at* at the end.

8. The teacher explains the process of looking for like characteristics: some groups may have a meaning focus, some may have grapho-phonic focus, and others may have a grammatical focus such as *go, going, gone.* She asks the students to create groups of words that share the same characteristic (open word sort).

9. Each group explains how their words go together.

10. Next the teacher directs all the groups to find words that share the same letter patterns.

11. Each group explains their categorizations.

Modification   For each group, the teacher can create a set of word cards that have similar letter patterns, word meanings, or grammatical functions. She asks the groups to arrange the cards according to the pattern and be able to tell how the words are alike. This word sort is closed because the teacher chooses the words to reinforce a concept that is being learned.

Further Diagnostic Applications

Basic View of Reading   Reading is a socio-interactive process in which learners share their thinking about how words are categorized based on their meaning, grapho-phonic similarity, or grammatical function. As students discuss how words are alike, they increase their active thinking.

Patterns of Strengths and Strategies   Word sorts are most appropriate for young readers who are developing a recognition vocabulary. For these students, categorizing words according to their distinctive features as well as their meaning enhances decoding by both meaning analogies and decoding analogies.

Learner Patterns That Produce Increased Engagement

1. For a simultaneous learner who easily sees relationships but often does not look at the word patterns, this approach focuses the student on likenesses among words rather than on their differences.

2. For a social learner who learns more readily with a partner or in a group, this approach can be effective because his friends help him focus, in this case, on distinctive features that are alike in words.

*3. For a passive learner who needs to select key features so he can remember what the words look like, the sorting provides a tool for talking about how words look alike.

Using the Technique as a Diagnostic Teaching Lesson   For word sorts to be effective, a majority of the following statements must be answered in the affirmative:

Yes   No

____   ____   1. The student can identify key visual or meaning features.

____   ____   2. The student can create analogies among words easily.

____   ____   3. The student discusses key features with a partner or in a group.

For Further Reading

Gillet, J. & Temple, C. (1994). *Understanding reading problems* (4th ed.). Glenview, IL: Scott Foresman.

Roskos, K. & Walker, B. (1994). *Interactive handbook for understanding reading diagnosis.* Englewood Cliffs, NJ: Merrill/Prentice Hall.

Word Walls

Description   Word walls are used to help readers develop their understanding of words. On large sheets of paper, the teacher writes critical and puzzling words for the students. The features of these words are discussed along with their meaning. Students can use the word walls when they write or read during classroom activities.

Targeted Reading Levels   1–4

Text   Single words

Predominant Focus of Instruction

1. Processing focus: print
2. Instructional phase: before and after reading
3. Response mode emphasized: oral
4. Strategy emphasized: elaboration
5. Skill emphasized: word identification and word meaning
6. Source of information: reader-based
7. Type of instruction: implicit
8. Type of cognitive processing: successive and simultaneous

Procedure

1. The teacher hangs a long sheet of paper on a wall and titles it, "Word Wall for _____." It could be a story, theme, or skill lesson.

2. The teacher introduces the word wall and writes key words for reading the story large enough for all students to read them.

3. After reading the teacher and students suggest other important story words and then write them on the word wall.

4. If students write the word on the wall, the teacher corrects spelling errors and discusses word features as students use these words when they write.

5. At this time, the teacher reviews spelling and word features as well as meaning.

6. For younger children, the teacher can add a small picture.

7. At the end of a unit, the teacher reviews all the words in the lesson, saying and spelling each word and putting it on an index card. The cards are collated on metal rings and put in the writing center.

8. The words can be sorted (see "Word Sort" in this chapter) for phonic patterns. For example, all the words beginning with the same letter would be one sort, then rhyming words would be another sort, etc.

Further Diagnostic Applications

Basic View of Reading   Learning to read means understanding words that influence stories. Readers need to use their knowledge of word features and word meanings to figure out story understanding; therefore, reading is an interactive process. By studying words, the students can elaborate their understanding of word meaning and word features.

Patterns of Strengths and Strategies   The word wall approach is most appropriate for students who learn word meaning and word features easily. This technique builds on their strength and allows them to develop a system for analyzing words.

Learning Patterns That Produce Increased Engagement

1. For a simultaneous thinker who readily uses what he knows and what's important to understanding new information, this technique promotes understanding the relationship words have to meaning.

*2. For a passive learner who needs help focusing on words to understand stories, this technique uses attention to meaning and word features to enhance reading.

*3. For a successive learner who can match sounds to letters but does not think about the meaning of individual words, this technique helps him develop a system for using what he knows to figure out word meaning and word features.

Using the Technique as a Diagnostic Teaching Lesson   For the word walls approach to be effective, a majority of the following statements must be answered in the affirmative:

Yes   No
_____   _____   1. The student can segment sounds.
_____   _____   2. The student can match sounds to letters.
_____   _____   3. The student applies decoding analogies to both known and unknown words.

For Further Reading

Cunningham, P. M. & Cunningham, J. W. (1992). Making words: Enhancing the invented spelling-decoding connection. *The Reading Teacher, 46,* 106–107.

Snow, C. E., Burn, M. S., & Griffin, P. (1998). *Preventing reading difficulties in young children.* Washington, DC: National Academy Press.

Epilogue

This text has included the means that effective teachers have used to adapt instruction to individual student needs. Intuitively, teachers have always changed their instruction as they encountered problems in teaching. Diagnostic teaching recognizes this decision-making power and places assessment in the hands of effective teachers.

Some Points for Assessment

Although different from the traditional forms of assessment, diagnostic teaching produces practical, efficient, and valid information about the learner.

1. It is practical because suggestions for instruction can be incorporated immediately into the instructional program.

2. It is efficient because reading instruction and learning do not stop in order to test; instead, they become an integral part of assessment.

3. It is valid because diagnostic teaching assesses reading in the same kind of instructional situation that is used throughout the student's classroom experience.

Some Final Points on Instruction

1. Selecting techniques from the tables in Chapter 10 should be considered tentative and subject to confirmation through teaching.

2. The student's response to instructional techniques changes as the student learns.

3. The student's response to instruction is an interaction among instructional variables in the reading event. Every event has a different set of interactions.

4. Instructional placement is based not only on how the student performs with aided instruction (mediated level) but also on the degree of task modification and teacher investment. The basic premise for placement is: "If I can find a way to teach easily what the student needs to know, I can place the student at a higher reading level."

Appendix 1
Administering an Informal Reading Assessment

Here are directions for administering an informal reading assessment (IRI).

1. Select texts that sample a range of reading levels, or use a published informal reading inventory.

2. Establish the readability of the text, if necessary.

3. Prepare questions that focus on important information, coherent textual structure, and key concepts. If you use a published

Table A–1 *Scoreable Errors (to be used in computing error rate)*

Substitutions or mispronunciations (the replacement of one word for another): Mark the mispronounced word by drawing a line through it and writing the substitution above the word.

want

"The man ~~went~~ to the store," said Ann.

Omissions (leaving out words): Circle the word omitted.

"The man went to (the) store," said Ann.

Insertions (adding extra words): Draw a carat and write the inserted word above it.

away

"The man went ^ to the store," said Ann.

Transpositions (changing the word order): Mark with a _____.

"The man went to the store," said Ann.

Prompted words (words that have to be prompted or supplied by the teacher): Write the letter *P* above these words.

P

"The man went to the store," said Ann.

Table A–2 *Recordable Errors (not computed in the error rate for an IRI)*

Repetitions (words or phrases that are repeated more than once): Draw a line over the word and write the letter *R* over the line.

R

"The man went to the store," said Ann.

Repeated repetitions (words for phrases that are repeated several times): Draw a line over the word or phrase and mark it with a *2R* over the line.

2R

"The man went to the store," said Ann.

Self-correction: If the child corrects an error, a line is drawn through the previously marked error and the letter *C* is written at the end of the line.

want C

"The man went to the store," said Ann.

Pauses: Long pauses that are used to gain meaning are marked with slashes.

"The man/went to the store," said Ann.

Punctuation errors (ignoring punctuation symbols): Draw a circle around the omitted punctuation mark.

"The man went to the store," said Ann."Then he went home."

informal reading inventory, be sure to check the questions for coherence and importance.

4. Establish rapport quickly and begin assessment.

5. If necessary, use a word recognition list to establish a beginning level for assessment.

6. Start with a passage that you think will be at the student's independent level of difficulty.

7. Have the student read the passage orally.

8. Using the coding system in Table A–1 and Table A–2, record the student's performance as she reads. Both scoreable errors (Table A–1) and recordable errors (Table A–2) are coded. Scoreable errors determine whether a passage was read at the independent, instructional, or frustration level. Recordable errors are additional errors used to evaluate a reader's strategies but are not computed in the error rate.

9. Assess comprehension by asking the prepared questions.

10. Find the oral accuracy score by calculating the error rate (Table A–3) or the percentage of oral accuracy (Table A–4).

Table A–3　*Calculating Error Rate*

1. Determine the number of scoreable errors per passage read.
   Example: Brian made 4 scoreable errors.

2. Estimate the total number of words in the passage read.
   Example: Brian read 86 words.

3. Divide the total number of words by the number of scoreable errors.
   Round off the quotient to the nearest whole number.
   Example:

$$4\overline{)86} \quad 21\, r\, 2 = 21$$

4. The quotient determined in Step 3 becomes the denominator in the
   error rate and the number 1 becomes the numerator.
   Example: Brian read the passage with 1 error every 21 running words;
   the error rate is 1/21.

Table A–4　*Calculating Percentage of Oral Accuracy*

1. Estimate the number of words read.
   Example: Brian read 80 words.

2. Count the number of scoreable errors.
   Example: Brian made 4 errors.

3. Subtract the number of scoreable errors from the number of
   words read.
   Example: 80 words – 4 errors = 76 words

4. Divide the number of words read correctly by the number of
   words read.
   Example:

$$80\overline{)76.00} \quad .95$$

5. Multiply the resulting decimal number by 100 to find the percentage
   of oral accuracy.
   Example: .95 × 100 = 95%

11. Compute the comprehension percentage score for the passage by
    (a) dividing the number of questions answered correctly by the
    total number of questions asked, and (b) multiplying the resulting
    decimal number by 100. Example: Brian answered 8 of 10 ques-
    tions correctly.

$$(a) \quad 10\overline{)8.00} \quad .80$$

$$(b) \quad .80 \times 100 = 80\%$$

12. Administer another passage on the same level. Have the student
    read the paragraph silently.

Table A–5 *Scoring Criteria by Performance Grade Level Suggested by W. R. Powell (1978)*

Reading Level	Word Recognition Error Rate	Comprehension Percentage
Independent		
1–2	1/17+	80+
3–5	1/27+	85+
6+	1/35+	90+
Instructional		
1–2	1/8–1/16	55–80
3–5	1/13–1/26	60–84
6+	1/18–1/35	65–90
Frustration		
1–2	1/7–	55–
3–5	1/12–	60–
6+	1/17–	65–

Note: From *The Finger Count System for Monitoring Reading Behavior* (pp. 7–11) by W. R. Powell, 1981, unpublished paper. Adapted by permission.

13. Assess comprehension by an oral retelling followed by direct questioning.

14. Decide the level of performance for each passage the student read. Use either Powell's criteria (1978) from Table A–5 or Betts's criteria (1946) from Table A–6. Use fluency rating as well.

15. Using the information from step 14, decide how to continue the assessment.

    a. If the student is reading at an independent level, move her up to the next level.
    b. If the student is reading at an instructional level, move her down to the next level to establish independent reading.
    c. If the student is reading at a frustration level, consider moving her down two levels to establish independent and then instructional reading experiences.

Table A–6 *Scoring Criteria Suggested by Betts (1946)*

Reading Level	Word Recognition	Comprehension
Independent	99%+	90%+
Instructional	95%	75%
Frustration	90%–	50%–

Table A–7   Informal Reading Inventory Summary Sheet

**Informal Reading Inventory
Summary Sheet**

Student's Name _____ Age _____ Grade _____

Examiner _____ Date _____

IRI Used _____ Form _____

Levels of Performance   **Oral**   **Silent**

Independent Level   ____   ____
Instructional Level   ____   ____
Frustration Level   ____   ____

Level	Fluency Rate	Scoreable Errors Error Rate	Percentage of Comprehension Oral	Silent
pp				
p				
1				
2				
3				
4				
5				
6				
7				
8				
9				
10				
11				
12				

16. Continue using this procedure, alternating between oral and silent reading at each level until a passage is read at frustration reading level for both oral and silent reading.

17. Summarize the results, using the Informal Reading Inventory Summary Sheet, reproduced in Table A–7.

Appendix 2
Computer Programs

Reading Stories—Books on Disc

Wiggle Works (Scholastic): A total emergent reading program that contains leveled predictable books on CD-ROM. These discs also provide models for framed writing of each book.

Living Books: A set of storybooks on screen. The text is read along with words highlighted on the page so the student can read along.

Discus Books: A set of predictable stories and poems that are on CD-ROM. These books also have the added feature of action in the storybook picture and naming objects in the picture to facilitate language development.

Smart Books (Scholastic): Books on an interactive CD-ROM program arranged by themes.

Working with Words

Phraze Krase (Macintosh): A software version of the "Wheel of Fortune" to help students focus on letters and letter patterns in words.

Mapping and Organizing Programs for Writing and Reading Comprehension

Kid Pix (Broderbund): Provides students a tool for visualizing concepts and then labeling them. The student can create semantic maps, outlines, or diagrams to organize thinking.

The Literary Mapper (Teacher Support Software): Includes predeveloped maps for character, setting, and action so that students can complete them as they read or write a story.

The Semantic Mapper (Teacher Support Software): Allows students to create their own maps and label them.

Drafting and Editing in Writing

Bank Street Writer (Scholastic): Word processing program in which the teacher can supply customized prompts for the students' own writing.

Magic Slate II (Sunburst): Word processing program in which the teacher can supply customized prompts for the students' own writing.

Language Experience Primary Series: Teachers can record children's dictated stories. Synthesized speech available.

Story Maker (Scholastic): Assists students in learning how to construct sentences, paragraphs, and stories.

Publishing

Print Shop (Broderbound): Prints cards, invitations, and posters with layout and graphics.

Children's Writing & Publishing Center (The Learning Company): A desktop publishing program. Includes graphics.

Comprehensive Literacy Programs for Beginning Readers and Writers

These comprehensive programs are for early reading instruction including reading and writing for the early grades.

Writing to Read (IBM)
Foundations in Learning (Breakthrough)
Early Reading Program (Waterford)
Little Planet Series (Young Children' Literacy Project)

Appendix 3
Predictable Book List

Level	Title	Author	Publisher
Beginning of First Grade			
	Look What I Can Do	Aruego, Jose	Scribner
	Do You Want to Be My Friend?	Carle, Eric	Harper Collins
	Have You Seen My Cat?	Carle, Eric	Philomel
	Spider, Spider	Cowley, Joy	Wright Group
	If You Meet a Dragon	Cowley, Joy	Wright Group
	Pancakes for Breakfast	de Paola, Tomie	Harcourt Brace Jovanovich
	Rain	Kalan, Robert	Greenwillow Books
	Brown Bear, Brown Bear	Martin, Bill	Holt, Rinehart, & Winston
	I Love You, Sun I Love You, Moon	Pandell, Karen and Tomie de Paola	Putnam
	Roll Over	Peek, Merle	Clarion
	Have You Seen My Duckling?	Tafuri, Nancy	Greenwillow Books
	Cat on the Mat	Wildsmith, Brian	Oxford University Press
	All Fall Down	Wildsmith, Brian	Oxford University Press
	I Went Walking	Williams, Sue	Harcourt Brace Jovanovich
	Where Is My Friend?	Ziefert, Harriet and Simms Taaback	Grossett & Dunlap

Level	Title	Author	Publisher
Near the Middle of First Grade			
	Bears on Wheels	Berenstain, Stan	Random House
	The Big Toe	Cowley, Joy	Wright Group/ Story Box
	It Looked Like Spilt Milk	Shaw, Charles	Harper
	Quick as a Cricket	Wood, Audrey	Child's Play International
	The Chick and the Duckling	Ginsburg, Mirra	Macmillan
	Sam's Cookie	Lindgren, Barbro	Morrow
	Five Little Ducks	Raffi	Crown
	Five Little Monkeys Jumping on the Bed	Christelow, Eileen	Clarion Books
	I Love Mud and Mud Loves Me	Stephens, Vicki	Scholastic
	Go Dog Go	Eastman, P. D.	Random House
	The Big Fat Hen	Baker, Keith	Harcourt Brace Jovanovich
	Where's Spot? (also in Spanish)	Hill, Eric	Putnam
	Buzz Said the Bee	Lewison, Wendy	Scholastic
	The Foot Book	Dr. Suess	Random House
	Fresh Fall Leaves	Franco, Betsy	Scholastic
Middle of the First Grade			
	A Dark Dark Tale	Brown, Ruth	Dial Press
	Have You Seen the Crocodile?	West, Colin	Harper & Row
	Spot's First Walk	Hill, Eric	Putnam
	Just Like Daddy	Asch, Frank	Prentice-Hall
	Mousetrap	Snowball, Diane	Scholastic
	Lady with the Alligator Purse	Westcott	Houghton Mifflin
	Rosie's Walk	Hutchins, Pat	Macmillan
	Whose Mouse Are You?	Kraus, Robert	Macmillan
	Just for You	Mayer, Mercer	Dial
	Just Me and My Baby-sitter	Mayer, Mercer	Dial
	Sheep in a Jeep	Shaw, Nancy E.	Houghton Mifflin
	Each Peach, Pear, Plum	Ahlberg, Janet and Allan	Viking Press

Level	Title	Author	Publisher
	More Spaghetti, I Say	Gelman, Rita	Scholastic
	Itchy, Itchy Chicken Pox	Maccarone, Grace	Scholastic
	The Great Big Enormous Turnip	Tolstoy, Alexei	Watts
End of First Grade			
	I Was Walking Down the Road	Barchas, Sarah	Scholastic
	Seven Little Rabbits	Becker, John	Scholastic
	Goodnight Moon	Brown, Margaret Wise	HarperTrophy
	Are You My Mother?	Eastman, P. D.	Random House
	Big Dog, Little Dog	Eastman, P. D.	Random House
	Good Night Owl	Hutchins, Pat	Macmillan/Greenwillow
	Leo, The Late Bloomer	Kraus, Robert	Windmill Books
	Just a Mess	Mayer, Mercer	Dial
	Jump, Frog, Jump	Kalan, Robert	Greenwillow
	Green Eggs and Ham	Dr. Seuss	Random House
	Hop on Pop	Dr. Seuss	Random House
	Nobody Listens to Andrew	Guilfoile, Elizabeth	Modern Curriculum Press
	Fortunately	Charlip, Remy	Macmillan
	Noisy Nora	Wells, Rosemary	Dial Books for Young Readers
	The Napping House	Wood, Audrey	Harcourt Brace Jovanovich
Between First and Second Grade			
	The Very Busy Spider	Carle, Eric	Philomel Books
	The Very Hungry Caterpillar	Carle, Eric	Philomel Books
	The Little Red Hen	Galdone, Paul	Seabury/Clarion
	The Three Bears	Galdone, Paul	Clarion Books
	The Doorbell Rang	Hutchins, Pat	Greenwillow
	George Shrinks	Joyce, William	Harper & Row
	Mouse Soup	Lobel, Arnold	Harper & Row
	Mouse Tales	Lobel, Arnold	Harper & Row/ HarperCollins
	Owl at Home	Lobel, Arnold	Harper & Row
	Chicka Chicka Boom Boom	Martin, Bill	Simon & Schuster

Level	Title	Author	Publisher
	There's Something in My Attic	Mayer, Mercer	Dial
	Little Bear	Minarik, Else	Harper & Row
	The House That Jack Built	Peppe, Rodney	Delacorte/Holiday House
	The Cat in the Hat	Dr. Seuss	Random House
Second Grade			
	Nana Upstairs & Nana Downstairs	de Paola, Tomie	Putnam/Harcourt Brace Jovanovich
	May I Bring a Friend	DeRegniers, Beatrice Schenk	Atheneum
	Over in the Meadow	Galdone, Paul	Prentice Hall
	Danny and the Dinosaur	Hoff, Syd	Harper
	Don't Forget the Bacon	Hutchins, Pat	Greenwillow
	The Very Worst Monster	Hutchins, Pat	Greenwillow
	Frog and Toad are Friends	Lobel, Arnold	Harper & Row
	Frog and Toad Together	Lobel, Arnold	Harper & Row
	Stone Soup	McGovern, Ann	Scholastic
	If You Give a Mouse a Cookie	Numerhoff, Laura	Harper & Row
	One Fine Day	Hogrogian, Nonny	Macmillan
	Henry and Mudge	Rylant, Cynthia	Aladdin Books
	Chicken Soup with Rice	Sendak, Maurice	Harper & Row
	Caps for Sale	Slobodkina, Esphyr	HarperCollins
	I Know a Lady	Zolotow, Charlotte	Greenwillow

Appendix 4
High Interest Series Books

Reading Level	Title	Author
First and Second Grade		
	Clifford, The Big Red Dog	Norman Bridwell
	Jullian Jiggs	Phoebe Gilman
	Arthur books	Lillian Hoban
	Frog and Toad	Arnold Lobel
	George and Martha	James Marshall
	Little Critters	Mercer Mayer
	Little Bear	Else Minarik
	Amelia Bedilia	Peggy Parish
	Curious George	H. A. Rey
	Henry and Mudge	Cynthia Rylant
	Mr. Putter and Tabby	Cynthia Rylant
	Marvin Redpost	Louis Sachar
	Harry (The Dirty Dog) books	Gene Zion
Second and Third Grade		
	Amber Brown	Paula Danziger
	Pee Wee Scouts	Judy Delton
	Kids of Polk Street School	Patricia Reilly Giff
	Horrible Harry	Suszy Kline
	Kids on Bus 5	Marcia Leonard
	Junie B. Jones	Barbara Park
	Nate the Great	Marjorie Sharmat
	Boxcar Children	Gertrude Warner
	Magic Tree House	
	Magic School Bus	

Bibliography

Allington, R. L. (1984a). Content coverage and contextual reading in reading groups. *Journal of Reading Behavior, 16*(2), 85–96.

Allington, R. L. (1984b). Oral reading. In P. D. Pearson (ed.), *Handbook of reading research* (pp. 829–864). New York: Longman.

Allington, R. L. (1995). Literacy lessons in the elementary schools: Yesterday, today, and tomorrow. In R. L. Allington & S. A. Walmsley (eds.), *No quick fix* (pp. 1–18). New York: Teachers College Press; Newark, DE: International Reading Association.

Allington, R. L. & Cunningham, P. M. (1996). *Schools that work: Where all children read and write*. New York: HarperCollins.

Almasi, J. F. (1994). The nature of fourth graders' sociocognitive conflicts in peer-led and teacher-led discussions of literature. *Reading Research Quarterly, 29,* 304–307.

Almasi, J. F. (1996). A new view of discussion. In L. B. Gambrell & J. F. Almasi (eds.), *Lively discussions! Fostering engaged reading* pp. 2–24). Newark, DE: International Reading Association.

Alvermann, D. E. (1989). Effects of spontaneous and induced lookbacks on self-perceived high- and low-ability comprehenders. *Journal of Educational Research, 81,* 325–331.

Alvermann, D. E. & Phelps, S. E. (1994). *Content reading and literacy*. Boston: Allyn & Bacon.

Au, K. (1993). *Literacy instruction in multicultural settings*. Fort Worth, TX: Harcourt Brace Jovanovich.

Bagert, B. (1991). Act it out: Making poetry come alive. In B. Cullinan (ed.), *Invitation to read: More children's literature in the reading program* (pp. 14–23). Newark, DE: International Reading Association.

Barr, R., Blachowicz, C., & Wogman-Sadow, M. (1995). *Reading diagnosis for teachers: An instructional approach* (3rd ed.). White Plains, NY: Longman.

Betts, E. A. (1946). *Foundations of reading instruction*. New York: American Book.

Bond, G. L. & Dykstra, R. (1967). The cooperative research program in first-grade reading instruction. *Reading Research Quarterly, 2,* 1–142.

Bromley, K. D. (1996). *Webbing with literature: Creating story maps with children's books* (2d ed.). Boston: Allyn & Bacon.

Brophy, J. (1984). The teacher as thinker: Implementing instruction. In G. Duffy, L. Roehler, & J. Mason (eds.), *Comprehension instruction: Perspectives and suggestions* (pp. 71–92). New York: Longman.

Clay, M. M. (1993). *Reading recovery: A guidebook for teachers in training.* Portsmouth, NH: Heinemann.

Cunningham, P. M. & Allington, R. L. (1999). *Classrooms that work: They can all read and write* (2d ed.). New York: Longman.

Daneman, M. (1991). Individual differences in reading skills. In R. Barr, M. Kamil, P. Mosenthal, & P. D. Pearson (eds.), *Handbook of reading research, Vol. 2* (pp. 512–538). New York: Longman.

Davis, S. J. (1990). Breaking the cycle of failure through thematic experience approach. *Journal of Reading, 33*(6), 420–423.

DeCarlo, J. E. (ed.). (1995). *Perspectives in whole language.* Boston: Allyn & Bacon.

Deci, E. L., Vallerand, R. J., Pelletier, L. G. & Ryan, R. M. (1991). Motivation and education: The self-determination perspective. *Educational Psychologist, 26,* 325–346.

Dole, J. A., Duffy, G. G., Roehler, L. R., & Pearson, P. D. (1991). Moving from the old to the new: Research on reading comprehension instruction. *Review of Educational Research, 61,* 239–264.

Dowhower, S. (1989). Repeated reading: Research into practice. *The Reading Teacher, 42,* 502–507.

Duffy, G. G. (1993). Rethinking strategy instruction: Four teachers' development and their low achievers' understanding. *Elementary School Journal, 93,* 231–246.

Duffy, G. G. & Roehler, L. R. (1987). Teaching reading skills as strategies. *The Reading Teacher, 40,* 414–418.

Dybdahl, C. S. (October 1983). *Comprehension strategies and practices.* Paper presented at the Annual Conference of the College Reading Association, Atlanta, GA.

Dybdahl, C. S. & Walker, B. J. (1996). *Prediction strategies and comprehension instruction.* Unpublished paper, University of Alaska, Anchorage, AK.

Elkind, D. (1983). Stress and learning disabilities. In D. Carnine, D. Elkind, A. D. Hendrickson, D. Meichenbaum, R. Sieben, & F. Smith (eds.), *Interdisciplinary voices in learning disabilities and remedial education* (pp. 67–80). Austin, TX: Pro-ed.

Fountas, I. C. & Pinnell, G. S. (1996). *Guided reading: Good first teaching for all children.* Portsmouth, NH: Heinemann.

Fitzgerald, J. (1989). Research on stories: Implications for teachers. In K. D. Muth (ed.), *Children's comprehension of text* (pp. 2–36). Newark, DE: International Reading Association.

Gambrell, L. (1996). What research reveals about discussion. In L. B. Gambrell & J. F. Almasi (eds.), *Lively discussions! Fostering engaged reading* (pp. 25–38). Newark, DE: International Reading Association.

Gambrell, L. B. & Jawitz, P. B. (1993). Mental imagery, text illustrations, and children's story comprehension and recall. *Reading Research Quarterly, 28,* 264–276.

Gambrell, L. & Marinak, B. A. (1997). Incentive and instrinsic motivation to read. In J. T. Guthrie & A. Wigfield (eds.), *Reading engagement: Motivating readers through integrated instruction* (pp. 205–217) Newark, DE: International Reading Association.

Garcia, G. E. & Pearson, P. D. (1990). *Modifying reading instruction to maximize its effectiveness for all students* (Technical Report No. 489). Champaign, IL: University of Illinois, Center for the Study of Reading.

Gaskins, I. W., Ehri, L. C, Cress, C., O'Hara, C., & Donnelly, K. (1996–1997). Procedures for word learning: Making discoveries about words. *The Reading Teacher, 50,* 312–327.

Gentile, L. M. & McMillan, M. (1987). *Stress and reading difficulties.* Newark, DE: International Reading Association.

Gillet, J. W. & Temple, C. (1986). *Understanding reading problems* (2d ed.). Boston: Little, Brown.

Gillet, J. & Temple, C. (1994). *Understanding reading problems* (4th ed.). Glenview, IL: Scott Foresman.

Gipe, J. P. (1995). *Corrective reading techniques for the classroom teacher* (3rd ed.). Scottsdale, AZ: Gorsuch Scarisbrick.

Glazer, S. M. (1992). *Reading comprehension: Self-monitoring strategies to develop independent readers.* New York: Scholastic.

Glazer, S. M. & Brown, C. S. (1993). *Portfolios and beyond: Collaborative assessment in reading and writing.* Norwood, MA: Christopher-Gordon.

Goldenberg, C. (1992–1993). Instructional conversations: Promoting comprehension through discussion. *The Reading Teacher, 46,* 316–326.

Goodman, K. (1996). Principles of revaluing. In Y. M. Goodman & A. M. Marek (eds.), *Retrospective miscue analysis: Revaluing readers and reading* (pp. 13–21). Katonah, NY: Richard C. Owen Publishers, Inc.

Goodman, Y. M. & Marek, A. M. (1996). Retrospective miscue analysis. In Y. M. Goodman & A. M. Marek (eds.), *Retrospective miscue analysis: Revaluing readers and reading* (pp. 39–49). Katonah, NY: Richard C. Owen Publishers, Inc.

Gunning, T. G. (1998). *Assessing and correcting reading and writing difficulties.* Boston: Allyn & Bacon.

Haenggi, D. & Perfetti, C. A. (1992). Individual differences in reprocessing of text. *Journal of Educational Psychology, 84,* 182–192.

Hansen, J. (1994). Literacy portfolios: Windows on potential. In S. W. Valencia, E. H. Hiebert, & P. P. Afflerback (eds.), *Authentic reading assessment: Practices and possibilities* (pp. 26–40). Newark, DE: International Reading Association.

Hansen, J. (1995). Literacy portfolios: Helping students know themselves. In J. E. DeCarlo (ed.), *Perspectives in whole language* (pp. 302–305). Boston: Allyn & Bacon.

Hare, V. C., Rabinowitz, M., & Schieble, K. M. (1989). Text effects of selected text features on main idea comprehension. *Reading Research Quarterly, 24,* 72–88.

Hiebert, E. H. (1994). Becoming literate through authentic tasks: Evidence and adaptations. In R. B. Ruddell, M. R. Ruddell, & H. Singer (eds.), *Theoretical models and processes of reading* 4th ed., (pp. 391–413). Newark DE: International Reading Association.

Johns, J. L. (1997). *Basic reading inventory* (8th ed.). Dubuque, IA: Kendall-Hunt Publishing Company.

Johns, J. L. & Lenski, S. (1997). *Improving reading: A handbook of strategies* (2d ed.). Dubuque, IA: Kendall/Hunt.

Johnston, P. H. & Allington, R. (1991). Remediation. In R. Barr, M. Kamil, P. Mosenthal, & P. D. Pearson (eds.), *Handbook of reading research, Vol. 2* (pp. 984–1012). New York: Longman.

Jordan, A. (1989). *Diagnostic narrative.* Unpublished journals of lessons. Eastern Montana College.

Juel, C. (1984). An evolving model of reading acquisition. In J. Niles (ed.), *Changing perspectives on research in reading/language processing and instruction* (pp. 294–297). Rochester, NY: National Reading Conference.

Juel, C. (1988). Learning to read and write: A longitudinal study of 54 children from first through fourth grades. *Journal of Educational Psychology, 80,* 437–447.

Juel, C. (1998). What kind of one-on-one tutoring helps a poor reader? In C. Hulme & R. M. Joshi (eds.), Reading and spelling: Development and disorders. (pp. 449–472). Mahwah, New Jersey: Lawrence Erlbaum Associates, Publishers.

Macon, J. M., Bewell, D., & Vogt, M. (1991). *Responses to literature: Grades K–8.* Newark, DE: International Reading Association.

Malone, L. D. & Mastropieri, M. A. (1991–1992). Reading comprehension instruction: Summarization and self-monitoring training for students with learning disabilities. *Exceptional Children, 58,* 270–279.

Manzo, A. V. & Manzo, U. (1990). *Content area reading: A heuristic approach.* Englewood Cliffs, NJ: Merrill/Prentice Hall.

Manzo, A. V. & Manzo, U. (1995). *Teaching children to be literate: A reflective approach.* Fort Worth, TX: Harcourt Brace.

Marek, A. M. & Goodman, Y. M. (1996). Understanding the reading process. In Y. M. Goodman & A. M. Marek (eds.), *Retrospective miscue analysis: Revaluing readers and reading* (pp. 21–39). Katonah, NY: Richard C. Owen Publishers, Inc.

Marvuglio, M. J. (1994). A celebration of learning: Student-led conferences. *Colorado Reading Council Journal* (Spring), 21–24.

Mason, J. M. & Au, K. H. (1990). *Reading instruction for today* (2d ed.). Glenview, IL: Scott Foresman.

McCormick, S. (1992). Disabled readers' erroneous responses to inferential comprehension questions: Description and analysis. *Reading Research Quarterly, 27,* 54–77.

McCormick, S. (1995). *Instructing students who have literacy problems.* Englewood Cliffs, NJ: Merrill/Prentice Hall.

McKenna, M. C. & Robinson, R. D. (1993). *Teaching through text: A content literacy approach to content area reading.* New York: Longman.

McNeil, J. D. (1992). *Reading comprehension: New directions for classroom practice* (3rd ed.). New York: HarperCollins.

Mills, R. E. (1956). An evaluation of techniques for teaching word recognition. *Elementary School Journal, 56,* 221–225.

Morrow, L. & Walker, B. (1997). *The reading team: A handbook for volunteer tutors K–3.* Newark, DE: International Reading Association.

Newell, G., Suszynski, K., & Weingart, R. (1989). The effects of writing in a reader-based and text-based mode of students' understanding of two short stories. *Journal of Reading Behavior, 21,* 37–57.

Ogle, D. (1989). The know, want to know, learn strategy. In K. D. Muth (ed.), *Children's comprehension of text* (pp. 205–223). Newark, DE: International Reading Association.

Oldfather, P. (1992, December). Sharing the ownership of knowing: A constructivist concept of motivation for literacy learning. Paper presented at the 42nd Annual Meeting of the National Reading Conference. San Antonio, TX.

Oldfather, P. & Wigfield, A. (1996). Children's motivation to read. In L. Baker, P. Afferbauch, & D. Reinkin (eds.), *Developing engaged readers in school and home communities* (pp. 84–114). Hillsdale, NJ: Erlbaum.

Palincsar, A. S. & Brown, A. L. (1989). Instruction for self-regulated reading. In L. B. Resnick & L. E. Klopfer (eds.), *Toward the thinking curriculum: Current cognitive research* (pp. 19–40). Alexandria, VA: Association for Supervision and Curriculum Development.

Paris, S. G., Lipson, M. Y., & Wixson, K. K. (1994). Becoming a strategic reader. In R. B. Ruddell, M. R. Ruddell, & H. Singer (eds.), *Theoretical models and processes of reading,* 4th ed. (pp. 788–811). Newark, DE: International Reading Association.

Paris, S. G. & Oka, E. R. (1989). Strategies for comprehending text and coping with reading difficulties. *Learning Disability Quarterly, 12,* 32–42.

Paris, S. G., Wasik, B., & Turner, J. (1991). The development of strategic readers. In R. Barr, M. Kamil, P. Mosenthal, & P. D. Pearson (eds.), *Handbook of reading research, Vol. 2* (pp. 609–640). New York: Longman.

Pauk, W. (1993). *How to study in college* (5th ed.). Boston: Houghton Mifflin.

Pearson, P. D. (July 1985b). *The triple read method for expository text.* Seminar presentation, Eastern Montana College, Billings, MT.

Pearson, P. D. & Camperell, K. (1994). Comprehension of text structures. In R. B. Ruddell, M. R. Ruddell, & H. Singer (eds.), *Theoretical models and processes of reading,* 4th ed. (pp. 448–468). Newark, DE: International Reading Association.

Pearson, P. D., Roehler, L. R., Dole, J. A., & Duffy, G. G. (1992). Developing expertise in reading comprehension (pp. 145–199). In S. J. Samuels & A. E. Farstrup (eds.), *What research has to say about reading instruction.* Newark, DE: International Reading Association

Peterson, B. (1991). Selecting books for beginning readers. In D. E. Deford, C. A. Lyons, & G. S. Pinnell (eds.), *Bridges to literacy: Learning from reading recovery.* (pp. 119–138). Portsmouth, NH: Heinemann.

Peterson, R. & Eeds, M. (1990). *Grand conversations: Literature groups in actions.* Richmond Hill, Ontario: Scholastic.

Pinnell, G. S., Fried, M. D., & Estice, R. M. (1990). Reading recovery: Learning how to make a difference. *The Reading Teacher, 43,* 282–295.

Powell, W. R. (1981). *The finger count system for monitoring reading behavior.* Unpublished paper. University of Florida, Gainsville, FL.

Powell, W. R. (1984). Mediated (emergent) reading levels: A construct. In J. Niles (ed.), *Changing perspectives on research in reading language processing and instruction* (pp. 247–251). Rochester, NY: The National Reading Conference.

Powell, W. R. (1986, December). *Emergent (mediated) reading levels: A new construct for placement from a Vygotskian view.* Paper presented at the National Reading Conference, Austin, TX.

Purcell-Gates, V. (1991). On the outside looking in: A study of remedial readers' meaning-making while reading literature. *Journal of Reading Behavior, 23,* 235–253.

Rasinski, T. V. & Deford, D. E. (1988). First graders' conception of literacy: A matter of schooling. *Theory into Practice, 27,* 53–61.

Rasinski, T. & Padak, N. (1996). *Holistic reading strategies: Teaching children who find reading difficult.* Englewood Cliffs, NJ: Merrill/Prentice Hall.

Ray, D. D. (1970). *Ray reading methods test* (experimental ed.). Stillwater, OK: RRMT Publications.

Reed, J. H., Schallert, D. L., & Goetz, E. (1992). Exploring the reciprocal relationship among comprehensibility, interestingness, and involvement in academic reading tasks. Paper presented at the annual meeting of the American Educational Research Association, San Francisco, CA.

Reutzel, D. R. & Cooter, R. B. (1996). *Teaching children to read: From basals to books,* 2d ed. Englewood Cliffs, NJ: Merrill/Prentice Hall.

Reutzel, D. R. & Hollingsworth, P. M. (1988). Highlighting key vocabulary: A generative-reciprocal procedure for teaching selected inference types. *Reading Research Quarterly, 23,* 358–378.

Roller, C. (1998). *So . . . What's a Tutor to Do.* Newark, DE: International Reading Association.

Roskos, K. & Walker, B. J. (1994). *Interactive handbook for understanding reading diagnosis*. Englewood Cliffs. NJ: Merrill/Prentice Hall.

Roskos, K. & Walker, B. (1998). Teachers' understanding and adaptation of their discourse as instructional conversation through self-assessment activity. Paper presented at the annual meeting of the American Educational Research Association, San Diego, CA.

Ruddell, M. R. (1997). *Teaching content reading and writing* (2d ed.). Boston: Allyn & Bacon.

Ruddell, R. B. & Unrau, N. J. (1997). The role of responsive teaching in focusing reader intention and developing reader motivation. In J. T. Guthrie & A. Wigfield (eds.), *Reading engagement: Motivating readers through integrated instruction* (pp. 102–127). Newark, DE: International Reading Association.

Ruddell, R. B. & Unrau, N. J. (1994). Reading as a meaning-construction process: The reader, the text, and the teacher. In R. B. Ruddell, M. R. Ruddell, & H. Singer (eds.), *Theoretical models and processes of reading* (4th ed.) (pp. 996–1056). Newark, DE: International Reading Association.

Samuels, S. J., Schermer, N., & Reinking, D. (1991). Reading fluency: Techniques for making decoding automatic. In S. J. Samuels & A. E. Farstrup (eds.), *What research has to say about reading instruction* (pp. 124–144). Newark, DE: International Reading Association.

Santa, C. M., Danner, M., Nelson, M., Havens, L., Scalf, J., & Scalf, L. (1986). *Content reading including study systems: CRISS*. Kendall-Hunt.

Schallert, D. L. & Reed, J. H. (1997). The pull of the text and the process of involvement in reading. In J. T. Guthrie & A. Wigfield (eds.), *Reading Engagement: Motivating Readers Through Integrated Instruction* (pp. 68–85). Newark, DE: International Reading Association.

Schunk, D. H. & Zimmerman, B. J. (1997). Developing self-efficacious readers and writers: The role of social and self-regulary processes. In J. T. Guthrie & A. Wigfield (eds.), *Reading Engagement: Motivating Readers Through Integrated Instruction* (pp. 34–50). Newark, DE: International Reading Association.

Sharan, Y. & Sharan, S. (1989–1990). Group investigation expands cooperative learning. *Educational Leadership, 47,* 17–21.

Short, K. G., Harste, J. C., & Burke, C. (1996). *Creating classrooms for authors and inquirers*. Portsmouth, NH: Heinemann.

Singer, H. (1989). An instructional model for reading and learning from text in the classroom. In R. A. Thompson (ed.), *Classroom reading instruction* (pp. 3–12). Dubuque, IA: Kendall-Hunt.

Snider, M. A., Lima, S. S., & DeVito, P. J. (1994). Rhode Island's literacy portfolio assessment project. In S. W. Valencia, E. H. Hiebert, & P. P. Afflerback (eds.), *Authentic reading assessment: Practices and possibilities* (pp. 71–88). Newark, DE: International Reading Association.

Snow, C. E., Burn, M. S., & Griffin, P. (1998). *Preventing reading difficulties in young children*. Washington, DC: National Academy Press.

Spiegel, D. L. (1998). Silver bullets, babies, and bath water: Literature response groups in a balanced literacy program. *The Reading Teacher, 52,* 114–124.

Stahl, S. (1998). Saying the "P" word: Nine guidelines for exemplary phonics instruction. In R. Allington (ed.), *Teaching struggling readers* (pp. 208–216). Newark, Del: International Reading Association.

Stanovich, K. E. (1981). Attentional and automatic context effects in reading. In A. M. Lesgold & C. A. Perfetti (eds.), *Interactive processes in reading* (pp. 241–262). Hillsdale, NJ: Lawrence Erlbaum Associates.

Stanovich, K. E. (1986). Matthew effects in reading: Some consequences of individual differences in the acquisition of literacy. *Reading Research Quarterly, 21,* 360–406.

Stowell, L. P. and Tierney, R. J. (1995) Portfolios in the classroom: What happens when teachers and students negotiate assessment? In R. L. Allington & S. A. Walmsley (eds.), *No quick fix,* pp. 78–96. New York: Teachers College Press; Newark, DE: International Reading Association.

Taylor, B., Harris, L., Pearson, P. D., & Garcia, G. (1995). *Reading difficulties: Instruction and assessment.* New York: McGraw-Hill.

Tierney, R. J., Carter, M. A., & Desai, L. E. (1991). *Portfolio assessment in the reading-writing classroom.* Norwood, MA: Christopher Gordon.

Tierney, R. J. & Pearson, P. D. (1994). A revisionist perspective on "Learning to learn from text: A framework for improving classroom practice." In R. Ruddell, M. Ruddell, & H. Singer (eds.), *Theoretical models and processes of reading* (4th ed.) (pp. 514–519). Newark, DE: International Reading Association.

Tierney, R. J., Readence, J. E., & Dishner, E. K. (1995). *Reading strategies and practices: A compendium* (4th ed.). Boston: Allyn & Bacon.

Tompkins, G. E. (1998). *50 literacy strategies: Step by step.* Englewood Cliffs, NJ: Merrill/Prentice Hall.

Turner, J. (1997). Starting right: Strategies for engaging young literacy learners. In Guthrie, J. & Wigfield, A. (eds.) *Reading engagement: Motivating readers through integrated instruction* (pp. 183–204). Newark, DE: International Reading Association.

Valencia, S. W. & Place, N. A. (1994). Literacy portfolios for teaching, learning, and accountability: The Bellevue literacy assessment project. In S. W. Valencia, E. H. Hiebert, & P. P. Afflerback (eds.), *Authentic reading assessment: Practices and possibilities* (pp. 71–88). Newark, DE.: International Reading Association.

Vygotsky, L. S. (1978). *Mind in society.* Cambridge, MA: Harvard University Press.

Walker, B. J. (1985a). Right-brained strategies for teaching comprehension. *Academic Therapy, 21,* 133–141.

Walker, B. J. (1990a). A model for diagnostic narratives in teacher education. In N. Padak, T. Rasinski, & J. Logan (eds.), *Challenges in reading* (pp. 1–10). Kent, OH: College Reading Association.

Walker, B. J. (1990b). *What research says to the teacher: Remedial reading*. Washington, DC: National Education Association.

Walker, B. J. (1996). Discussions that focus on strategies and self-assessment. In L. B. Gambrell & J. F. Almasi (eds.) *Lively Discussions! Fostering Engaged Reading* (pp. 286–296). Newark, DE: International Reading Association.

Walker, B. J. (1999). *Supporting struggling readers* (2d ed.). Markham, Ontario: Pippin Publishing Limited.

Wigfield, A. (1997). Children's motivations for reading and reading engagement. In J. T. Guthrie & A. Wigfield (eds.), *Reading engagement: Motivating readers through integrated instruction* (pp. 14–33). Newark, DE: International Reading Association.

Wilkinson, P. A. & Patty, D. (1993). The effects of sentence combining on the reading comprehension of fourth grade students. *Research in the Teaching of English, 27,* 104–125.

Wood, K. D., Lapp, D., & Flood, J. (1992). *Guiding readers through text: A review of study guides*. Newark, DE: International Reading Association.

Zutell, J. (May, 1988). *Developing a procedure for assessing oral reading fluency: Establishing validity and reliability*. Paper presented at 33rd Annual Convention, International Reading Association, Toronto, Canada.

Index

About The Author

Barbara J. Walker is professor of Reading at Oklahoma State University where she teaches courses in reading difficulties and coordinates the Reading and Math Center. Dr. Walker received her Ed.D. from Oklahoma State University in Curriculum and Instruction, specializing in reading difficulty. Prior to returning to Oklahoma, Dr. Walker was a professor in the Department of Special Education and Reading at Montana State University, Billings, where she coordinated the Reading Clinic. She was a reading specialist in the elementary schools of Stillwater, Oklahoma; organized and taught the college reading program at Vernon Regional Junior College in Vernon, Texas; and coordinated the educational program at the Hogar Paul Harris in Cochabamba, Bolivia.

Dr. Walker's research interests focus on teacher development, early literacy intervention, and reading difficulties. Her publications include *Supporting Struggling Readers* (1999), *Tips for the Reading Team* (1998) and *The Reading Team: A Handbook for K–3 Volunteer Tutors* (1997) with Lesley Morrow, and *Interactive Handbook for Understanding Reading Diagnosis* (1994) with Kathy Roskos. Dr. Walker received the College Reading Association's 1997 A. B. Herr Award for outstanding contributions to reading education and was a distinguished finalist for the International Reading Association's 1991 Albert J. Harris Award for research in reading disabilities.

Dr. Walker is a state, national, and international professional leader having served on the board of directors of the International Reading Association, College Reading Association, and Montana State Reading Council. Most important to her, however, is preparing teachers to work with struggling readers. In this capacity, she has helped more than 2,000 struggling readers improve their literacy.